D0848442

The Ring of Truth

The Ring of Truth

And Other Myths of Sex and Jewelry

WENDY DONIGER

OXFORD
UNIVERSITY PRESS

OXFORD
UNIVERSITY PRESS

Oxford University Press is a department of the University of Oxford. It furthers the University's objective of excellence in research, scholarship, and education by publishing worldwide. Oxford is a registered trade mark of Oxford University Press in the UK and certain other countries.

Published in the United States of America by Oxford University Press
198 Madison Avenue, New York, NY 10016, United States of America.

Library of Congress Cataloging-in-Publication Data
Names: Doniger, Wendy, author.
Title: The ring of truth and other myths of sex and jewelry / Wendy Doniger.
Description: New York : Oxford University Press, 2017. | Includes
bibliographical references and index.
Identifiers: LCCN 2016055313 (print) | LCCN 2017007846 (ebook) |
ISBN 9780190267117 (cloth) | ISBN 9780190267124 (updf) |
ISBN 9780190267131 (epub) | ISBN 9780190621759 (online content)
Subjects: LCSH: Rings—Folklore. | Rings in literature.
Classification: LCC GR950.R5 D66 2017 (print) | LCC GR950.R5 (ebook) |
DDC 398.28—dc23
LC record available at https://lccn.loc.gov/2016055313

1 3 5 7 9 8 6 4 2

Printed by Sheridan Books, Inc., United States of America

For my niece, Emma Doniger

Contents

Acknowledgments

I STARTED COLLECTING stories and ideas about rings over the years when I was writing *The Bedtrick* (2000). Along the way, I published "Jewels of Rejection and Recognition in Ancient India" (1998) and "The Ring of the Forgetful Husband in World Mythology" (1999). And after that I continued to publish articles about rings: "Gli Anelli Magici della Memoria" (2001); "Magic Rings and the Return of the Repressed" (2006–7); "Narrative Conventions and Rings of Recognition" (2009); "The Rings of Budur and Qamar" (2013); "Myth, Reason, and Rationality" (2016); and "Menander, Terence, and the Rape of the Clever Wife" (2017). I'm grateful to the publishers of these books and journals for permission to cite materials that first appeared therein. Rings were major players in the penultimate draft of *The Woman Who Pretended to Be Who She Was* (2005), until my eagle-eyed editor, Cynthia Read, saw that I had tangled up two books, one about self-imitation and one about rings, and that the rings were just getting in the way in the self-imitation book and needed a book of their own—this book. I owe her a lot for that alone, but she also actually contributed a number of texts, translations, and news items to this book, as well as tightening my sentences, generally separating the chaff from the wheat, and even finding the perfect image for the cover. They really don't make editors like that any more.

Over these years, wherever I went, no matter what people asked me to talk about, I talked about rings, and I took furious notes not only in the Q & A but during the lecture itself, as the adrenaline generated new ideas even while I was telling the audience the old ones. I tried out bits and pieces of it on unsuspecting audiences in a number of venues: the Plenary Address, Millennial Meeting of the American Philosophical Society, Philadelphia, 1999; the John R. Adams Lecture in the Humanities, San Diego State, 1999; the Jane Ellen Harrison Memorial Lecture, Newnham College, Cambridge University, England, 2000; the Inaugural

Lecture for the Center for Gender Studies, School of Oriental and African Studies, 2001; the First Annual Memorial Barry Ulanov Lecture, Union Theological Seminary, March, 2003; the Henry Myers Lecture at the Royal Anthropological Institute, London, 2004; the Humanities Open House Lecture, University of Chicago, 2004; the President's Lecture, Radcliffe Institute, 2004; the Presidential Lecture, Stanford Humanities Center, 2004; and then lectures throughout England, Europe, India, the United States, and South Africa, culminating at the American Academy in Berlin, in December 2015, where Gerhard Casper, Lorraine Daston, and Philip Kitcher made me rethink important points. Everywhere I went, people helped me sort out my ideas about the book and often brought me more stories. I am grateful to those who attended the lectures and responded with many of the ideas that I have incorporated in this book.

I particularly benefited from discussion of parts of the book at a number of seminars, beginning with the Gauss Seminars at Princeton University in 1999; I wish particularly to thank my host, Michael Wood, as well as Elena Wood, Walter Lippincott, Debra Malamud, Frank Lewin, James Boon, Froma Zeitlin, Bernard Lewis, Stephen Teiser, Elaine Pagels, George Kateb, Jeff Stout, and Victor and Mickey Glasser. At Stanford University, in the autumn of 2010, I was privileged to talk about the project with the Andrew W. Mellon Scholars in the Humanities: Sarah Carey, Julie Draskoczy, Kate Elswit, Brendan Fay, Shana Goldin-Perschtbacher, Andrew Goldstone, Danielle Heard, Minku Kim, Seth Kimmel, Yann Robert, Hannah Rohde, and Karen Zumhagen-Yekplé; and especially my host, R. Lanier Anderson, director of the program in 2010.

At the Work in Progress Seminar, King's College, Cambridge, 2010, I enjoyed spirited feedback from Bert Vaux (my host) as well as John Forrester, Chris Prendergast, Simon Goldhill, Bill Burgwinkle, Anastasia Norton-Piliavsky, Lorraine Daston, Robin Osborne, Elisabeth Giselbrecht, Giovanni Ciotti, Paolo Visigalli, Humeira Iqtidar, Elisa Ganser, Hugo David, Imma Ramos, Julius Lipner, and James Clackson. At the University of Chicago Divinity School faculty retreat in 2011, I learned a great deal from Simeon Chavel, Margaret Mitchell, and Clark Gilpin; Bruce Lincoln expertly and tactfully guided me to and through the Norse sources.

At a seminar with the Department of Classical Studies at Boston University, in 2011, I learned much about Menander and Terence from Stephanie Nelson, Stephen Scully, Ann Vasaly, Laurie Glenn, Jeffrey Henderson, Leslie Lemire, Pat Larash, Patricia Johnson, Sophie Klein, and

Dustin Dixon. In England in November 2013, Rachel Dwyer, Arshia Sattar, and Lucy Lunt gave me some great stories. I am grateful to Ann Rower for sharing her manuscript, and her memories, about Leo Robin; and to Gary Tubb and Sheila Kennedy for giving me a first edition of Charles Edwards's *The History and Poetry of Finger-Rings* (1855), which kicked off a paper chase on which I discovered many other wonderful old books about rings. I owe thanks to Marina Warner for her help with the *Arabian Nights*, to Nicholas Rudall for his good advice about Menander and Terence, to Philip Kitcher for new ideas about Wagner, and to the late Mary Douglas for many long talks about ring composition and much else. The two readers for Oxford University Press, Velcheru Narayana Rao and Stuart Blackburn, offered me not only erudite encouragement but also important corrections (minute and not so minute) and a larger vision of the book to which the details had blinded me; I have gratefully taken their advice.

In addition to my official research assistants over those years— Katherine Ulrich, Greg Spinner, Amanda Huffer Lucia, Blake Wentworth, Jeremy Morse, Charles Preston, Nabanjan Maitra, and Sunil Singh— I have been privileged to have two spectacular unofficial research assistants: Professors David Tracy and Lorraine Daston. David and Raine brought me obscure and arcane tidbits of information about rings from all sorts of places that I could never have ventured into myself, and came up with ideas, too, that would never have occurred to me; their influence is palpable on every page.

I am grateful to Alfred Music Publishing for permission to use the lyrics to "Diamonds Are Forever" (from the film *Diamonds Are Forever* [1971, directed by Guy Hamilton]), Music by John Barry, Lyrics by Don Black, © 1971 United Artists Music Ltd., copyright renewed by Emi Unart Catalog Inc. Exclusive print rights controlled and administered by Alfred Music. All rights reserved. Reprinted by permission.

And I am grateful to Music Sales Corporation for permission to use the lyrics to "Diamonds Are a Girl's Best Friend," words by Leo Robin and music by Jule Styne, Copyright © 1949 (Renewed) by Music Sales Corporation (ASCAP). International copyright secured. All rights reserved. Reprinted by permission.

The Excerpt from "Glitter and Gay" is from *Collected Poems 1943–2004* by Richard Wilbur. Copyright © 2004 by Richard Wilbur. Reprinted by permission of Houghton Mifflin Harcourt Publishing Company. All rights reserved.

I am grateful to New Directions Publishing for permission to reprint Denise Levertov's poem, "Wedding Ring," from *Life in the Forest* (New York: New Directions Publishing Corporation, 1978).

Finally, I would like to dedicate the book to my niece Emma Doniger, who knows all about jewelry and who listened with eager (or tactful) attention to so many of my stories and then taught me another story, about the women of her generation who prefer to buy their own jewelry.

Zingst, on the Baltic, December 13, 2015

Preface

My Family Jewels and Other Tall Tales

*The ring, man, the ring: that was what he came back for. If
we have no other way of catching him, we can always bait
our line with the ring.*

SHERLOCK HOLMES, in Arthur Conan Doyle's *A Study in
Scarlet*, Chapter 4

I ALWAYS BELIEVED that my mother's brother Harry was a fence, though
she insisted that he was a "gemologist." Every weekday of his life, well
into his eighties, he went from his home in New Jersey into the Diamond
Exchange in New York City; he also claimed to have invented a way of making perfect diamonds, very cheap, and to have been somehow cheated, or
threatened, out of his formula by the De Beers cartel.[i] Whenever Uncle
Harry came to our house for dinner, after the dessert plates were cleared
he would take out of his inside breast pocket a rolled-up piece of black
velvet, which he would unroll and unfold to reveal a series of pockets, each
containing a piece of lovely jewelry, or a few unset gems, particularly fire
opals, all suspiciously inexpensive, no questions to be asked. My father
would be pressured into buying some of them, and I still have several
pieces that I cherish, though every time I wear one of them I glance about
nervously in fear that someone will come up to me and claim ownership
of it. So the dicey side of jewelry is in my blood.

---

i. See chapter 10, p. 258. Throughout this book, footnotes (indicated by Roman numerals)
will be used for cross-references; endnotes (marked by Arabic numerals) will contain biblio-
graphic and occasionally nonessential but too-good-to-cut information.

On the other side of the family, my uncle Leo wrote "Diamonds Are a Girl's Best Friend."[ii] More precisely, Leo Robin was a kind of shirttail relative, the brother of my aunt Irma (Robin), the woman my father's brother Simon Doniger married, so he was not exactly, technically, my uncle, just an uncle by marriage, once removed. But I knew him from family gatherings when I was a little girl, and he really did write the lyrics to all of *Gentlemen Prefer Blondes* (and many other great songs, including "Thanks for the Memory" and "Beyond the Blue Horizon"). So stories about jewelry are also part of my family heritage.

Stories often surrounded, like gift-wrapping, the jewelry that came to me. When my great-grandmother Franzi Baruch owned and ran the Hotel New York in Marienbad from 1903 to the 1930s, a Russian prince, short of the cash to pay his bill, allegedly paid by giving her his seven-piece harem ring, each piece adorned with a diamond, emerald, ruby, and small pearl, and she kept it through the years. The Hotel New York in Marienbad is no more,[1] and Russia has lost its princes, but that ring was passed down in my family and came to me.

And there are stories about some of the jewelry that my father gave my mother (cooler than the hot pieces that he got from Uncle Harry). When my parents were first married, during the Depression, there was not enough money for any ring at all. But years later, when my father had become a successful publisher, he had Cartier make a gold ring for her, studded with diamonds and rubies, a kind of retrospective wedding ring. It was in the form of a "gimmel" ring,[2] from the Latin *gemelli*, "twins": two rings joined together by a pivot so that when united they constitute a single ring. Often there is a hand on each circlet,[3] and when they are brought together the hands clasp. Sometimes there is a third ring, with a heart, which appears when the hands are separated, and on which are usually inscribed the names of the lover and his beloved, "Antony to Cleopatra." This was the form of the ring my father gave my mother. But he had the heart inscribed "REF to SHU," which was her favorite volume of the eleventh edition of the *Encyclopedia Britannica* (1911), with its superb essays on Renaissance, Romanticism, Schiller, Schubert, Shakespeare, and so forth.

There's a different sort of story about a gift from my father to my mother that happened in the summer of 1958, when the three of us were in Vienna and I went with my father to a store on the Ringstrasse where

---

ii. See chapter 10, p. 261.

he bought three pieces of jewelry; at Christmas, he gave one to my mother and another to me, and I always wondered if he gave the third to a mistress, a figure whose existence we had other reasons to suspect, but without any hard evidence.

There's a story behind each piece on the charm bracelet to which my father added year after year—the ballet dancer that twirls, the windmill that turns; I could tell them like a rosary. After his death, my mother took my charm bracelet and added it to hers and wore the two of them as a necklace (including a little gold book which opened to say, "To Wendy from Daddy"), which I eventually inherited at her death. She also had another charm bracelet of which she said each charm—and there were many— came from a different lover of the courtesan who had owned the bracelet.

It was my mother's idea to take my father's Phi Beta Kappa key and my Phi Beta Kappa key and have them made into a pair of earrings, which she (who had never finished high school, a fact that she bitterly resented) wore for years and I now wear. (It was, I realized years later, one of my mother's many feminist gestures: the keys were designed for watch fobs that men would wear on their three-piece suits; she found a way for women to wear them too.) My mother had a great deal of good jewelry, but she also loved costume jewelry, plastic pins and earrings with Mickey Mouse or Mr. Peanut on them, glass beads and necklaces of shells. She particularly delighted in mixing the real and fake jewelry together, to *épater* the sort of people who set great store on the difference between them.

Not all the stories that jewelry tells are true. When my husband and I honeymooned on Crete in 1965, we found in a little shop there an ancient carnelian stone carved with a centaur, which he later had made into a signet ring for me (another retrospective wedding ring). Now, many years after a bitter divorce, the loving inscription that he had had engraved inside it is certainly a blatant lie, but I still wear the ring. After all, I did love him once, and it's a charming centaur.

There is also a story behind my bracelet of ancient Indian gold coins from the Gupta Empire (c. fifth century CE). John Marshall, who had excavated much of India in the early twentieth century, had given it to Penelope Chetwode when he wooed her back in the 1930s; she married another man (John Betjeman) but kept the bracelet. One day in 1968, when she and I were riding on the Berkshire Downs in England, our Arabian horses spooked and bolted. Penelope was wearing the bracelet, which got tangled in the reins and fell off somewhere over the considerable distance of grassland that we traversed before we were able to pull up. The sun was setting;

the bracelet seemed hopelessly lost. But Penelope said a prayer to Saint Antony, patron saint of lost or stolen things: "St. Antoine de Padou, grand voleur, grand filou, vous qui retrouvez tout, rendez-nous ce qui n'est pas à vous" ("St. Antony of Padua, you big thief, you robber, you who find whatever is lost, give back to us what does not belong to you." An Italian American version goes: "Tony, Tony, look around. Something's lost and can't be found.")[4] And she vowed to give the bracelet to me right then and there if we found it. (She had previously planned to leave it to me in her will.) As we cantered back over the path the horses had taken, the last rays of the sun picked out the gleaming gold in the high grass, and I still wear the bracelet.

The rest of this book will not be about my own stories but about the stories that other people have told, throughout recorded history and all over the world, about pieces of circular jewelry, particularly rings. Yet my personal anecdotes do silhouette the book's themes. The mutual imitation of real and fake, legal and illegal, marital and extra-marital jewelry is a pervasive motif. Marriage, jewelry, and faking it are joined at the hip in such folk wisdom as the old joke: "What's the difference between the first wife and the last wife?" Answer: "With the first wife, the jewelry is fake, and the orgasms are real." The circular form of rings and bracelets, miming the circle of eternity, persists in the face of human ephemera: lovers come and go, marriages end, Russian princes are no more, but rings remain. The fairy tale of the miraculously lost-and-found piece of circular jewelry carries mythic overtones: would Saint Anthony have come through had Penelope Chetwode not generously pledged the bracelet to me should it be found? The jewelry in the stories I've collected here, like my own, preserves (and sometimes erases) true and false memories, making promises that come true and that lie.

Introduction

The Signifying Ring

WHY ARE SEX and jewelry, particularly circular jewelry, particularly finger rings, so often connected? Why do rings keep getting into stories about marriage and adultery, love and betrayal, loss and recovery, identity and masquerade? What is the mythology that makes rings symbols of true (or, as the case may be, untrue) love? As I seek answers to these questions, each chapter of this book, like a separate charm on a charm bracelet, will consider a different constellation of stories. The first seven chapters are about rings throughout history; in particular, they are all recognition stories in which a ring is a vital clue. They deal with sexual rings (chapter 1), rings found in fish and found (with children) in the ocean (chapter 2), rings of forgetful husbands (chapters 3, 4, and 5) and clever wives (chapters 6 and 7). Chapters 1 and 2 are broadly cross-cultural (though largely Anglophone) and deal with a number of relatively short texts; the next three chapters concentrate on fewer stories discussed in greater depth, taken from individual cultures: India (chapter 3), medieval Europe (chapter 4), and the Germanic world (chapter 5). Chapters 6 and 7 deal with a single theme— the "clever wife"— in cross-cultural distribution. Chapters 8 and 9 veer ever so slightly into stories about necklaces in particular cultures and particular historical periods: a treacherous royal necklace in eighteenth-century France (chapter 8) and true-and-false necklaces in nineteenth-century English novels and twentieth-century American films (chapter 9). The final two chapters return to rings, to the invention of the mythology of diamond engagement rings in twentieth-century America (chapter 10) and a concluding consideration of the cash value of rings and the clash between reason and convention in myths about rings of recognition throughout the world (chapter 11).

Some of the rings in the stories that we will encounter throughout this book originally belong to men, and just about all the jewelry that women have, they get from men (sometimes they inherit it from their mothers, but not often). But both men and women tell the stories (though men are usually the attributed authors of the earlier texts). These stories drive my arguments about six basic points, three about the content of the plots and three about the function of the narratives:

1. Most of the stories take for granted what I am calling the "slut assumption," that women get jewels only from men they sleep with (husbands or lovers).
2. Women use jewelry to their advantage in the stories, often to win (or win back) their husbands, while men use (or try to use) rings to wriggle out of promises to women.
3. Men's concern for the paternity of their children, and women's for their children's legitimacy, drive many of the myths of rings of recognition.
4. By overcoming reason, the myths allow us to believe what we want to believe about the power and endurance of sexual love and about our ability to rebalance the moral world.
5. The tension between hard evidence ("reason") and the soft power of myth ("rationality") experienced by an audience is mirrored by a similar tension in the story itself.
6. Different versions (or variants, or tellings) of much-retold stories supply us with a cumulative mass of different psychological details that together suggest deeper meanings of the myth. And comparing earlier and later variants allows us to see myths in the making, a process that we can then recognize in such contemporary examples as the invented tradition of diamond engagement rings.

I must warn you at the start, in the spirit of full disclosure, that there are many sorts of rings, and stories, that this book is *not* about. It is *not* about the Scandinavian lore of the ring of power, the ring that allows the wearer to rule the world or become master of time and space, the evil ring that the bad guys want to possess and the good guys want to destroy. This is the ring that eventually ends up in the hands of Frodo via J. R. R. Tolkien, but you will not find that sort of ring here, for this book is about the interactions of men with women, and there are no women to speak of in *The Lord of the Rings*; it's all about guys.[1] The rings that women get from men are also, in a way, rings of power, but of another type—the power to ensure that your integrity is above suspicion, that you are in charge of your own body, and that your child will inherit. In stories of clever women, for example,[i] as long as the man has the ring, he controls her; when she gets the ring, she gets back control of her own sexuality. Political power, too, may sometimes be at stake here, for the woman who sleeps with the king (as many of our heroines do) knows that if her son becomes crown prince, she will be the queen mother. But the rings in this book always also have some connection with love and/or sexuality.

When I was growing up, during and after World War II, we sent away for magic rings that had a secret password and a secret compartment in which to hide messages or forbidden substances, which in those innocent days were usually beetles, though we knew that in centuries gone by there actually were rings with concealed compartments full of poison (for the Borgias) or, in my day, Nazi, anti-Nazi, Communist, or anti-Communist microfilm. Heroes and superheroes, too—Dick Tracy, the Green Hornet— had and have magic rings. This book is not about those rings, either. Yet every ring in these stories does carry a message, albeit not necessarily in a secret compartment.

For rings are signifiers, semiotic objects. Robert Benchley, in his "Opera Synopses," satirized the multi-valence of the Wagnerian ring;[ii] Benchley's heroine seeks "the magic zither which confers upon its owner the power to go to sleep while apparently carrying on a conversation; . . . [and a] *Tarnhelm* or invisible cap which will enable her to talk to people without their understanding a word she says. For a dollar and a half extra Dampfboot throws in a magic ring which renders its wearer insensible."[2] The many powers of Benchley's ring and its accessories include, as usual, unconsciousness but also the power to confound and confuse both vision and words. For there are magic rings that cloud the mind with invisibility, forgetfulness, and memory, and some are just as destructive as poison rings or spy rings. This book is about them.

---

i. See chapters 6 and 7, pp. 137–205.

ii. See chapter 5, pp. 120–123.

The Ring of Truth

I
_____

Marriage Rings (and Adultery Rings)

Rings in History

Rings have been around for a long time. The ancient Greeks used rings as love tokens, though not as marriage rings.[1] The Romans, too, used rings for love rather than marriage; some Roman rings, usually of iron (later of gold), with no gemstone, were associated with betrothal, though still not with marriage, and with no long-term commitment. Later, such a ring was called the *annulus pronubus* (literally, "the finger-ring for marriage"). The early Christian church authorities were the first to approve the ring as a token of commitment to marriage, now regarded as more than a dissoluble secular contract,[2] and by the thirteenth century, rings came to play an important role in marriage.[3] The giving of a ring on the occasion of marriage is mentioned in the 1559 Book of Common Prayer.

We have datable archaeological records for other forms of jewelry, which first appear in sites dated around 70,000 years ago, some 30,000 years before cave paintings and mammoth-tusk figurines. They are necklaces: usually shells or animal teeth with holes bored in them.[4] Some paleo-anthropologists regard this moment when we started using personal ornamentation—rather than the moment when we first developed language or created painted images—as the moment when we became genuinely human: Homo Adornatus. Since these necklaces were made long before the invention of the mirror, and one can't keep looking down at one's own necklace all day without becoming cross-eyed, to get the full effect one had to read the admiration in the expression of other people, very early evidence of a theory of mind (taking the perspective of someone else), of wearing jewelry in order to affect another person.

The Meaning of Rings

Tiffany's one-line ad,[i] proclaiming, "Each Ring Has a Story to Tell,"[5] echoes a remark made by Elizabeth Taylor, who, in an interview on the occasion of the publication of her memoir, *My Love Affair with Jewelry*, in 2002, said, of her many jewels, "Each one tells me a story." Stories about rings are linked through a common cluster of meanings. In one early German text, perhaps ninth century, Brynhild[ii] sends to her brother, Attila the Hun, a ring twined round with wolf's hair as a kind of signal, which he does not understand (nor do scholars of the text).[6] A ring that sends a signal that no one understands—how postmodern can you get? But though some people in some stories misread a ring's signal, others do get it, and we can try to get it too.

Some of the meanings of the rings in love stories are suggested by the unbroken circular shape of the ring, which promises a love that is infinite, constant, eternal. "I gave my love a ring that had no end. . . . How can there be a ring that has no end? . . . A ring when it's rolling, it has no end," says the old "Riddlesong," and then, in some versions, it adds, "The story that I love you will never end." Henry Swinburne, a lawyer specializing in matrimonial law in the sixteenth and seventeenth centuries, remarked, "It skilleth not at this day what metal the ring be of, the form of it being round and without end doth import that their love should circulate and flow continually."[7] Other meanings of the ring of love are suggested by its substance, metal, originally iron but later usually gold: the ring that promises love is as pure as gold (or fool's gold, as the case may be). Thus Swinburne also praised the espousal ring's "metal hard and durable, signifying the durance and perpetuity of the contract"[8] (though gold, as we know, is relatively soft). These features integral to the ring seem to nominate it for its role of vouchsafing integrity and fidelity. Jewelry lasts much longer than a wedding dress, or even a marriage certificate.

The ring differs from most other circular jewelry, necklaces and bracelets, in two significant ways: a ring needs no clasp for you to take it on and off, breaking the circle, and a ring often remains on your hand constantly, in contrast with more cumbersome jewelry that you usually take off at bedtime. (The same is true of bangles, which often share the symbolism of rings and are a commonplace in stories about women, sex, and marriage.)[9]

---

i. See chapter 10, p. 268.

ii. See chapter 4, p. 110.

In a folktale version of the "ring-in-a-fish" story[iii] recorded in Kashmir in 1892, the ring is a nose-ring.[10] Rings of all sorts certify the unbroken constancy of love in ways that necklaces and bracelets generally do not.

Like the link of a chain, any form of circular jewelry may fetter the wearer to the giver. A Victorian poem "To Her Ring" exhorts the ring, "Now, as thou bind'st her fingers, bind her heart."[11] Shakespeare's Posthumus, in *Cymbeline*,[iv] wrongly suspicious of Imogen's fidelity to him, refers to the bracelet that he gives her as "a manacle of love" (1.2.53). The sadomasochistic apotheosis of the ring as fetter appears in Pauline Réage's (Anne Desclos) Sadeian novel, *Story of O* (1954), where O's lover permanently affixes between her legs two rings, engraved with the names of O and of Sir Stephen, sealing off her sexuality like a chastity belt and attached to a chain by which any man can control her like an animal.[12]

The symbolism of a circle of gold is complicated by the fact that rings are often bi-polar, ambivalent, signifying, like so many symbols, two opposite things at the same time.[13] Sometimes a single ring takes on double meanings simply by being alternatively present and absent, first received, then lost, then found again. A ring may have opposite meanings for two different people in a story, or it may set up a masquerade until a second ring unmasks it. And rings tend to clone or breed in the dark, subject to a kind of ongoing fission, like amoebas. When Otto Rank and Anais Nin exchanged rings, he gave her one that he had received from his mentor, Freud, and she gave him one that had been her father's. But the two rings, patriarchal symbols, soon became three, as she hired a jeweler to duplicate from the ring she gave to Otto Rank a third ring, which she gave to her duplicate lover, Henry Miller.[14]

The ring of truth is shadowed by the ring of lies. Wedding rings can be used to tell useful lies: married men in search of extra-marital pleasures often take off their wedding rings when they go on the prowl, while Catholic priests who do not want to inspire the attentions of women will often put on wedding rings when they go out in mufti.[15] Rings are also lexically associated with truth and falsehood through several English words that are mere homonyms rather than philologically related but nevertheless echo one another in English stories of finger rings. The "ring of truth" in a statement can be traced back to what the *Oxford English Dictionary*

---

iii. See chapter 2, p. 25.

iv. See chapter 4, p. 106.

(*OED*) calls "the resonance of a coin or (less commonly) glass vessel by which its genuineness or inherent purity is tested." Significantly, one of its earliest attestations in this sense is in a statement about a woman: "She was a false coin, which would not stand the test of a ring."[16] On the other hand, according to the *OED*, a "ringer" (primarily American and Australian slang) is "a person who fraudulently substitutes one thing [usually a dog, horse, or athlete] for another." But "ringer" (particularly "dead ringer") also means, more significantly for several recurrent plots in our corpus, "a person or thing that looks very like another; a double." And Shakespeare seems to have coined the term "ring-carrier" (in *All's Well That Ends Well)*[v] as a pejorative term for a go-between or panderer.

Thus, over and above the meanings suggested by their shape and substance, rings pick up other meanings the way some fabrics pick up scent or dog hair. George Frederick Kunz, writing about rings in 1917, put it well: "While we may regard as superstition any fancy that the material ring possesses any magic quality, that lent to it by association or by memory is none the less real though it is only in the brain or heart of the wearer."[17]

The Signet Ring

The ring as a signifier of identity is a material token; it doesn't change when we change, and so it is regarded as a guarantee of identity across time: if Solomon has Solomon's ring,[vi] he's Solomon.

Sometimes the ring is carved in a special way or set with a distinctive stone that makes it unique. Many of the rings in our stories are men's signet rings or seal rings, carved with the owner's name or initials or insignia—literally a signifier. The Assyrians used signets or seals to seal letters and documents; the Minoans picked up the custom from the Assyrians. At first these seals were probably free-standing cylinders, but the Greeks converted the cylindrical seals into flat ovals set into rings.[18] And the Greeks probably brought signet rings into India with the armies of Alexander, from the third century BCE. Seals, as we will see,[vii] have a rich range of meanings and a history of symbolism, and rings have another. They combine in signet rings.

---

v. See chapter 6, p. 159.

vi. See chapter 2, p. 27.

vii. See chapter 7, p. 202.

The first signet rings belonged to kings and were rings of power; "to bestow one's ring is to bestow a power," Heinrich Zimmer remarked, "the authority to speak in one's name."[19] Of course, many of the men in the old stories are lovers as well as kings, and they often use their signet rings to entrap innocent women. A legend tells that King John of England fancied the wife of the baron Eustace de Vesci; he "borrowed" de Vesci's seal ring on the pretext of having a copy made and sent it to de Vesci's wife with a request that she meet him immediately. Seeing the ring, she obeyed, but happened to meet her husband on the road; when he saw how they had been tricked, de Vesci "resolved to find a wanton and put her in apparel to personate his lady."[20] (This ruse is a bed-trick, which we will encounter often in these stories: someone substitutes for someone else in bed, fooling the sexual partner.)[21]

Another king who attempts in vain to seduce his courtier's wife uses a signet ring to "prove" that he had succeeded, in a story that the Agrawal caste tell about the origin of the goddess Shila Mata who is worshipped in their temple:[viii]

> The Shah of Agroha married his only daughter Shila to Mehta Shah, the minister of the state of Sialkot. When the King of Sialkot heard of her great beauty, he sent Mehta Shah to another state, while he himself went to meet Shila and attempted to "spoil her chastity." When she resisted his advances, the thwarted king ordered Shila's maidservant to put his ring in Shila's bed. When Mehta Shah returned home he discovered the king's ring in his bed and thought Shila had been unfaithful to him. Immediately he ordered her to return home to her father's house at Agroha. Some years later, the maidservant confessed to Mehta Shah that it was she who had put the ring in their bed and that Shila had, indeed, been faithful to him. Mehta Shah then rushed to Agroha to retrieve his wife and ask her forgiveness; but on the way to Agroha he collapsed and died. When Shila

---

viii. Note to the reader: Against the usual convention, throughout this book I will use indentation not to indicate a direct quote but to summarize a story in my own words, condensing and rewording, though adding nothing; within such summaries, material within quotation marks (including direct quotations) represents text reproduced verbatim. Where I quote an entire text verbatim, I will enclose it in quotation marks, interspersing my own summaries within square brackets. And I will put the citation for all of the direct quotations at the end of each story. Texts marked as poetry will be reproduced verbatim but not enclosed in quotation marks.

learned of her husband's death she joined him on his funeral pyre. A temple was built on the site of their cremation, which came to be known as the Shila Mata Shakti Mandir.[22]

The spiteful king uses his ring, in revenge, to frame the good woman who spurned him. He rightly assumes that her husband will assume that the king either lost his ring in her bed or gave it to her, but in either case slept with her.[23]

Queens, too, sometimes have signet rings. According to a much told, and much denied, legend, Queen Elizabeth I, when she loved Robert Devereux, Second Earl of Essex (1565–1601), gave him a ring and told him that if ever he was in trouble, he should send it to her and she would help him; or (in other versions) that no matter what charges might be brought against him, she would pardon him.[ix] Things went badly between them, and he was imprisoned for treason and condemned to death. He sent her the ring, but Lady Nottingham, who was to deliver it to the queen, was prevented from doing so.[24] (The reasons are differently narrated in different versions.) Years later, Lady Nottingham, on her deathbed, sent for the queen, gave her the ring, and told her what had happened. The queen, full of remorse, died soon after. So the legend goes. The diary of John Manningham (covering the years 1602–3), the only contemporary who alludes to a ring in connection with Essex's relations with Elizabeth, states only that "the queen wore till her death a ring given her by Essex."[25]

Signet rings are the stamp of recognition. In the Hebrew Bible (Genesis 38),[x] Judah's "seal" by which Tamar identifies him is a signet, presumably a signet ring,[26] which, together with the cord and staff, according to Robert Alter, "as the legal surrogate of the bearer would have been a kind of ancient Near Eastern equivalent of all a person's major credit cards."[27] To lose them (as Judah does) would amount to what we call identity theft.

Signet rings therefore play an important role in many myths of masquerade and recognition, a major genre that often intersects with our themes of love and betrayal.[28] The ring of recognition must be unique to a single person in order to establish the identity of the wearer. Stith Thompson, the Linnaeus of folklore, included in his wide survey of folktale motifs (a cross between the periodic table and the Dewey Decimal

---

ix. This motif bears a suspicious resemblance to several episodes in the medieval European romances; see chapter 4, p. 87.

x. See chapter 6, p. 152.

System) an entire Tale Type (TT 560), "The Magic Ring," but also noted several widely distributed motifs involving (non-magic) rings of recognition (such as "H 94: Recognition by ring"). Oscar Wilde's *The Picture of Dorian Gray* (1890) is about a man whose disfiguring sins are magically transferred to a painting, while he remains always the same; when he dies, he suddenly takes on the hideous form of the transfigured painting, which returns to its pristine form. The story concludes: "It was not till they had examined the ring that they recognized who it was." In real life, too, a metal ring is often all that is left to identify a dead person when the body has decayed or been destroyed.

Rings also sometimes convey erotic powers. Signet rings worn by men in sixteenth-century Italy were often set with stones that were engraved with erotic images of naked women and were said to give them the power to command women. The image of a nude woman with her hair down to her breast, "facing a man who showed signs of love," gave the wearer the power to make any woman he touched with it do whatever he wished.[29] Were these stones to fall in the hands of a woman, however, they would have no power whatsoever.[30]

In Arthur Conan Doyle's "The Case of Lady Sannox" (1893), Lord Sannox tricks his wife's lover (a surgeon) into cutting off her lower lip in order to punish, and prevent, her adulteries; he claims that the lip must be cut off in order to save her from death from a cut she has received from a poisoned dagger, but when the surgeon has done his work, Lord Sannox confesses: "The wound, by the way, was from nothing more dangerous than my signet ring." He has used his signet ring to brand her as his property, just as sadistically as the lover of O used his ring as a chastity belt.

A song made famous by Elvis Presley expresses unabashedly the possessive aspect of the ring:

> She wears my ring to show the world that she belongs to me
> She wears my ring to show the world she's mine eternally
> With loving care I placed it on her finger
> To show my love for all the world to see
> . . .
> That's why I sing, because she wears my ring.[31]

In our day (well, in my day, at least), the sexual marking power of signet rings lived on in the custom by which a young man in high school or college would give his class ring or fraternity ring to his girlfriend, who generally wore it on a chain around her neck. These rings changed hands (or necks) quite often. In the film *Dear Heart* (Delbert Mann, 1964), the character played by Glenn Ford shows a friend his fraternity ring. "Fun and games," he says, and then, "Look what happens when you turn it around; it becomes a wedding ring." The tension between "fun and games" and weddings is what much of this book is about.

The Ring on Her Finger

The signet ring is an extension of the hand, with its handwriting and, later, fingerprints.[32] Rings sometimes become part of your finger; you wear a ring for many years and never take it off and then you discover that, as you grow older and your joints swell, the ring grows tighter, until you actually can't take it off. Sometimes it leaves a mark on your hand, thus becoming a scar.

The finger and the ring are closely associated as signs of natural and cultural identity, respectively; as Posthumus says in *Cymbeline*, "My ring I hold dear as my finger, 'tis part of it" (1.4.134).[xi] And in *The Merchant of Venice*,[xii] Portia says to Gratiano, speaking of the ring his wife had given him, "Your wife's first gift; / A thing stuck on with oaths upon your finger / And so riveted with faith upon your flesh" (5.1.168). Bassanio then says, speaking of losing the ring that Portia had given him, "Why, I were best to cut my left hand off / And swear I lost the ring defending it" (5.1.177–178). Rings worn on the body are therefore legally almost as inalienable[xiii] as a limb—or a pound of flesh, for that matter.

The ring was often regarded as a part not merely of the finger but of the heart. A tradition attributed variously to the Greeks, Romans, and Egyptians, and still current in northeast Scotland in the nineteenth century,[33] made the fourth finger on the left hand the ring finger and held that it was directly connected to the heart by a vein called the vein of love, *vena amoris*. Macrobius, in the fifth century CE, remarked, "Because of this nerve, the newly betrothed places the ring on this finger of his spouse, as though it were a representation of the heart."[34] The sixteenth-century Dutch physician Levinus Lemnius said that this finger was called *Medicus*;

---

xi. See chapter 4, p. 106.

xii. See chapter 4, p. 107.

xiii. See chapter 10, p. 279, for the legal disposition of jewelry.

the old physicians would stir up their medicaments and potions with it, "because no venom could stick upon the very outmost part of it but will offend a man and communicate itself to the heart."[35]

The ring finger often played a macabre role in folklore and literature. The Welsh *Mabinogion* (1300–1425) tells a chilling story about the amputation and mutilation of a woman's finger that bore a ring. As the story is rather long, I will summarize the main points that concern us here:

> Elphin boasted to the king of his wife's chastity; the king imprisoned Elphin and sent his own son, Prince Rhun, to test the continence of Elphin's wife. She had, however, been warned by Elphin's bard, the magician Taliesin. She dressed one of the scullery maids in her own clothing and adorned the maid's fingers with her own best rings, including the signet ring that Elphin had sent to her as a token a short time before. Rhun drugged the maid so that she didn't even feel him cutting off her little finger, on which was the signet ring. He had his way with her, and afterward he took the finger—with the ring on it—to the king as proof that he had violated Elphin's wife's chastity and cut off her finger as he left. The king summoned Elphin and showed him the ring and the finger as evidence that the one who had cut it off also lay with his wife. To this Elphin replied: "Indeed, there is no way I can deny my ring, for a number of people know it. But, indeed, I do deny vehemently that the finger encircled by my ring was ever on my wife's hand." The finger was much larger than his wife's, he pointed out, the nails had not been pared for a month (and his wife pared them every day), and there was rye dough on it, which his wife never kneaded. Taliesin freed his master from prison, verified the chastity of his mistress, and silenced the bards so that none of them dared say a single word.[36]

The text does not tell us how Taliesin "verified the chastity" of Elphin's wife, but perhaps he merely testified to the bed-trick he had staged (very much like the one used by King John on de Vesci's wife). Nor does it explain (for it cannot) how a woman's amputated finger proves that her chastity was violated. (Inverted, displaced, transferred castration? Upwardly displaced defloration?) Here, the evidence of the ring is separated from that of the finger, in this case a sign not so much of personal identity, which the signet ring theoretically establishes, but of class: the owner of that finger is a working girl, not a lady. The king seems to believe the ring, though it

is false—not in the sense that tin may masquerade as silver but because
the ring appears to be a proof when in fact it is not, and the finger is. The
king at first accepts the "proof" conventionally provided by the old myth of
the ring of recognition because he wants to dishonor Elphin. And Elphin
acknowledges the logical reasoning behind that proof: a number of people
know the ring. But the hard evidence provided by the finger finally breaks
through the convention of the story,[xiv] a convention that the storyteller also
constantly undercuts with a series of cynical asides ("the story says that"
and "if the tale can be believed," etc.).

An amputated finger with a ring (again with a bed-trick) also appears
in *The Changeling*, a seventeenth-century play by Thomas Middleton and
William Rowley.[37] And in a story collected in the nineteenth century from
a village in the Auvergne, a telltale ring on the mutilated paw of a wolf
reveals the true identity of what had appeared to be a human woman.[38] In
other stories a witch masquerading as a cat is revealed by the same mutilation of the hand/paw.[39]

The Sexual Ring

Jewelry is often imagined as part of the body. Think of all those metaphors
that liken a woman's body parts to jewels: pearly teeth, ruby lips, eyes shining like diamonds, golden hair. Philip Roth, in *Sabbath's Theater*, rhapsodizes on the clitoris and concludes: "Why do they need jewelry, when they
have that? What's a ruby next to that?" On statues of goddesses (I know the
South Indian bronzes best, but it is true much more broadly), the bracelets
and anklets seem part of their skin, more a part of them than any garment
could be; this is especially true of statues of nude goddesses, even of naked
women, who often wear nothing but jewelry. One of the earliest images of
this sort that I know comes from the ruins of Mohenjo-daro in the Indus
River Valley (now in Pakistan), from a great civilization that thrived c. 2000
BCE. It is a tiny (10 cm.) bronze image of an impudent, defiant dancing girl,
totally naked save for a chunky necklace and an assortment of bangles.

In the *Yogavasishtha*, a Sanskrit text from Kashmir in the eleventh
century CE, a woman named Chudala uses her magic powers to transform
herself into a man by day and back into a woman by night; as she changes
into a woman, at sunset, she exclaims, "I feel as if I am falling, trembling,
melting. I am so ashamed as I see myself becoming a woman. Alas, my

---

xiv. See chapter 11, pp. 302–324.

chest is sprouting breasts, and jewelry is growing right out of my body."[40] Jewelry in this culture was an essential part of a woman's physical reality. Indeed, it was part of a man's body, too; the ancient Indian warrior Karna was born with golden earrings and golden armor that were part of his skin; when he grew up, he was tricked into cutting them off, a bloody and excruciating, but not fatal, operation.[41] There is only one form of ornamentation even more closely bonded to the body than jewelry, and that is tattooing. The women of the village of Kanker, in Chhattisgarh, central India, always say that tattooing "is the ornamentation that no one can take from you, the only ornaments that go with you in death."[42]

These visceral connections between jewelry and the body are particularly true of rings. Nowadays some people get rings tattooed on their fingers instead of buying metal rings. The naturally close association between rings and fingers (and the heart) underlies stories in which a ring conjures up a person in his or her physical entirety. When, in the ancient Indian epic the *Ramayana*, the princess Sita,[xv] separated from her husband Rama, sees his ring, she feels "as happy as if she had been reunited with her husband,"[43] and a commentator remarks that "this beloved ring would inevitably remind her of his hand, the memory of which would in turn conjure up for her his arm, which in turn would evoke his whole body. Thus," he continues, "she fantasizes seeing her husband before her and makes as if to embrace him."[44]

The ring as the body of an absent lover appears in several Christian texts. Red marks in the shape of rings (called "espousal rings") were said to have appeared miraculously around the fingers of a number of women in the Middle Ages, symbols of their marriage to Christ.[45] A nun named Sister Benedetta Carlini (c. 1623) cited such an "espousal ring" as proof that Christ had married her; on the fourth finger of her right hand was "a circle, the width of an ordinary, inexpensive gold ring . . . and on the top side there were five points . . . of an almost dark red color."[46] But others claimed that she had imagined it, or that her lover was the devil or a kind of incubus who masqueraded as Christ. Benedetta complicated matters by testifying that a demonic masquerader of this sort did in fact appear to her—not instead of Jesus, but in addition to him, two months after the display of the first ring, at which time another ring appeared on her right hand, not nearly as beautiful and brilliant as the

---

xv. See chapter 3, p. 63.

first.[47] Benedetta's own testimony about the masquerader is vivid and revealing:

> "Another time there came one young man with a ring to tell her that he wanted her to be his bride and she answered him that she wanted to be the bride of Jesus. He wanted to put the ring on her finger by force, telling her companion to hold her hand. . . . She never wanted that young man to touch her hand to put the ring on it."[48]

Benedetta was so sure that this was not the true bridegroom that she resisted and was symbolically raped by him with the ring. Finally, however, doubt was cast upon the evidence of the first ring: some of the nuns noticed that Benedetta's adjoining fingers were sometimes stained with the same shade of yellow as the ring, and that the ring appeared sometimes very bright and at other times faded. Finally, Benedetta's companion, Bartolomea, found a small brass box containing diluted saffron: "She surmised that Benedetta used the saffron to paint the ring and that she used her own blood for making the red stones."[49] So the ring was an artificial scar, transformed, unsuccessfully, into a supernatural sign.

The ring from Christ takes an even more vivid form in the story of Catherine of Siena (who died c. 1380). She had, according to the hagiographies, visions of a ring made of silver or of gold, ruby-encrusted and diamond-studded, but she herself said, in several letters, that "we do not marry Christ with gold or silver but with the ring of Christ's foreskin, given in the Circumcision and accompanied by pain and the shedding of blood. . . . She even said that the ring of flesh with which Christ marries us in the Circumcision is a sign that he is the spouse of our humanity."[50] The reference to male genitalia sexualizes the ring, while the reference to a divine, spiritual marriage rather than a human, carnal union desexualizes it. The scar that a wedding ring makes on a finger is the next thing up from circumcision, as a form of sexual marking.

Indeed, a ring was more broadly regarded as a symbol of the male sexual body. Words for the male genitalia often refer to jewelry, as in the expression "the family jewels." The Tibetan word for the male genitals is "jewel" (*nor bu*), and the word *schmuck* means "jewel" in German and "genitals" in Yiddish (and, then, also in Yiddish, comes to designate a man who is a contemptible jerk, a creep—in a word, a prick). Ovid's *Amores* includes a poem on "A Ring," specifically a signet ring, which plays the part of the male sexual organ in this supremely erotic passage:

> Ring, to encircle my beautiful girl's finger,
> appreciated only in terms of the giver's love,
> go as a dear gift! Receiving you with glad heart,
> may she slide you straightaway over her knuckle:
> . . .
> Lucky ring, to be touched by my lady:
> now I'm sadly envious of my own gift.
> O if only I could, suddenly, be my present,
> by the art of Circe or old Proteus!
> Then, when I wanted to touch my girl's breasts
> and slip my left hand into her tunic,
> I'd glide from her finger, however tight and clinging,
> and with wonderful art fall into the loose folds.
> Again, so I could seal a secret letter,
> the sticky wax not freeing from a dry gem,
> I'd be touched first by the lovely girl's wet lips—
> so that sealing the work would give me no pain.
> . . .
> Wear me, when you drench your body in the hot shower,
> and let the falling water run beneath the jewel—
> though, I think, your naked limbs would rouse my passion,
> and, as that ring, I'd carry out a man's part.[51]

But far more common than the association with male genitalia is the representation of women's genitalia as a ring. The wearing of a ring has obvious sexual meanings, perhaps on the analogy between putting your finger through a ring and putting one sexual organ into another. Since Shakespeare's time, "ring" has been a slang term for the female genitalia,[52] just as "jewel" (*bijou*) is in French. In the very last line of *The Merchant of Venice*,[xvi] Gratiano, punning on the finger ring that has played an essential part in the plot, promises: "Well, while I live I'll fear no other thing / So sore as keeping safe Nerissa's ring" (5.1.306–307). About which David Bevington delicately comments, "As Gratiano bawdily points out

---

xvi. See chapter 4, p. 107.

in the play's last line, the ring is both a spiritual and a sexual symbol of marriage."[53]

Throughout the Slavonic oral tradition, the vagina is represented as a golden ring.[54] In one story, a husband (named Staver Godinovich) fails to recognize his wife, who is masquerading as a male warrior, until the warrior "lifts his garment up to the very belly button and then the young Staver Godinovich recognised the golden ring."[55] In a Russian tale recorded by A. N. Afanasiev, a magic ring on a young man's finger, like a kind of proto-Viagra, made his penis grow longer, the lower down on his finger he put the ring. When a thief who was riding in a carriage slipped the ring down to the middle of his finger, he got an erection that "knocked the coachman off his box, passed over the horses and extended five miles in front of the carriage."[56]

The association of the ring with female genitals underlies a naughty French satire on the motif of the ring "fished up" from vast waters.[xvii] It was published c. 1462, in *The One Hundred New Tales (Les cent nouvelles nouvelles)* collected by Antoine de la Sale:

A miller had a beautiful but rather stupid wife, whom a clever knight tricked into allowing him to bed her on several occasions. The miller decided to take revenge on the knight. When the knight was away from home for a month at least, the miller called on the knight's wife. Knowing that she was in her bath, he brought a fine pike to her and insisted on presenting it to her himself. She thanked him and sent it to the kitchen to have it prepared it for supper. Meanwhile the miller saw a large, beautiful diamond ring sitting on the edge of the tub, where the lady had placed it before bathing. The miller stole it and left. Only later did the lady discover that she had lost the ring, and she was deeply upset, for the knight, her husband, had given it to her on their wedding day. Finally she summoned the miller, who assured her that he knew nothing about the diamond but then suggested that, since she had left her diamond at the edge of the bathtub, it must have slipped from her finger, fallen into the water, and worked its way into her body. He asked her to lie on her bed, examined her, and claimed that he could see the ring and would extract it. "Begin, then, handsome miller," she replied. Then,

---

xvii. See chapter 2, p. 25.

"The miller even made use of the same type of tool as the knight had used, in order to fish for the diamond." It took several attempts, and she begged him to keep fishing until he found it. Finally, "the miller fished so diligently that he returned madam's diamond." When she told the knight what had happened, he realized that the miller had repaid him heartily. When they met again, the knight greeted the miller with, "May God keep you, fisher after diamonds!"[57]

The fish is brought to the house and is sent down to dinner, where anyone who knew the old story of the ring-in-the-fish might expect to see someone open the pike and find the ring. Not so; the tale moves in another direction, brilliantly satirizing the idea that a woman might lose her wedding ring in the deep waters of her own insatiable (and naive) sexuality and find it only in the course of an adultery. It may also be a blasphemous take on the disciple Peter, whom Jesus said he would make a "fisher of men." Here the fisher after diamonds is a fisher of women.

Hans Carvel's Ring

The symbolic equation of ring and vagina is grotesquely clear in a story first collected and published in 1470 by Poggio Bracciolini (1380–1459, also known as Poggio Fiorentino, "Poggio of Florence") in his book of jokes, in Latin, *Facetiae*:

> Franciscus Philelphus, jealous of his wife (*zelotypus uxoris*), was worried that she might go to bed with some other man, and so he watched her day and night. One night, in a dream (for we often dream about what has concerned us when awake), he saw a certain demon, who promised him a way to be certain of his wife.... "Take this ring and keep it carefully upon your finger; for as long as your finger is in the ring, your wife will never sleep with another man without your knowledge of it." Philelphus, awakened by joy, realized that he had his finger in his wife's vagina. That ring indeed allows a jealous husband to be sure that his wife will not be unchaste without his knowledge.[58]

It is worth noting that Poggio leaves a loophole for the husband to let his wife sleep with another man with his permission; it protects him only from her adultery without his knowledge.

De la Sale, who also told this tale, remarks that the jealous husband let his wife sleep undisturbed, "perhaps because he had so many fancies and whims in his head that nature was restrained."[59] François Rabelais, to whom the story is usually attributed, may have drawn upon the de la Sale version when he retold the story in *Gargantua and Pantagruel* (c. 1533), though the tale was freely circulating by then. But Rabelais changed the husband's name to Hans Carvel and made him the jeweler of the King of Melinda (in East Africa).[60]

Rabelais says that Hans Carvel, here evidently a Muslim, in his old age married the bailiff Concordat's daughter, a young, attractive, ardent girl, much too friendly to friends and neighbors. Suspecting that his wife might be unfaithful to him, Carvel, jealous as a tiger, gave her a chain enriched with pure Oriental sapphires. Still, he was worried, and Satan appeared and gave him the ring: "Grammercy, My Lord Devil," said Hans Carvel. "I renounce Mahomet if ever it come off my finger." When he awoke to find his wife protesting, he "thought only that someone was trying to steal his ring."[61]

It's strange that Rabelais, of all people, followed de la Sale in using a coy locution for the place where the husband found his finger (*trouva qu'il avoit le doigt on comment a nom? de sa femme*).[62] One English translator renders it quite literally as "his wife's what-do-you-call it."[63] Poggio, protected by the shield of Latin, had been much more straightforward: *sensit se digitum habere in uxoris cunno*. But the story itself then became yet another coy locution; in nineteenth-century England, "Hans Carvel's ring" (or just "Carvel's ring") came to be a slang term for a vagina.

The story continued to be retold by others, including Jean de la Fontaine (1621–95)[64] and Matthew Prior (1664–1721). Prior's version has some charming doggerel in it. He too turns the demon into Satan, who appears in the form of a barrister, from Lincoln's Inn:

> And giving Him a Magick Ring,
> Fit for the Finger of a King;
> Dear Hans, said He, this Jewel take,
> And wear it long for SATAN'S Sake:
> 'Twill do your Business to a Hair:
> For long as You this Ring shall wear,
> As sure as I look over LINCOLN,
> That ne'er shall happen which You think on.[65]

FIGURE I.I Jean-Honoré Fragonard's illustration of the story of Hans Carvel's ring (as told by la Fontaine), executed between 1765 and 1777. The Devil hovers in the form of a cloud over Hans, whose right hand is groping under the bedclothes.

Source: © Petit Palais/Roger-Voillet

Sigmund Freud and D. E. Oppenheim retold this story in their collection of folktales, using Poggio's version rather than Rabelais's: a demon, rather than "the devil," visits the man (who is not named).[66] Oddly, though, Freud omits Poggio's very Freudian observation that "we often dream about what has concerned us when awake."[67] The power of the ring is projected (as Freud taught us to see); within the dream, the man puts the ring not on his wife's finger, as we might expect if it were to function as a fetter, but on his own, in a transposed replication of the sexual act. (Magic powers are often projected in this way: in ancient India, placing a magic ointment on *your own* eyes made you invisible to others.)[68] Outside the dream, however, his wife—or the part of her that concerns him—*is* the ring, which therefore belongs on his finger, not hers.

The Vagina Monologues

The French tradition of Rabelais also developed in other directions, not merely equating the vagina itself with a ring but giving another ring the power to reveal the truth of that first ring, the woman's jewel. The story in this form plays upon an equation between a woman's mouth and her lower mouth, a widespread motif that Freud called "upward displacement."[69] A thirteenth-century text by Garin, *Le Chevalier qui faisait parler les C—et C—ls*,[70] was retold in 1747 in a brief tale attributed to Count Anne Claude de Caylus. In this story a fairy gives a young knight, Amador, the power to make women's sexual organs speak.[71] In 1875, Denis Diderot published a novel based on the Caylus story: *Les bijoux indiscrets* (*The Indiscreet Jewels*).[72] Diderot set his story in the world of Orientalism that was in place even in the time of Rabelais and was rife in eighteenth- and nineteenth-century Europe. In the pseudo-genre of the *Arabian Nights*, *Les bijoux indiscrets* revels in a miscellaneous mélange of sultans in mosques who worship the Hindu god Brahma and deal with duplicitous Brahmins (since all Orientals, Hindu and Muslim, apparently look alike in the dark).

Diderot also added a ring to Caylus's story. Now, talking rings were nothing new. The satirist Lucian, in the second century CE, quotes a man who was said to have "a ring set with an engraved signet bearing the head of the Pythian Apollo and to have boasted that the ring literally 'spoke' to him." Lucian says this was a lie, and he cites the story just to show what stupid fables some people believed.[73] In Diderot's allegory, a genie named Cucufa discovers at the bottom of his pocket a tiny silver ring, which he gives to Prince Mangogul with this user's guide: women speak, but not through their mouths; put this ring on your finger, turn the stone toward some woman, and it makes her "jewel" talk; on another finger, the little finger, it makes you invisible; and you can also say, "I will be there," and it transports you wherever you like.[74] (This is quite a ring, more multi-tasking even than Benchley's[xviii] or Wagner's:[xix] the ring of invisibility, of truth, and of sexuality, with seven-league boots thrown in for good measure.)[75] Diderot tells us that women's "jewels" always speak, but too softly to be heard; the ring just amplifies the volume.[76] As soon as the jewels talk, someone devises a muzzle to make them stop talking, but they have their uses: a woman who lied about rape because she was jealous of her lover's new girl-friend is found out when her jewel tells the truth; the man is set free, and she is condemned to wear a chastity belt (another ring) forever.[77]

The ring works on other mammals, too; Prince Mangogul turns the ring on his mare, to make it speak like a woman,[78] thus combining the magic rings that allow the wearer to understand the speech of animals (King Solomon had the most famous of these)[xx] and those that understand vagina monologues.[79] Since vaginas were often given the slang name of animals (*chatte* in French, pussy/beaver/coney in English, etc.), it is easy enough to see the animal-language-rings as the source of the vagina-language-rings. Chantal Thomas points out that the vaginas in Diderot's story do not, in fact, express women's thoughts or experiences: "The jewels, far from saying what they like, what gives them pleasure, how they have orgasms, are essentially bookkeepers. They tally the register of visitors and *their* orgasms."[80] Yet, Thomas admits, "To the extent that this ring is presumed, according to the Freudian analytic scheme, to give voice to the forbidden ... Diderot ... reveals himself here with surprising candor, perhaps *unwittingly*, just as the jewels do."[81]

Michel Foucault used the Diderot story to introduce his *History of Sexuality*:

"The aim of this series of studies? To transcribe into history the fable of *Les bijoux indiscrets*. Among its many emblems, our society wears that of the talking sex. The sex which one catches unawares

---

xviii. See the Introduction, p. xxi.

xix. See chapter 4, p. 120.

xx. See chapter 2, p. 27.

and questions, and which, restrained and loquacious at the same
time, endlessly replies. One day a certain mechanism, which was so
elfin-like that it could make itself invisible, captured this sex and, in
a game that combined pleasure with compulsion, and consequently
with inquisition, made it tell the truth about itself and others as
well. For many years, we have all been living in the realm of Prince
Mangogul: under the spell of an immense curiosity about sex, bent
on questioning it, with an insatiable desire to hear it speak and be
spoken about, quick to invent all sorts of magical rings that might
force it to abandon its discretion. . . . Our problem is to know what
marvelous ring confers a similar power on us, and on which master's finger it has been placed. . . . It is this magical ring, this jewel
which is so indiscreet when it comes to making others speak, but
so ineloquent concerning one's own mechanism, that we need to
render loquacious in its turn."[82]

And that is one of the purposes of this book of mine, too.

The Rings of Wives and Courtesans

The patterns that link jewelry and the sexuality of women have intricate
historical and sociological implications, but a ruthless structuralist can
group the narratives of circular jewelry into two contrasting paradigms.
Though they are ancient types, I will name them after the two film icons
who seared my soul when I was a teenager in the 1950s: Doris Day (1924–)
and Marilyn Monroe (1926–62). The Doris Day/professional virgin scenario of legitimation ("Get the *wedding* ring before you go to bed with him")
is challenged by the Marilyn Monroe / gold-digger scenario of illegitima-
tion ("Get *lots* of rings [or bracelets, or necklaces] before [and after] you go
to bed with him"). These two paradigms have different historical trajecto-
ries, one from the regulation of marriage by religion and the other from the
survival strategies of women outside the confines of religion. The tension
between them is the driving force behind the narratives. But both of them
are grounded in what I would call the slut assumption: when a woman
has a piece of jewelry, she must have gotten it by sleeping with some man.
Many of these tales (particularly but not only those about clever wives)[xxi]

---

xxi. See chapters 6 and 7, pp. 137–207.

are about inheritance, and others (particularly but not only the nineteenth-century stories)[xxii] are about heirlooms. But most of them involve payment for services rendered.[xxiii] Fay Weldon, in *The Bulgari Connection*, put it well: "She was a working girl, he was a wealthy man, and he loved her and must prove it. That's why she expected him to buy her expensive jewelry." Ultimately, this paradigm reduces women to whores.[83]

The mythology of women and their jewelry often raises issues of authenticity. The (wedding) ring, on the one hand, the Doris Day ring, makes the wife a good woman; it's official, marital, given to her by the unique man she is supposed to love, her legal man, her husband, in return for sleeping only with him. And she damn well better keep it; if she loses it, she might lose her authenticity. Some married women, according to the nineteenth-century historian Charles Edwards, were "so rigidly super-stitious or firm" that they would never ever take off their wedding ring, "extending the expression 'till death do us part' even to the ring."[84] This also applies to men in some of our stories: if the husband loses his ring (or, more particularly, gives it to a woman he thinks is not his wife—Tamar, Helena),[xxiv] he loses his authenticity and validates hers.

By contrast with the married woman, another sort of woman gets other forms of circular jewelry, necklaces or bracelets (or anklets), or other kinds of rings—the Marilyn Monroe jewelry—from men (plural), lovers or serial husbands, in payment for sleeping with them, which makes her lose her chaste authenticity. I would call these women courtesans, in the European sense of a woman of notorious beauty, often a famous actress or dancer, sometimes called a demi-mondaine; she is the mistress of a wealthy lover (or a series of lovers, or husbands, but only one at a time) who gives her valuable gifts, principally jewelry. (The word "courtesan" in American English has overtones of crass prostitution that I wish to exclude; think Madame du Barry or Mata Hari, rather than Belle Watling or Polly Adler). The great courtesans—Dumas's Camille (Marguerite Gautier), Verdi's Violetta, Elizabeth Taylor, Mae West—have an authenticity different from that of the monogamous women, because their fabulous jewelry proves that they have many rich/famous lovers/husbands and thereby authenti-cates their beauty and their charm.

---

xxii. See chapter 9, p. 228.

xxiii. See chapter 11, p. 294.

xxiv. See chapter 6, pp. 152, 160.

The much publicized number and value of the jewels worn by such women is the equivalent of the collection of garters that a certain sort of man used to show off, or the notches that he cut on his bedpost. A vividly mythologized instance of the female form of this tradition appears in Mary de Morgan's 1880 fairy tale, "The Necklace of Princess Fiorimonde": the beautiful, evil princess refused to marry for fear that her husband would make her give up the magic that kept her beautiful; so she turned each of her suitors into a bright, beautiful bead strung on the gold circlet that she always wore around her neck. She did this twelve times until, finally, the thirteenth suitor tricked her and made her the thirteenth bead, thereby releasing the other twelve suitors from the necklace.[85] Significantly, the necklace had no clasp, and "just fit over her head"; in effect, it was a ring.

In the 1958 film musical, *Gigi*, based on a 1944 novella by Colette, a young girl who is being tutored in the art of a courtesan, and in particular in the ways to get jewelry from lovers, sings, with great disapproval:

> A necklace is love
> A ring is love
> A rock from some obnoxious little king is love.[86]

And in the 1956 operetta *Candide*, the much-seduced Cunegonde seems at first to be haunted by the same sort of shame over her ill-gotten jewelry that troubles Gigi. In one verse of a song, lyrics by Richard Wilbur, she sings:

> Pearls and ruby rings,
> Ah, how can worldly things
> Take the place of honor lost?
> Can they compensate
> For my fallen state,
> Purchased, as they were, at such an awful cost!
> Bracelets, lavalieres,
> Can they dry my tears?
> Can they blind my eyes from shame?
> Can the brightest brooch
> shield me from reproach?
> Can the purest diamond purify my name?

But she quickly makes her peace with her jewels in another verse:

> And yet, of course, these trinkets are endearing!
> I'm oh so glad my sapphire is a star.
> I rather like a 20-carat earring!
> If I'm not pure, at least my jewels are.[87]

And that is the courtesans' creed.

So there is a tension between the two forms of authenticity that jewelry offers the married woman (validating her chastity) and the courtesan (validating the devotion and wealth of her conquests). Trouble arises only when the wife, from paradigm A, strays into the territory of the courtesan, in paradigm B, and obtains jewelry that she cannot account for.[xxv] But even then, sometimes the jewels a married woman gets from her lover validate her in a different way, because her lover really loves her, and her husband may merely own her. And the jewelry that a masquerading "clever wife"[xxvi] gets from the man she sleeps with proves that she is actually virtuous, not promiscuous, since it proves that her lover is her husband.

In many tales of this corpus, beauty is a legitimating or, more often, illegitimating criterion. Translators know the old sexist saying, often attributed to George Bernard Shaw: translations are like women: if they are beautiful, they can't be faithful, and if they're faithful, they can't be beautiful. The circularity of jewelry, beauty, and jealousy is reduced to its logical absurdity in Isak Dinesen's 1934 short story, "The Roads Round Pisa" (a story all about circularity), when a man who prides himself on his knowledge of jewelry buys for his wife, an insanely jealous woman, a pair of particularly fine eardrops, "to set off the beauty of his young wife, who wore them so well." Then:

> "He had been so pleased to have got them that he had fastened them in her ears himself, and held up the mirror for her to see them. She watched him, and was aware that his eyes were on the diamonds and not on her face. She quickly took them off and handed them to him. 'I am afraid,' she said, with dry eyes more tragic than if

---

xxv. See chapter 9, p. 253.

xxvi. See chapter 6, p. 137.

they had been filled with tears, 'that I have not your taste for pretty things.' From that day she had given up wearing jewels."

As the author comments in despair, "She is indeed jealous of her own jewels."[88]

In Anthony Trollope's novel *The Eustace Diamonds* (1871), the protagonist Lizzie Greystock refuses to relinquish the diamond necklace that her late husband, the aged Sir Florian Eustace, had given her; and when she sets out to snare another rich husband, she wears the diamonds to highlight her beauty. In the Guy de Maupassant story, "The Necklace" (1885),[xxvii] Mathilde borrows a diamond necklace to make herself beautiful in hope of entrancing a rich man who will marry her and give her diamond necklaces. Jewelry and beauty play a game of doubles here: if women are beautiful, men give them jewelry, which they want in part because jewelry makes them more beautiful, so that they can attract more men, to give them more jewelry—or, perhaps, a wedding ring, which magically transforms the Marilyn Monroe type into the Doris Day type. Popular music, as usual, cuts to the chase, this time in lines of a lyric from the musical *Kismet*, entitled "Baubles, Bangles, and Beads":

> [S]omeday he may
> Buy me a ring, ring-a-ling-a,
> I've heard that's where it leads,
> Wearing baubles, bangles and beads.[89]

Women use jewelry to get men to buy them jewelry. It's a circle, like the circle of a ring.

---

xxvii. See chapter 9, p. 234.

The Ring Fished from the Ocean

The Story in the Fish

The ring in the fish is one of the all-time top-ten narrative hits, topping the charts since at least the time of the ancient Greeks. Fish are the ultimate lost-and-found of the folklore world. Stith Thompson notes many variants within his motif entitled "fish recovers ring from sea."[1] The fish is one particular species in the more general genus of helpful animals who enable the hero to accomplish difficult tasks, often in gratitude for a favor that the hero did for the animal in the past.[2]

These stories generally regard as a benevolent miracle the return of the ring from the ocean, a place from which everything eventually returns but you cannot expect any particular thing to return. This optimism may be what e e cummings had in mind when he wrote, "For whatever we lose, like a you or a me, it's always ourselves we find in the sea."[3] That cheerful attitude also marks this Chinese Buddhist tale:

> There was once a married woman who used to say all the time, "I never lose anything." Her son took his mother's ring and threw it into the water; then he went to ask his mother where her gold ring was. She said to him: "I never lose anything." The next day, his mother invited three Buddhist sages to dinner; she sent a man to the market to buy a fish. When the man returned, they prepared the fish and in its stomach they found the gold ring. The mother said to her son, "I never lose anything." Her son, delighted, went to the spot where the Buddha was staying and asked him: "What is the cause of my mother's good fortune in never losing anything?" The Buddha explained that, in an earlier birth, his mother had lived alone in

the northern mountains, and when, every winter, all the inhabit-
ants went south, she was so poor that she was not able to leave; she
stayed there all alone and kept in order all the utensils and goods of
the tribe; every spring, all the men came back and the mother gave
each object, without exception, back to its owner. Because of that,
she attained this good fortune of never losing anything.[4]

The return of the objects each spring after the hard winter is here analo-
gized, superficially, to the miraculous return of the ring and, more pro-
foundly, to the return of the woman's good fortune in a better rebirth.

The return of a ring from deep water is also compared with the return
of the dead in an old Irish story about a salmon, the protagonist of most
Irish and Scottish fish stories:

Findabair fell in love with Froech, against her parents' will, and gave
him a thumb ring that her father, Ailill, had given her; she told her
father that she had lost it. But Ailill found the thumb ring one day in
Froech's wallet and recognized it and threw it into the river; Froech
saw him do this and also saw a salmon leap for the ring and catch
it in its mouth. Froech leapt after the salmon and caught it by the
gills. He sent the salmon to Findabair with instructions to her to
cook it well, for he knew the thumb ring was inside the salmon and
thought that it might be demanded of her that night. Indeed, Ailill
asked Findabair to give him the ring and said, "I swear by the god
my people swear by, you will die unless you restore it. That is why I
demand it of you—I know you cannot produce it. That ring will not
come from where it has been put until the dead come to life."

Findabair sent her maid to look for the ring; the maid brought a
platter into the royal house, and the salmon was on it. Findabair had
cooked it well, and the gold thumb ring lay upon it. And so Froech
won Findabair.[5]

The translator remarks that Findabair's father "has accused her of giving her ring (and by implication herself) to Froech."[6] And Froech himself
says, "She said that she would give me her love for a year" in exchange for
the ring. We have seen how often a ring is equated with the sexuality of a
woman, and this is so even when the ring ends up in a fish.

The illogical but apparently very deep-seated hope that a fish can
retrieve both a ring and the true love that the ring represents lies behind

an old German folktale, which tells of a man who deliberately threw his ring into the Rhine river in the hope that a fish would swallow it and be brought to the king's table, where his sweetheart would recognize the ring and bring it back to him. This is the "Rhine Legend," recorded in *Des Knaben Wunderhorn* ("The Youth's Magic Horn"),[7] a collection of anonymous German folk poems that was assembled, reworked, and published between 1805 and 1808.[8] The ring in this legend functions as a kind of shiny lure both for the fish and for the desired sweetheart; the pieces of the puzzle are the same as usual, but the causal links are different.

The identification of the ring in the fish with a beloved woman is made startlingly explicit in the film *Big Fish* (2003, Tim Burton), when a man whose ring is swallowed by a fish remarks, "My wedding ring, the symbol of my fidelity to my wife, soon to be mother of my child, was now lost in the gut of an uncatchable fish." And then he further muses: "We called it a him, whereas in fact it was a her. She was fat with eggs, gonna lay them any day. Sometimes the only way to catch an uncatchable woman is to offer her a wedding ring." The fish has become not only female (in contrast with the generally ungendered or male fish in most of these stories) but the speaker's beloved, pregnant like his wife. And suddenly this female fish conjures up, from the basic ring-in-fish scenario (you must get *back* the ring from the fish to get *back* the woman), the Doris Day scenario:[i] you need to *give* the woman (fish) a ring in order to mate (catch) her.

Solomon's Ring

Since rings are so closely connected with identity, to lose your ring is also to lose significant aspects of your identity, and to find it again (especially inside a fish) is to rediscover, or to prove, who you are.

One of the most famous tales of this genre is the story of King Solomon's ring, a small finger ring with a seal consisting of an engraved stone, a ring that Solomon received from the archangel Michael, according to one tradition,[9] or from four angels, according to another.[10] A number of texts insist that this magic ring enabled Solomon to understand the language of animals.[11] The Hebrew Bible does not mention such a ring, but it tells us that Solomon "spake also of beasts, and of fowl, and of creeping things, and of fishes" (1 Kings 4.33).[12] A misreading of this text may have given rise to the

---

i. See chapter 1, p. 20.

belief that Solomon could converse not *about* but *with* animals, a legend
that Rudyard Kipling, among others, perpetuated:

> There was never a king like Solomon
> Not since the world began.
> Yet Solomon talked to a butterfly
> As a man would talk to a man.[13]

Konrad Lorenz, who entitled his classic work on animals *King Solomon's
Ring* (1952), queried not Solomon's gifts but his ring: "I am quite ready
to believe that Solomon really could [talk with animals], even without the
help of the magic ring which is attributed to him by the legend in question, and I have very good reason for crediting it; I can do it myself, and
without the aid of magic, black or otherwise. I do not think it is very sport-
ing to use magic rings in dealing with animals."[14] We will often encounter
this hardheaded resistance to the magic powers of rings.

King Solomon's ring was said to have been stolen and thrown into
the sea but later found in the stomach of a fish that was served at his
table, a particularly appropriate fate for a ring that enabled the wearer to
understand the language of animals, presumably including fish, though
Solomon is not said to talk to this fish. There are several versions of the
story of Solomon's ring in the Hebrew and Arabic traditions. According
to one Muslim version, Solomon "thoughtlessly took it off his hand when
he was in the bath and it was carried away by a malevolent genius. At the
end of the forty years it was found again in the body of a fish served on
the monarch's table."[15] An Arabic text cited by Richard Burton elaborates
upon this plot, presenting an extreme form of the ring of identity; this ring
transforms not just the wearer's ability to prove who he is but his actual
physical appearance:

> Solomon was so much infatuated with a female prisoner named
> Aminah, the daughter of a gentile prince, that he entrusted to her
> care his precious signet, given to him by the four angels that pre-
> sided over the four elements. A mighty Jinn succeeded in gaining
> possession of the ring and, by its power, assumed Solomon's form,
> at the same time changing Solomon's appearance to such an extent
> that his people no longer recognized him and drove him from his
> kingdom. However, one of Solomon's ministers saw through the
> disguise of the Jinn and exorcised him by reciting certain verses of

the Law. The Jinn fled in terror and dropped the ring into the sea, where it was swallowed by a fish. In due time Solomon, who had become a fisherman, caught this fish, found his ring, and regained his kingdom.[16]

A woman is part of the solution, not the problem, in a Jewish variant in which, again, Solomon must wear his ring in order to look like himself, but now also in order to exercise his magic powers:

Solomon used his magic ring to capture the demon Asmodeus, who promised to tell Solomon the secret of the power of all demons if he would lend him the magic ring. But as soon as Solomon had given up his protecting ring, Asmodeus threw it into the sea, where a fish swallowed it. Then Asmodeus flung Solomon more than a thousand miles away from Jerusalem, and palmed himself off as the king. Solomon wandered about in far-off lands, among strangers, begging his daily bread. People thought him a lunatic, because he kept insisting that he was Solomon. But it was even worse when he met someone who recognized him, stirring up memories that made his present misery almost unendurable.

After three long years, Solomon took a job as chief cook in the kitchens of the King of Ammon, and the king's daughter, Naamah, fell in love with him. The Ammonite king had the lovers taken to a barren desert, in the hope that they would die of starvation there. Solomon and Naamah wandered through the desert until they came to a city by the seashore, where they purchased a fish. When Naamah prepared the fish, she found in its belly the magic ring belonging to Solomon, who recognized it, put it on his finger, and transported himself to Jerusalem. He drove out Asmodeus and ascended his throne again.[17]

Some people do recognize Solomon without his ring in this version, but without the ring even they cannot help him regain his throne. Nor does his stint as cook give him access to the ring-bearing fish; that possibility of the motif dead ends, and Solomon has to buy the fish. His status as cook merely makes the King of Ammon despise him and try to kill him. Nor is it said that Naamah recognizes him, just that she falls in love with him. It takes the magic ring to turn him back into his recognizable self.

Louis Ginzberg expands upon the partial recognitions in another version that seems to offer an alternative, less magical ending. In this telling, while the real Solomon was wandering far away, the members of the Sanhedrin (the religious assembly of men) noticed the false king's peculiar behavior and investigated the matter. Here again the women are part of the solution: the wives of Solomon and his mother Bath-sheba informed the members of the Sanhedrin that the behavior of the king had completely changed, and that he never allowed anyone to see his feet (for fear, of course, of betraying his demonic nature, since demons' feet, as everyone knows, point backward). The Sanhedrin gave the king's magic ring to the wandering beggar who called himself King Solomon and had him appear before the pretender on the throne. As soon as Asmodeus caught sight of the true king protected by his magic ring, he flew away.[18] Here, it is the *behavior* of Solomon and Asmodeus, not their superficial appearance, that identifies them to thoughtful people, Solomon's wives and the men of the Sanhedrin. But, despite these reasonable considerations, they still need the magic of the ring to reveal the true form of Solomon before they can accept him. Reason, as usual, yields to magic.

Polycrates's Ring

The stories we have considered so far belong to the dominant branch of the ring-in-fish genre, call it Type A, in which the ring is lost against the owner's will and is miraculously regained, to the owner's relief and delight, often bringing with it the desired mate (or, in variants that we will soon consider, child) that was feared lost forever. In the other branch of the ring-in-fish story, the polar opposite of the story of Solomon—call it Type B—the ring is something that the owner would wish to destroy if possible, something that is thrown away into deep water but returns against the owner's wish. The defining ring of this type in European mythology is the ring of Polycrates, ruler of Samos,[19] whose story the Greek historian Herodotus tells (c. 485–420 BCE):

> "Polycrates had extraordinary good fortune but was advised to forestall the jealousy of the gods by taking what he valued most, and which, when lost, would cost him the most agony of soul, and casting it away where it would never come to the world of men again. Polycrates had a signet ring that he wore continually; it was bound in gold, its stone was an emerald, and it had been made by a great

craftsman. Polycrates ordered a boat, went in it himself, and, when he was far from his island, threw his ring into the sea. Five or six days afterwards, a fisherman caught a fish so large and beautiful that he thought he should give it to the king. When the royal servants cut up the fish, they found in its belly Polycrates' signet ring. Polycrates realized that it was impossible for one man to deliver his fellow man from what is fated to happen to him; he knew he would not end well."[20]

Polycrates is ambivalent: he is very fond of his signet ring, so he both does and does not want to get it back, though his fear of the ring is the dominant emotion. Polycrates was eventually killed (probably impaled and/or crucified), so he did indeed come to a bad end.

A variant of the Polycrates myth may be seen in a legend told in explanation of the historically attested custom of the "Marriage with the Sea," in which the Doge of Venice annually casts his gold ring into the Adriatic in token of that marriage. One version states that when he did this on one occasion, "This ring later was found in a fish that was served at the table of the Doge almost a year after the ceremony. The legend holds that this recovery was an omen of the eventual downfall of the Venetian Republic."[21] The Adriatic had served the Doge with divorce papers, and returned his ring.[ii]

The Bishop of Glasgow's Salmon

"The Bishop of Glasgow's Salmon" sounds like the beginning of an off-color joke, or a limerick ("There once was a Bishop of Glasgow ..."), but it simply names two of the main dramatis personae in the hagiography of the founder of the See of Glasgow, the seventh-century bishop Saint Kentigern, popularly known as Mungo.[22] The figure of a salmon with a ring in its mouth appears on the coat of arms of the city of Glasgow, as well as on the armorial bearings of several of the bishops of that city from the early fourteenth century.[23] A popular Catholic source says this about the fish: "The Fish was one caught by Saint Kentigern in the Clyde River. When it was slit open, a ring belonging to the Queen[24] was miraculously found inside it." The king had suspected the queen both of "intrigue" and

---

ii. See chapter 10, p. 279.

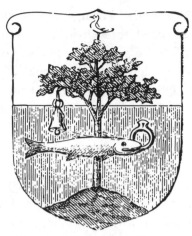

FIGURE 2.1 The Coat of Arms of the City of Glasgow: a salmon with a ring in its mouth.

Source: © Hein Nouwens/Shutterstock.com

of losing the ring that he had given her. "She had asked Saint Kentigern for help, and he found and restored the ring in this way to clear her name."[25]

One Scottish legend adds more details and changes the queen to a commoner:

> "A married woman by ill-chance let her wedding ring fall into the river Clyde. On her return home her husband noted its absence and, believing she had given it to a lover, became furiously jealous, used the harshest language to her and even threatened her life. In her despair the innocent wife went and cast herself at the feet of St. Kentigern, Bishop of Glasgow, supplicating him to render her faithfulness manifest. The Bishop prayed, and in a few hours, a fisherman came to him bearing as a gift a large salmon he had just caught, and in the mouth of the fish was found the lost ring. The husband, convinced of his injustice, was kinder to his wife than ever before, so as to make good the wrong he had done her."[26]

Although in this version of the story the woman is presumably innocent, the mere loss of the wedding ring is a cause for suspicion, and she is saved only by the lucky advent of the salvific salmon.

But other texts, including the *Acta Sanctorum* (a hagiography of Catholic saints, begun in the seventeenth century), assume that the woman was in fact guilty. Joycelyn, a monk of Furness (1175–1214), told this story, identifying the woman as the wife of King Rederech (also called Riderch or Rockerick).

> Queen Languueth desired a certain young soldier and easily made him sleep with her. Foolishly and shamelessly, she gave him a gold ring with a precious gem, which her husband had given her "as a special sign of his marital love." Even more foolishly, her lover wore the ring, and the king saw it on his finger one day when the soldier was asleep. Barely controlling his impulse to kill the soldier, the king took the ring off the soldier's finger and threw it into the river. The soldier thought nothing of the ring.
>
> When the king asked the queen to show him the ring, she sent word to the soldier, but he replied that he had no idea where he had lost it. The king had the queen imprisoned, and she sent for Saint Kentigern and told him all, though he already knew what had happened. He ordered the messenger to cast a hook into the river Clyde and bring back the first fish that he caught. He brought back a salmon, which Kentigern had cut and gutted; he found the ring in it and sent it to the queen by that same messenger. She sent it to the king, who knelt and asked her publicly to pardon him for having unjustly accused her. She went to Kentigern, confessed her guilt to him, and "restrained her feet from another such fall." But not until after her husband's death did she tell anyone "the sign by which the Lord magnified his mercy."[27]

The husband's desire to kill the man who cuckolded him is deflected first to the ring, which he throws into the river, and then to his wife, who invokes a saintly bishop to deflect from her, in turn, the punishment for adultery. Instead of killing her, the king subjects her to what is in effect, an ordeal: if you can find your lost ring, you are proved innocent. She is *not* innocent but is proven innocent by the rigged ordeal.[28] Her caddish lover doesn't even notice the loss of the ring and does not come to her defense. (In a close parallel, King Mark finds his adulterous wife Isolde[iii] asleep beside her lover Tristan, and takes the wedding ring from her finger, but instead of throwing it into a river he replaces it with another ring, thus avoiding, or at least postponing, the need for a trial or ordeal.)

---

iii. See chapter 4, p. 101.

Bishop Kentigern plays the role of the champion for the wife of King Rederech, perhaps because Kentigern himself was said to have been born of a mother who, falsely accused of unchastity, survived a double ordeal.[iv] Kentigern's tale therefore appropriately finds its place within the corpus of medieval courtly epics, where notorious adulteresses like Guinevere and Isolde find ways to prove their innocence by manipulating ordeals that depend upon miracles, the equivalent of the miracle of the ring in the fish.

The (Not-So-) Fortunate Farmer's Daughter

Another dark, if not tragic, variant of the story of the ring in the fish and the accused woman is a tale that has been called "The Fish and the Ring, or the Cruel Knight and the Fortunate Farmer's Daughter."[29] A Victorian English text, published in 1842, tells the story of Dame Rebecca Berry, who died in 1696:

> Sir John Berry, passing a cottage, heard the cries of a woman in childbirth. His knowledge in the occult sciences informed him that the child to be born was destined to become his wife, but he determined to evade the decrees of fate. When the child had reached the age of marriage, he took her to the seaside, intending to throw her in; but he relented, and threw his seal ring into the sea instead. He forbade her ever to see his face again, on pain of death, unless she recovered the ring. She became a cook in a noble family. One day as she was preparing a codfish for dinner she found the ring in the fish. She brought the ring to the knight and became his wife. In memory of this event, the arms of Sir John Berry bear a fish and a ring.[30]

The husband's rejection of his destined wife is presumably based on his class snobbery, his desire "to avoid so ignoble an alliance" (as William Jones, who recorded this version, puts it). But his revulsion is amplified to a point so extreme that he tries to kill her (Jones describes other frustrated attempts to destroy her from early childhood), and he does so for another reason—in a vain attempt to resist fate, as Polycrates tried to do, also in vain. The prospective husband's fury is deflected, however, from

---

iv. See chapter 4, p. 90.

the woman to the ring; as was implicit in the tale of the Kentigern ordeals, and is now here explicit, the ring substitutes for the accused woman. He hopes she will *not* bring back his ring, while of course she hopes that she will. Where he is Polycrates, she is Solomon. (This pattern extends to a number of the stories of lost rings in which the man wants to forget and the woman wants him to remember.)[v]

An expanded version of the basic plot was published in ballad form in 1860. Here the knight, simply called "the Yorkshire Knight," does not wait for the girl, a farmer's daughter, to grow up, nor does he resist his first impulse to kill her; he takes the newborn infant and throws her into the river, where she floats on the tide until a fisherman finds her and adopts her. We learn why the knight hates her:

> Says he, "If you live, you must needs be my wife;
> But I am resolved to bereave you of life:
> For 'till you are dead I no other can have,
> Therefore you shall lie in a watery grave."

When she is "aged eleven full years" and "her sweet beauty began to appear," the cruel knight finds her again, takes her from the fisherman and, after a foiled attempt to have her killed by his brother, again takes her to a river and tells her to strip, "for this hour is your last." She begs him to spare her, but:

> He hearing the pitiful moan she did make,
> Then from his own finger a ring he did take,
> And unto this maiden in anger did say,
> "This ring in the water I'll now throw away;
> Pray look on it well, the posey is plain,
> And when you see it may know it again.
> I charge you for life, ne'er come more in my sight,
> For if you do, I shall owe you a spite;
> Unless that you bring the same ring unto me."
> With that, he let the ring drop into the sea. . . .
> She was a cook maid, and forgot all things past,
> But here is a wonder now comes at the last.

---

v. See chapter 5, p. 133.

As she a fish dinner was dressing one day,
And opening the head of a cod, as they say,
She found a rich ring, and was struck with amaze;
And then she with wonder upon it did gaze.
At viewing it well, she did find it to be
The very same ring the knight threw into the sea.
She smil'd when she saw it, and bless'd the kind fate
But did to no creature the secret relate. . . .

Eventually she finds the Knight, who says:

"This hour's your last, to the world bid good night,
For being so bold to appear in my sight."
Said she, "In the sea, sir, you flung your own ring,
And bid me not see you, unless I could bring
That ring unto you, and I have it," said she,
"Behold, 'tis the same that was thrown into the sea!"
When the knight saw the ring, he did fly to her arms;
He kissed her, and swore she had a million of charms.
Said he, "Charming creature, I pray pardon me,
Who has often contrived the ruin of thee.
Tis in vain to alter what fate has decreed,
For I find thou wast born my dear bride to be."[31]

The doggerel embroiders the tale with a number of stock themes that
we will often encounter, such as the childless couple who fish the baby
from the water. But again the theme of inevitability—from blind fate or
a watchful deity—is sounded: "Tis in vain to alter what fate has decreed."
Suddenly the knight discovers that his bride is charming, and he makes
her a lady, and they live happily ever after. The sudden sharp change of
emotion is as unconvincing here as it is in a closely related story, the tale
of the clever wife,[vi] in which a husband who hates his wife challenges her
to get his ring, and suddenly declares his love for her when she succeeds.

    The ordeal of retrieving the ring, in the Kentigern cycle, is designed
to determine whether or not the woman who had lost it was guilty of
adultery.[32] In some variants, the suspect, or a champion, is forced to

---

vi. See chapter 6, p. 137.

search for the ring (sometimes by being thrown into the water himself or herself).[33] Generally, however, only the ring is thrown into the water; we see the transition from the woman to the ring actually in process from the Yorkshire knight, who actually *does* throw the infant into the water as well as (later) the ring, to Sir John Berry, who throws only the ring.

The moral of both variants of the tale of the Fortunate Farmer's Daughter seems to be that the million to one odds of finding your ring in a fish are the same as the odds that the husband who abandons you like that will return to you. This moral holds true even when the genders are reversed so that a woman calls the shots, as in the case of Peter Güldenstern. He asked his beloved for her hand, but she threw her ring in a pond and said: "As unlikely as I am to find this ring again, so unlikely am I to become your wife." The ring was found in the belly of a fish, and Güldenstern was able to fulfill the condition—though she also made him build her a new house.[34]

The Child and the Ring in the Water

In some variants of the ring-in-fish story, a lost child, rather than (or as well as) a ring, is retrieved from the fish's maw, like Jonah from the whale; the fish serves as a surrogate womb.[35] In this fifteenth-century CE Indian story, a child, without a ring, is found in a fish:

Krishna's infant son Pradyumna was stolen by a demon who threw him into the ocean. There the child was swallowed by a large fish, which was caught and brought to the palace kitchen of a great magician. The magician's wife, Mayavati ("Mistress of Magic"), found the child inside the fish. She raised the boy, but she was so entranced by his extraordinary beauty that she fell in love with him. When he grew to manhood and realized how attached to him she was, he said, "Why are you acting like this, instead of acting like a mother?" (In one variant, the magician catches them *in flagrante* and says to Mayavati, "You crazy whore, have you lost your mind, making love with your own son?")[36] Then she said to him, "You are not my son; a demon stole you from your father, Krishna, and threw you into the ocean, where a fish swallowed you. I took you out of the fish's belly, but your own mother is still weeping for you." Eventually it was revealed that Pradyumna and Mayavati had been husband and

wife in a previous life, and that in this life, too, Mayavati was the
true wife of Pradyumna.[37]

Mayavati, whose name tells us that she controls illusion (*maya*) rather
than being controlled by it, knows the truth all along. She therefore has
no need of a ring to reveal the true identity of the child she finds in a fish.

But more often, the ring is essential to the identification. A ring, supplemented by the services of two bangle-sellers, is needed as evidence in
a modern Tamil folktale, despite the fact that the hero takes elaborate pre-
cautions to ensure the recognition of his true love:

> A young boy was swallowed by a huge fish. A man found the fish
> and sold it to a raja's house. When the boy cried out for rice, they
> fed the fish rice, which the boy ate. The boy grew up inside the
> fish and one day asked to be married to a young woman. The raja's
> people offered money to any woman who would marry the fish; a
> bangle-seller who had two daughters, the elder born of his first wife
> who had died, the second born of his present wife, gave the older
> daughter to the fish as his wife.
>
> One day she spied on him when he was bathing and had taken
> off his fish skin; she stole the skin and burned it. They lived together,
> and she became pregnant and was about to go to her parents' home
> to have her child, when her husband told her to put her clothes away
> where she could find them on her return. And he said, "Make your
> handprint on the wall with this sandal paste. Take my ring, and give
> me yours." She did, and both of the rings fit them both.
>
> When she went home, her stepmother pushed her down a well,
> dressed her own daughter in the older girl's sari and jewels, and
> took her to the fish-boy. "When they arrived, the husband saw that
> the ring she was wearing didn't fit her," and so he knew she wasn't
> his wife. Then he asked her to get the things his wife had hidden,
> but she said, "How am I supposed to know where they are?" He
> asked her to put her hand on the print made on the wall with sandal
> paste, but her hand didn't match it. He realized that his in-laws had
> substituted her for his wife, but he didn't know where his wife was.
> So he kept quiet and refused to speak to the substitute wife. Inside
> the well, the girl gave birth to a boy, who grew up down there.
>
> One day another bangle-seller came by and fitted the boy with
> bangles. Then he went to the raja's house and told the fish-boy of

the boy and the woman in the well. The fish-boy buried the false wife up to her head and she died. The bangle-seller led the fish-boy to the well, where he found his wife. After they were reunited, the fish-boy tested her: "She was wearing his ring; her hand fit the handprint on the wall; and she got the things from their hiding place. . . . [They] were happy as husband and wife."[38]

Despite the harder evidence of fingerprints, and the softer evidence of factual memory, the ring (which the true wife apparently manages to get back from the false wife, we are not told how) is still needed to prove the case.

This tale incorporates the motif of the animal husband (more often an animal bride),[vii] whose partner removes the animal skin to reveal the true human form within.[39] We will soon encounter variants of the tale of Cinderella, who often takes on an animal disguise (Donkeyskin, Catskin, etc.); the animal skin that conceals the heroine in many of these stories is a minimal version of the entire animal form assumed by the woman in tales of the wolf-wife[viii] and the swan maiden,[ix] and by the boy who lives inside the fish in the Tamil story.

Sometimes the lost child (with or without the ring) is fished directly out of the water, not out of a fish, yet the plot still toes the line of the ring-in-fish story, as in this fairy tale entitled "Princess Carpillon," told by Marie-Catherine Le Jumel de Barneville, Baroness d'Aulnoy (1650–1705):

The infant Princess Carpillon was kidnapped. After some years, the girl escaped, but fell into a lake; some fishermen found her in the nets they had cast for catching carp, mistaking her for a big carp. When they saw her they were disappointed, but a childless king and queen adopted her. She delivered into the keeping of the queen a diamond ring that she had had from infancy. One day the queen, suddenly remembering the diamond ring Carpillon had given her, said to the king, "I always forgot to show you a ring the young shepherdess delivered to my keeping." "Is the stone beautiful?" said the king. "I only looked at it for a moment," said the queen, "but here

---

vii. See chapter 5, p. 128.

viii. See chapter 1, p. 10.

ix. See chapter 5, p. 129.

it is." She gave him the ring, and no sooner did he see it than he exclaimed, "O God! What do I see? Do you not recognize a present I received from you?" So saying, he pressed a spring of which he knew the secret; the diamond flew back, and the queen saw a portrait of herself she had had painted for the king and had tied round her little girl's neck for a plaything when she was an infant. As the joyous queen remarked to the girl, "The ring you gave me has solved the enigma."[40]

The ring is not a king's signet but something even better: it is a portrait of the child's mother that only the king knew how to find.

The Family Romance

The child and ring found in water is a subset of a much broader range of recognition narratives of children lost and then found, with a ring left as an identifying token, often but not necessarily in water. Sometimes the child is abandoned because the mother is accused of adultery; the presumed bastard is thrown out but returns, with the ring, to vindicate the mother.

In stories told from ancient Indian epics[x] and ancient Greek and Roman comedies[xi] to the present day, rings serve to identify the lost child and to connect the child with the parents. In a group of medieval Irish texts, a fairy lover from another world visits a human woman, impregnates her with a child (usually a son), names the child, and departs, giving the mother "a recognition-token (perhaps a ring), which on a specified occasion is to be delivered to the son, who is then to search for his father in the latter's country, using the gift as a means of identification."[41] In the *Cath Maige Tured*, a fifteenth-century Celtic manuscript, the lover tells the mother "that she should not part with [the ring] by sale or by gift, save to one whose finger it should fit." When the son grows up, his mother finds that the ring fits his finger.[42]

In the *Ethiopika* of Heliodorus, who lived in Syria in the third or fourth century CE, Persinna, queen of the Ethiopians, abandons her daughter because the child is, unlike her mother, white, and the queen fears

---

x. See chapter 3, p. 61.

xi. See chapter 7, pp. 172–181.

accusations of adultery.[43] Years later, the final proof of the daughter's identity is provided by two rings: the cultural ring that her mother had left her as a token (the ring that Persinna's husband had given her at their wedding) and a natural ring, the daughter's birthmark, "like a ring of ebony staining the ivory of her arm!"[44] Thus she is black after all, at least in that natural mark from her mother that answers to the cultural ring of patriarchy.[45]

In one branch of this story, a child's high-born parents lose him (it is usually a boy in this variant) or attempt to destroy him, but years later, after he has been raised by low-born people or animals, he finds his parents and comes into his inheritance, having established his noble birth, often proven by a piece of jewelry.[46] Freud called this the Family Romance,[47] citing as a paradigmatic example the tale of Oedipus (which has no ring but does have a highly significant long gold pin, with which Oedipus blinds himself).[48] The story often involves incest: Oedipus thought he was sleeping with an unrelated older woman but discovered, to his horror, that she was his mother. By contrast, in the tale of Mayavati that we have considered, Pradyumna thinks he is being seduced by his mother but discovers, to his delight, that she is an unrelated older woman. The Indian text transforms the Oedipus story from tragedy to romance.

The Pope's Ring and the Fish

Incest lurks in the background of a surprising number of stories in this corpus, not so surprising, perhaps, when we consider that one excuse for incest is that the two parties involved do not recognize that they are child and parent (or, sometimes, siblings)—until they find the identifying ring (sometimes with the help of a fish).

A letter and a key, as well as a ring (and *two* episodes of fishermen fishing out lost objects), identify the lost child in one particularly complex and incestuous variant of the lost-child-and-fish story, *Gregorius vom Stein* (*Gregory of the Rock*), a German narrative poem. The Minnesinger Hartmann von Aue (c. 1165–1210) wrote it around 1190,[49] as an object lesson in religious renunciation:

> An orphaned brother and sister fell prey to their passion and had a son; the father went on a pilgrimage to repent of his sins, and died. The mother put the child in a box, with twenty gold pieces and a tablet detailing his incestuous lineage, and pushed it out into the

ocean. There two fishermen in the service of an abbot found the box; the abbot opened it, found the child, and told one of the fishermen to raise the boy as his own son, Gregorius, together with the fisherman's natural son. He kept the tablet.

One day Gregorius broke his foster brother's nose with the blow of his seal ring; the fisherman's wife, infuriated, blurted out the secret of Gregorius's birth and added, "Curse the fish that didn't snap him up when he was thrown away!" Gregorius started asking questions; he went to the abbot, read the tablet, and learned of his true birth. He left, taking the tablet with him, and became a wandering knight; he called himself the knight of the fish and had a fish embroidered on his coat of arms. He rescued a besieged woman, married her, and fathered two daughters. Eventually his wife discovered the tablet and recognized it as the one that she had put into the box with her child; and so she realized that she was Gregorius's mother, as well as his wife. When he learned of this, he left to devote himself to a life of poverty.

He asked a fisherman in Aquitania to row him out to a rock, chain his legs to the rock, and throw the key into the lake. The fisherman said that if he ever found the key, he would know that Gregorius was a holy man and that God had forgiven him. A fish swallowed the key. Seventeen years later, the fisherman caught the fish and found the key in it. He unlocked Gregorius, who was taken away by two elderly clergymen who had been sent from Rome to find the next pope on a rock in Aquitania. Gregorius became pope and was given the Fisherman's Ring. One day his mother came to visit the pope; she did not recognize him, but he recognized her and told her who he was, and that God had forgiven them.

Gregorius's signet ring is just about the only object in the story that is *not* thrown into deep water, but it initiates the episode in which Gregorius discovers his true identity, in the way that signet rings are supposed to reveal identities. Its peripheral importance to the main plot makes all the more significant the implication that Hartmann felt he must somehow include it, even in such an offhand way. In place of the ring, the tablet, which tells the whole story, again and again, is the official source of identity.

The fish appears in multiple guises; when Gregorius takes it as his coat of arms, he means it to indicate that he came from a fisherman's hut, but it's also the fish that did *not* swallow him as an infant, a non-existent fish that, when conjured up by the curse of the fisherman's wife, is an essential part of Gregorius's discovery of his identity. What Gregorius cannot yet know when he puts a fish on his coat of arms is that a fish will someday find the key to his freedom and that he will someday wear the ring known as the Fisherman's Ring (Annulus Piscatoris), the gold seal ring of the pope, originally engraved with an image of Saint Peter, the fisherman.[50] The fish, which has been a Christian symbol from the earliest days, is therefore highly over-determined in this story, though only loosely connected with a ring.

Rings of Incest

A ring is the key to a Jain didactic text composed just a century or so after the tale of Gregorius; the Jain story depicts an even more horrendously convoluted incest scenario and is told, like Hartmann's tale, in the service of religious renunciation. It involves two signet rings belonging to identical twins with identical names (so that we will need to use an "ā" at the end of the feminine name to distinguish it from the masculine):

> A courtesan named Kuberasena bore a son and daughter, twins, and nursed them for eleven days, but her madam insisted that she abandon them. She made a signet ring for the boy inscribed with the name Kuberadatta, and a similar ring for the girl, marked with the name Kuberadattā. And then, terrified of the madam, she placed the two children in a casket studded with jewels and set the casket afloat in the waters of the Yamuna River.
>
> A pair of merchants found them, and each took one of the children home, naming them after the names on the rings. When the children were grown, the two merchants married the boy and girl to one another, "even though they seemed indeed to be twin brother and sister." One day Kuberadatta placed his own ring in his wife's hand; astonished, Kuberadattā said to him, "How is it that these rings are so like each other, just as our names are so similar? I fear that we are in truth brother and sister, and that we are not the two children of those merchants at all." They asked the merchants, and heard the story, and "they deeply regretted their marriage."
>
> Both of them were filled with the desire to renounce life. Kuberadattā became a Jain nun and hid her jeweled signet ring.

Kuberadatta became a trader and went to the city of Mathura, where he met Kuberasena, his mother, but neither recognized the other. He became her lover and she bore him a son, named Kubera.

Kuberadattā had developed supernatural knowledge and knew "the terribly improper things" that her brother was doing. She showed her signet ring to her superior and told her about herself and went to Mathura. She met Kuberadatta's son, Kubera, and told him everything; he realized that Kuberasena was both his grand-mother and his mother, and that Kuberadattā was both his sister and his aunt. Then she gave him the jeweled signet ring, and "by that signet ring, . . . Kubera became enlightened and became a monk." Kuberadatta also renounced the householder's life and went into the forest. He meditated and went to heaven. "Even Kuberasena saw how topsy-turvy the world of sense objects is, and she became disgusted with life in this world and took on herself the vows of the Jain householder."[51]

The incest here spans two generations, doubling back to involve both sib-lings and parents. But what is most significant for our central theme is that neither the fact that the children are found together, nor the fact that they look alike, nor the fact that they have the same names (but for an a/ā variation) is sufficient to identify them as people who must not wed; only the signet rings are taken as hard evidence of the incest that has already taken place, and the ring is what enlightens the final child in this twisted lineage.

A ring facilitates rather than exposes incest in a tale composed by the Egyptian writer Yousef Idris (1927–1991), "House of Flesh,"[52] a short story about a blind man who marries a recently widowed thirty-five-year-old woman who has three daughters between sixteen and twenty years old. Usually she does not wear the ring that he gave her when they married. When he remarks, one day, that she has started wearing it, she realizes that one of her daughters has worn the ring to masquerade as her mother in the blind man's bed. Eventually each girl asks to wear the ring for a day, to take "her turn in the game of the ring. . . . In silence, the finger sneaks. The one whose turn it is puts on the ring, also in silence."

The blind man notices the difference between his partners in bed:

"At first he would say to himself that it is women's nature that refuses to stay the same; for one time she is fresh and graceful like a drop of dew, worn and depleted another, like water in a stagnant pond. . . . True, the ring is always there, but the finger that it encircles is different every time. He almost knows, and they certainly all know. . . . With silence, he began to confirm to himself that his partner in bed was always his spouse and lawful wife, true and pure, wearing his ring, young one moment and old the next, alternatively soft and hard, sometimes thin, sometimes fat. . . . *No blame is there on the blind.* Is there?"

And that is how the story ends. The women know that they know, and the man pretends that he does not know. He blames the ring.

In contrast to this modern tale, all of the incestuous pairings in the Jain story and in the tale of Oedipus are innocent, unknowing; an unkind and unavoidable fate dooms these abandoned children to their unhallowed pairings and leads them ultimately to the cynical realization of "how topsy-turvy the world of sense objects is," as the Jain text puts it. This is also true of all the surviving characters in the German story—except for Gregorius's mother, who knew perfectly well what she was doing in the first pairing, though even she was innocent of incestuous intent in the second pairing. She alone, therefore, not Gregorius, is a "sinner," because she alone knows the sinful story from the start. Kuberadattā, too, understood what was going on before the men did, though not from the start. But the overwhelming point of all of these stories is the power of chance to destroy even the consciously innocent and ignorant, and the power of rings and fishes to bring to light the buried, sinful, unconscious past.

Cinderella's Ring

Though Freud, and most subsequent literary analysts (particularly Otto Rank and Joseph Campbell),[53] concentrated on the fate of the male child in the Family Romance, the stories can also be read from the standpoint of the mother, the woman who gives birth to the hero, abandons him in infancy, and then, sometimes, marries him. And by far the most retold and widespread of all the Family Romances is about a girl: Cinderella.

The element of incest is almost always erased from the Disneyfied variants told to children, but it is a prelude to the central plot in many other versions of the story: Cinderella's mother dies when she is very young, and her father vows to marry only a woman who looks just like her, or whose finger fits her wedding ring; when Cinderella grows up and turns out to be that woman, she flees from her father. (Sometimes the brother, rather than the father, proposes an incestuous liaison with the Cinderella-figure.)[54] Then the better-known story takes over: Cinderella disguises her beauty, works as a menial servant, is magically transformed into a gorgeous princess, meets the prince, and so forth.

Although a slipper is usually the key to Cinderella's identity in the versions best known in the French and Anglophone world, a ring[55] supplies the vital clue in many variants.[56] We have noted the sexual symbolism of putting a finger into a ring;[xii] others have noted the sexual symbolism of putting a foot into a shoe.[57] The ring functions differently, however, depending upon whether it appears in the prelude (where the heroine resembles her mother and flees from her father) or the central story (where she resembles a princess and flees from the prince). In the prelude, the ring is a part of the problem: it lets her father identify her.[58] But in the main story, the ring is part of the solution: it lets the prince identify her.

The folklorist Alan Dundes has suggested that these Cinderella stories reflect "the common fantasy of a girl wishing to literally replace her mother—with respect to being her father's mate."[59] This is certainly true of one modern version: *Peau d' Âne (Donkeyskin)*, a 1970 French musical film written and directed by Jacques Demy, starring Catherine Deneuve as Donkeyskin. Donkeyskin's father has a donkey that excretes jewels (perhaps including rings), and this is the beast that her fairy godmother skins to disguise her. Her father proposes marriage to her, and she can't see anything wrong in marrying him; indeed, the Lilac Fairy remarks, "Every little girl wants to marry her daddy; it's a great idea." But the fairy prevents Donkeyskin from fulfilling this desire, not because of any concern about incest but simply because the fairy had had an affair with him herself years ago and admits that she now holds a grudge against him for leaving her; in the end, the fairy marries the father. Trust the French to come up with this sort of variant. But meanwhile, Donkeyskin takes the ring that her father gave her when he proposed to her and puts it into the cake she cooks for the king, who tries the ring on the finger of every woman in the land.

For where, in the Disneyfied version, the heroine inadvertently gives the prince her slipper, in many tellings the prince gives her a ring on purpose, and after they have become separated she cooks a unique dish and, accidentally or on purpose, slips the ring into it.[60] Cinderella uses her

---

xii. See chapter 1, p. 8.

cooking sometimes to conceal a ring, sometimes to reveal her identity in other ways, and the prince recognizes her not by the size of her foot or her finger but by her skill as a cook. Food, after all, is a richly evocative carrier of memories, as storytellers knew long before Marcel Proust called up the remembrances inspired by those little tea-infused cakes from Combray.[61] Food provides another link to the motif of the ring in the fish, for by the time the ring in those stories is found, the fish who swallowed it has usually been cooked.

A ring hidden in food is the clue in the Scottish variants of Rashin-Coatie and Cap o' Rushes. In one telling (recorded in dialect) the prince is pining away for his lost love, and Cap o' Rushes, in the kitchen, who is that lost love, sends him a cup with his ring in it:

> "The young man he drank it and he saw the ring at the bottom. 'Send for the cook,' says he. [Cap o' Rushes appeared.] 'Where did you get this ring,' says he. 'From him as gave it me,' says she. 'Who are you, then?' says the young man. 'I'll show you,' says she. And she offed with her cap o' rushes, and there she was in her beautiful clothes. Well, the master's son he got well very soon."[62]

Here the ring behaves like the signet ring of the clever wife,[xiii] to prove to the man that he has known the woman before. In some stories, such as the Indian tale of Shakuntala,[xiv] the man does not want to know what the ring tells him; but in the Cinderella story, he is delighted to know.

In an American telling of the Donkeyskin story, the ring is not the prince's but her own, an atavism from her previous (and real) high birth, bringing the plot closer to that of the male versions of the Family Romance. This version also significantly increases the list of things that the ring can do. While Donkeyskin is in hiding as a lowly cook, a prince comes to the house and she cooks for him:

> "She cooked a real good dinner, and she forgot there had been a diamond on her finger, and it slipped off and went into some soup. . . . Well, the prince he was eating this soup and he found this ring. And he just put it down in his pocket and didn't think much more about

---

xiii. See chapter 6, p. 137.

xiv. See chapter 3, p. 69.

it." The fairy godmother made the girl beautiful for thirty minutes; the prince saw her and fell in love with her. Then Donkeyskin went away. "Well, he went all over the world to see if he could find whose finger this ring would fit. He thought that the ring he had found was hers." Finally he found Donkeyskin. "And they went and slipped that ring on her finger and it fit. And she changed back into that girl that he had fell in love with. They were married and lived happily ever after."[63]

Donkeyskin's ownership of the ring apparently not only identifies her as a lady with small fingers (as in the Welsh tale of Taliesin)[xv] but somehow hints to the prince that the ring belongs to the beautiful lady he has fallen in love with; finally, it magically changes her back into that lady.

The same sort of transformation seems to take place in another American version in which, again, the ring is not his but hers.[64] The ring serves many purposes in this text, beginning as an impossible wedding gift, designed to keep her father away from her: When the woman's father insisted on marrying her, "She went an' tol' her godmother an' she said, 'Now you tell him to find you a ring that will fit the finest bird that flies in the air.' So the father found the ring." This is the ring that she eventually slips into the prince's cake, so that the ring that begins as an attempt to keep the wrong man away (her father) is thus transformed into a ring that unites her with the right man.

Cinderella's Fish

In the tale of Findabair and the salmon, and in variants of "the Fortunate Farmer's Daughter," a cooked fish serves as the locus of somatic memory, and several stories of the Cinderella type invoke the ring-in-fish motif. Here is one recorded in Kashmir in 1892:

> A young woman bathing lost her nose-ring, and a fish swallowed it; the fish was caught, brought to the palace, and the cook, surprised to find the nose-ring, showed it to the king. The king made a proclamation asking anyone who lost a nose-ring to come to him. He found the woman, was charmed by her, and married her.[65]

---

xv. See chapter 1, p. 9.

A variant recorded in North India (place unspecified) in the same period (1893) even brings in the telltale shoe, while keeping the ring and the fish:

> A young merchant saved the lives of four animals, who helped him to get a magic ring that put the services of four demons at his disposal. With their aid, he married a princess, and they went to live in a palace on the banks of a river. One of her shoes fell in and was carried downriver to the realm of a king; a fish swallowed it; a fisherman caught it; and the cook found in its stomach a shoe so beautiful that he brought it to the king. The king said that the wearer of the shoe must be his queen. An old woman in his service found the princess by sailing up the river in the direction that the fish had come from; she tricked the princess into getting her husband's magic ring away from him. The king then captured the princess and threw her husband, the merchant, in prison. But the animals got the ring back for him and restored everything.[66]

The fish swallows the shoe instead of the ring and is then replaced by other animals, grateful animals who bring back not the shoe but the ring, though the king, as usual, searches for the owner of the shoe. Everyone gets into the act in this potpourri variant whose themes have been shuffled by a storyteller who senses that they all belong together but can't quite sort them out.

A lock of hair replaces the shoe in a Tamil story that incorporates several of the Cinderella motifs:

> A young man saved the life of a cobra and was rewarded with a magic signet ring that granted the wearer any wish. He wished for a beautiful girl with long hair; she appeared and they married. "One day, a hair from the wife's beautiful long braid fell into the river, a fish ate it, a man caught it and then sold it to the raja's cook who cut it open and saw the hair wound around a stick. He unwound it and measured it—it was sixty feet long! 'If her hair is this lovely, think what the woman herself must be like!' said the raja." An old woman promised to bring the woman to the raja. She went to where the woman's husband was bathing and had taken off the ring; the old woman persuaded the wife to let her put on the ring. "Let her go to the raja," wished the old woman, and the young woman appeared before the raja, "who saw that she

was the woman whose hair he had found in the fish." The raja kept the woman and locked the ring in seven nested boxes. One day, the woman's husband passed the room where she was kept and saw a photo of himself and her that she had posted outside her room. With the help of a group of rats, who gnawed through the boxes, the man got the ring, put it on, wished to have his wife back, and lived a happy life with her.[67]

The motifs are shuffled and jumbled in this variant, in which the fish swallows not the ring but the telltale characteristic of the heroine—very long hair—which identifies her to the king; and she identifies herself to her husband through the modern technique of photography. The ring, though a signet, never identifies anything at all; it just grants wishes.

Shakespeare's Rings I: The Lost Child
Pericles

Aspects of the Cinderella story shadow Shakespeare's *Pericles* (1607–8), a late romance in which jewelry, including a man's ring, plays a crucial part in the recognition of parents and their children. An incestuous father, a staple of Cinderella stories, haunts this play, which begins when a king, Antiochus, commits incest with his daughter. But another daughter's resemblance to her mother serves not to prompt incest but to identify her. When Pericles, the prince of Tyre, meets his long-lost daughter Marina, he remarks that she might be mistaken for his long-lost wife Thaisa: "My dearest wife / Was like this maid, and such a one / My daughter might have been: my queen's square brows; / Her stature to an inch; as wand-like straight; / As silver-voiced; her eyes as jewel-like . . ." And then, to Marina, "Thou look'st / Like one I loved indeed" (5.1.7–11, 125–126).

A combination of physical resemblance and corroborating memories identifies Marina to Pericles. Struck by her resemblance to Thaisa, but lacking any hard evidence such as a letter or a ring, Pericles submits Marina to a grueling, super-rational cross-examination involving proper names and narrative details, about her breeding, parentage, and so forth; and she gives all the right answers. Yet still he wavers, and finally he asks for the crucial name: "What was thy mother's name? tell me but that, / For truth can never be confirm'd enough, / Though doubts did ever sleep" (5.1.201–3). Only when Marina names Thaisa does he believe her.

Thaisa had given birth to Marina during a storm at sea and then apparently died of the childbirth. At this point Thaisa usurps the motif of "child put in a box at sea with identifying jewelry," which rightfully belongs to her newborn babe, Marina. But there is no need for Pericles to give the infant Marina the sort of jewels or letters of identification that abandoned infants usually have in fairytales, since he does not abandon her but takes her ashore himself and hands her over to a friendly king to care for her until he returns.

Having thus dealt with Marina's birth, Pericles turns his attention to Thaisa's (supposed) death. He calls for "spices, ink and paper, / My casket and my jewels" (3.1.65) and has Thaisa placed in a box and consigned to the sea. Unconscious, she floats to shore and is revived and adopted by a fatherly physician/magician, Cerimon. Cerimon notes that Thaisa is "shrouded in cloth of state; balm'd and entreasured with full bags of spices! A passport too!" (3.2.66–67). The "passport" is a note, written by Pericles, that identifies Thaisa as his (dead) wife and asks the finder to bury the queen: "Besides this treasure for a fee, The gods requite his charity!" (3.2.73–74). Cerimon revives her and says, "Madam, this letter, and some certain jewels, / Lay with you in your coffer which are / At your command. Know you the character?" (that is, the handwriting) (3.4.1–2). And she replies, "It is my lord's." So the letter invites a double recognition: Cerimon discovers that this is Pericles's wife, and Thaisa learns that her husband thinks she died in the storm (just as she had assumed that he died there).

But Thaisa's jewelry goes on to play a more complex role. In an inspired Shakespearean innovation, Cerimon says that Thaisa herself is the jewelry: "Her eyelids, cases to those / Heavenly jewels which Pericles hath lost, / Begin to part their fringes of bright gold. / The diamonds of a most praised water / Doth appear to make the world twice rich" (3.2.100). The cliché of a woman with eyes like emeralds and so forth[xvi] here exposes and mocks the cliché of the recognition plot: her face itself is the gem by which a woman really ought to be identified.

The actual jewels do their work years later, when Pericles finds Thaisa again but does not at first recognize her (supposing her dead), whereupon Cerimon says, "Early in blustering morn this lady was / Thrown upon this shore. I op'd the coffin, / Found there rich jewels; recover'd her" (5.3.22).

---

xvi. See chapter 1, p. 10.

Cerimon does not mention the letter. Pericles seizes upon the mention of the jewels, and says, "May we see them?" (5.3.25). Before he can see the jewels, however, Thaisa speaks, and he recognizes her voice. Still he hesitates, and she looks at his ring and says, "When we with tears parted Pentapolis, / The king my father gave you such a ring." And Pericles cries out, "This, this: no more," and embraces her (5.3.40). But in fact he *does* ask for more, as he continues to test her as he had tested Marina, asking her the name of his second-in-command, and only then, when she gives the right answer, remarking, "Still confirmation" (5.3.54). The conventional evidence of the jewelry thus both does and does not prove who Thaisa is; as with Marina, other forms of hard evidence, including specific knowledge (the predecessor of the security questions on modern websites), are also demanded.

The Winter's Tale

Much of this plot reappears in *The Winter's Tale*, which Shakespeare wrote a few years after *Pericles*. The jealous Leontes, thinking that the daughter his wife Hermione has just borne was sired by another man, orders his servant Antigonus to have the child abandoned. When Antigonus, shipwrecked after a storm at sea, unwillingly carries out the order, he consoles himself by citing the folktales about abandoned children nursed by kites and ravens, wolves and bears. And he names her Perdita, because she was lost at sea (just as Pericles had named his daughter Marina, because she was found at sea). The bears in this case ignore the child but not, alas, Antigonus, who, after leaving the child on the shore of Bohemia, is said, famously, to "exit, pursued by a bear" (3.3.53). It is human shepherds, not sheep (or other animals), who find the child and raise her.

Antigonus leaves something with Perdita that he refers to as "these, / Which may, if fortune please, both breed thee, pretty, / And still rest thine" (3.3.48–49) (i.e., pay for your good upbringing and still be there for your dowry). The meaning of "these" becomes generally apparent soon after, when shepherds find the child and speak of "a bearing-cloth for a squire's child!" and becoming "rich by the fairies" and, finally, "Gold! all gold!" (3.3.113–118). But the detailed description of "these" comes only near the end of the play, when the shepherd says that the box found with the infant contains "such secrets ... which none must know but the king" (4.4.759). And what is in the box? "The mantle of Queen Hermione's, her jewel about the neck of it, the letters of Antigonus found with it which they know to be his character..." (5.2.32–36). These are the same sorts of things that were found with Thaisa (though not with Marina): a jewel and a letter from the king. The material objects are supported by the other common factors in fairytale recognition, physical resemblance and signs of nobility: "The majesty of the creature in resemblance of the mother, the affection of nobleness which nature shows above her breeding, and many other evidences proclaim her, with all certainty, to be the king's daughter" (5.2.37–40).

But before Leontes had any idea that Perdita was his daughter, he was in danger of committing incest. Leontes felt attracted to Perdita, and when Antigonus's widow chided him and reminded him that his long-dead queen was once "more worth such gazes / Than what you look on now," Leontes replied, "I thought of her, / Even in these looks I made" (5.1.226–227). And then Perdita's mother, Hermione, who, like Thaisa, had been presumed dead all these years, was discovered alive.

Queen Hermione's "jewel" in Perdita's possession may or may not be a ring, but another ring supplies another piece of the puzzle in the final scene. Someone asks, "What, pray you, became of Antigonus, that carried / hence the child?" The answer is, "He was torn to pieces with a bear" (5.3.64–67), and a handkerchief and rings are cited in evidence. Setting aside the handkerchief, which might perhaps be used as evidence in some other play, we are left with the rings.

The Ring (and Child) in the Fish in the News

Lost rings are found surprisingly often in fish—not only in stories but in recorded history. The many stories in which a magic ring is found in the belly of a fish are the mythical expression of a perfectly banal happening: fisherman fish many things up out of the deep. Indeed, there are a number of anecdotes, in the Ripley's Believe-It-or-Not genre, testifying to the fact that fish really do swallow rings;[68] fish, after all, swallow all sorts of stuff (recall the contents of the stomach of the shark in the film *Jaws* [Steven Spielberg, 1975]) and are particularly attracted to shiny lures. "Stomach Contents of a Man-eating Crocodile" was the title of an exhibit I saw once in the Science Museum in Kolkata; it was full of rings and bangles and necklaces, some presumably the remains of the men that the crocodile had eaten. There's a folk tradition in America that you should not wear flashy diamonds or shiny gold jewelry when you go swimming

because you'll look like a shimmering fish in trouble and attract sharks[69]—
not to mention the possibility of losing your jewelry. And if you go to the
snorkeling beach at Hanuma Bay, in Honolulu, the guide there warns you
to take off your wedding ring, as the cold water shrinks your fingers and
many rings fall off and are never recovered, perhaps swallowed by fish.[70]
Sherlock Holmes used the metaphor of a ring attracting a fish when he
remarked (in *A Study in Scarlet*), "We can always bait our line with the
ring."

Yet in contemporary America, "true" stories of rings in fish have
become practically synonymous with flagrant lies; the Free Dictionary
defines a "fish story" in general as "a great big lie," referring to the tendency of fishermen to exaggerate the size of their catch. A ring often gets
into the fish story, making it even fishier. Irony and cynicism characterize
the use that Hollywood films make of the theme. In *Big Fish* (2003, Tim
Burton), a boy's father tells a lot of tall stories, and his favorite is the one
about how a great big catfish swallowed his wedding ring when he used it
as bait on the end of a line that the fish snapped off. He got it back when
he again caught the fish, who spit it up and then vanished back into the
deep. His son says, "It never happened!" and calls it an "amusing lie" and
an "elaborate mythology"; he complains: "When I realized of course that
everything you said was impossible, I felt like a fool to have trusted you."
Yet in the end, the son (supported by the director's eye view, inviting us to
join him) regards the story of the ring in the fish as true and tells the even
more mythological ending himself: he carries his dying father down to the
river (the father hands his wedding ring to his wife as he goes in), where
the father becomes the great catfish and swims away.

Many putatively true stories of rings in fish are attested in the modern period. The *London Gent's Magazine* in January 1765 carried this item
about a Mrs. Todd, of Deptford, who, on a boat traveling to Whitstable,
took off her gold ring and threw it into the sea, to make a point:

> "She said that, 'It was as much impossible for any person to be poor,
> who had an inclination to be otherwise, as for her ever to see that
> ring again.' The second day after this, and when she had landed, she
> bought some mackerel, which the servant commenced to dress for
> dinner, whereupon there was found a gold ring in one. The servant
> ran to show it to her mistress, and the ring proved to be that which
> she had thrown away."[71]

Note the realistic touch that it is in the process of dressing, not serving, the fish that the ring is found. (In real life, you clean a fish before you cook it. Some of the rings in these old stories appear in the fish as it is cleaned in the kitchen, but more often they are discovered when the fish is served on the table. But how did it get to the table with the ring still in its belly?) And note, too, the upper-class vow, damning the poor, that inspires the mock ordeal.

Jump ahead two centuries, and consider this headline for an Associated Press item printed in the *New York Times* on October 23, 1934: "Texan Claims Ring Found in Cod as One Lost in 1906." This is how it went:

"Dateline Boston. A ring found in the stomach of a codfish by a Boston fisherman last week was claimed today by the Rev. E. T. Drake of the First Presbyterian Church of Orange, Texas, as one lost by him while swimming at Corpus Christi, Texas, twenty-eight years ago.... The ring bore the inscription, 'Pat D,' the abbreviation of his mother's name, Patricia Drake.... Fishermen along the waterfront, however, were debating the possibility of the codfish being twenty-eight years old, although many have been known to live more than thirty years, they said. Besides, they said, it's a long swim from the Gulf of Mexico to the fishing ground."

By the twentieth century, one can detect a certain cynicism in the reportage, even when (or because?) a clergyman is the witness.

The heyday of ring-in-fish journalism/mythology was two decades earlier, when the *New York Times*, on January 26, 1913, proclaimed, "Found His Ring in a Fish: A Perennial Romance." The story was long, but here are the highlights:

"Telegraphic dispatches last week announced the good fortune of a man in New Jersey, appropriately named Gold, who went to Barnegat recently and caught a lot of fish. This was gratifying; but it was more than counterbalanced by the loss of a fine diamond ring which was dropped overboard while the enthusiastic disciple of old Izaak was making his lucky haul. On the day of the dispatch, however, he joyously displayed the ring to his wondering mates at the engine house—for he is a fireman when he is not a fisherman—and explained that the friend with whom he had shared his piscatorial triumph at Barnegat had sent him the day before a fine fish. It came by parcel post, and his wife at once set about preparing it for supper. Inside this apparently innocent fish was the lost ring."

Mr. Gold met with some skepticism, but the reporter came to his defense:

"The story was received with incredulity by the other firemen, and is still discredited in certain parts of the commonwealth of New Jersey. Their skepticism is an evidence that these people are not well read in history. The record of the world is full of instances which would testify to the truth—or at least the plausibility—of the Jersey fisherman."

And the article then cites, as historical precedents, the tales of Solomon, Polycrates, and the Bishop of Glasgow, among others, and concludes: "In view of such a wealth of cumulative and venerable evidence is it possible longer to doubt the Barnegat incident?" Surely not. Such are the uses of history, or, rather, mythological history.

In real life, the odds are strongly against the possibility that among the rings that any given fish has swallowed will be the ring that you may have lost in the ocean. In real life, you don't look for your lost ring in a flounder. All of the ring-in-fish stories are both counterfactual and counterintuitive, promising a happy ending that could seldom have been the case.[xvii] But that way madness lies; the point of the story, and the reason for its extraordinary popularity, must be found elsewhere than in the actual habits of gold rings and fish.

A contemporary variant on the theme of the ring (or child) found in the fish[xviii] is the story of the message in a bottle cast out to sea and washed back to shore after many years. A real-life instance of this story began on December 27, 1984, when a seven-year-old boy threw a Pepsi bottle into the Gulf of Mexico in Clearwater, near St. Petersburg, Florida. The bottle was sealed with electrical tape and there was a message in it: "To whoever finds this letter please write me a letter and let me know. Roger J. Clay, 890

---

xvii. See chapter 11, p. 308.

xviii. See chapter 2, p. 37.

Linwood Ave., Fairfield Ohio, 45014." A Florida man named Don Smith found the bottle in Tampa Bay on July 4, 2003, almost twenty years later. He went onto the Internet and discovered that Roger had been killed in a motorcycle accident on July 10, 1998, when he was twenty-one. Smith contacted Roger's parents. Roger's father said, "It was like he was trying to remind us he was still with us." His mother said, "He's still playing tricks on me."[72] Smith said he had told Roger's mother, "What I can tell from this is that Roger's letting you know that, 'Hey, I'm OK. And guess what? I can still find you.'"[73] The message *inside* the bottle is banal: let me know if you find this. But the message *of* the bottle is far from banal: it is interpreted as a voice from the other side of the barrier of death, a reassurance that nothing is ever lost, not the boy, not his mother. The bottle proved nothing; the story proved everything. The people who experienced the event knew how the myth should go.

The poet Denise Levertov (1923–1997) also knew how the myth should go and translated it into her own life in her poem "Wedding-Ring," written in 1978, some four years after her divorce. The ocean in her poem is a basket filled with lost objects, more precisely, objects that have lost their meaning:

> My wedding-ring lies in a basket
> as if at the bottom of a well.
> Nothing will come to fish it back up
> and onto my finger again.
> It lies
> among keys to abandoned houses,
> nails waiting to be needed and hammered
> into some wall,
> telephone numbers with no names attached,
> idle paperclips.
> It can't be given away
> for fear of bringing ill-luck.
> It can't be sold
> for the marriage was good in its own
> time, though that time is gone.
> Could some artificer
> beat into it bright stones, transform it
> into a dazzling circlet no one could take

for solemn betrothal or to make promises
living will not let them keep? Change it
into a simple gift I could give in friendship?[74]

The ring that "can't be given away for fear of bringing ill-luck" could have
belonged to Solomon or Polycrates; the solemn betrothal undone by promises that can't be kept could belong to any of so many of the husbands and
lovers that we will encounter throughout this book.

The Token Rings of Lost Children

In actual recorded history, a heartbreaking collection of tokens left with
abandoned children can be seen in the Foundling Museum in Brunswick
Square, London, on the site of a home for abandoned babies who were
raised and educated by the institution. Thomas Coram established the
home in 1739; in 1954 the last children were placed in foster care. When
the Hospital for the Education and Maintenance of Exposed and Deserted
Young Children opened in 1741, the founders wrote, "A note should be
made of any 'particular writing' or 'peculiar thing' that was left with a
child, as an identifier in case the child was later claimed."[75] Presumably
the parents believed that the hospital offered the child a better future than
they could themselves, but it must have been a heart-wrenching decision,
and many parents hoped that they might someday get back on their feet

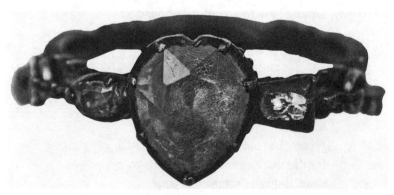

FIGURE 2.2 Child's ring token with a heart, from the Foundling Hospital in
London.

Source: © Foundling Museum, London

and be able to reclaim their child.[76] Some of the parents (most, but not all, mothers) of these children left a token as a means of establishing the parents' identity and connection with the child. They left scraps of fabric, small metal objects, or bits of jewelry; they left a thimble, a padlock, even a hazelnut. One parent left an admission ticket to a lecture about science by Dr. Erasmus King to be given at his home in Dukes Court, Westminster.[77]

After 1758, written receipts began to be issued to parents, but many still chose to leave a token as a "tangible link with the child they left behind."[78] Moreover, since many of the parents could not read, such tokens were often the only sort of document they could produce, bearing an unspoken message something like, "I have nothing else to give you, but you can keep this as a reminder that I exist, or exchange it for something else and forget about me." Some are inscribed. One metal heart reads, "You have my Heart Tho wee must Part, Nat. 6: Sep.r 1759."[79] Others seem to be "repurposed sentimental objects from love affairs . . . left with the infant who was the result of the affair,"[80] like the ring with a heart inset, inscribed on the interior of the band: "He who neglects me loses me." Such a ring might have been passed down through the mother's family or given to her by the child's father or a previous sweetheart.[81]

A ring given by an abandoned child's father plays a crucial role in Charles Dickens' *Oliver Twist*.[82] Oliver's mother, dying in the workhouse, was wearing around her neck a chain with a gold locket that contained a gold wedding ring, two locks of hair, and the name Agnes. (The physician attending her noted that she was not wearing a wedding ring and concluded that it was "the old story.")[83] The woman attending her "stole from the corpse, when it had hardly turned to one, that which the dead mother had prayed her, with her last breath, to keep for the infant's sake."[84] Clearly she meant the locket with the ring to be used as a token eventually to reunite the child with his father, who had given the locket to Agnes, intending to marry her. "They would have treated him better, if they had known it all!" another woman remarks.[85] But the father died, the tokens were concealed by Oliver's half-brother in order to keep the father's estate for himself, and it was not until years later that the tokens did, finally, establish Oliver's identity and restore him to his fortune.[86] Significantly, the tokens include the wedding ring that, had Agnes worn it on her ring finger, would have made all the difference.

The fact that so many tokens remain in the Museum is evidence that very few parents ever managed to take their children back; only about one child in a hundred was ever reclaimed.[87] The others left the hospital when they reached adulthood, probably never having seen the ring or other token that was their only link to their parents.[88] It's only in the stories that the children are always found again.

3

Shakuntala and the Ring of Memory

WE LEARN, FROM the tales of Solomon[i] and others, that you may lose your official identification, and hence your persona, your personal identity, if you lose your ring (identity theft). But in many stories, this straightforward fact leads to the quasi-magical idea of losing your memory of who you are, or your memory of your connection with a lover, if you lose a ring that was a gift from that lover. When you find the ring, you remember again. In this way, two sets of symbols, of personal identity and recognition on the one hand (the signet ring) and of sexual union on the other (the marriage ring), unite in a genre of myths about the identity of a sexual partner.

Tom Zoellner writes of the engagement ring he gave to the first girl he loved: "It had a memory inside of it that could not be erased, at least not as long as it remained attached to the owner. It was a living reliquary."[1] It is an old custom in America and Europe to move a ring from one hand to another (or tie a piece of string around a finger) to remind you about some trivial duty. The things that rings make people forget and remember in the stories of rejection and recollection—things like women and children—are far from trivial.

Among all the stories of rings of forgetfulness and memory (and of rings found in fish), one of the oldest and most famous is the ancient Indian tale of Shakuntala, best known from a Sanskrit play written by the poet Kalidasa in the fourth century CE. But before we listen to this story, let's touch down for a moment in ancient India, to consider the broader mythology of rings and other jewelry in that culture. The first two chapters of this book have provided a wide transcultural, synchronic survey

---

i. See chapter 2, p. 27.

of some of the basic stories told about rings in many times and places, without regard for geographical context or historical development.[2] In this and the next few chapters, we will dig deeper within particular cultures, and clusters of cultures, all the while looking to see how these stories change in response to new needs that arise through changing historical circumstances.

Rings in Ancient India

Charles Edwards, in the nineteenth century, rather naïvely reported that "signets of lapis lazuli and emerald have been found with Sanscrit inscriptions, presumed to be of an antiquity beyond all record."[3] But in recorded history, signet rings appear in Indian texts only from the third century BCE,[4] after the arrival of the Indo-Greeks in the wake of Alexander's aborted invasion of northwest India in 326 BCE. A signet ring is used to forge a royal document in a quasi-historical political play, Vishakhadatta's *The Minister's Seal-ring*, composed in South India probably during the seventh century CE.[5]

Seal rings, of both men and women, played a part in romantic assignations, according to the *Kamasutra*, the third-century CE Indian textbook of erotic love:

> "When the king arises from his afternoon siesta, the women attendants who keep track of the roster come to him followed by the servants of the woman whose turn it is to spend the night with the king, of the woman who has been passed over on her night, and of the woman who is in her fertile season. And they present the king with scented oils, each marked with the stamp of the woman's seal ring, and tell him whose turn it is to sleep with him that night and who is in her fertile season. Whichever one among these oils the king takes, he announces that the woman who owns it will sleep with him that night."[6]

It's worth noting that the women as well as the king have seal rings, which here identify them as potential sexual partners. On the other side of the harem wall, a lover sending a message to a woman in the harem is advised to give her his seal ring marked with an impression.[7] (The commentator explains that he leaves a ring with his name on it, marked with traces of his nails and teeth.)

The cultural connections between women and circular jewelry in India are complex. In Shudraka's play, *The Little Clay Cart,* also from the third century CE, the courtesan and wife use jewelry in ways that challenge European stereotypes: the courtesan lends her casket of jewelry to a poor man whom she loves, and when it is stolen from him his wife gives him her pearl necklace to pay back the courtesan. Eventually the stolen jewelry is found, and the courtesan returns the pearls to the wife. The usual roles are reversed here: the stereotypical courtesan milks a man of everything he has[8] and is the bitter enemy of his wife, often usurping a wife's place or masquerading as a wife;[ii] but here the courtesan lends the man jewelry, and the wife's necklace redeems the courtesan's jewels.

A piece of circular jewelry, an anklet, plays a key role in the ancient Tamil epic, *The Tale of an Anklet (Cilappatikaram),* traditionally believed to have been composed in the fifth century CE by Ilanko Atikal, a Tamil prince.[9] It tells the tale of Kovalan, who, having squandered all his money on a courtesan, travels to Maturai, the capital of the Pandyan kingdom, to sell one of the gold anklets of his wife, Kannaki. Falsely accused of having stolen the anklet of the Pandyan queen, he is executed. When Kannaki learns of her husband's death, she rushes to the palace in a fury, accuses the king of murder, and proves that the anklet was hers by breaking it open and revealing rubies inside, where the queen's anklet contained nothing but pearls. (In this South Indian land of pearl-fishers, rubies are less precious than pearls, and lack their symbolic value.)[iii] The king acknowledges his guilt and dies; the queen follows him.[10] The less valuable circular jewelry in this story proves the innocence not of the woman but of her husband.

Sita's Jewels

These and other Indian traditions about women and jewelry are assumed in the tale of Sita and Rama in Valmiki's *Ramayana,* an ancient Sanskrit epic poem (composed between 200 BCE and 200 CE) that has remained central to Hinduism from the time of its composition to the present day. In this text, when prince Rama goes into exile, he takes his wife, Sita, with

---

ii. See chapter 6, p. 158.

iii. A similar contrast between a true circlet of one gem and a false circlet of another marks several nineteenth-century European stories about true and false necklaces. See chapter 9, pp. 230–241.

him. At first she starts to give away all her jewels, but she balks at the prospect of going away in rough garments, and in the end she wears her jewelry into the forest. Indeed, her jewels play an essential role in the plot at several points.

Ravana, king of the ogres, schemes to carry Sita away. He transforms Maricha, one of his ogres, into a golden deer studded with jewels, like something made by Bulgari; even when Maricha later resumes his true ogre form, he remains covered with jewels.[11] When Sita sees the jewel-studded deer she insists that Rama go after it for her. In Rama's absence, Ravana lures her away, and as he carries her off through the air, her jeweled anklet and her pearl necklace fall to the earth on a mountain.[12] Then she purposely throws down other jewels (other fairytale heroines have used breadcrumbs or, more wisely, pebbles), hoping that a group of monkeys that she sees below will find them and tell Rama;[13] that is, she expects the jewels to identify her. Eventually, a group of these talking monkeys do find the jewels and take them to their king, who tells Rama, "I saw Sita, adorned with jewels, being carried away by Ravana, as she writhed in his arms and tore the jewels from her body." Later, the monkey Hanuman tells Sita how upset Rama was when he saw the jewels that she had thrown down from Ravana's chariot; when Rama saw them he burst into tears, clutching the jewels to his chest, crying out, "O my beloved!"[14]

Rama's brother Lakshmana has gone with Rama and Sita into the forest. Rama shows the jewels to Lakshmana, saying, "These are surely Sita's jewels." But Lakshmana replies, "I cannot recognize her ear and hair ornaments; I only know her anklets because I would touch her feet every morning."[15] By this he affirms that he, Lakshmana, has never looked at Sita's face or body and has therefore never desired her for himself; he thus testifies both to Sita's chastity and to his own. Jewelry, as usual, has a two-edged power to identify a woman as chaste (or unchaste).

Later, when Rama sends Hanuman to Sita in her captivity on Ravana's fortress island, Lanka, the jewelry gives self-contradictory evidence. Hanuman first sees another woman wearing fine jewelry. He knows she cannot be Sita because Sita (following classical Hindu law) would never adorn herself except in her husband's presence;[16] and, indeed, when he sees Sita, she is wearing a dirty, soiled, worn-out garment, and no jewelry, the perfect image of the chaste wife in exile.[17] (An ally of the ogre Ravana at one point had suggested to him that he tempt Sita with diamonds,[18] but he doesn't.) The poet remarks, "It was only with great difficulty that

Hanuman was able to recognize Sita without her ornaments, as hard as to understand the meaning of a word that was used out of context."[19]

But then, "after a closer examination,"[20] Hanuman decides that she is definitely Sita, because he sees that she is in fact wearing all the ornaments Rama had described, the earrings and the other jewelry studded with pearls and gems, "all in their proper places." The jewels no longer sparkle. They have dimmed with constant wear, but Hanuman is sure they are the very ones Rama had described to him. "The ornaments which fell on the mountain are missing," he realizes, "but the others are exactly as Rama had said."[21] So basic to the *Ramayana* are the episodes involving the monkey Hanuman and Sita's jewels that they are among the few episodes that survive the journey to the Chinese translation of much of the *Ramayana* in a great sixteenth-century epic poem about (among other things) a monkey.[22]

Two motifs clash in this episode: the tradition that a good woman must not wear jewelry in her husband's absence,[23] and the tradition that a great lady can always be identified by her jewelry. The phrase "dimmed with constant wear" is a compromise move (as was her ambivalence about wearing jewelry into the forest in the first place). In general, the married woman who wears jewelry in her husband's absence is a bad wife. But since Sita is a princess, jewelry is an essential part of her being; therefore, she remains a good wife even when she wears her jewelry in exile from her husband.

In Nina Paley's brilliant animated film version of the *Ramayana* (called the *Sitayana* or *Sita Sings the Blues* [2008]), one of the male Hindu interlocutors on the soundtrack remarks at this point in the story, "She drops her jewelry along the way; it went all the way up to Lanka. [We see an image of a big ring with an enormous solitaire diamond falling from the sky to earth, followed by other jewelry.] She has a lot of jewelry in the forest." They laugh. But the woman remarks, "No, do you remember, she's not wearing any jewelry, because she left everything in Ayodhya; she just came in her *sannyasi* [ascetic] clothes." And the male voice replies, "Don't challenge these stories." Wise advice. Clearly Sita's jewelry in this episode remains a problem.

Now Sita must validate the messenger from her husband. Again jewelry comes to the rescue: Hanuman gives Sita Rama's signet ring,[24] a priceless ring with Rama's name etched on it, by which she recognizes that the messenger does in fact come from Rama:[25] "Sita took her husband's ring and felt as happy as if she had been reunited with her husband."[26] (The commentator here tells a story about a quarrel in which Sita threw down the ring and, later, wanting to make up again, used the ring as an excuse.)[27]

Finally, Sita in turn gives Hanuman a jewel she has been wearing in her hair; she says, "Rama will recognize this token. It will make him remember me and our parents." Hanuman takes it and places it on his finger.[28] He fleshes out Sita's speech to him when he repeats it to Rama: "She said, 'Give Rama this jewel which I have taken great pains to look after and preserved in my hair. And tell him that when I see it, even in my misery, I feel better, for I feel as if I am seeing Rama.'" Rama takes it, begins to weep, and says, "My heart melts at the sight of this jewel. Sita's father gave her this jewel when she got married. . . . My beloved's beauty enhances the splendor of this jewel and today, when I look at it, I feel as if I am looking at her." Both Rama and Sita feel that the other is somehow present (with their parents) in their jewelry.

As Hanuman leaps over the ocean to the island of Lanka, a fish swallows his shadow, and Hanuman enters the fish to get it back.[29] In some later tellings, he engenders a child at the same time.[30] In a contemporary South Indian variant of this episode, the storyteller says that Hanuman dropped Rama's ring into the ocean; then the storyteller asks his listeners, "How can Hanuman retrieve the ring?" Someone in the audience (within the story) jumps up, runs to the ocean, finds the ring, and returns it to the storyteller, who then continues his narration.[31] In this postmodern version, someone on the outermost frame of the narrative, in place of the customary fish, retrieves the ring from the ocean.[iv]

Ratnavali, the Lady with the Necklace

The association between fine jewelry and women of a certain class underlies the plot of a Sanskrit drama, The Lady of the Jeweled Necklace, attributed to King Harsha, who ruled much of North India in the seventh century CE:[32]

> The princess Ratnavali ("[Woman with a] Jeweled Necklace"), on her voyage to become one of King Udayana's wives, was shipwrecked and fished out by a merchant. He brought her to Udayana's minister, who recognized her by the jeweled necklace that she always

iv. See chapter 2, p. 25.

wore. Not wishing to anger the chief queen, he put her in the queen's service as a handmaid named Sagarika ("Ocean Woman"). She met the king and they fell in love. But she would not agree to keep meeting him, and the king said, "My beloved, who is like a jeweled necklace found by chance, slipped out of my hand before I could hang her around my neck."

The queen imprisoned Sagarika, who gave her jeweled necklace to the Brahmin jester; the jester realized from its value that Sagarika must be of noble birth. Then the chief councilor of Ratnavali's father arrived; when he saw the necklace on the jester he thought he recognized it as Ratnavali's but decided that this might be sheer coincidence. Then Sagarika appeared, still in chains. The councilor, looking at Sagarika, said, "She looks just like the princess." And, recalling the necklace, he decided that this must in fact be Ratnavali. The jester said, "As soon as I saw the jeweled necklace I knew that this was the property of no common person." The queen had Ratnavali's chains taken off, embraced her, and adorned her with her own ornaments.

Sagarika, the Ocean Woman, is rescued out of the ocean—like a ring, or a fish. Her jeweled necklace suggests, if it does not prove, that she is Ratnavali, and it brings with it, as it surfaces, the usual submerged recognition. Like a signet ring, the necklace is here associated with a hidden name: Ratnavali at first is *like* a necklace (which the king fears he has lost), then is known to *have* a necklace (by which the king's minister recognizes her before the play begins, and her father's councilor half-recognizes her at the end), and finally is recognized as being *named* a necklace.

The necklace is at first taken as evidence but is then ruled inadmissible. When the chief councilor of Ratnavali's father arrives and sees the jeweled necklace, he remarks, "I know that necklace! It's the very one that the king gave the princess at the time of her departure." But then he decides that this might be sheer coincidence, thinking, "There are so many jewels in a royal family that it is not hard to find a 'speaking resemblance' of ornaments."[33] The word he uses is *sam-vada*, literally a conversation, a form that "talks together." The commentator glosses it as "resemblance" (*sadrishyam*) and says that the councilor means that it might be another, similar jewel. Thus the councilor invokes coincidence to explain away the striking resemblance between the necklace last seen on Ratnavali and the necklace now seen on the jester: princesses have so many jewels.

The argument about the "speaking resemblance" deflects the power of the jewelry so that it isn't the essential clue, the single clue by which all stands or falls, after all, but merely one piece in a more complex puzzle of mistaken identity. The text simultaneously presents the traditional, formulaic symbol of identity (the piece of jewelry that identifies the person in disguise) and mocks it: a piece of jewelry is a stupid way to identify someone. Thus common sense intrudes, momentarily, into the romanticism of the myth, and a reasonable, rather flat-footed realization challenges the equally flat-footed assumption that if she's wearing the same ring or necklace, she must be the same person. When Sagarika appears, the councilor says, "She looks just like the princess." And then, aside, "Since the necklace bears such a strong resemblance, and since this girl came from the ocean, it's clear that this is Ratnavali, the daughter of the King of Simhala."[34] The jewelry is a part of the cumulative weight of evidence.

Though the hard evidence of the jewelry is undermined, the "soft" evidence of somatic memory is validated in the end. The truth that the necklace reveals from the start is not Ratnavali's identity (which is finally established by her face) but her class. (The connection is supported by the near-homonym of the Sanskrit words for noble birth [abhijana] and recognition [abhijnana].) As the jester remarks to himself at the end, "I knew that this was the property of no common person." She is the daughter of a foreign king, masquerading as someone of a lower class, the princess as the pauper—but wearing a necklace no pauper could afford.

Here the text suddenly plays the harsh light of reason on a traditional romantic theme: *anyone* who has a fabulous necklace of emeralds and rubies must be a princess, if not necessarily the particular princess you are looking for. (The flip side of this argument —the proof, in a finger with a ring, that the woman is *not* a lady—prevails in the Welsh tale of Taliesin.)[v] And Sagarika's class is eventually the key to her individual identity. In the end, class reconciles the queen to her fate: the knowledge that the Ocean Woman is in fact the Lady of the Jeweled Necklace forces the queen to welcome her as a co-wife.

---

v. See chapter 1, p. 9.

The Rejection of Shakuntala

The tension between royal jewelry and an innocent girl of the forest, joined through the folk motif of the ring in the fish,[vi] is at the heart of the tale of Shakuntala and the ring of recognition. Here again the king's signet ring, like Rama's, is an essential clue (as it is throughout the genre of kings who use signet rings to seduce their female subjects),[vii] but unlike Sita and Ratnavali, the heroine of this story has no jewelry of her own.

The story of Shakuntala draws upon the broader Hindu mythology of fish. The fish appears in Indian texts quite early (c. 900 BCE) as the hero of the flood myth: he saves from the cosmic doomsday flood waters a few good people, including a man who had saved the fish when it was little and at the mercy of the bigger fish.[35] The myth of the flood extends the motif of the salvific fish to include not merely the local flood, which washes away, in each individual death, one memory within a single lifetime, but the universal flood, which washes everyone away at doomsday, the deadly phase of the great life cycle of the cosmos. Even then, the myth assures us, the human race survives; the memory of the tradition survives.

The fish is an ancient symbol of liminal consciousness in India. The Upanishads, in the fifth century BCE, tell us: "As a great fish goes along both banks of a river, both the near side and the far side, just so the dreamer goes along both of these conditions, the condition of sleeping and the condition of waking."[36] And as a fish swims deep in the ocean, it symbolizes a deeply submerged consciousness, underpinning both dreaming and waking, memory and forgetting.

Neither a fish nor a ring appears in the earliest version of the story of Shakuntala, in the great ancient Sanskrit epic poem the *Mahabharata* (composed between 300 BCE and 300 CE):

> When King Dushyanta[37] was hunting in the forest, he came to a hermitage where he met a beautiful young woman named Shakuntala, the daughter of a sage and a celestial nymph who had abandoned her. He persuaded her to marry him by the rite consisting of nothing but private, mutual desire,[38] but she made him promise that if she bore him a son the boy would become king. Then he left, promising to send for her.

---

vi. See chapter 2, p. 25.

vii. See chapter 1, p. 5.

Shakuntala gave birth to a boy, and when he was six years old she brought him to court, saying to Dushyanta, "This is your son. Remember the promise you made long ago when we lay together." When the king heard her words, he remembered perfectly well, but he said, "I do not remember. Whose woman are you, you evil ascetic? I don't remember ever having had anything to do with you." She replied, "You know very well, your majesty; why do you say that you don't, lying like a common man? Your heart knows the truth, and knows your lie. A man who does something wrong thinks, 'No one knows me,' but the gods know. If you do not do what I ask, your head will burst into a hundred pieces." She discoursed at length on the reasons a man should honor his wife, quoting the dharma texts, and concluding, "The son born from his wife is like a man's face in a mirror. Why do you reject your son, who comes to you of his own accord and looks at you with affection? Look on my son as your other self, as your reflection seen in a clear pond. What evil deeds did I do in a previous life so that I was abandoned in this life, first by my mother and now by you? I will go home now, but do not reject your own son."

Dushyanta replied, "I do not recognize this son that you have. Women are liars. Who will trust what you say? Your son is too big, and too strong, to have been born as recently as you claim. Your own birth is low, and you look to me like a whore [pumschali]. All that you are saying makes no sense to me. I do not recognize you. Go where you like." Again she tried, in vain, to explain the moral law to him, and then she left. At that moment a disembodied voice from the sky said, "The mother is the father's leather water-bag; the son belongs to the man who begets him. The mother brings forth a son and her own body is split into two. Support your son, and do not reject Shakuntala." Then Dushyanta said to his court-iers, "I knew all of this perfectly well, knew that he was my own son. But if I had accepted him as my own son just from her words, there would have been doubt among the people." And he said to Shakuntala, "People would think that I had a bond with you because you are a woman, and that I had chosen this son for the kingdom. That is why I argued." Then he accepted his son and forgave Shakuntala for the harsh words she had spoken to him in her anger.[39]

Dushyanta does not want to remember either Shakuntala or his awkward promise about the succession. (King Shantanu, also in the *Mahabharata*, incurs the same problem when he desires a woman whose father will not let him marry her until he promises, against custom, to make her son king.[40] And Rama's stepmother, in the *Ramayana*, uses sexual blackmail as the last of several arguments to get Rama's father to put her son on the throne.[41] This is an endemic problem in ancient Indian fiction.) No explanation is given for Dushyanta's decision to lie about her other than his own weak rationalization. In one recension of the text, he says, "I don't sleep with a woman without a good reason. I don't recall being together with you."[42] And the narrator in this recension remarks, candidly, "Because he was attached to enjoyment of other women, Shakuntala and her son disappeared from his mind."[43] But a divine voice from the sky, a kind of Indian deus ex machina, forces the king to acknowledge his son, whose extraordinary size and strength had previously led the king not to accept him as divinely blessed but to reject him as begotten by some other, previous lover. That voice's statement about the importance of mothers is hardly feminist—it is of the "hen as a way for an egg to make another egg" school of embryology. But its surprisingly violent image of a woman split in two in childbirth evokes sympathy for mothers and suggests a widespread mythical response of a woman to a double-dealing man: her own literal bisection into two women or, less violent and more common, her performance of two women,[44] herself and the woman she pretends to be.[viii] Surely there is irony in the text's statement that the king magnanimously forgave *her* for speaking to him in anger.

The Ring of the Bodhisattva

The Buddhists told the story of Shakuntala (without mentioning her name) in two of the texts called Jatakas (stories of the Buddha's previous births), sometime between the fourth century BCE and the fifth century CE.[45] These stories are notoriously difficult to date precisely, so we cannot use them as steppingstones between the *Mahabharata* and the later text of Kalidasa. Rather, it is best to regard them simply as variants that develop

---

viii. See chapter 6, p. 165.

certain aspects of the story, in particular introducing the theme of a ring. One of the Jatakas tells this story:

> King Brahmadatta of Varanasi was wandering in his pleasure groves when he saw a woman and fell in love with her. He seduced her and she conceived a child who was the future Buddha, the Bodhisatta. He gave her the signet ring from his finger and dismissed her with these words: "If it is a girl, spend this ring on her nurture; but if it is a boy, bring ring and child to me." She gave birth to a boy, and when he was growing up the children teased him, calling him "No-father." He asked his mother about his father, and she told him. At his request, she took him to the palace and said, "This is your son, sire." The king knew well enough that this was the truth, but shame before all his court made him reply, "He is no son of mine." "But here is your signet-ring, sire; you will recognize that." "Nor is this my signet ring." Then said the woman, "Sire, I have now no witness to prove my words, except to appeal to truth. Wherefore, if you be the father of my child, I pray that he may stay in mid-air; but if not, may he fall to earth and be killed." So saying, she seized the Bodhisatta by the foot and threw him up in the air. The child, suspended in the air, told the king he was his son. The king stretched out his hands and cried, "Come to me, my boy! None, none but me shall rear and nurture you!" A thousand hands were stretched out to receive the Bodhisatta, but it was into the arms of the king and of no other that he descended, seating himself in the king's lap. The king made him viceroy, and made his mother queen-consort. At the death of the king his father, he came to the throne, was called King Katthavahana, and after ruling his realm righteously, passed away to fare according to his deserts.[46]

This text introduces a gender bias: if the child is a boy, you can use the ring to secure his patrimony, but if it's a girl, you can use it for her dowry. Thus the ring serves both as a proof of identity and as a kind of child support; this version recognizes the hardheaded value of a ring, a very early instance of the argument that diamonds are a girl's best friend.[ix] And when the king simply denies that the woman's ring is his, he demonstrates the obvious fact that jewelry doesn't actually prove anything at all unless other people acknowledge it.

---

ix. See chapter 10, p. 266.

These reasonable considerations lead back into irrational religion, an act of truth reminiscent of the voice from the sky in the *Mahabharata* tale of Shakuntala: a miracle, a suspension of the law of gravity, which proves the identity of the child and epitomizes, like the judgment of Solomon (1 *Kings* 3.16–27), the liminality of the child torn between two parents. But whereas Solomon's proposal to split the child, which would kill it, smoked out the true mother in protest, and the voice from the sky in the *Mahabharata* spoke of the mother herself being split in half, the father here quite blithely accepts the possibility that his son may crash and die. (The mother has faith that since the child really is the king's, he will be safe). This text spells out, as the *Mahabharata* does not, the king's total disregard for the child as well as the mother.

Another Buddhist version in another Jataka story reverts to the more conventional assumption that the ring is an incontrovertible proof: when the seducer, this time the king's Brahmin chaplain, says to the child, "I gave your mother a token; where is it?" the boy hands him the ring, which the Brahmin recognizes and acknowledges. But he also goes on to test the boy on his knowledge of dharma, the same knowledge that Shakuntala used in vain, in the Epic, to prove to Dushyanta who *she* was. And after they have recited stanzas back and forth to one another, the chaplain accepts the boy not merely as his son (which he had already done on the basis of the ring) but as a Brahmin worthy to succeed him as royal chaplain (which he decides on the basis of the boy's knowledge).[47] The child must use his achievements as well as his ancestry to ensure his recognition by his father. And although the woman in both versions of this story has no name, the son is named; indeed, each of the Buddhist texts is named after the child in that text. In the transition from the *Mahabharata* to these Buddhist texts, Shakuntala has lost both her name and her ability to discourse on dharma, both of which have been transferred to her son.

A Buddhist tale from the Tibetan tradition also makes the mother a silent player:

> King Bimbisara, a notorious philanderer, had a liaison with the wife of a very rich merchant who was away on business, and she became pregnant. She informed the king, who sent her a signet ring (*anguli-mudraka*) and a brightly colored chiffon cloth, telling her that if the child was a girl it could remain with her, but if it was a boy she should dress him in the fabric, bind the seal ring around his neck and send the boy to him. After nine months had passed, she gave birth to a beautiful

son. She fed him with ghee and honey, bound the seal ring around his neck, covered him with the cloth, and placed him in a chest. She gave the chest to her serving-maid, telling her to take it to the gate of the royal palace, light a circle of lamps around it, and stay off to one side until someone took the child. The maid did as she was told. The king saw the lamps, sent for the chest, had it opened, recognized the signet ring and the cloth, and took the child into the palace.[48]

The text remarks, a propos of the mother's successful plan, that "women, even without receiving instruction, are full of knowledge," which is simultaneously a put-down, denying women the right to education and literacy, and an acknowledgment that even illiterate women know how the story goes. Of course, the king knows the story too. But this woman, still unnamed, does the right thing: she sends the double proof, the ring now supplemented by a cloth, that will assure her son's recognition at the palace, even though she herself never appears there (presumably never to be recognized as the child's mother) and never says a word to the king (though she does speak to the servant girl). The ring says it all for her.

The Recognition of Shakuntala

The poet Kalidasa, writing in the fourth century CE, was under the patronage of the Gupta dynasty, who traced their lineage back to the child of Shakuntala and Dushyanta, a child named Bharata—from whose name is derived the word used to designate India in most Indian languages to this day. Kalidasa had his work cut out for him to transform Bharata's father from a lying seducer to a sympathetic lover, and he fell back upon the tried and true device of the magic ring of memory and the curse of forgetfulness.

Here let's pause and note that there are three different sorts of rings interacting in these stories. First is the ring of identity, the signet ring, already well known in India, as we have seen, and in particular the signet ring that a woman uses to prove her assertion that a certain man has impregnated her, a theme that the Jatakas introduced into the Shakuntala story. Second is the ring that is lost and then found in a fish, a ring that we know from other stories, including Indian ones.[49] And third is the magic ring that bewitches memory and forgetfulness, well known from the European medieval tradition[x] but not attested in India before Kalidasa.

---

x. See chapter 4, p. 87.

The new version of the story of Shakuntala combines all three of these rings. The first two were already widely known in the ancient world, lying right at hand for Kalidasa to pick up, like so many lost rings; he just had to draw the ring-and-fish out of the storytellers' ocean of tricks, through the technique that Claude Lévi-Strauss called "bricolage," the myth-maker's ability to take a piece of one story to mend another story.[xi] But Kalidasa needed to conjure up some sort of magic to get the king out of his dilemma, and he made use of the third type of ring. This is what he came up with:

> King Dushyanta met Shakuntala in the forest, and they fell in love. She did not yet know that he was the king (he told her he was the king's minister in charge of religious affairs); then he offered her his signet ring with his name engraved on it. When her friends read the name on the ring and reacted with surprise, he said, "Do not misunderstand; the ring is a gift from the king." Shakuntala refused the ring at first, but eventually, after she had found out that he himself was the king, she slept with him. As he left to return to court, he placed his ring on her finger, telling her to count off one day for each letter of his name, and at the end he would send for her.
>
> Shakuntala, daydreaming about the king, slighted a short-tempered sage, who cursed her: "Since you were so lost in thought of some man that you had no mind for anyone else, he will not remember you even when you try to awaken him, just as a drunk does not remember the story that he told before." Shakuntala didn't hear the curse, but her friends did, and persuaded the sage to put limits on it: "The power of the curse will cease the moment she presents some ornament as a token of recognition." When the king failed to send for her, and Shakuntala discovered that she was pregnant, she set out for court. Her friends advised her, "If the king is slow to recognize you, be sure to show him the ring inscribed with his name."
>
> Meanwhile, at court, the king's neglected queen was heard singing a sad song: "How have you forgotten your love?" The king, knowing that she was singing about him, was touched by her delicacy and sent his jester to her with a courtly reply. But then, suddenly alone, he felt the pangs of separation from someone he loved though he knew of no such lost love. He thought to himself, "Even a happy

---

xi. See chapter 11, p. 301.

man may be overcome by passionate longing when he sees beautiful things or hears sweet sounds. Perhaps he is remembering something he was not conscious of before that moment, the loves of a former life, firmly rooted in the impressions of lingering emotions."

When the king saw Shakuntala, who was veiled, he wondered who she was; when he was told that she was pregnant with his child, he was full of doubt; and when she removed her veil, he said, "Did I take this beauty before, or not? No matter how hard I try, I cannot remember ever making this woman my own. And how can I accept her when she shows clear signs of pregnancy and I have doubts about being the one who sowed the field, as it were?" Shakuntala thought to herself, "When his passion has undergone such a change, what good would it do even if I were to make him remember? But I must prove my own purity." And she said to the king, "If you have doubts, thinking that I am another man's wife, I will dispel your doubt by this token of remembrance. . . . Oh no! My finger is not wearing the ring!" Her chaperone said, "It must have been lost when you went into the water at the shrine." The king smiled and said, "This is why people say that women are so cunning, like cuckoos who let other birds nurture their eggs." But he continued to waver: "Am I deluded, or is she lying? This is my quandary. Which is worse for me, to desert my wife or be defiled by the touch of another man's wife?"

The chaplain made a helpful suggestion: "Since it has been predicted that the king's son will be a sovereign of the world, wait until Shakuntala has the child and see if he has the marks of sovereignty." The king agreed, but Shakuntala ran away and was snatched up to heaven by the celestial nymph who was her mother. The king lamented, "Though I do not remember the sage's daughter, or any marriage, still my aching heart contradicts me."

Guards dragged in a fisherman and charged him with having in his possession the royal signet ring and with having invented the tale that he found it inside a fish. But the king rewarded the fisherman and gladly received the ring. As soon as the king saw the ring, he remembered that he had married Shakuntala and had denied her in the delusion that overcame him when she had lost the ring. But, one of the women argued, "Such a passion should not need a token of remembrance or recognition." To which the king replied, "So, let me blame the ring."

One day, in heaven on an errand for the gods, Dushyanta met the child that Shakuntala had borne. When a bystander remarked, "Miraculous, astonishing, the speaking resemblance between this boy and you," the king began to suspect that it was his own son. The boy had lost his bracelet while playing with a lion cub, and the king picked up the bracelet, to the astonishment of two bystanders, who recalled that it was a magic bracelet that no one but the boy or his parents could pick up; if anyone else touched it, it would change into a serpent and bite that person. The skeptical king asked, "Have you yourself ever been eye witnesses to this transformation, with your own eyes?" To which the two women replied, "Many times." But the king was convinced only when the boy said, "You are not my father; Dushyanta is my father." Then Shakuntala entered and said, "Even after I heard that the bracelet didn't turn into a serpent, I was afraid to believe it." But when she saw the king she said, "He is not like my husband. Who is this man who defiles by the touch of his limbs my son, who was protected by that bracelet?" The boy said, "Mommy! This stranger embraces me and calls me his son." Then Shakuntala and the king began to argue:

Dushyanta: "My dear, it is only fair that you should turn my cruelty to you against me, as I see that you now refuse to recognize me. The light of memory has pierced the darkness of my delusion . . ."

Shakuntala: "It must have been the ripening of my past deeds that made you, who had been so compassionate, become so cold. But how did you come to remember unhappy me? Ah, I see your ring."

Dushyanta: "Yes, it was by getting back this ring that I got back my memory. It does seem to me strange that through a loosening of my memory, I denied Shakuntala and then, afterwards, as a result of seeing the ring, I understood that I had formerly married her."

Shakuntala: "Thank goodness! My husband did not refuse me without any reason. But I don't remember being cursed. Could I have been cursed without knowing it, when my mind was distracted by the separation? Is that why my friends advised me to show the ring to my husband?"

Then a god explained it to her: "Your husband rejected you because of the curse that obstructed his memory; the reflection does not assume a shape on the surface of a mirror when its brightness is masked by dirt, but it finds its place there easily when it is cleaned."

Dushyanta's amnesia is not total; it leaves traces, clues for the king to follow. Shakuntala in the *Mahabharata* spoke of a son as the reflection of
his father; here the clouded mirror reflection symbolizes the incompletely
erased mental image, Dushyanta's only half-lost memory of his wife
and son. The twist here consists in the fact that although the king gave
Shakuntala the ring to make *her* remember *him*, its loss makes *him* forget
her; the magic of the loss of the ring on her finger is projected, as it were,
into his mind many miles away, like the ring that Hans Carvel put on his
own hand in order to control his wife.[xii] To put it differently, Shakuntala's
mistake (a trivial breach of ascetiquette) injures Dushyanta's mind. As
Robert P. Goldman put it, Dushyanta "is made to suffer for the actions
of another, actions of which he is completely innocent. This functional
sharing or even transfer of the fruits of one person's actions is a recurrent
theme in accounts and illustrations of the workings of *karma*."[50]

Karma, in the sense of the moral record of good and bad actions committed in this life and former lives, is often transferred in this way,[51] and
it is alluded to in the king's reference to "impressions of lingering emotions," the veiled memories that act like perfumes (*vasanas*) carried on the
transmigrating soul, often causing a sense of *déjà vu*.

A transfer of this sort takes place when Shakuntala offers the king
an easy out through the projected blame for his caddishness. In the
Mahabharata, Shakuntala worries aloud if she might have committed evil
deeds in another life that caused her to be abandoned first by her mother
and now by her lover. In Kalidasa, too, she blames the ripening of her
past deeds for his coldness. In both cases, she thinks it must have been
her own fault somehow. But Kalidasa *makes it* her fault, not in a previous
life inevitably forgotten but in her slight to the sage that resulted in his
curse—which she did not forget but simply never knew about.

Both Shakuntala and Dushyanta are oblivious of the curse (and the
offense that inspired it), subject to a focal amnesia that often affects victims of karma or curses (frequently both together).[52] Both the curse and
karma are in play here: she is cursed, and both she and Dushyanta have
intimations of a past life, while he is oblivious not only of the curse but of
his entire encounter with her. As Romila Thapar suggests, both the curse
and the signet ring that restores the memory that the curse has erased
are "stereotypical items of folk literature," and they are in "a contrapuntal

---

xii. See chapter 1, p. 15.

relationship: the curse acts as an impediment to the action, the ring as a token of recognition resolves the problem."[53] The magic effect of the curse seems to be an exaggeration of a rather banal psychological insight widely recorded in folklore and superstition, including stories in the "Bishop of Glasgow" cycle:[xiii] the belief that if you lose your wedding ring you somehow jeopardize your marriage. Shakuntala's loss of the ring "could be suggestive of a certain casualness on her part."[54] But, one might argue prosaically, the ring was made for a man's hand, and would be too big for a woman, making it quite likely that she would lose it.

Dushyanta lies about the ring at the start, denying that it is his, just as he will later deny that Shakuntala and her son are his (fearing that, like a cuckoo, she wants to insinuate some other man's egg into his, Dushyanta's, nest—to cuckold him, as the cuckoo metaphor functions in English) and just as the king in the Buddhist tale denied the ring even *after* the woman returned to him. Even the spectacularly naïve Shakuntala expresses her distrust of the ring. But then Dushyanta forgets her because of the ring; the curse is a very convenient and rather suspicious excuse, as the cynical ladies in the court point out: "Such a passion should not need a token of remembrance or recognition." The king's reply, "So, let me blame the ring," is about as close to an admission of guilt as that sort of ruler, indeed that sort of man, will ever get.

When he recovers the ring found in the fish, he insists that he rejected her because of delusion, or madness, or a dream, or a demon, or fate; and he regards his amnesia as a dream from which he has now awakened, though now he meets her only in his dreams. The king has done this before, as we know from the neglected queen who sings of forgotten love. Shakuntala, who has begun to understand him better, is persuaded that "when his passion has undergone such a change," it would be no use to try to remind him of it. This is tantamount to saying that she does not believe he has forgotten her but, rather, fears that he no longer loves her. Later, she pretends not to recognize him at first, subjecting him to his own treatment.

In the *Mahabharata*, Shakuntala is a wise woman who discourses on dharma; in Kalidasa, she is hardly more than a child and says little when the king accuses her of lying; indeed, most of her words reach us only because the king tells us she said them. In the *Mahabharata*, when

---

xiii. See chapter 2, p. 31.

Shakuntala meets the king at court, she has already borne the child that legitimates her. Kalidasa's Shakuntala, by contrast, goes to the forgetful king so quickly—at *his* suggestion, constrained by the number of symbols on *his* ring—that at her first confrontation with him she is merely pregnant, indeed barely pregnant. There is no child to back her up; all that she has is the ring, and since that is lost, she runs away. Only later, when the child is a few years old, can he legitimate his mother, as he does in the Buddhist stories and in some of the tales of clever wives.[xiv]

But there is more to it than this. In the *Mahabharata*, Shakuntala is the daughter of the celestial nymph Menaka,[55] and she claims that she herself can fly.[56] When she is pregnant, she is snatched up by her celestial mother, just as Sita is when Rama has abandoned her, also pregnant. Indeed, the parallel with Sita may be extended: both women are daughters of supernatural women (Sita is the daughter of the Earth), both come from another world (Sita from the "green world" or the subterranean world) to bear the king a son (twin boys, in the case of Sita), and both disappear when the king abuses them. Dushyanta says he rejected Shakuntala because of his fear of public disapproval, an argument that rings equally hollow when Rama uses it to reject Sita.[57] This is a pattern we know well from world folklore and religious literature:[58] the story of the swan maiden,[xv] the woman who comes from another world to bear a special son and returns to her own world when her husband abuses her.

The story in the *Mahabharata* is about power and inheritance, but Kalidasa turns it into a story about desire and memory. In this new form, the story simultaneously plays upon our sympathy with Dushyanta when he suffers from his amnesia and our sympathy with Shakuntala when she suffers because of it. Unlike Dushyanta in the *Mahabharata*, who with calculating common sense rejects the son who is unnaturally big and strong for his putative age, Dushyanta recognizes his son by a similarly unnatural quality, his ability to play with a young lion. Clearly this "proof" can be used by either side and is therefore no proof. But there are other signs of recognition as well. The ring is doubled here not, as it often is, by a second ring but by another piece of circular jewelry, the magic bracelet that identifies the boy's parents—a kind of proto-DNA that, in mass production, would

---

xiv. See chapter 6, p. 139.

xv. See chapter 5, p. 128.

put an end to all tales of changelings, all Family Romances.[xvi] The king is skeptical about this trick, as is Shakuntala, who won't believe the evidence of the bracelet and thinks that the king "defiles by his touch" the boy whose bracelet was intended to prevent the touch of anyone but his father—until she sees the king with her own eyes. The king's skepticism seems to challenge the assertion that the bracelet turns into a snake ("Have you yourself ever been eye witnesses to this transformation, with your own eyes?" the king asks the onlookers), until, to our astonishment, they reply, "Many times." Both the ring and the bracelet do tell the truth. Bystanders also note the "speaking resemblance," literally a "form that talks together" (the same term that was used to speculate about Ratnavali's necklace) between the boy and his father, just as Shakuntala in the *Mahabharata* had said that a man's legitimate son is like his face in a mirror.

Kalidasa's Dushyanta responds instinctively to his son, even when his memory does not know that it is his son: "How is it that I feel love for this little boy as if he were the son born of my own loins? If my limbs thrill so to his touch, what bliss must he give to the man whose body gave him life?" In the same way, when the king first falls in love with Shakuntala, who is apparently of another class, he hopes that she may in fact turn out to be of his own class. He reasons: "Surely she is fit to be the wife of a man of royal birth, since the heart of a nobleman like me yearns for her; for the inner inclinations of good people are their authority to distinguish doubtful objects." And Dushyanta's "aching heart" remembers his marriage to Shakuntala when his memory does not, attributing his tantalizing half-memory to a loose thread trailing from a previous life. Later, when all has become clear, he says: "Just as a man in doubt might say, 'There is no elephant,' even as it walks past him before his very eyes, but then, seeing its footprints, he might be satisfied—my mind underwent changes just like that."[59]

The fish story gets Kalidasa out of what subsequent Indian scholars recognized as a true moral dilemma. In 1920, Rabindranath Tagore argued that the amorous Dushyanta would have deserted Shakuntala "in real life . . . as the natural consequence of his character," but because this desertion "would have been so extremely cruel and pathetic as to destroy the peace and harmony of the whole play," Kalidasa introduced the device of the sage's curse. Nevertheless, Tagore continued, "The poet has left a small

xvi. See chapter 2, p. 40.

rent in the veil through which we can get an idea of the royal sin." And this glimpse is the moment when, hearing his neglected queen singing about her sad loss of his love, the king explains to the jester, "We desert our loves after a short spell of love-making."[60]

Thapar has pointed out that the ring "frees the king from any blame for rejecting the woman he had married," so that "Dushyanta cannot be blamed for his behaviour as he is under a spell; ... To all these accusations the king can innocently reply that he is not guilty, since he has no recollection of Shakuntala."[61] She asks, "Were the curse and the ring also introduced because they gloss over the real tension between Shakuntala and Dushyanta, namely, the paternity of her child?"[62] But, as we learn from the Buddhist traditions, the ring is a traditional part of the paternity riddle; the curse of forgetfulness is what "gloss[es] over" the tension. Thapar goes on to raise another question: "Is Kalidasa avoiding the moral issue of condemning Dushyanta's action in rejecting Shakuntala, and would such an avoidance not have been regarded as contemptible in those times?" In 1938, Akhtar Husain Raipuri, who translated Kalidasa's play into Urdu, argued that Kalidasa, being a man of his time and identifying with Brahminical high culture, changed the original epic story in an attempt "to save the king from being seen for what he really was—a man who refused to accept responsibility for seducing an innocent woman" (and, I would add, abandoning her).[63]

A. K. Ramanujan simultaneously invokes and mocks the convention of the ring and the fish in the tale of Shakuntala in his poem, "No Amnesiac King" (1986), of which one stanza goes:

> One cannot wait anymore in the back
> Of one's mind for that conspiracy
> Of three fishermen and a palace cook
> To bring, dressed in cardamom and clove,
> The one well-timed memorable fish,
> So one can cut straight with the royal knife
> To the ring waiting untarnished in the belly,
> And recover at one stroke all lost memory.

As the poem continues, the fish "in its dead white belly / has an uncooked signet ring and a forest / legend of wandering king and waiting / innocent, complete with fawn under tree."[64] The "wandering king" needs the "forest legend" to tell his story the way it has to be told.

But he also needs the "uncooked signet ring" to get back his own lost memory.

Dushyanta's loss of memory is notorious in later Sanskrit literature. When a man disguised as a king seduces a woman, and the real king later honestly denies having had her, she says to him, "Did you marry me by the ritual of mutual desire and then forget me, as Dushyanta forgot Shakuntala, long ago?" And the king replies, "Truly, I never married you at all; I just came here now."[65] Yet India, and the rest of the world, continued to generate stories in which rings, rather than kings, took the burden of guilt for seducing and abandoning women.

The Return of the Repressed

Our texts express two different views of the resurgence of the past—past loves, past memory—as it is symbolized by the ring retrieved by the fish: that it is harmful, something to be feared (the ring of Polycrates),[xvii] and that it is beneficial, something to be desired (the ring of Solomon, or Shakuntala). In both branches of the story, the ring in the belly of the fish reminds us that we cannot escape our fate, whether we fear it or desire it. But in both cases, the ring that is symbolic of clouded memory is inevitably found, because it is an integral part of the person who loses it. Polycrates, whose ring came back even when he threw it into the ocean, is reincarnate in the Victorian Cruel Knight, who tried in vain to drown, and then to lose, both his ring and his future wife, with the moral clearly spelled out for us: "Tis in vain to alter what fate has decreed."[xviii] Oedipus learned this lesson the hard way: the prediction about his mother and father made him run away . . . to his mother and father and his complex. The circular workings of fate force us back to the place where we are meant to be, however fast we may run in the other direction.

Freud explored one variant of this myth of the strangle grip of the past in his theory of the return of the repressed (*Wiederkehr des Verdrängten*), a concept that illuminates several variants of the myths of the ring in the fish.[66] Freud touched upon it in his discussion of Oedipus in *The Interpretation of Dreams* (in 1899)[67] when he warned us that when faced with the same evidence in our lives that Oedipus faced in his, like him "we

---

xvii. See chapter 2, p. 30.

xviii. See chapter 2, p. 34.

may all of us well seek to close our eyes to the scenes of our childhood,"[68] which is to say, to repress those memories, to throw the ring of memory back into the ocean of the unconscious. He spelled this out years later (in 1937) in *Moses and Monotheism*:

> "What a child has strongly experienced and not understood by the time he has reached the age of two he may never again remember, except in dreams. Only through psychoanalytic treatment will he become aware of those events. At any time in later years, however, they may break into his life with obsessional impulsiveness, direct his actions, force him to like or dislike people, and often decide the choice of his love-object by a preference that so often cannot be rationally defended."[69]

We repress unconscious thoughts and/or feelings that we find too painful, but this repression requires fairly heavy psychic maintenance, and the repressed thought may break out at a moment of psychic trauma, particularly when stirred up by an event that somehow resembles the original trauma. The formation of symptoms at a later time indicates the return of the repressed, though it appears in a distorted form in these symptoms. Freud's scenario of recovering childhood memories appears in our myths as the recovery of a child, thought lost forever, from the ocean[xix]— the ocean of stories, as the great Hindu narrative compendium calls it (*Kathasaritsagara*), now mythologized until it has what Freud elsewhere[70] called the "oceanic feeling" of religion.

And the ring, when we do get it back out of the water, is not the same. It has undergone "a sea-change, / into something rich and strange," like the submerged body of the drowned king imagined in Shakespeare's *The Tempest* [1.2.402]. Ramanujan saw this as the point of the Shakuntala story: "Nothing is lost, only transformed."[71] (He may have been paraphrasing Ovid: "Everything changes, nothing perishes.")[72] And Freud expressed another aspect of this insight when he remarked, "The finding of an object is in fact the refinding of it."[73] (Or, as the Buddhist mother puts it, "I never lose anything.")

The positive and negative aspects of this repression, and the corresponding negative and positive aspects of its return, are mythologized in the two

---

xix. See chapter 2, p. 50.

forms of the tale of the ring-retrieved-by-a-fish, the Polycrates syndrome and the Solomon/Shakuntala syndrome. Repression is to some extent a Bad Thing (it causes guilt, neurosis, and so forth), and the retrieval of the repressed thought (through dreams or psychoanalysis) may be therapeutic for the individual (the Solomon/Shakuntala syndrome). But the repression may be healthier for society in general; and even for the individual, the breakthrough of a repressed emotion may have tragic consequences, for its original force may be distorted and multiplied by an intensity built up through the years in prison.

Both aspects of the myth, and the theory, are embodied in rituals related to our mythology of precious things lost and found in water. On the Jewish New Year of Rosh Hashanah there is a ceremony called Taslich, during which Jews traditionally go to the ocean or a stream or river to pray and to throw into the water bread crumbs symbolic of their sins, which they hope the fish will devour rather than bring back to them. But the Hebrew Bible (Ecclesiastes 11.1), advises us, "Cast thy bread upon the waters: for thou shalt find it after many days." Which will happen? Which do we *want* to happen?

The Lost and Found of Rings

In the tales of lost rings found in fish, the fish becomes the symbol of the recovery and persistence of memory, primarily because of the metaphor of retrieval from the depths of the ocean but also, perhaps, because the fish's staring eyes suggest a consciousness that never falters for a moment, as ours does when we alternately sleep and wake—or, in some views, die and are reborn. Indo-Europeans measure time by the blink of an eye (cf. the German *Augenblick*, the Sanskrit *nimesha*); but for fish, who do not blink, time does not erode memory.[74] Gail Hinich Sutherland put it well: "The magic fish [is] the symbol of the remote possibility, the unlikely occurrence, the finding of something which had been irretrievably lost, the silvery receptacle of the lost ring, and the reminder to humans that nothing can ever be permanently forgotten, ignored, or submerged in ignorance or non-being."[75]

The British poet James Fenton pointed out a strange paradox about rings lost and found:

"When, as often happens, rings are dropped or lost, or when they are deliberately buried with the dead, their chance of survival increases. This is the paradox of the valuable object. If it is not lost, it gets melted down as styles change or as necessity arises. But if it is hidden in a hoard, or dropped in a peat bog, or somehow allowed to lie forgotten, it may one day be retrieved."[76]

Or, as Freud would have insisted, if it is "somehow allowed to lie forgotten," it *will* one day be retrieved.

For a ray of hope shines through this dark view of the inevitable return of repressed memories, and that is the more positive counterpart to Polycrates's ring, namely, the ring of Solomon/Shakuntala. That ring holds out the hope that the return of the desired mate, and/or the child, that we had feared lost forever, will be healing, and the hope that we ourselves will not be lost when we die, that our children, or our words or works, will survive and, with them, something of our memory. For, of all the things that we lose, memory is the most precious; it is also the most recoverable, if one knows how to go about it, and is lucky.

4

Rings of Forgetfulness in Medieval European Romances

The Man Who Forgot His Wife
When He Lost His Ring

We begin to see how the tales of circular jewelry come to intersect so often with the mythology of sexual deception in marriage, when jewelry identifies a sexual partner. Some of the rings in these stories identify adulterers while others reveal true lovers and/or marriage partners. And still others restore memory, or, when lost, induce forgetfulness.[i] When a ring is lost, it may make the wearer forget both identity and love, which is to say the identity of both the wearer and the beloved.

But there are also rings explicitly designed to make people forget rather than remember. In the twelfth-century Anglo-Norman story of Yonec, a ring makes a jealous husband forget his wife's adultery:[1]

A woman was married to a rich man who locked her up but could not keep her from falling in love with a knight. The lovers were discovered together, the woman imprisoned, and the knight fatally wounded. As he died he gave her a ring and assured her that, as long as she kept it, her husband would not remember anything that had happened, nor would he continue to imprison her. He also gave her his sword and made her swear that no man but their as yet unborn son (Yonec) would ever possess it. She kept the ring and the sword, and they comforted her. She continued to live with her

i. See chapter 3, p. 83.

husband for many years, but he never accused her of infidelity, nor ever insulted or abused her.[2]

This is a very useful sort of ring to have, even without the powers of filial identification that it has, in this story, bequeathed to the sword.

The same sort of ring of forgetfulness is given to the wife rather than the husband in the thirteenth/fourteenth-century *Gesta Romanorum*:

> "Fredericus, who reigned in a Roman city, had been a long time without offspring. Finally, by the advice of wise counselors, he married a beautiful girl in parts far distant and lived with her in an unknown land and had offspring. After this, he wished to return to his realm but could not obtain his wife's consent; indeed, she always repeated that if he abandoned her she would kill herself. Hearing this, the emperor caused two splendid rings to be made, and had engraved upon two gems images of the following efficacy: one of remembrance and the other of forgetfulness. Having set these in their appropriate rings he gave one—that of forgetfulness—to his wife, and kept the other for himself.... The wife began straightway to forget the love of her husband, and the emperor, noting this, journeyed back to his realm with great joy, and never returned to his wife. He ended his life in peace."[3]

This text reverses the convenient assumption in Kalidasa's version of the Shakuntala story,[ii] the romantic belief that it's only because the lover *forgets* the mother of his child(ren) that he leaves her. The effect is much the same, of course; during the period in which Shakuntala loses the ring of memory, it becomes a ring of forgetfulness, though it resumes its primary role of memento when it is found. But the cynical tale of Fredericus argues, instead, that it's because the king *remembers* the mother of his children, and makes sure that *she* forgets *him*, that he leaves her. Like the husbands in the stories of clever wives,[iii] this king forges a ring of memory and abandons the woman he impregnates. The twist comes in the doubling and inverting of the ring, so that here he keeps the ring of memory and gives her the ring of forgetfulness.

---

ii. See chapter 3, p. 74.

iii. See chapter 6, p. 137.

Such rings of forgetfulness, which often replace or are replaced by drugged goblets of wine, come into play in several related medieval cycles from Welsh, Celtic, French, German, and early English literature: the story of Lancelot and Guinevere, of Owein (or Yvain) and the Lady of the Fountain, of Tristan and Isolde, and (to be treated in a separate chapter)[iv] Siegfried and Brünnhilde. Each story is told in a number of different texts, and the stars of one often make cameo appearances as bit players in another. Both Yvain[4] and Arthur[5] appear, for example, in the defense of Isolde, and Tristan pretends to have a sister named Brunehild.[6] Each text tends to spell the names of the protagonists in a slightly different way; to simplify matters, I will standardize the spellings as Tristan, Isolde, Guinevere, Lancelot, Siegfried, Brünnhilde, and Yvain.

Let's begin with Yvain.

Yvain, the Knight of the Lion, and the Lady of the Fountain

Yvain (called Owein in the Welsh historical texts) was a historical king of the late sixth century, the son of Urien of Rheged, in what is now northwest England and southwest Scotland.[7] Well known from Welsh poetry and prose (particularly *The Dream of Rhonabwy*), he is called Iwenus, Ewen, Owein, Owain, Owain mab Urien, or Yvain in the earliest known texts of the tale often called "The Lady (or Countess) of the Fountain" (in the Welsh sources)[8] or "The Knight of the Lion" (in the French).[9] Geoffrey of Monmouth, writing in 1136, mentions him (as Iwenus) only in passing, but *The Lives of Saint Ninian and Saint Kentigern*, written in Scotland between 1147 and 1164, depicts Ewen (as he is called there) as a villainous cad, who courted a British princess named Thenaw (or Thaney or Theneva or Teneu), daughter of the Brythonic king Leudonus (Lothian):

> She refused to marry him, and in retaliation her father sent her to work as the servant of a swineherd. Desperately in love with her, Yvain sent a woman to try to persuade Thaney to grant him her affection; when this failed, he disguised himself as a woman and met her near a fountain. Through trickery, he led her away to an isolated spot and raped her, as a result of which she conceived a

---

iv. See chapter 5.

child. Yvain then abandoned Thaney. Her father punished her for becoming pregnant by having her thrown from a mountaintop, but she survived unharmed, after which a clear fountain, no doubt a token of her innocence, sprang up miraculously. Then Thaney was set adrift in a boat on the Firth of Forth; she survived and gave birth to the future bishop Kentigern.[10]

No ring, no loss of memory, just plain old rape, pregnancy, shame, and persecution, plus two fountains: one a witness to the scene of the rape and the other a miraculous testimony to it. Thaney's pregnancy is unwanted, but the child that results from this unplanned parenthood became Bishop of Glasgow (a.k.a. Saint Kentigern, who once found a ring in a salmon).[v]

The child drops out of the later variants of the tale of Yvain, and so does the physical violence of the rape, which gives way instead to an emphasis upon the mental and psychological harm done to the woman who has been seduced and abandoned. Thaney's miraculous fountain—and little else—remains in Chrétien de Troyes's tale of Yvain (composed, in French, around 1177). But, like Dushyanta,[vi] the rehabilitated Yvain now has need of a magic ring:

> As Yvain entered a fortress, the gate dropped down, catching the saddle and the horse's haunches, which it cut off clean, trapping Yvain (and the front half of his horse) between this gate and the inner gate. There he met a woman named Lunette, who told him that she recognized him, as she had been to the court of King Arthur, where Yvain alone of all the knights had treated her courteously. Then she said, "Accept this little ring, and if you please return it to me when it's done its work, and you're free." She gave him the little ring and told him it had the power to conceal anyone who wore it, as long as he turned the stone into his palm. Then she led him to safety and kept him in her room. From his hiding place he saw the Countess of the Fountain, Laudine de Landuc, and fell in love with her; he met her and married her.
>
> After a while, he longed to go with Gawain to Arthur's court. Laudine made him promise to return after precisely one year,

---

warning him that her love would turn to hate after that. He protested that he could not know the future, that he might become ill
or be held prisoner, that events might detain him. Still she swore,
"If our Lord keeps you from death, nothing will stand in your way
as long as you never forget me." And she loaned him a ring with
a magic power in its stone: "No true and loyal lover can be captured, or lose any blood, nor have any evil come to him. As long as
he wears it and holds it dear he will remember his beloved. . . . No
knight has ever had it from my hand. I give it you only because of
my love."

Yvain rode off. His body might follow the king, but his heart
remained with her, joined to her own. Gawain, however, kept him
so long that a year passed, and months after that. Then all of a sudden, when King Arthur came and was seated in their midst, Yvain
was struck by an overwhelming thought; he realized all at once
that he'd broken his promise and stayed beyond the time they'd
agreed. Laudine sent a woman who accused him of being "disloyal,
and a traitor, and a liar, and a deceiver, who'd deserted his wife and
betrayed her. . . . You've forgotten it all, you couldn't be bothered to
remember a thing. . . . She sends me to tell you never to come back,
but only return her ring." And she took the ring from his finger.

Yvain lost his senses and wandered for a long time. Another
countess sent her maid to anoint him with a special ointment that
cured him, so that his mind and memory recovered. She very much
wanted to be his mistress or his wife, but he took his leave of her.

One day he came upon a serpent who had gripped a lion by the
tail and was burning him up. Yvain cut the serpent in half and freed
the lion. After that he took the road as before, and the lion stayed
with him always. Eventually, Yvain came to Laudine's fountain. Sad
and weary, he fainted, and his sword slipped from its scabbard and
wounded him on the cheek. No metal mesh is perfect: the tip of the
sword slipped through his shining mail and slit his skin, and he
bled. As he recovered he bitterly accused himself for exceeding his
year's leave and making his lady hate him.

He found Lunette imprisoned by Laudine, who blamed her for
Yvain's treachery. Yvain told Lunette who he was and offered to
defend her, but insisted that no one should know his name. With
the help of his lion, Yvain won the battle against Laudine's knights
to vindicate Lunette, and Laudine forgave her. Though Laudine still

did not recognize Yvain, she begged him to stay with her until he and the lion recovered from the wounds they had incurred in Lunette's defense. He refused, however, saying, "I could not stay here unless my mistress pardoned me, forgave me, and forgot her anger and displeasure." When he was gone, Laudine swore: "I swear, and you have my word, if he'll come to me here, without deception or deceit I'll do everything I can to bring about this peace.... I'll help him return to the love and the grace he once knew with his lady." Then Yvain returned and Lunette said, "My lady! Forget your anger! His only mistress is you. This is Yvain, your husband." The lady trembled at these words and said: "May God save me! You'll make me love him in spite of myself, though he neither loves nor respects me." Yvain forgot all his worries.[11]

The seed of Yvain's moral rehabilitation appears at the start of this text, when Lunette helps him out of his tight spot because he alone among the knights was not a snob, was kind to the servant Lunette. (In a fourteenth-century story from the Welsh *Mabinogion*,[12] she simply comments that he is the handsomest man she has ever seen; "If you had a lover," she says, "she would be the best of lovers.") The text thus invokes a common fairytale motif: befriend a fairy when she is disguised as a lowly person (and Lunette's magic powers are evident in her ring of invisibility) and she will reward you with supernatural gifts.

Despite this more promising start, Yvain continues to behave as a bounder (if not nearly as great a bounder as Ewen is in the Scottish texts), blithely breaking his promise to his wife. New things happen to him, and change him, but despite the moral improvement that his character undergoes in the increasingly selfless adventures he undertakes,[13] he gets up to his old tricks right to the very end. The "deceptive oath" (as Chrétien calls it) that Yvain tricks Laudine into making is needed because he has, magically and conveniently, forgotten about her for so many years; he blames the ring, but he also, rightly, blames his own fickleness. Since Laudine's ring prevents him from forgetting her, he must have remembered her when he nevertheless remained in Arthur's court; he only forgets her when she takes back the ring. His amnesia then lasts not long enough to get him into the sort of unconscious deception that embroils Dushyanta in Kalidasa's play, but long enough to inspire him to carry out the kind of conscious deception that Dushyanta enacts in the *Mahabharata*. In the end, he forgets that he forgot her; the story concludes, "He remembers none of his troubles, as they are driven from his mind by the joy he finds in his dearly beloved mistress." Chrétien does not tell us whether or not his dearly beloved mistress still remembers that (as she had complained to Lunette, quite recently) "he neither loves nor respects me."

As is so often the case, the ring is double, here dividing up the qualities of identity/memory and invisibility. If you lose the ring of identity, other people don't know who you are; if you lose the ring of memory, you don't know who you are; and if you have the ring of invisibility, other people don't know that you are at all. Rings of memory and forgetfulness are closely related to rings that bestow invisibility, perhaps on the principle of "out of sight, out of mind." Or, to put it differently, the ring may prove the physical identity of the wearer (if he has this ring, he is who he says he is), or conceal it from himself (when he loses it, it makes him forget who he is), or conceal it from others (it makes him invisible).

The first ring that Lunette gives Yvain makes him invisible, and the second ring controls his memory of his lady. Lunette asks Yvain to give back the ring of invisibility when he has finished with it (when could one ever be finished with such a ring?); we never see him return it, but he does not use it again. Laudine gives him a second ring expressly in order to see if he has been unfaithful; this ring is designed not to make him remember her but, on the contrary, to protect him ("from imprisonment, illness, loss of blood, and danger in battle," according to another reading) only as long as he remembers her. He forgets her, and so her servant woman takes the ring back again.

When Yvain finally remembers his wife, it happens for no reason at all, "all of a sudden," "all at once." This first awakening is not, however, the last; the removal of the ring in this text does not restore his memory of the "adventure" with Laudine; au contraire, it drives him mad, so that he forgets again, and this second amnesia is eventually reversed by a magic ointment. But, mercifully, a part of his memory is still withheld, and the text remarks: "It would have been worse had he known everything he'd done." This final piece of the past becomes available to him through a magnificent metaphor for memory breaking back out through the barriers of forgetfulness: the sword that slips through his armor. Only then does he bitterly accuse himself for making his lady hate him. The sliver of light from the past that is freed by the penetrating sword symbolizes what Freud would call "the return of the repressed."[vii] The breakthrough

---

vii. See chapter 3, p. 83.

is inevitable; or, as our text so wonderfully puts it, "No metal mesh is perfect." Nor, Freud would have added, any mental mesh, either.

The ring is never blamed for Yvain's forgetfulness, a lapse that is highly over-determined. Even before he leaves, he equivocates, anticipating reasons why he might not keep his promise to return, and Laudine warns him that the ring will not work if he forgets her, as she seems to know he will. But the text suggests another reason for Yvain to remain in court and to forget his wife: the strong pull of the male world of the Round Table. Yvain leaves Laudine not for another woman but for Gawain, with whom he later jousts in mutual disguise, "hating where he loves, loving where he hates," just as he maneuvers with his wife in ambivalence and in disguise. His horse split in two and a serpent split in two are double images of Yvain halved, torn between his love for Gawain and his love for Laudine; they supplement the violent image of his heart separated from his body when he rides away from her to join Gawain.

We may also recognize here, in the pull of the world of the court, the undeveloped traces of a very old and widespread folk motif: a hero who falls in love with a magic woman from another world but insists upon visiting his own land again against her will, and while he is home is tricked into remaining there forever, alive or, more often, dead.[14] Somewhere in the traditions from which the elements of the story are derived, the Lady of the Fountain may have been a fairy and her kingdom an Otherworld realm.[15] This might be yet another reason that Yvain forgets his lady.

A Celtic story of this type, part of the same corpus as the tales of Yvain and Arthur, is told of Ogier the Dane, a paladin of Charlemagne, known from the *chansons de geste*:

> The fairy Morgana (Morgan le Fay) met Ogier the Dane and wanted him. She placed on his head a crown of flowers which made him instantly lose his memory; his combats, his glory, Charlemagne and his court, all vanished from his mind; he saw only Morgana, he desired nothing but her. They made love blissfully for more than a hundred years, and neither of them aged at all until, one day, Morgana forgot herself and playfully snatched the crown from his head. Ogier regained his memory and lost his contentment; he missed Charlemagne and his own relatives and friends. Reluctantly, Morgana agreed to let him go, at least for a time, to

revisit Charlemagne's court. Eventually, when he had forgotten Morgana and was about to marry another woman, the jealous fairy snatched him back and took him to live with her on the island of Avalon.[16]

According to another variant, the fairy gives Ogier not a ring of flowers for his head but a ring for his finger, which, like the ring of flowers, destroys both his memory and his aging: it makes him appear to be a man of thirty, though he is in fact 100 years old. Two hundred years later, still looking good, Ogier appears at the court of France, where the old Countess of Senlis finds out about the properties of the ring; while making love to him, she draws the ring from his finger and places it on her own, whereupon she instantly blossoms into a young woman while Ogier sinks into instant senility until, eventually, he gets his ring back.[17] Ogier is the mere pawn of the fairy, whose gifts keep him alive and account for both his loss of memory and his eventual return to her.

The tales of Yvain and Ogier share the themes of the ring, the jealous fairy, and the unfaithful knight; the variables are the intimately related qualities of memory and aging. The cumulative story stands as a parable for the tragic interaction of sexual love, jealousy, and betrayal, on the one hand, and aging, memory, and a ring, on the other.

Lancelot and Guinevere

Several episodes in the medieval European cycle of Arthur, Lancelot, and Guinevere involve a ring of forgetfulness. The story is best known from the *Morte d'Arthur* (1470) of Malory, based on earlier sources.[18]

In one episode, Arthur is the victim of a magic ring employed by a false Guinevere. The thirteenth-century *Lancelot of the Lake* tells us that every day for two weeks Arthur was given a potion that made him fall in love with a woman who had taken the form of Guinevere.[19] When the false Guinevere claimed to be the true Guinevere, she showed Arthur a ring that seemed to be the one he had given to the true Guinevere when they were married. But when the ring of the true Guinevere was found, identical to the imitation, the masquerader was unmasked. The false ring in this story proves a dud, but false rings have much better luck in stories about Guinevere not with Arthur but with Lancelot.

The *Lancelot* tells of a knight named Bors who undertook a vow of perpetual chastity and therefore rejected the marital overtures of Claire, the
daughter of King Brandegoris. Then:

> Spurned by Bors, Claire asked her governess to help her. The gov-
> erness, an old lady skilled in magic, said, "Here is a ring that I will
> take to him on your behalf. It has such great power that he will love
> you whether he wants to or not." The old lady went to Bors and told
> him that Claire had sent him the ring in the hope that he would
> wear it from now on, to remember both her and his mistreatment
> of her. So Bors took the ring and placed it on his finger. As soon as
> he had put it on, his heart changed completely. "If earlier his heart
> had been cold by nature and virginal in thought and deed, now it
> desired what it had formerly shunned." The governess took him to
> Claire's bedroom, where he impregnated her. Then Bors went back
> to his own room and began to rub his hands together in joy, until it
> happened that the ring, which was a little too big, fell off and slipped
> onto the bed. Bors then realized that he had been deceived. He was
> chagrined.[20]

The ring given to Bors is a ring of love and forgetfulness masquerading
as a ring of memory; it makes him forget not some previous lover but, in
effect, God, to whom he has vowed his chastity. It functions as a drug, producing a spell from which, when the ring slips off his finger, he awakens
and is, understandably, miffed.

In 1470, Thomas Malory told the same story, *mutatis mutandis*, about
Lancelot and Elaine, but he split the function of the alibi ring in two, giv-
ing half to the ring and half to a drug in the form of a magic cup of wine.
The relevant episode begins at a moment long after Guinevere had lured
Lancelot out of his vow of chastity and they had become lovers, cuckolding
King Arthur:

> King Pelles knew that Sir Lancelot would beget upon Pelles's daugh-
> ter, Elaine, a son who would be Sir Galahad, the knight who would
> win the Holy Grail. Dame Brisen, Elaine's maid, told Pelles that
> Sir Lancelot loved only Queen Guinevere, but that she could make
> him lie with Elaine and think that he was with Guinevere. She sent
> a man whom Lancelot knew well, with a ring that Guinevere often
> wore and the news that she was at a nearby castle.

Brisen told Sir Lancelot that she would bring Guinevere to him; she brought him a cup of wine, and when he had drunk it he could not wait to go to bed; and he thought that Elaine was Queen Guinevere. They lay together until morning; and all the windows and holes of that chamber were stopped so that no daylight came in. But as soon as Lancelot opened the window the enchantment was gone, and he knew his mistake. He forgave Elaine, but vowed that, if he could find Brisen, "she shall lose her head for witchcrafts, for there was never knight deceived so as I am this night."

Elaine gave birth to Galahad, and people in Camelot said that Lancelot was the father, which angered Guinevere. Then Lancelot told the queen how he was made to lie with Elaine "by enchantment in likeness of the queen. So the queen held Sir Lancelot excused."[21]

Lancelot had actually met Elaine before: he had rescued her from a boiling cauldron when she was "naked as a needle," and he thought that "she was the fairest lady of the world, but if it were Queen Guinevere."[22] But in the "enchantment" (which consists of nothing but wine and darkness, which are dispelled as soon as he sobers up and opens a window), he does not know that she is not Guinevere; the ring and the wine together do their usual work—the ring (falsely) identifying the woman, the wine making him unable to see who she really is. He needs no deeper magic to make him forget (like Bors) his vow of fidelity to someone else (God or Guinevere, as the case might be). Guinevere is at last persuaded that Lancelot was truly fooled; the ring gets him off the hook. In any case she may take comfort from the fact that he regards Elaine as merely the *second* most beautiful woman in the world. Elaine, too, is innocent; she is merely her father's dupe. All is well, for a while, until Lancelot lets Elaine trick him into bed *again*—but that is another story.

Tristan and Isolde

The ring as a sign of identity and memory again works in tandem with a drug of forgetfulness in the tales of Tristan and Isolde, of which there are many versions. I will concentrate on the German text by Gottfried von Strassburg (1210), supplementing it with several others, particularly those of the Norman poet Béroul (c. 1191) and Thomas of Britanny (c. 1160 CE); and I will call the lovers by their German names.[23] The tale of Tristan and

Isolde is a part of the same medieval cycle of courtly romances that preserved the tales of other forgetful lovers; there are strong parallels between Tristan and Lancelot and less direct ones with Yvain.[24] The lady's maid (Lunette, Brisen, Brangane) in all three stories also plays a crucial, though very different, role in bringing the lovers together.

Gottfried's Tristan[25] has two Isoldes: Isolde the Fair and Isolde of the White Hands.[26] (I will refer to Isolde the Fair as Isolde, and Isolde of the White Hands as the other Isolde.)

> Tristan, the nephew of Mark, King of Cornwall, fell in love with Mark's wife, Isolde the Fair, and they became lovers. When Mark could no longer pretend that he did not know about the affair with Isolde, Tristan fled from Cornwall to Arundel, where he lived with Isolde of the White Hands (the other Isolde). She fell deeply in love with him and constantly pressed him to marry her. He stayed with her for some time, but he resisted the temptation to sleep with her or marry her. One day, however, he addressed a soliloquy to the absent Isolde, complaining that he was wretched while she was happy; that he was forgoing the pleasures of love for her sake, while she indulged in them as often as she pleased, with her partner, Mark. Knowing that Isolde was sleeping with Mark, he began to think that this freed him to sleep with the other Isolde, which he very much wanted to do.[27]

That is all that Gottfried tells us; his text ends here. But in the French text by Thomas of Britanny, Tristan's soliloquy progresses to the rationalization that allows him to marry the other Isolde: "Were I not so much desired by a new love I could better endure my longing for Isolde, and I fear unless she give heed to it, I may give up my longing for very weariness. Since I cannot have my true love, I shall have to take what I can."[28] And so forth and so on. (In Eilhart von Oberg's *Tristant und Isalde*, c. 1180, Caerdin, the brother of the other Isolde, tells Tristan that Isolde has probably forgotten him,[29] thus projecting upon Isolde the forgetfulness that is in fact Tristan's proven weakness.) Eventually, Tristan yields to the urgings of the other Isolde, and marries her. But as soon as Tristan betrays Isolde with the other Isolde (by marrying the other Isolde), he betrays the other Isolde with Isolde (by refusing to consummate his marriage with the other Isolde). And it is in this second betrayal (or, if you prefer, un-betrayal) that a ring plays a decisive role.

Isolde gives him a ring at their final parting, when they vow eternal love and fidelity. In Béroul's version of the story, she tells him to take her ring, made of green jasper engraved with a seal, and assures him that if he does not send her the ring, she will not believe what is said to her, but as soon as she sees the ring, she will do whatever he asks. The poem breaks off before she has a chance to keep her promise.[30] In Gottfried's version of that parting, Isolde says to Tristan, "See to it that no living woman ever comes between us to prevent us from remaining always fresh in our affection, in which we have been so perfect all this long time. Now accept this ring. Let it be a witness to our love and our devotion. If you should ever be moved to love any thing but me, let this remind you of how my heart now feels. . . . Do not forget me for anyone."[31] Isolde's negative phrasing here— not "remember me" but "do not forget me"—is reminiscent of the prescient worries of the Lady of the Fountain. These medieval noblewomen knew their men all too well.

Isolde's fears are well founded: though Tristan wears what is supposed to be a ring of remembrance (and though, according to the Norwegian adaptation of the story, he later had it engraved with the words of the oath that Isolde spoke at their final parting, when they vowed eternal love and fidelity),[32] he forgets Isolde while he is wearing it, for he has it on when he promises to marry the other Isolde; only when it falls off does he remember Isolde. In the twelfth-century *La Folie Tristan d'Oxford*, too, she gives him a ring; he leaves her and she thinks he is dead and that (when he returns in disguise) the man before her is a fool pretending to be Tristan— until he shows her the ring.

Gottfried's text does not go on long enough to tell us what becomes of the ring, but Thomas's does. After Tristan has married the other Isolde, he goes to bed with his bride on the wedding night:

> They bring the maiden to bed, and Tristan has himself divested of the tunic that he is wearing, which is tight around the wrists. As they take off his robe they pull from his finger the ring that Isolde had given him on the last day he ever saw her. Tristan sees the ring and enters on a new train of thought. Seeing the ring on his finger, he recalls the agreement which he made at their parting, when he had to go away, and he heaves a deep sigh from his heart: "I do not know to which I should be false, since I must trick, betray, and deceive one, or, so it seems, play false to both together! For this girl has come so close to me that Isolde is already betrayed. I have loved

the Queen so much that the girl is betrayed, and I, too, am greatly betrayed. . . . Both are in love with me, and I am breaking faith with both of them."[33]

Only when the ring is removed from his hand, removed from his body, does the promise inscribed in it enter his mind. (This is a variant of a pattern we know from Bors, who came to when an enchanted ring fell from his finger.) When Tristan takes off the ring, it seems to enter his field of vision for the first time, moving, as it were, from his hand to his eyes; and then it stirs his memory and his guilt. Other variants of the story also note Tristan's reaction to the ring. When he sees the golden ring, a new thought enters his head, and he is "sore abashed" as he remembers the covenant that he made at that parting in the orchard, when she had implored him not to violate his love for her. He says to himself that, though it grieves him, he must lie with the other Isolde; yet he is caught in the middle: he should neither betray Isolde nor leave the other Isolde.[34] He does not know what to do.[35]

Eilhart von Oberg's telling is more elaborate:

"The ring of green jasper fell from his finger. It sounded on the stones, and Tristan saw it. Then his heart awoke and he knew that he had done wrong. For he remembered the day when Isolde the Fair had given him the ring, and he was bitter with himself that ever he had accused her of treason; for now it was he that had betrayed, and he was bitter with himself also in pity for this new wife and her simplicity and beauty. See how these two Isoldes had met him in an evil hour, and to both had he broken faith."[36]

In Thomas's text, Tristan goes on with his self-flagellation for several pages until, finally, he decides on an excuse, a way out of his dilemma: he tells his bride that he has a wound in his side that pains him (which is true)[37] so that he cannot make love (which has certainly not been true). He promises her, "We shall have our fill another time, when you and I both wish it," and she replies, "I am more sorry for your ailment than for any other ill in the world. But I will and can well forgo the other thing I hear you speak of."[38] Or, according to Eilhart von Oberg, Tristan turns away and tells his bride he has made a vow to "abstain from embracing and kissing my wife" for a year.[39] The other Isolde suffers from the denial of carnal pleasure; she has no delight of her husband, nor does she love another. She is (Thomas tells us) "quite the opposite to Mark, since Mark can have his pleasure of Isolde though he cannot change her heart."[40] Yet Isolde also sighs in her chamber for Tristan, whom she so much desires.[41]

Once the ring comes off his finger, and forever after, Tristan knows he is betraying not only both Isolde and the other Isolde but King Mark, whom he is cuckolding, a far more serious crime (in that world, and in ours) than two-timing the women. In Béroul's telling, Mark, who strongly suspects that Tristan and Isolde are betraying him but does not wish to acknowledge his suspicion, enters into the symbolism of the rings one day when, surrounded by his court, he discovers Tristan and Isolde asleep side by side, fully dressed, in apparent chastity. (According to Gottfried, Tristan, suspecting that they might be discovered, drew his sword and placed it naked between them. When King Mark found his wife and nephew lying on their bed, separated by a naked sword, he assumed that this could only be a sign of their fidelity and loyalty toward him: her fidelity as a wife and his loyalty as an honorable knight. And so he brought them back to his court, restoring both to their former positions.) In order simultaneously to make a public statement of his trust in them and to give them a private warning, Mark takes from Isolde's finger the ring of gold and emeralds that he had given her on her wedding day and puts in its place the ring that Isolde had once given him.[42] These two legitimate rings belong not to the lovers but to the wife and her lawful husband, doubling the adulterous rings.

On another occasion, Tristan again removes Isolde's ring from his finger, but now to employ it in its more conventional function as a sign—not for him this time but for her, and not once but twice. Tristan wants to see Isolde, and he gives her ring to Caerdin (the brother of the other Isolde), telling him to make sure that she sees it; she does, and arranges for a rendezvous, and Tristan comes to her.[43] The ring identifies Caerdin as Tristan's messenger, as it will again on a later occasion. In a French poem that narrates just this one episode, Tristan himself comes to Isolde, in disguise. When she fails to recognize him but the dog does, Tristan complains to the dog (disguising his voice): "You have bidden me better welcome than she whom I so loved. She will not recognize me. Will she at least recognize this ring which she gave me? This little ring of jasper has never left me." At this point, Isolde sees the ring, opens wide her arms, and says, "Come! Take me, Tristan!" But Tristan continues to complain, this time to her, in his own voice: "Friend, how could you so long have failed to recognize me, longer than this very dog? What mattered this ring? Do you not feel how

far sweeter it would have been to have been recognized at the very mention of our former love? What mattered the sound of my voice? You should
have overheard the sound of my heart."[44] In mocking the convention of the
ring, Tristan is wrenching the tale out of the genre of the folktale into the
genre of the medieval courtly epic, demanding romantic criteria of recognition ("the sound of my heart") over two of the traditional criteria—not
just the ring, but the dog.[45] His argument is very like that of the women in
Dushyanta's court who argued, "Such a passion should not need a token
of remembrance," to which the king replied, "So, let me blame the ring."[viii]

Gottfried's Tristan uses the ring one final time to bring Isolde back
to him. One day Tristan was mortally wounded by a poisoned spear. He
knew that he would die of the poison if he did not send for Isolde, who had
magic healing powers, but he could not do that himself. He sent Caerdin
to bring Isolde to him secretly, saying:

> "Take this ring with you—it is our secret token. . . . Be sure that she
> sees this ring; for as soon as she has set eyes on it and recognized
> you, she will seek a subtle pretext for talking with you. Hide it from
> your sister so that she may have no suspicion of our love. I cannot
> love your sister, nor shall I ever be able to love her, or any other, so
> long as I shall love the Queen. I love Queen Isolde so much that
> your sister remains a maiden."[46]
>
> The other Isolde overheard this speech and learned at last "why
> she loses her joy of him." When Isolde saw the ring she at once rec-
> ognized Caerdin, who then, alone with her, persuaded her to come
> back with him to save Tristan's life. She sailed with him, but the
> other Isolde tricked Tristan into believing that Isolde was not on
> board the ship. Tristan cried out, "Dearest Isolde," and died. Isolde
> arrived, took his dead body in her arms, and died at his side.[47]

Tristan dies as he lives; his final words are a bitter pun, "Dearest Isolde,"
referring ostensibly to the woman with him, but actually to the woman
who is not with him. He had betrayed them both and together they
killed him.

When Richard Wagner retold the story of Tristan and Isolde in his
opera, *Tristan and Isolde,* he simplified matters greatly: there is only one

---

Isolde. Wagner's Tristan is never unfaithful to Isolde, and Wagner's Isolde shuns the bed of her husband King Mark; thus Wagner preserves the physical fidelity, if not the moral fiber, of the two notorious adulterers. Most relevant to our inquiry, Tristan is entirely exculpated by a love potion, which the maid, Brangane, slips into their drinks (in place of the poison that Isolde had instructed her to use). The magically spiked drink, like ordinary wine in other stories, supplies the irrational rationalization for their behavior: why would they fall in love, unless they were drunk (or drugged, or magically cursed), when Isolde hated Tristan and was betrothed to another man? Why, indeed.

The potion occurs in some of the earlier versions, too, and Béroul puts a spin on its effects, stipulating that Isolde's mother made its spell to last only three years. At the exact moment the time was up, both of the lovers were assailed by second thoughts, not about the morality or legal consequences of their actions, but about the inconvenience: Tristan suddenly longed to be back at court (just as Yvain did)[ix] and wanted to give Isolde back to Mark if he could; Isolde began to mutter to herself that she had wasted her youth—or, as we would say, given him the best years of her life. She bitterly regretted that no one was treating her like a queen any more.[48] They still loved one another—and eventually resumed their affair—but they were no longer crazy about each other. Suddenly, they got very practical. When Brangane later tells Mark the secret of the love potion, Mark is overjoyed to learn that his friend Tristan was free from guilt, and he resolves to give Isolde to him in marriage. Like Arthur, however, Mark is eventually forced to punish the lovers, and the story always ends in their death.

The Ring on the Statue

Tristan commissioned a statue of his beloved Isolde so lifelike that it was taken for real, and he gave his statue of Isolde a copy of the ring that symbolized their love.[49] This latter detail is picked up in a medieval tale about a man who does not create a sculpture but finds one and gives it a love-ring that brings it to life—whereupon it falls in love with the sculptor. This inversion of the Greek tale of Pygmalion, who fell in love with the statue he had created, is a much-told tale;[50] there are versions by Felix Brentano,

---

ix. See chapter 4, p. 91.

Heinrich Heine, Gabriele d'Annunzio, Gustave Flaubert, and Joseph von Eichendorff (in *Das Marmorbild*).[51]

William of Malmsbury told the story in 1125,[52] and Robert Burton retold it in his *Anatomy of Melancholy* (1621), in a story that he dates to 1058:

> "A young Gentleman of Rome, the same day that he was mar-
> ried, after dinner with the Bride and his friends went a walking
> into the fields, and towards evening to the Tennis Court to rec-
> reate himself; whilst he played, he put his ring upon the finger
> of a statue of Venus, which was thereby, made in brass; after he
> had sufficiently played, and now made an end of his sport, he
> came to fetch his ring, but Venus had bowed her finger in, and
> he could not get it off. Whereupon loath to make his company
> tarry at present, there he left it, intending to fetch it the next day,
> or at some more convenient time, went thence to supper, and
> so to bed. In the night, when he should come to perform those
> nuptial rites, Venus stepped between him and his wife (unseen
> or felt of her) and told him that she was his wife, that he had
> betrothed himself unto her by that ring, which he put upon her
> finger."[53]

Burton's hero was eventually able to get rid of Venus by magic, as was the hero of another version by the poet Thomas Moore (1779–1852), "The Ring: A Tale," a poem whose plot could be summarized thus:

> On the day when Rupert was to wed Isabel, he played tennis,
> wearing the ring that he intended to give to her that night. Fearing
> that he might break the gem or lose it, he fastened the ring on
> the finger of a statue that had long stood there, of a heathen god-
> dess or queen. When he went to retrieve it, he found the marble
> finger bent, the hand closed upon the ring; when he went back
> to it later, the hand was open and the ring was gone. That night,
> in bed with Isabel, he felt, though neither he nor Isabel could
> see it, a cold carcass between them; it embraced him and kissed
> him and told him that he was her husband, wed by the ring. This
> happened a second night, until Rupert sought the help of a holy
> man named Austin, who conjured up a lascivious female fiend
> at a crossroad.

The poem ends:

> The female fiend no sooner heard
> Than, with reluctant look,
> The very ring that Rupert lost
> She from her finger took.
> And, giving it unto the youth,
> With eyes that breath'd of hell,
> She said, in that tremendous voice,
> Which he remembered well,
> "In Austin's name take back the ring,
> The ring thou gav'st to me;
> And thou'rt to me no longer wed,
> Nor longer I to thee."
> He took the ring, the rabble pass'd,
> He home return'd again;
> His wife was then the happiest fair,
> The happiest he of men.[54]

When Prosper Mérimée retold the story in *La Vénus d'Ille*, in 1837, the goddess proved more intractable:

> A man placed his wedding ring on a statue of the goddess Venus during the athletic games played to celebrate his marriage. Later he could not retrieve the ring from the statue, for he had unwittingly pledged himself to the goddess. What is worse, the statue came to life, fell in love with him, and came between him and his bride on the wedding night, claiming him for herself, preventing the consummation of their union, and, finally, crushing him to death. When they found the dead man, they found on the rug the diamond ring.[55]

In a Christianized telling, the knight puts his ring on the finger of a statue of the Blessed Virgin, who clasps it and will not give it back; and so he renounces the world and enters a monastery as the betrothed of the Virgin.[56] Henry James narrated a variant much closer to *La Vénus d'Ille* in *The Last of the Valerii* (1874), in which Count Valerio (who is himself likened to "a statue of decadence") worships a recently unearthed statue of

Juno and turns away from his wife; the pagan goddess destroys the marriage. Venus, Mary, a mysterious heathen goddess (or queen), Juno—in each case, her stony fingers close around the ring and keep the hero from his bride, and the story that began with a happy ending becomes tragic. As Maurizio Bettini remarks upon the shift from Venus to Virgin, "These are curious, even bizarre, cultural combinations—the result of playing games with the traditional tale, capriciously altering the characters' costumes and roles."[57] The name of the game is intertextuality.

Shakespeare's Rings II: The Lying Ring

Robert Burton's version of the ring on the statue was composed in 1621, some five years after the death of Shakespeare, and Shakespeare participates in many of the same mythologies that underlie the medieval Romances, particularly the role of jewelry in supporting true or false allegations of adultery.[x] *Cymbeline* and *The Merchant of Venice* make fine use of this mythology.

Even a greatly simplified summary of *Cymbeline* (1608–10), concentrating only on the theme of falsely incriminating jewelry, is still quite complicated:

> Imogen married Posthumus and gave him a diamond ring, whereupon he gave her a bracelet. Iachimo bet Posthumus that Imogen would commit adultery with him, Iachimo; he persuaded Posthumus to wager his diamond ring. Iachimo won his bet by entering Imogen's bedroom, hiding in a locked chest when she was asleep, then emerging and taking detailed notes on the contents of the room and the marks on her body, and stealing the bracelet. When Iachimo presented these "proofs," Posthumus resisted at first but was finally persuaded by Iachimo and gave him the ring.
>
> Then Posthumus sent a man to kill Imogen, but the messenger spared her; she disguised herself as a man and escaped. Eventually, Imogen and Posthumus, both in disguise, were brought into the presence of the king. When Imogen saw Iachimo wearing the ring, she demanded that he tell where he got it (5.5.137: "That diamond upon your finger, say / How came it yours?"). This prompted Iachimo to tell everyone the story of the falsification, which vindicated Imogen at last.

---

x. See chapter 2, p. 36.

Imogen says, as she gives Posthumus the ring at the start, "This diamond was my mother's: take it, heart; / But keep it till you woo another wife, / When Imogen is dead" (1.2.42–44). And he gives her in return the bracelet that he calls "a manacle of love" (1.2.53). Thus Imogen unknowingly predicts the circumstance under which Posthumus will give away her ring, and he uses a metaphor of imprisonment that betrays the sort of jealousy that leads a man to lock up his wife. The double jewelry—the ring and bracelet—is highly sexualized: Posthumus says to Iachimo, "My ring I hold dear as my finger, 'tis part of it" (1.4.134), and Iachimo says, producing the bracelet for Posthumus, "It must be married / To that your diamond" (2.4.99).

When Iachimo springs his trap, Posthumus at first dismisses the evidence about the contents of the room ("This you might have heard of here, by me, / Or by some other" [2.4.77–79]), and even when Iachimo shows him the bracelet, Posthumus's friend Philario, invoking common sense, reasons with him, "It may be probable she lost it; or / Who knows if one of her women, being corrupted, / Hath stol'n it from her?" (2.4.115–117). (Philario, at least, has read *Othello*, in which this is precisely what happens; Imogen's bracelet is the equivalent of the smoking handkerchief in Othello.) Agreeing with this at first, Posthumus says to Iachimo, "Render to me some corporal sign about her, / More evident than this; for this was stolen" (2.4.119–120), but then he rejects this argument, concluding: "She would not lose it; her attendants are / All sworn and honorable: they induced to steal it? / And by a stranger? No, he hath enjoy'd her" (2.4.124–126). And when Iachimo describes the mole under Imogen's left breast, claiming to have kissed it, and concludes, "You do remember / This stain upon her?" Posthumus replies, "Ay, and it doth confirm / Another stain" (2.4.137–140). Yet the villain is unmasked in the end. This is *Othello* as told by Melina Mercouri[58]— everyone goes to the seashore—or by Gioachino Rossini, in whose 1816 opera version Desdemona persuades Othello of her innocence and survives.

The Merchant of Venice

In *The Merchant of Venice* (1596–7), the plot involving rings (supplementing the more famous plots involving the three caskets and Shylock's pound of flesh) could be summarized like this:

> Portia marries Bassanio, and Nerissa, Portia's lady-in-waiting, marries Gratiano; each woman gives her husband a ring. When the

men sail away to aid their friend Antonio, the women dress as a
lawyer and her clerk and follow them. The "lawyer" saves Antonio's
life and demands Bassanio's ring as payment; Bassanio resists but
gives it to her; similarly, Nerissa gets Gratiano's ring. When the men
return, the women berate them for giving away their rings, presumably to women, but finally reveal the story of their disguises and give
back the rings.

The ring plot is echoed in the other two plots: when Portia's suitors are
asked to choose between caskets of gold, silver, and lead in order to win
her, Bassanio, wisely choosing the lead casket (in which Portia's portrait is
found), remarks: "The world is still deceived with ornament" (3.2.74), not
knowing that he, too, will be deceived with a (golden) ornament. Shylock's
insistence that flesh can be the equivalent of gold resonates with the
repeated statements that rings are part of the body,[xi] as when Portia refers
to Gratiano's ring as "your wife's first gift, / A thing stuck on with oaths
upon your finger / And so riveted with faith upon your flesh" (5.1.165–168).
The image of a ring as a part of one's flesh is echoed when Bassanio, unable
to produce the ring that Portia had given him, says, "Why, I were best to
cut my left hand off / And swear I lost the ring defending it" (5.1.177–178).
    But the rings also carry their conventional meanings of sexual posses-
sion and betrayal. When Portia gives her ring to Bassanio she says, "This
house, these servants, and this same myself / Are yours,—my lord's!—I
give them with this ring, / Which when you part from, lose, or give away, /
Let it presage the ruin of your love" (3.2.170–173). As is so often the case,
even as she gives the ring to him she rightly predicts that he will give it
away, and that she will take that as a sign that he no longer loves her. His
reply also anticipates the loss, even as he denies it: "But when this ring /
Parts from this finger, then parts life from hence" (3.2.183–184). The rings
are inscribed with short mottos called "posies." When Gratiano admits he
gave away Nerissa's ring he calls it "a hoop of gold, a paltry ring, / That
she did give me, whose posy was / For all the world like cutler's poetry /
Upon a knife, 'Love me, and leave me not'" (5.1.146–150), thus mocking
the inscription and, presumably, the sentiment it conveys. Nerissa replies
in defense of that sentiment: "What talk you of the posy or the value? /
You swore to me, when I did give it you, / That you would wear it till your

xi. See chapter 1, p. 10.

hour of death, / And that it should be with you in your grave" (5.1.151–154). Portia, too, defends all that the ring stands for: "If you had known the virtue of the ring, / Or half her worthiness that gave the ring, / Or your own honor to contain the ring, / You would not then have parted with the ring" (5.1.199–203).

Above all, the rings are taken as direct proof that a sexual act has taken place (and, later, that another will take place). First, the women pretend to believe that their husbands slept with the people to whom they gave their rings. Then Portia links her own sexuality with her ring, as she threatens, "By heaven, I will ne'er come in your bed / Until I see the ring!" (5.1.191), a line worthy of Doris Day.[xii] Then, speaking of the "lawyer" to whom Bassanio says he gave the ring, she swears: "Since he hath got the jewel that I loved, / And that which you did swear to keep for me, / I will become as liberal as you, / I'll not deny him anything I have, / No, not my body nor my husband's bed" (5.1.224–230). Portia invokes the paradigm of obsessive jealousy so often associated with the controlling symbolism of the ring, even while she evokes the many stories in which women sleep with men in exchange for rings. And then, when she gives the ring back to him, she says, "By this ring, the doctor lay with me" (5.1.259). The final line of the play (5.1.307) also makes an off-color joke about rings, punning on both "sore" (in the sense of the adverb "severely" as well as the adjective "painful") and "ring" (the ornament and the woman's sexual organ):[xiii] "Well, while I live I'll fear no other thing / So sore as keeping safe Nerissa's ring." The defense rests.

---

xii. See chapter 1, p. 20.

xiii. See chapter 1, p. 10.

Siegfried's Ring and Wagner's Ring

Siegfried and Brünnhilde

The love triangle formed by Mark, Isolde, and Tristan parallels, in a number of details (you might say forms a triangle with), two other great medieval triangles, that of Arthur, Guinevere, and Lancelot (which we have encountered in passing)[i] and that of Gunther, Brünnhilde, and Siegfried (a triangle somewhat squared by Gutrune, Gunther's sister), which we will consider now. As the transactions with rings in the many variants of this story become so complex that even the actors within the story cannot always keep track of them, the reader may be forgiven for having to check back from time to time.

The story is found in many different texts. We will consider here three thirteenth-century sources—the Norse *Thidreks Saga*[1] and *Völsunga Saga*,[2] and the Austrian *Nibelungenlied*[3]—and two from the nineteenth century: Henrik Ibsen's Norwegian *The Vikings at Helgeland* (1858) and Richard Wagner's German opera cycle, colloquially known as *The Ring* (more fully, *The Ring of the Nibelung*), which he produced between 1848 and 1876.[4] The characters have different names in different texts, but to simplify matters I will generally call them by the names they have in Wagner: Siegfried,[5] Brünnhilde,[6] Gunther,[7] and Gutrune,[8] making an exception for the Norse names when quoting scholars writing about those texts (which call them Sigurd, Brynhild, Gunnar, and Gudrun) and Ibsen (who calls the women Hjördis and Dagny).

---

i. See chapter 4, p. 95.

The Man Who Lost His Ring
When He Forgot His Wife

Three consecutive episodes concern us here.[9] First, Siegfried wins Brünnhilde, then leaves her and marries Gutrune. Second, disguised as Gunther, Siegfried wins Brünnhilde for Gunther. And third, Siegfried's deception is exposed through the evidence of a ring that he had taken from Brünnhilde during the first or second episode.[10] What is unclear, and the texts differ about, is precisely what Siegfried does to "win" Brünnhilde in the first and second episodes, and when and where he gets the ring that, as usual, proves the sexual encounter. In some versions he deflowers her in the first episode, in some in the second, and in others it is unclear when he does it, or even whether he does it at all. In some versions, Siegfried takes the ring from Brünnhilde, in some he gives it to her as a kind of "linen-fee" or "morning-gift" in exchange for her virginity, if he deflowers her, or as a betrothal ring, if he doesn't. In others he does both, either taking back the same ring he has given her, or giving her a second ring after taking hers (but where does the second ring come from?).

In addition to the five full texts that we will consider, there are a number of fragmentary ones, as well as "the missing and hypothetical 'Great Lay of Sigurd,' "[11] known only from accounts in other ancient sources. Since this is apparently the text that would have told us precisely what happened to Sigurd in bed with Brynhild, I think "Great Lay" is a doubly significant title (though it might better have been called the "Great Lay of Brynhild"). The extant sources make various guesses about this crucial episode, the irritating grain of sand that keeps generating different pearls of variants. Tom Shippey summarizes the problems well:

> "But what did happen in that lost, original, complete version? The story has baffled ancient and modern rewriters alike. In brief, it is agreed that King Gunnar asked his friend Sigurd to win for him the valkyrie Brynhild behind her ring of fire, and he did so, taking Gunnar's shape. Why, if he had already woken her and been betrothed to her? He was given a potion of oblivion by Gunnar's witch-wife mother, and promised the hand of Gunnar's sister Gudrún. How did he win Brynhild? Just by crossing the ring of fire, or was something else involved? . . . And the critical point: how does Brynhild find out? Again, there is general agreement that Gudrún, provoked by a clash over precedence, tells her, and proves it by

pointing to a ring. But what is the ring? [And] who is wearing it, Brynhild or Gudrún, and what in the world is it supposed to prove? The ancient sources do not agree, the author of the Nibelungenlied seeming especially baffled, and Wagner after him."[12]

Why do the texts keep fiddling with the story? Shippey puts his finger on it: "The trouble is, there is an answer no one wants to admit.... Where does it leave Sigurd? As a sexual predator, who furthermore betrays his friend and blood-brother. The neat solution has therefore proved unacceptable."[13] The neat but unacceptable solution is that Sigurd/Siegfried *knowingly* does all these things. The texts therefore keep trying to cloud his moral responsibility with rings and potions. Claude Lévi-Strauss pointed out long ago that the reason myths keep repeating the same stories, with variants, over and over,[ii] is because they pose problems that cannot be solved.[14] This is surely true of the tale of Siegfried and Brünnhilde.

Each new telling views these acts in a different moral light. In later variants, the introduction of the ring (or its alter ego, the magic potion) lets Siegfried off the hook in a manner that we recognize from the revisionist version of the tale of Dushyanta and Shakuntala[iii] and the tales of the bewitched Lancelot.[iv] Yet in all the extant versions of the story of Siegfried and Brünnhilde, the ring is taken as proof of the identity of the man in Brünnhilde's bed: she may not have known him in the dark, but when she sees the ring later on, she knows who her bedmate was.

Wagner's opera *Siegfried* was caught up in this quandary on the levels of both text and hypertext: Siegfried cannot entirely repress (to use Freud's term)[v] his personal past (his mistreatment of Brünnhilde) nor can Wagner repress Siegfried's textual past (the Norse and German texts that tell of that mistreatment). The history of the text re-emerges, summoned by the magic ring; the repressed historical tradition returns to stain the hoped-for moral purity of the noble German hero. The two repressions— of Siegfried's past and the *Nibelungenlied*'s past—converge and emerge when Wagner transforms the ambiguous past of the textual tradition into a metaphor for the inescapable ambiguities of the personal past of his

---

ii. See chapter 11, p. 301.

iii. See chapter 3, p. 69.

iv. See chapter 4, p. 95.

v. See chapter 3, p. 83.

hero: a ring. The ring of golden fire that returns to the Rhine in the final flood is the return of the repressed on a cosmic scale.

Let us trace the ring through five stages of the myth, before turning to another Wagnerian ring saga, the tale of Wieland the Smith, which sheds light from a different angle on the sexual connotations of the ring.

Stage One: *Thidreks Saga*

In the *Thidreks Saga*, Siegfried kills a dragon and bathes in the dragon's blood, making his body invulnerable except in the spot between his shoulders where he cannot reach. (It is worth noting, in light of Siegfried's stupidity and caddishness, that he is literally thick-skinned, more precisely horny-skinned, as a result of the dragon's bloodbath.) Then he tastes the dragon's heart, which gives him the ability to understand what the birds are saying.[15] Siegfried meets Brünnhilde but merely tames her horse Grane (which only he can do). He mounts the horse and rides away. After leaving Brünnhilde, Siegfried meets Gutrune and marries her. Then Siegfried persuades Brünnhilde to marry Gunther. On the wedding night Brünnhilde will not allow Gunther to consummate the marriage, and so the two men decide that Siegfried should deflower Brünnhilde but conceal his identity from her. Siegfried and Gunther exchange clothes. Siegfried swiftly rapes Brünnhilde and, when morning comes, draws a gold ring from her finger and substitutes another. Gunther and Siegfried swap clothes again, and no one else knows what has happened. Siegfried later gives Brünnhilde's ring to his wife, Gutrune. When Brünnhilde sees her ring on the hand of Gutrune and learns that it was a gift from Siegfried, not Gunther, she realizes that it was Siegfried, not Gunther, who had raped her.

This text makes a distinction between the sin of the deception (and rape) and the sin of adding insult to injury by telling people about it. Siegfried promises Gunther that he will not rape and tell. Some time later, however, the two women fight. When Brünnhilde insists that Gunther had taken her maidenhead, which she believes to be the truth, Gutrune displays Brünnhilde's ring as proof that it was Siegfried, not Gunther, who first took Brünnhilde, got her ring, and then gave it to Gutrune. The evidence of the ring explains, apparently, how Gutrune knew about Siegfried's trick without him telling her: he gave her Brünnhilde's ring. The reader might well wonder why in the world a man would take a ring from a woman he has raped and give it to his wife, and all I can say is that other men in this corpus of stories do it too.[vi] Moreover, in this particular case it may well be that the real Siegfried, the unbewitched Siegfried, really does want his wife to know, really does want to blow up the false marriage and return to his true love. And it is this Siegfried who works, beneath the radar of the magic spell, to make the ring tell the true story.

Stage Two: *Völsunga Saga*

In the *Völsunga Saga*, Siegfried again kills a dragon and bathes in the dragon's blood, but this time the dragon is named Fafner, and Siegfried takes a golden ring from Fafner's hoard. He also obtains the great horse Grani[16] (which, in the *Thidreks Saga*, he got later, from Brünnhilde).

Only then does Siegfried encounter Brünnhilde. He comes to a mountain surmounted by a castle glowing with fire. He rides Grani through the ring of flames, enters, and awakens the sleeping Brünnhilde. He swears that he will marry her or no one else, gives her the dragon's golden ring as a token of his love, and rides away. Perhaps under growing Christian influence and in order to avoid the promiscuity of the *Thidreks Saga* (in which both men bed Brünnhilde), the *Völsunga Saga* goes out of its way to insist that Siegfried most definitely does *not* rape Brünnhilde; he places his sword between them in the night (a symbolic action that we have also seen Tristan employ, when he *had* been Isolde's lover).[vii]

But now Grimhild, the mother of Gutrune and Gunther, drugs Siegfried to make him forget Brünnhilde and marry Gutrune.[17] Gunther, seeking to marry Brünnhilde himself, fails to penetrate the fire (as he failed to penetrate Brünnhilde's maidenhead in the *Thidreks Saga*). Siegfried and Gunther exchange shapes (Grimhild tells them how) and Siegfried-as-Gunther rides Grani through the flames (again), finds Brünnhilde (again), and asks her to be "his" wife (again)—though this time he means Gunther's wife. He takes from her the ring that he had given her (as Siegfried), and now (as Gunther) he gives her, in exchange, a second ring, also taken from the dragon. After this he rides away back through the fire to his companions, and he and Gunther change back into their own shapes. Brünnhilde marries Gunther. Siegfried thus becomes,

---

vi. See chapter 7, p. 173.

vii. See chapter 4, p. 97.

in effect, and like Dushyanta,[viii] a man who forgets his wife when he loses his ring.

Eventually, Siegfried awakens from the drug. But only some time later does Brünnhilde learn the truth:

> One day, as they were bathing in the river, Gutrune told Brünnhilde that it was Siegfried, not Gunther, who "rode the wavering flames when you thought it was King Gunther. He lay with you and took from your hand the ring [that] you can now see here for yourself." Brünnhilde recognized the ring and became pale as death. She upbraided Gutrune for marrying Siegfried when he had promised to marry her, Brünnhilde, and she accused Gutrune of betraying her, because Siegfried was the better man. (When Gutrune had earlier told Siegfried that she meant to ask Brünnhilde whom she had most wanted to marry, Siegfried asked her not to do it, or she would be sorry.) Brünnhilde also cursed Grimhild, because "she brought Siegfried the ruinous ale, so that he could not remember my name."
>
> Then Brünnhilde went to bed and lay as if dead. When Gunther came to her she said, "What did you do with the ring I gave you? My foster-father gave me this ring at our last parting." Gunther did not answer this, and she then told him that she knew that Siegfried had won her, riding through the fire, and that she loved only Siegfried and greatly regretted that she was not married to him.

Brünnhilde lies doubly, in an attempt to entrap Gunther in a lie, when she says that her foster-father gave her the ring that she gave to him. As we know, it was Siegfried who gave it to her (in their first encounter) and it was Siegfried-as-Gunther, not Gunther, to whom she gave it in the second encounter. Gunther could not possibly begin to answer her question. Clearly, the ring is playing a more important role here, and its implications are becoming more complex, and murkier.

Stage Three: *Nibelungenlied*

The Austrian *Nibelungenlied* combines the *Thidreks Saga* and the *Völsunga Saga*. It is awash in ambivalence and seems to be trying to cover up the

---

viii. See chapter 3, p. 69.

rape.[18] In this version, as usual, Siegfried kills a dragon and bathes in its blood. But now, in a separate incident, he fights with the Nibelungs, human kings, and wins from them some gold, a sword, and (in place of the ring he wins from the dragon in other variants) a cap or hooded cloak of invisibility (*Tarnkappe*, which also gives him the power of twelve more men). Then he meets Gutrune before he has ever met Brünnhilde. This change greatly mitigates Siegfried's guilt, since he now cannot be said to two-time Brünnhilde.

When Gunther says he wants to win Brünnhilde, Siegfried agrees to help him, on condition that, if he succeeds, Gunther will let Siegfried marry Gutrune. Siegfried then uses his magic cloak to stand beside Gunther in a contest to win Brünnhilde, invisibly augmenting Gunther's ability to hurl a boulder and leap a great distance. When (as in the *Thidreks Saga*) Gunther is unable to force Brünnhilde to submit to him on their wedding night, he gets Siegfried to masquerade as him, wearing the magic cloak. But this time he makes Siegfried promise not to actually deflower her. Gunther watches from behind a curtain as Siegfried subdues Brünnhilde after a violent fight and draws a golden ring from her finger in such a way that she does not notice it. He also takes her belt, a symbol of defloration, but he does not deflower her. Gunther then takes Siegfried's place and consummates his marriage with Brünnhilde, whereupon she loses her supernatural strength. Later, Siegfried gives Brünnhilde's ring to Gutrune. At this point the poet says, "I do not know whether it was his pride made him do it. Later he gave [it] to his wife, and well did he rue it!" And indeed he does, as he does in the *Thidreks Saga*, where, as here, the ring comes not from a dragon but from Brünnhilde.

Years later, the women quarrel, and Gutrune mocks Brünnhilde, saying, "My dear husband Siegfried was the first to enjoy your lovely body, since it was not my brother who took your maidenhead. Where were your poor wits? It was a vile trick. . . . I prove it with this gold ring on my finger here which my sweetheart brought me when he first slept with you." Brünnhilde summons Gunther and the court and says, "I accuse your sister before you of having *said* for all to hear that her husband made me his paramour." Gunther asks Siegfried, in public court, to swear—not that he didn't *do* it but that he didn't *tell*: "My lady Brünnhilde tells me some tale of your having boasted you were the first to enjoy her lovely person—so your wife, lady Gutrune, avers." And Siegfried replies, "I am willing in the presence of your vassals to rebut with my most solemn oaths that I ever— *said* this to her." In this way, neither Siegfried nor Gunther ever actually says that Siegfried did or did not take Brünnhilde's maidenhead, but their carefully hedged words allow both women to go on thinking that he did.

Brünnhilde is totally powerless at this moment in the *Nibelungenlied*; she never accuses either of the men of doing her any harm, but merely brings the equivalent of a libel suit against Gutrune (which she loses). Brünnhilde suffers public humiliation on two counts: that Siegfried tricked her and that his wife has been shooting off her mouth about it. Gunther—who in the *Thidreks Saga* made Siegfried promise not to *tell* that he had deflowered Brünnhilde and in the *Nibelungenlied* not to *do it*— hedges. Evidently he does not want the truth about his quasi-cuckolding to be made public. As for Siegfried, presumably he merely gave Gutrune the ring and she figured it out herself, so he wasn't actually lying. It may be the literal truth that he never did actually *tell* Gutrune anything, but of course he let the ring speak for him. As we have seen, rings often supply the voices for women's sexual organs.[ix]

Stage Four: Ibsen's *The Vikings at Helgeland*

The Vikings at Helgeland, a play in four acts that Henrik Ibsen wrote in 1858, works fascinating changes into the plot. Now Brünnhilde (here called Hjördis) is the foster sister of Gutrune (Dagny). Ibsen's plot turns upon an intimate conversation between the sisters that contains a stunningly frank piece of sexual psychology. Hjördis is a proto-feminist (a figure we know from other, later Ibsen plays) and the mother of a little boy. As for the ring, though the women wear it on their arms, Ibsen always refers to it as a ring of gold rather than a bracelet, surely in homage to the ancient myth. Here is how the part of the plot that concerns us unfolds:

> One night, when Hjördis (Brünnhilde) was drinking with Sigurd (Siegfried) and Gunnar (Gunther), and was "heated with the mead," she vowed that no warrior could have her as his wife unless he could kill the white bear that guarded her bedroom door and then carry her away in his arms. Gunnar confessed to Sigurd that he couldn't live without Hjördis but did not dare to attack the bear. So Sigurd, wearing Gunnar's armor, killed the bear. Hjördis thought he was Gunnar and gave him a golden ring from her arm. They spent the

---

ix. See chapter 1, p. 18.

night together in her bedroom, and before dawn, he carried her to Gunnar's ship. Sigurd then married Dagny (Gunnar's sister) when Gunnar married Hjördis, and Sigurd gave Hjördis's ring to Dagny. Gunnar and Hjördis had a son, Egil.

But Sigurd was secretly in love with Hjördis, and she with him, though they expressed only hostility to one another. Trouble arose between Sigurd and Gunnar, and Sigurd told Dagny that it was he, not Gunnar, who had killed the bear and taken the ring, which he begged her to throw away "to the very bottom of the sea," so that Hjördis would never see it. He admitted that he had spent the night with Hjördis, but insisted that he had kept his sword between them all night long. Dagny refused to get rid of the bracelet—she said it was too precious to her, because of her love for him—but she promised to keep it hidden from all eyes, and never to reveal what he had told her.

One day, however, Hjördis asked Dagny if she had ever felt an irresistible urge to fight alongside the men, and when Dagny replied, "Never! How can you think that? I, a woman?" Hjördis said, "A woman, a woman . . . ! Ah, nobody knows what a woman is capable of!" But then, without drawing breath, she told Dagny that only once in her life had she felt a "shuddering ecstasy"[19] in a man's arms, as her blood burned and her bosom throbbed, and that was the night when Gunnar killed the bear and crushed her in his arms until his breastplate burst. Knowing, as Hjördis did not, that it was Sigurd with her that night, Dagny became suspicious and jealous.

Hjördis felt ashamed of having been married by force, and kept urging Gunnar to do deeds of valor that would bring her honor to wipe out her shame. When they were again all drinking together, Hjördis insisted that Gunnar was a greater hero than Sigurd, since Gunnar was the only one who had been able to kill the bear. Dagny, unable to brook this, shouted out, "The sword that lay drawn between you and the bear-slayer hangs at my husband's side—and the ring you took from your arm you gave to Sigurd. Here it is!" Gunnar admitted that this was true, and that he was a coward.

Hjördis and Sigurd confessed their love for one another and she persuaded him that they must both die, that it was not possible for them to stay married to people they did not love. Seeing in the sky a vision of two black horses approaching in the gathering storm — "One for you, and one for me!"—she killed Sigurd, who said to her, as he died, "My life has been heavy from the hour I tore you out of my own heart and gave you to Gunnar." She cried out, "There is no hiding-place for me—except at the bottom of the sea!" and threw herself over a cliff. Learning that Hjördis had killed Sigurd, Dagny said, "So she hated him that much," and Gunnar concluded, "Then she loved me after all." The child Egil had a vision of his mother, Hjördis, riding off at the head of a herd of black horses, bearing the dead to Valhalla.

Ibsen has complicated Hjördis's jealousy of Dagny by revealing her frustrated desire to fight like a man, indeed her scorn of traditional women's roles. Hjördis assures Sigurd that she much prefers death to the fate that would have been hers if they had married and she "had sat in your homestead weaving linen and wool for you and bearing you children." And when Sigurd protests that she is "soul-sick," and warns her that their enemies may be killing her son, she replies, "Let him die—my shame dies with him!" Though she herself throws down the gauntlet of physical conquest to any man who wants to marry her, she later resents having been married "by force." Ibsen directly and brilliantly links this twisted, ambivalent feminism to her sexual frustration—more precisely, to her subconscious knowledge (which Dagny understands as Hjördis does not) that she was sexually fulfilled only with Sigurd, never with Gunnar. When Dagny finally blurts out the truth of the ring, she is revealing the truth of Hjördis's sexuality.

Ibsen's Sigurd is exonerated in his sexual masquerade with Hjördis not by being drugged himself but, rather, by finding Hjördis drunk, apparently too "heated by mead" either to know who she is in bed with or to remember, later, whom she gave her ring/bracelet to. And it is Dagny, not Sigurd, who, also apparently in her cups, breaks her promise not to tell about the seduction by proxy. Sigurd is thus exculpated of the sin of indiscretion by both of the women he sleeps with: Hjördis is in a mental fog the night they go to bed together, and Dagny indiscreetly blurts out the secret. (Though Sigurd has also committed an indiscretion in revealing it to her, he is not, in this text, violating a promise to Gunnar not to tell it.) Hjördis too reveals a secret, though she (unconsciously again) doesn't know what she is saying, when she speaks of her sexual experience with the man that she doesn't realize is Sigurd.

But was Sigurd telling Dagny the truth about the sword in the bed, or just cribbing an excuse from the *Völsunga Saga* (or, indeed, from Tristan, who put the sword between himself and Isolde after they had in fact become lovers)? Did he merely hold Hjördis in his arms to produce her sexual ecstasy, or did he do more, as Dagny fears? The ring/bracelet as usual is taken as proof of the consummation of a sexual act, but, as we know, it often lies. This golden band shares the implications of Polycrates's ring:[x] Sigurd says it should stay forever in the bottom of the sea (where Hjördis says she, too, belongs). It brings only trouble.

Stage Five: Wagner's *The Ring of the Nibelung*

The ring itself comes from the bottom of the sea and returns to it in the end, in Wagner's version of the story. Wagner's opera *Siegfried* premiered at the Bayreuth Festspielhaus on August 16, 1876. It is the third in the tetralogy of *The Ring*. The basic plot follows that of the *Völsunga Saga*, with only minor modifications, though it adds significant psychological details that go a long way toward cracking the Norse code of the old story. Siegfried gets the ring from the dragon Fafner (and bathes in his blood), but now he also gets from him the Tarnhelm (the descendant of the *Nibelungenlied's Tarnkappe*), the magic helmet that grants the wearer the powers of invisibility, shape-shifting, and instantaneous long-distance travel. He does not, however, know the powers that these magic objects have. Then, undisguised, unmagicked, he wins Brünnhilde for himself, climbing up through the ring of fire to get to her. He finds her asleep in her armor and mistakes her for a man until he removes her armor (and remarks, "This is no man!"[20]), whereupon she awakens and they fall in love. Perhaps because of some foreboding, he promises always to remember her, while she, with the same foreboding of forgetfulness that animates not merely the Brünnhilde of the *Völsunga Saga* but Isolde and the Lady of the Fountain,[xi] asks him merely to "remember yourself," and, she adds, "Remember the fire that blazed around my rock." He gives her the ring that he had taken from the dragon, and in exchange Brünnhilde gives him her horse Grane (an atavism held over from the *Thidreks Saga* horse, Grani).[21]

Then, in the concluding opera of Wagner's *Ring*, *Götterdämmerung* (premiered the day after *Siegfried*), Siegfried, still riding Grane, meets

---

x. See chapter 2, p. 30.

xi. See chapter 4, pp. 89, 97.

Gutrune. Gunther hears of Brünnhilde and wants to marry her but has been warned of the fire that encircles her rock, and so he gets Siegfried to win her for him, bribing Siegfried with the promise of his sister Gutrune. No mother appears in this version, and so the siblings themselves (abetted by their half-brother, Hagen) make Siegfried fall in love with Gutrune, drugging him with a magic drink that makes him forget that he has already married Brünnhilde and given her a ring. He is also magically transformed (by the Tarnhelm, whose powers Hagen explains to him) into the shape of Gunther, so that Brünnhilde does not know him. The Tarnhelm also transports him instantly to the flame-encircled mountain.

Siegfried-as-Gunther passes through the flames and accosts Brünnhilde. After a violent struggle, he seizes her and forcibly takes the ring from her, saying, "Now you are mine, Brünnhilde, Gunther's bride." He places his sword between them in the night. Then he brings her to Gunther and the two men change back into their own forms. When Brünnhilde arrives to marry Gunther, she is stunned to see that Siegfried doesn't recognize her, is about to marry Gutrune, and is wearing the ring that he gave her and that Gunther (as she thinks) has just robbed her of. She faints, into Siegfried's arms, but quickly recovers when she realizes that he does not know who she is.

The argument here is not between the two women, as in the other variants, but between Brünnhilde and her two lovers, Siegfried and Gunther. Gunther, genuinely perplexed, insists that he never gave a ring to Siegfried, but then he asks her, "But—do you really know the ring well?" This is a reasonable challenge: is it perhaps the wrong ring? She does not answer, and Siegfried insists that he never took the ring from any woman; he got it from a dragon. Gradually Brünnhilde realizes what has happened, and she cries out, "Betrayed! Shamefully betrayed!" And, to Gunther, "Away, betrayer, betrayer of your self."

The argument between Siegfried and Brünnhilde goes on and on like an Abbott and Costello routine ("You took that ring from me." "What ring?" "That ring." "This ring?" "Yes." "No, I didn't." "Yes, you did"). The inanity arises because Siegfried and Brünnhilde are talking past one another, switching back and forth between the two different seduction episodes that Wagner has conflated: the first, when Siegfried-as-Siegfried rode through the fire and gave her the ring (which he is talking about), and the second, when Siegfried-as-Gunther took the ring from her by force (which she is talking about).[22]

Later, Siegfried tells Gunther that he had not betrayed him; he wonders if somehow the Tarnhelm had let Brünnhilde see through the disguise. (This is Wagner's much-reduced version of what other tellings treat as Siegfried's broken promise not to *tell* about the trick—which Siegfried hedges, in those versions, by giving Gutrune the telltale ring). Eventually, Hagen kills Siegfried by striking him in the one place that missed the magic treatment when he bathed in the dragon's blood. Siegfried's betrayal of himself, as well as his beloved and his friend, is the moral equivalent of that one vulnerable spot on his back. Through that tiny physical and moral opening (like the gap in Yvain's armor[xii]), the spear pierces and kills him. Brünnhilde takes her ring from Siegfried's corpse and puts it on her finger. She calls for her horse, Grane; lights the pyre; cries, "Siegfried, your wife greets you!"; and rides Grane back into the circle of flames, to join Siegfried in death.

The Twilight of the Ring

The ring that Wagner's Siegfried gets from the dragon Fafner has a complex history: together with the Tarnhelm, it was made out of gold that originally belonged to the Rhinemaidens. The dwarf Alberich stole the gold from them and forced another dwarf to forge from it both the Tarnhelm and a ring that is said to give its owner the power to conquer the world. The gods stole the ring (and the Tarnhelm) from Alberich and gave them to the giants Fafner and Fasolt in order to ransom Freyja, the goddess of love, fertility, and youth. Alberich had put a curse on the ring: whoever obtains it will die. As if to prove the power of the curse, the giants quarreled violently over the ring. Fafner killed Fasolt and was transformed into a dragon, and that's the dragon that Siegfried kills to get the ring (and the Tarnhelm). Hagen, who stirs Gunther on to marry Brünnhilde and who kills Siegfried, is Alberich's son.

Wagner gave Siegfried's ring powers beyond those found in the Scandinavian sources, where magic rings generate wealth and carry curses.[23] Although the ring in Wagner does not in itself have the power it often has, to make the bearer invisible or a shape-shifter, it is made from the same gold as the Tarnhelm, the magic helmet that, as a kind of alter ego of the ring, gives the wearer both of these powers, plus the ability

---

xii. See chapter 4, pp. 91–94.

to travel great distances in an instant (like the extra power the cloak of invisibility has in the *Nibelungenlied*, to augment the wearer's strength). The Tarnhelm plays no part in the earlier sources; Wagner compounded it out of the ancient Greek helmet of invisibility, Gyges's ring of invisibility, and the medieval German cap or hooded cloak of invisibility that, in the *Nibelungenlied*, Siegfried wins from Alberich.[24] By making it a metal helmet rather than a cloth cap or cape, Wagner was able to give it the powers of the Rhinemaidens' gold. Together in Wagner, as they always are, twins born from the same magic source, the ring and the Tarnhelm do indeed convey great power. But there is more.

Wagner combined Polycrates's signet ring of destructive power with Shakuntala's wedding ring of love,[xiii] but he set the two functions against one another: those who would use it for power must renounce love. In Norse mythology, the giant who built Valhalla had asked for Freyja, goddess of love and sexuality, as his payment, but in order to keep Freyja, the gods killed him. In Wagner's telling, the gods do not kill the giant builders (now there are two) but offer them the gold ring instead of Freyja; thus Fafner must, like Alberich, renounce love to have the ring. Yet when Siegfried gets the ring, it does not seem to stop him from falling in love with two women and getting into the kinds of trouble that sort of thing usually entails. Most rings are for winning love; some are for forgetting love. The Wagnerian ring is said to be for forsaking love but is actually drawn back into the older mythology of the ring of power, and Siegfried both wins and forgets love because of the ring. Perhaps his ignorance of its power is balanced by his immunity to its curse against love.[25]

The tension between the ring used for power and the ring used for love is resolved in the theme of the forcing of love. In *Das Rheingold*, the first opera in the cycle, Fricka, the wife of Wotan (king of the gods) and sister of Freyja, asks the fire god Loge if a woman could use the ring to keep her man faithful, and Loge says no man could be unfaithful to a woman who had the ring. How, then, you may ask, can Siegfried fall for Gutrune while Brünnhilde still has the ring? Perhaps the answer is that Siegfried, the real Siegfried, is *not* unfaithful; only when he forgets himself (i.e., becomes Gunther) can he forget her. The bewitched Siegfried, who magically forgets Brünnhilde, has not only taken leave of his senses, he's taken leave of himself. He's no longer Siegfried.

---

xiii. See chapter 2, p. 30, and chapter 3, p. 79.

On the other hand, a man can harness the power of the ring only by giving up love altogether (though not sex, as the dwarf Alberich points out in a fine distinction: women will be forced by the lust of the dwarf whom they do not love). In *Die Valkyrie* (the second opera in the tetralogy), Wotan himself says he got tired of love (mere physical love) and went on to power, and he admits that he used love to force Erda (the earth goddess on whom he fathers the Valkyries) to tell him what he needed to know to maintain his power. Yet Wotan also protests against the marriage vow that unites those who do not love.[26] (We have seen that Ibsen's Hjördis objects to this too.) By contrast, Siegfried (though, in Wagner, at least, under the influence of the potion he is no longer truly Siegfried) colludes in first tricking Brünnhilde and then forcing her to marry Gunther, whom she does not love.

When Siegfried gets the ring (from the dragon who got it from Alberich), it resumes the significance it has for gods, in contrast with dwarfs: faithfulness in love. Siegfried gives the ring to Brünnhilde (whom he has both forced and won) as a token "of my faithfulness to you," and when one of the other Valkyries asks her to give the ring back to the Rhinemaidens, Brünnhilde says, "But Siegfried's love shines out of it to me, Siegfried's love!" (The ring, as usual, lies; Siegfried—bewitched—is soon to make love to Gutrune.) When Siegfried-as-Gunther comes to win her, Brünnhilde threateningly extends her finger with Siegfried's ring—*his* ring—and says, "You will never force me to shame as long as the ring protects me." But Siegfried now invokes the other aspect of the ring, the demonic ring that forces love: "Gunther will take his man's right, and you will marry him through the ring. . . . You now teach me how to take it from you." He seizes her and takes the ring from her. Even at the end of his life, Siegfried teases the Rhinemaidens with the ring, unwilling to return it to them but still entirely unaware of its power. He dies in ignorance of the nature of the ring, but Brünnhilde never forgets it. She takes it from his corpse in their final ring transaction, and restores it at last to the Rhine.

The powers of the ring are established in the first two operas of the tetralogy, *Das Rheingold* and *Die Valkyrie*. The ring is the star of the cycle. Siegfried is just a bit player, along with all the other humans, not to mention the gods and demigods. Siegfried's ignorance of the identity of his true wife is not nearly as important as his ignorance of the identity of the ring, which he took from the dragon without knowing its power. He himself says that he does not know its use, though by the time he gives it to Brünnhilde he can say, "Whatever deeds I have done, the virtue of them is enclosed in this ring." Still he gives it to her on their first date, somehow sensing that both the ring and this woman are very important to him, and on their second meeting he takes it back, not because he remembers or recognizes it (he does not) but because she has told him that while she has it, it will prevent him from accomplishing his goal, which is to take her for Gunther.

To Brünnhilde, the ring signifies not just the identity of the man who seduced her but retrospective ownership: whoever has the ring had her; or, rather, as the two men in question seem to regard the matter, whoever has her has the right to the ring. This is, after all, not any old gold band from Tiffany's but the ring that will bring about the end of the world, an end to which Brünnhilde is merely the means. As Jesse Byock points out, "Wagner united two stories, unconnected in their Norse forms: the tale of Siegfried and the account of Ragnarok, the downfall of the Norse gods."[27] And the bridge that he used to join the two stories was the ring.

In setting the start and finish of his opera cycle in the Rhine (not *on* it but *in* it), Wagner was drawing upon an Indo-European myth of cosmic destruction and regeneration, the Norse version of which is called Ragnarok. Brünnhilde's final equestrian leap into the fire triggers the destruction of Valhalla and the flooding of the world by the waters of the Rhine. The forces of Ragnarok, always waiting in the wings, find their tiny opening, the vulnerable spot, in Siegfried's moral and physical armor, and into that opening the heroine, assuming cosmic dimensions, rushes, taking the world with her.

The horse in the flames that are then quenched by the rising waters is a transformation of a complex symbol that belongs to the ancient Indian version of Ragnarok, in which a mare triggers the final fire and the final flood. Hindu mythology tells of a fire that threatened to destroy the universe until it was placed in the mouth of a mare that roams at the bottom of the ocean; the flames that shoot out of her mouth are simultaneously bridled by and bridling the waters of the ocean.[28] This delicate balance, this hair-trigger suspension, will finally be disturbed at the moment of doomsday,[29] when the signal will be given for the mare to gallop out of the ocean and set the world on fire. The now unbridled ocean will leave its bed and flood the ashes of the universe, which will lie dormant until the next period of creation.[30] The myth expresses the barely controlled tendency of the universe to autodestruct. (We may also see here a kind of pre-scientific theory of global warming: when it gets hotter, the icecaps will melt and there will be a flood.) The mare bears in her mouth the flaming seed of both the destruction and the ultimate recreation of the cosmos.

Brünnhilde, closely identified with her horse Grani, is the doomsday mare, the filly with the flame in her mouth. Ibsen's Siegfried (Sigurd) wants to throw the ring to the bottom of the sea, which is precisely where Ibsen's Brünnhilde (Hjördis) also intends to end up. When she jumps off the cliff, however, she joins the herd of wild black horses racing toward Valhalla. The astute reader will have noticed that in the Hindu story there is no ring at all. But the equine flame that is expelled to the bottom of the ocean, certain to return someday, becomes, in the Norse myths, a ring of fiery gold, and in Wagner's version that fiery ring is submerged deep in the Rhine.

It is unlikely that Richard Wagner knew the Indian sources of the myth of the submarine mare, though he had a vague, if passionate, acquaintance with Indian philosophy (via Schopenhauer, Schelling, and Nietzsche), enough to structure his ring cycle like the Hindu cycle of creation, which is more explicitly circular than the Norse myth. On the other hand, he was far more familiar with the Norse mythology of Ragnarok, and so he combined the Scandinavian tradition of the fire-breathing dragon (Fafner) in the watery depths with the German folk tradition of the Rhinemaidens. To this already rich mix he added the concept of the fire and flood from the Eddas.[31]

When Siegfried, in exchange for her horse, gives Brünnhilde the ring he took from the dragon Fafner, his action symbolically connects the two animals that are often combined in the Indo-European myth of the equestrian hero who kills the dragon (of whom Saint George is the most famous). And when, at the end of Wagner's cycle, Brünnhilde rides her horse into the ring of fire, which is then extinguished by the flood waters of the Rhine, the images are again conflated. Wagner had all the pieces of the puzzle in his hands: the Hindu cosmology, the Norse cosmology, and, finally, the myth of Brünnhilde the equestrian Valkyrie. The story seemed to cry out for just one twist, to let Brünnhilde ride her own horse back through the flames to Siegfried, and it took Wagner's genius to add that final twist. He re-arranged the elements to re-invent a wheel of cosmic death and transfiguration, to make his own myth.

In the end, as in the cosmic myth of regeneration, the world returns to its primeval state, with the Rhinemaidens singing happily and playing with their gold as they did at the start of the first opera in the cycle, *Das*

Rheingold. The narrative, too, is a ring. But it is a spiral, not a circle. The ring that goes back into the Rhine at the end has been reforged; it is a ring with a different history. The difference is the loss, the tragedy: Siegfried has betrayed his one true love, and the world, when it rises again out of the waters of the Rhine, will never be the same.

Wieland the Smith

In Wagner's cycle the ring plays its conventional role as the key to recognition. It does not provide an excuse for Siegfried, the husband who has forgotten his wife, or even wake him up, but it wakes *her* up, when she sees it on the hand of another woman. Though it ultimately unlocks the memory of a forgotten sexual episode, the ring is not blamed for the forgetfulness, which is sometimes simply taken for granted (as in the case of the medieval Tristan)[xiv] but at other times (for Tristan as well as Siegfried) attributed to the effect of a mind-altering drink. Yet in another of Wagner's works, which foreshadowed and even now illuminates the storyline of the *Ring* cycle, the ring is in itself a magic drug of forgetfulness straight out of the European romance cycles. This work is *Wieland the Smith* (*Wieland der Schmied*), written in the same year in which Wagner published his first draft of the Siegfried story (1848).

Wagner knew that the tales of Siegfried and Wieland (who is known as Volundr in the Norse, and Wayland in the old English sources) occur in all of the Germanic sources—Norse, German, and old English[32]—and that the themes of the ring and sexual betrayal are central to both of them. (They are also connected through Siegfried's sword, which some sources say Wieland made.) Wieland's ring splits its twofold magic along gendered lines, giving to women the power to inspire love and to men political power.[33] But different sources bring out different aspects of these two powers.

In the thirteenth-century *Volundarkvida* (one of the poems collected in the Norse Poetic Edda), the wife of Volundr the smith is, like Brünnhilde, a Valkyrie, a woman from the other world. She disappears, and so does a ring Volundr had made for her, which he later recognizes on the hand of the king's daughter: the king had stolen it. The king imprisons Volundr and cuts the tendons of his legs. Volundr escapes and in revenge murders

---

xiv. See chapter 4, p. 97.

the king's two sons, gets the princess drunk on beer, rapes her in her sleep, makes himself wings, and flies out of the story.[34]

In the *Thidreks Saga*, Volundr slips the princess a love potion, but her magic knife enables her to resist the potion. Again, the king imprisons Volundr and cuts the tendons of his legs. Here, however, Volundr merely seduces the princess instead of raping her, and he returns to her in the end, though he still murders her two brothers.[35] The hamstringing links Wieland to the ancient Indo-European mythology of artisan gods and blacksmiths who are lame, sacrificing their legs for the skill of their hands—or for the wings that their art gives them. The Greek Hephaestus is a prime example, and the dwarf Alberich another. Like Wieland, the lame artisan god is often cuckolded.[36]

Wagner wrote a libretto for the Paris Opera using the story of Wieland, but never set it to music. A shorter version of this draft, which he published as a prose essay in 1849,[37] combines several of the old themes with new ones that cast Wieland in a more ambiguous light:

> One day, as Wieland was bathing on the shore, a swan maiden came to bathe and took off her swan apparel, while her sisters continued their journey to the northern lands. Overpowered by love, the poet and smith Wieland wrestled with her and won her, and they lived in blissful union. She gave him a ring and warned him that if he let her get it back, she would leave him; for though she loved him, she still desired her freedom, and the ring gave her the power to fly. Wieland made a number of rings identical to hers and hid her ring among them, but one day she found hers and flew away.
>
> King Neiding ("Envy") captured Wieland so that he would work for him alone. He severed the tendons of Wieland's legs so that he could not escape. But Wieland forged wings and flew into the sky to join his wife. As he left, he shot arrows into King Neiding's heart.[38]

Now there is no princess to seduce or rape, and there are no brothers to murder, only the king who has maimed him. Presto change-o, Wieland has been morally rehabilitated. The rape still hovers over the text, however, in the way that Wieland "captures" the swan maiden. He maintains his power over her now not by hiding her "swan apparel," that is, her wings, the usual pattern in tales of swan maidens (destroying the obvious source of their power to fly), but by hiding the ring that she gives him, in place of the ring that he—who is, after all, a smith—gave her in earlier versions. (In the tale of Siegfried, too, the ring is sometimes given by her to him, sometimes by him to her.) The motif of apparently identical men or women standing in for one another (Siegfried for Gunther, for instance) here is transferred to the ring itself, now camouflaged among other, identical rings.

Wagner told a much expanded and rather different version of the story in another prose draft of the libretto:

> Swanhilde, a swan maiden, fell to earth while her sisters, as Valkyries, continued their journey to the northern lands. The poet and smith Wieland took her in. King Neiding's daughter Bathilde wanted Wieland for herself. She also knew, as Swanhilde did not, that the ring Wieland had made for Swanhilde had the power to give women the charm of love and men the strength for victory. Together with her brother Gram, Bathilde forced her way into Wieland's lodgings and stole the ring. Then she burnt the house to ashes, and Swanhilde took flight. Gram captured Wieland and Neiding kept him imprisoned. Bathilde used the ring's magic powers to cast magic fetters on Wieland so that he desired her and forgot Swanhilde. Yet, when he heard the sound of Swanhilde's name, Wieland began to recover his memory. But Gram, too, was in love with Bathilde, under the power of the ring, and she had promised herself to him. Still besotted, Wieland killed Gram, and Neiding cut his sinews.
>
> Then, one day, Bathilde asked Wieland to repair her ring, which he recognized as Swanhilde's. Only now did his memory of her return in full. He uttered the swan maiden's name and raised his hand to kill Bathilde, until Bathilde revealed that Swanhilde was still alive and had flown away to the west. The swan maiden called out Wieland's name from the sky. Wieland forged wings for himself, set fire to his forge (Neiding and his court perished in the flames), and rejoined Swanhilde in the ethereal vault.[39]

This is *Swan Lake*[40] in lederhosen: Tchaikovsky's swan maiden, Odette, is Swanhilde; her evil alter ego, Odile, is Bathilde; King Neiding is the evil sorcerer-father Rothbart, and the doomed couple achieve their final apotheosis in heaven. The parallel suggests that Brünnhilde, too, is not only a Valkyrie but a swan maiden (like Sita and Shakuntala),[xv] a woman from

---

the other world who comes to her earthly lover, is betrayed, and returns to her own world. The flames that surround Brünnhilde are prefigured here in the reciprocal arsons: first Bathilde burns down Wieland's house, and then Wieland burns down Bathilde's house. A long way from Ragnarok, perhaps, but within the same cosmology.

The king's daughter, who was there in the earlier texts but did not appear at all in Wagner's first telling, now reappears with a vengeance; she is responsible for the swan maiden's flight, she alone knows the power of the ring and manages to steal it, and she two-times Wieland (with her brother!). Again Wagner has elided many of Wieland's negative traits: now Wieland does not desire Bathilde until she bewitches him, and though he does sleep with Neiding's daughter and does kill Neiding's (one) son, both of these crimes are justified: the son and the daughter are guilty of incest, and the daughter has entrapped Wieland with magic. Where the poet of the *Volundarkvida* insisted that "he was more knowing than she," Wagner here not only shows that she is more knowing than he—she, not he, wields the power of the ring—but echoes the contrast between Bathilde and Wieland with an even more explicit contrast between Bathilde and Swanhilde, between the evil woman who knows the power of the ring and the good woman who does not.

Now the parallels with the *Ring* become clearer. The incestuous couple Bathilde and Gram foreshadow Gutrune and Gunther (as well as the incestuous siblings Siegmund and Sieglinde, Siegfried's parents). Swanhilde is Brünnhilde. Wieland removes Swanhilde's wings and discovers her identity as a woman, just as Siegfried removes Brünnhilde's armor and discovers hers. Both Siegfried and Wieland offer their love to a woman who offers a ring in return. The mechanism of Siegfried's selective amnesia is prefigured as well, the ring playing in *Wieland* a role analogous to that of the magic potion in *Siegfried*.[41] Here the Wagnerian ring needs no supplementary magic potion to cast the spell of forgetfulness that it produces in the medieval epics.[42] Swanhilde passes briefly through Wieland's thoughts, but it takes the ring to awaken him; in contrast, Siegfried only half-remembers Brünnhilde, and it is she, not he, who is awakened by the sight of the ring. One can hear, in the tale of Wieland, the seeds growing in Wagner's mind, and one can see him already manipulating the sources to erase the darker episodes in Wieland's record and make him no longer a murdering rapist but the blameless dupe of a woman who knows more than he does.

The Wieland sources, like those for the tale of Siegfried, gradually upgrade the hero's moral character, transforming the cad into an innocent victim. All of the sources mitigate Wieland's caddishness by stating that the man whom he kills had cut Wieland's leg tendons, imprisoning him until he was able to forge wings. Wieland's acts of violence against women are in revenge for this hamstringing, two men expressing their mutual hatred in violence that they inflict upon one another not directly but indirectly, by injuring the women who belong to them. This is a pattern that we will encounter again and again in transactions in which men trade women and jewelry in order to cement alliances between themselves.

The Rehabilitation of Cads

If we return to the mythology of Siegfried and Brünnhilde, and consider it alongside Wieland as well as the other medieval European narratives and the tale of Shakuntala and Dushyanta,[xvi] we see a pattern emerging. We might hazard a kind of historical development as we trace certain basic plots: in early variants, the man simply brazens it out, denying and rejecting the woman he has seduced, but later tellings exculpate the man by attributing his behavior to a convenient attack of amnesia. The men who forget their wives sometimes blame a drug or a drink but more often place the blame on a smoking ring: its loss or, on the other hand, its evil power, clouds the memory of the man who conveniently "forgets" that he is married. In many stories, the protagonist (I hesitate to call him the hero) who loses a ring and forgets his bride knows perfectly well who his bed-partner is at the time he seduces (and, often, impregnates) her, but later on he projects a kind of retroactive amnesia over the event, claiming that he was, in effect, tricked. The bewitching potion or ring lets the cad off the hook; plead temporary insanity and you can get away with murder.

Or we may be witnessing in these sequential texts not so much the rehabilitation of a cad as the invention of caddishness. In the early texts, a man could treat a woman any way he liked, and people (i.e., other men) naturally approved. But slowly, over the course of centuries, standards changed, and Siegfried's bad behavior had to be explained away. We will have a good look at another ancient society with an appalling toleration for

---

xvi. See chapter 4, p. 87, and chapter 3, p. 69.

caddishness when we consider certain Greco-Roman plays.[xvii] We might also attribute some of the mistreatment of women to the ancient Indo-European bond of *Männerfreundschaft*, which binds a man to another man more strongly than to any woman. We saw this bond at work when Yvain stayed with Gawain instead of returning to his Lady, and when Tristan's bond to Mark (like Lancelot's to Arthur) ultimately drove him away from Isolde (or, in the case of Lancelot, Guinevere).[xviii] The sword placed between the lovers[xix] proclaims the temporary triumph of that bond.

The move away from these ancient male bonds, and from the cult of the cad, may appear to indicate a growing concern for the feelings of women, a need to apologize for a man who breaks his promise; but it may also reflect increasing subjugation of women and concern for their chastity, which widens the gulf, the asymmetry, between the acceptable infidelity of a man and the unacceptable infidelity of a woman. The ring allows him, but never her, to be unfaithful. And in the end, she always forgives him. This process is therefore not necessarily a sign of moral progress. It is just change: one form of oppression is exchanged for another. To abandon a woman without lying poses one set of problems, while to lie about it poses another. We may argue about which is worse: shameless harm or dissembling harm.

We may also look for other developments of this sort. In the earliest versions of many of these stories, the man simply abandons the woman without any justification. In the revised version, he lies to society; social pressure makes him pretend to forget. But in the re-revised version, the man often actually thinks that he forgets; now he is lying not to society but to himself. (Or, one might say, he is repressing his knowledge of his guilt.)[xx] At this point, the hero is caught between changing ethics, between old-fashioned patriarchal polygyny and a new romantic sympathy for the woman who is betrayed.

Many stories suggest other forms of mental incompetence, offering other reasons for the clouding of reason, resorting to supernatural forces, ex machina, to extricate the plot from a human tangle: a curse, a magic potion. Love is something that may suddenly spring up, without warning

---

xvii. See chapter 7, p. 172.

xviii. See chapter 4, pp. 89, 95, 97.

xix. See chapter 7, p. 171.

xx. See chapter 3, p. 83.

or apparent cause. In the tale of Tristan,[xxi] that surprise too is translated into the sudden thrill produced by the magic potion.

Lorraine Daston provides a sharp psychological insight into the function of the rings in the nineteenth-century texts:

> "The ring of forgetfulness is a device not for changing character but for letting true desires surface, a bit like Freud's view of what happens in dreams—or, in this case, more like the collective unconscious intruding into the tidied-up 19th century retelling. And if ever history had a super-ego, it was the 19th century."[43]

In contrast with the medieval sources of the legend, the figures in Wagner's doomed triangle behave very nobly indeed. But they still need magic rings to transform them from cads to heroes.

The Alibi Ring: Oxytocin

In many of the stories of forgetful men, the narrator is caught on the horns of a dilemma: Kalidasa wants to whitewash Dushyanta for his patrons in the Gupta dynasty,[xxii] and the narrators of the medieval stories of Tristan and Siegfried were hard-pressed to rehabilitate a cad en route to becoming an ethnic hero. In such revisions, someone has to take the rap, and the ring of forgetfulness is the fall guy. In the cycle of Yvain,[xxiii] the earlier texts tell a story of rape, and there is no ring. Later, Yvain becomes an urbane courtier, and two rings get into his story, cleaning up his act. Sometimes— again Yvain is a prime example—the ring acts not as an alibi but as a complete exculpation: the protagonist tries to break away from the past, tries to break a promise, sometimes but not always a sexual promise, but the ring makes him circle back into the past, as Alice kept going back in the door from the garden in Looking-Glass Land.

In cultures that honor the narrative convention of the ring, the ring offers a socially acceptable reason for doing what you secretly want to do. Rings, which often come packaged in fishes,[xxiv] are fishy excuses. The ring

---

xxi. See chapter 4, p. 103.

xxii. See chapter 3, p. 74.

xxiii. See chapter 4, p. 89.

xxiv. See chapter 2, p. 25.

expresses, long before Freud, repression and ambivalence: it gives the hero permission to violate the promise of monogamy that the ring also represents. The ring says, I love only you, but it also says, it is not my fault if I forget that I promised to love only you. The ring of forgetfulness justifies the violation not only of monogamy but of adulterous relationships. The hero is not even true to the woman with whom he is betraying his wife (recall Tristan with two Isoldes). And it's not just a matter of a European courtly ethic using the ring/potion as an alibi required by a newly arrived high Christian ethic: it happens in ancient India too, where the ring justifies polygamy in a polygamous society where it should need no justification.[xxv]

In some of the medieval stories, exculpatory rings are supplemented or replaced by potions. But the earliest supernatural alibi for immoral erotic actions is what could be called the Aphrodite defense, after Penelope's argument, in Homer's *Odyssey*, book 23 (c. 800 BCE), that the goddess of love was entirely responsible for Helen of Troy's adultery with Paris. Lady Love made her do it; the god or goddess of lust made her do it. In the Strauss-Hofmannsthal opera *The Egyptian Helen*,[44] too, deities are responsible for irrational passion, and there are twin drugs as well: one to destroy memory, and another to restore it. We can see the Aphrodite alibi developing in Greek literature: Euripides, in his *Medea* (431 BCE), blames Medea for the crimes she commits when Jason jilts her, but Apollonius of Rhodes, in the third century BCE, blames Aphrodite. For centuries after that, lovers continued to speak of a *coup de foudre*, a metaphor that suggests supernatural intervention, Jove's thunderbolt, short-circuiting any possible moral qualms.

The ring, however, is folklore's drug of choice. "Forget me not," inscribed on so many rings, asks the lover not to forget that first intensity of feeling for the beloved. It is intended to ward against the mundane, gradual erosion of love. The myth transmutes this gradual process into the sudden amnesia produced by the negative magic of the ring.

As time passed, new techniques of magical amnesia were invoked, though they were still used in service of the same goals. In *Mirage* (Edward Dmytryk, 1965), the protagonist suffered from amnesia as a result of the shock of seeing his friend fall to his death from a twenty-seventh-story window; when the film was remade just three years later, as *Jigsaw* (James

---

xxv. See chapter 3, p. 66.

Goldstone, 1968), the drug LSD induced the loss of memory. Nowadays the magic potion that makes moral considerations irrelevant, or that allows you to pretend that your superego is/was asleep, can be alcohol, drugs, or an unhappy childhood.

Had Dushyanta, Yvain, Tristan, and Siegfried lived to our time, they might have attributed their memory lapses to another sort of a drug, and cited a study reported in an article in *Nature Genetics*.[45] Scientists at the Yerkes Regional Primate Research Center, in Atlanta, Georgia, concluded from their experiments that the hormone oxytocin seemed to enable male voles[46] to remember female voles "with whom they have had contact," as they so delicately put it. Apparently oxytocin, a hormone released during sex, produces attachment; more sex, more oxytocin, more love, the paradigm promises.[47]

In a *New Yorker* piece entitled, "Dept. of Mating. Science Explains Why Men Are Like That," James Collins cited the Yerkes study and suggested its application to human life. A man and a woman sleep together, and then "the call never comes. It's as if he'd completely forgotten about her. Well, maybe he really has completely forgotten about her, and maybe it's not his fault: maybe he simply has a neurological disorder." And so, Collins remarks, "It is possible, then, that some male humans may be deficient in oxytocin and simply don't remember the encounters they have had with females the night before. This could be the reason they never call. . . . Maybe it will make people think twice before engaging in a lot of negativity about 'caddishness' and 'big creeps.' "[48] Thus a quasi-scientific argument can be made in defense of men who forget women they have loved and left. Perhaps oxytocin was the secret ingredient in all those rings of memory.

Oxytocin aside, why are there so many stories about men who forget their women, and relatively few about women who forget their men?[49] Or, to put it differently, why do more cultures permit polygyny than polyandry? Some scholars would explain the gender imbalance in terms of biology (the different roles that men and women play in producing a child), others in terms of culture (the different roles that men and women play in society).[50] Our stories cannot settle this question. They can, however, furnish stunning evidence of the length and breadth of this inequality in the records of human history.

Gender aside, what is the connection between amnesia and fidelity? Memory is an intrinsic part of love. In Sanskrit one of the words for love (and for the god of love) is *Smara*, memory (the Sanskrit word is cognate with the English "memory"). Some myths imply that love is the true locus of memory, that to remember who your soul was in a previous life you must remember who you were in love with, that knowing/remembering your lover proves *your* identity, not just his or hers. To forget whom you loved, therefore, is to forget your very identity. Though few of us remember former lives or experience total amnesia, it is not uncommon for husbands to forget their wives, and wives their husbands, in the emotional if not literal sense, and the myths exploit that experience. Ralph Harper argues that memory can sometimes be not the locus of love but, on the contrary, merely a weak substitute for it: "And who would not rather be in the presence of someone alive whom he loved than in the presence of a memory or an illusion of presence? You cannot go to bed with a memory."[51] But I beg to disagree. If our myths prove nothing else, they prove that you *can* go to bed with a memory, indeed that you can hardly go to bed with anything *but* a memory. Yet those same myths stand behind Harper when he says: "I do not know which is worse: to remember real love lost or to remember the deceptions of a love that was never real."[52] Both, say the myths. Both.

6

Pregnant Riddles and Clever Wives

The Man Who Wouldn't Sleep with His Wife Until She Had Borne Him a Son

As men use rings to wiggle out of tight spots, women can use rings in their counter-subterfuges. In the stories of forgetful husbands, the ring eventually cures the man's forgetfulness, though it often justifies it as well. In the stories we are about to consider, the rings of the straying husbands ultimately bring them back to their wives, but not by jogging their memories. And where children were of little or no concern to Yvain, Lancelot, Tristan, Siegfried et al. (or their lovers),[i] children are the key to the stories in this chapter (as they were to Shakuntala and to the protagonists of Family Romances).[ii]

In the tale known to folklorists as "The Clever Wife" or "The Clever Wench," a husband challenges his wife to get a child (almost always a son) fathered by him, though he will never sleep with her. She succeeds by tricking him into bed, where she masquerades as another woman (a maneuver known as a bed-trick).[1] Usually he also challenges her to get his ring, which he will never take off. Sometimes he does not mention the ring, but she insists on having it before she submits to him so that later she can prove that she was the woman in his bed (or he in hers, depending on your point of view) and that her child is his.

---

i. See chapter 4, p. 87, and chapter 5, p. 110.

ii. See chapter 2, p. 40, and chapter 3, p. 69.

This myth has a very long shelf life indeed. As it travels through Europe, Asia, and the Middle East, numerous variations develop, which Carol Thompson Neely summarizes well:

> "The central task requires the production of an heir by the wife, and the supplementary tasks all involve obvious symbols of male and female sexuality—the obtaining of rings, swords, or the husband's stallion, the digging of a well . . . the filling of a trunk. In several of the tales, the wife in fact disguises herself as a man, gains access to her husband, beats him at cards, and offers to provide him with a woman. . . . To fulfill the female part of the bargain and to put to rest their husbands' sexual anxieties, the women . . . take on the roles of lower-class, powerless, or degraded women—a cowherd's daughter, a slave, an imprisoned princess, a poor Florentine maid— women who, like whores, can be used contemptuously to supply sexual satisfaction and abandoned with ease without concern for consequences or heirs."[2]

Behind the challenge is the husband's rejection of his wife, which led Stith Thompson to call the theme "The Rejected Wife as Lover" (while filing it under it the evocative title of AT 891D). Maggie the Cat in Tennessee Williams's *Cat on a Hot Tin Roof* is one in a long line of rejected wives who are determined to get pregnant nevertheless. Her husband, who has stopped sleeping with her, taunts her: "How in hell on earth do you imagine you're going to have a child by a man that can't stand you?" She replies, "That's a problem that I will have to work out."

We might define the skeletal plot of the tale of the clever wife as the story of a wife who manages to get pregnant by a husband who (a) refuses to consummate his marriage, (b) denies that her child (when she gets pregnant) is his, and (c) is forced, by the recognition of a ring, to acknowledge his wife and child. The British upper classes used to apply the word "clever" to a man (usually of a lower class, or Jewish, or, during World War II, Japanese) who was glib, not to be trusted, an arriviste, not a true gentleman ("too clever by half"). Here the word seems to carry an additional, misogynist value. The wife's cleverness is, in many variants, the problem as well as the solution: humiliated when she trumps his riddles at the start of the story, the husband vows to marry her precisely in order to take revenge. Thus in an oral Arabic version, recorded in the Nile valley in 1893, "He could find no better way to pay her back than to marry her."[3] In one

version, he vows to take vengeance on a low-caste woman for her impertinence in daring to "crack riddles" with him, a prince.[4] This is how the
ruling classes, or the dominant paradigm, regard what James C. Scott calls
the "weapons of the weak":[5] subversion, resistance, in this case, women
taking control in a patriarchal culture.

But there is more to it than that. Two different virtues are at stake: on
the one hand, the subversive virtue of actively resisting, fighting for what
you want, honestly or dishonestly; and, on the other hand, the noble, passive virtue of being innocent of sin. The clever wife, though spurned for
her wit at the start, is praised for it at the end. Defending her marital fidelity with a subversive intelligence, she proves that she is sinless as well as
clever.

Muladeva and the Brahmin's Daughter

One of the earliest versions of this story that I know is the tale of
Muladeva and the Brahmin's Daughter. It is the final tale, the ultimate
riddle, in a book rich in riddles, Somadeva's *Ocean of the Rivers of Story*
(*Kathasaritsagara*). This great compendium of tales, composed in Sanskrit
in Kashmir between the tenth and eleventh century CE, fed its streams into
yet another great narrative ocean, the *Arabian Nights*, and was enriched in
turn by stories from that tradition. In the tale that concerns us, a Brahmin
named Muladeva tells how he, a well-known trickster, was himself tricked:

> I went to Pataliputra with my friend, to test the cleverness of the
> people there. We saw a beautiful woman who made a fool of me
> with her riddles and embarrassed me. And I said to my friend,
> "I must certainly marry that clever woman. I must pay her back for
> making such fun of me."
>
> We found out her father's house and went there in disguise. He
> gave her to me in the proper way. That night, in the bridal chamber,
> I laughed and reminded my wife of our first encounter. When she
> heard that, she recognized me, and she smiled and said, "City slick-
> ers trick country hicks like that." Then I said to her, "I hope you're
> happy, you city slicker. This country hick is going to abandon you
> and go far away, I promise you." To which she, too, made a prom-
> ise: "I swear that you will be bound and brought back to me by
> means of a son fathered by you." When we had made these mutual
> vows, she turned her face from me and went to sleep, and I put

my own ring on her finger while she slept. Then I went back to my native city, Ujjain, in order to test her cleverness.

When the Brahmin's daughter awoke in the morning she did not see me but she found the ring with my name on it, and she realized, "He has kept his promise and abandoned me. Well, I will keep my promise, too, and abandon all regrets. His name, on this ring, is Muladeva, a famous trickster. Everyone says he lives in Ujjain. That's where I'll go." She lied to her father, saying, "My husband has already abandoned me. How can I live without him? So I will go on a pilgrimage, to torment this cursed body." Unwillingly, he gave her his permission.

She went to Ujjain, dressed as a courtesan named Sumangala, set up an establishment, and became famous there. But she turned away all of her suitors, including my friend, and I became curious and went to see her. I entered and saw my own darling, whom I did not recognize because she was wearing the clothes of a courtesan. But she recognized me again, and received me like a trickster courtesan. Then I passed the night with her, the most beautiful woman in the world, and I became so bound to her by passion that I could not leave the house. She, too, was bound to me through sexual passion, and never left my side until, after some days, the blackness of the tips of her breasts showed that she was pregnant. She then forged a summons from the king and left me to return to Pataliputra. Though I was in love with her, I did not follow her, because I supposed that she belonged to someone else.

She gave birth to a son. When he was twelve years old another boy said to him, "No one knows who your father is, for someone or other fathered you when your mother was wandering around in foreign lands." Embarrassed, the boy asked his mother, "Mommy! Who is my father, and where is he? Tell me!" And his mother, the Brahmin's daughter, thought for a moment and said to him, "Your father is named Muladeva. He abandoned me and went to Ujjain." When she told him the whole story, the boy said, "Mommy, I will bind him and bring him back, and so I will fulfill your promise."

He went to Ujjain and recognized me from the description his mother had given him. Then he stole my bed right out from under me while I was asleep, lowering me gently onto a pile of rags on the floor. When I woke up I felt a mixture of embarrassment, laughter, and amazement. I went to the market place and wandered around, and I saw the boy selling the bed. I asked him, "What price will you take for this bed?" But he replied, "You can't buy it for money, you crown-jewel of tricksters, but by telling me a marvelous tale never heard before." I said to him, "I will tell you a marvelous tale never heard before. If you understand it and admit that it is true, you may keep the bed. But if you do not, you must give me the bed. And you will have shown that you must be an ignorant bastard." The boy won the contest and said, "So I have conquered you, and you are my slave."

Then he bound me and took me back to his mother in Pataliputra. When she saw him she said to me, "My husband, today my promise has been fulfilled. You have been bound and brought here by a son fathered by you." And then she told the whole story, in front of everyone. Her relatives all congratulated her on having achieved her wish through her wisdom and having a son who had wiped away the stain on the family honor. And I, having achieved my goal, lived there with my wife and son for a long time, and then returned to Ujjain without them. So you see, there really are in this world some women of good family who love their husbands. Not all women misbehave always.[6]

The riddle of this story does not have to do with any of the riddling words exchanged by wife and husband (and son).[7] Other Indian variants use different riddles in those exchanges. But the real riddle lies in the situation itself, the quandary of the rejected wife: how can you get a child if your husband, in the euphemism of the Tennessee Williams play, cannot stand you?

Muladeva is said to be the author of "Muladeva's Verse": "What man would enter a house from which no lovely, full-breasted, wide-hipped woman looks out on the street for him, a house that is a prison without chains—unless he is made of stone?"[8] (The image of the prison is a telling one, for the challenge given to the clever wife is often made even more difficult by having her locked up, usually in a deep well, from which her father—or, occasionally, her mother—releases her so that she can proceed with her trick.) Muladeva himself, like the man in his verse, wants a beautiful woman in his house—but he has many houses. He is a famous Indian thief and trickster, the subject of many stories in both folk and courtly literature; even the Brahmin's daughter knows his name. He appears throughout the *Ocean of the Rivers of Story* not only as a thief but as a thief of love, particularly noted for his devious erotic adventures.[9] In another tale, he gives a lovesick friend a pill that turns him into a woman so that he can gain access to the harem.[10] He knows how to turn another man into a woman, but he does not how a woman can turn into another woman.

What identifies Muladeva's son as the true son of his father is his cleverness, his skill as a thief, his father's profession. He inherits his dud dad's ability to steal, which is proof of his paternity.[iii] He and his father recite riddles back and forth to one another like the child and the chaplain in the Buddhist tale of Shakuntala,[iv] where, as here, the child must prove himself his father's son. Muladeva's boy, an even greater trickster than his father, proves his identity not merely with words but with a most literal "bed-trick" that surpasses his mother's: he steals the bed out from under his sleeping father. In one variant, the boy plays a different literal bed-trick: he sneaks into his father's bed-chamber, spreads sleeping powder, and steals all the jewels. Finally, "he even undid the legs of the couch which were inlaid with precious coral, and instead put under the bed the strong plantain stalks! Then he disappeared into the night."[11] Muladeva, who knows nothing about the boy's actual parentage, casually remarks that if the boy can't answer the riddle, he will prove himself to be so ignorant that he must be a bastard (literally, "the son of a lover," *jarajata*), which is what the boy at first appears to be, rather than the legitimate son of a great trickster, which is what he really is. In one variant, the son becomes a famous thief who cannot be caught.[12] Even in versions where he is the son not of a thief but of a king, the old motif hangs on atavistically, and we are told that his mother, herself a princess, rejects her own father's offer to put the boy on the throne. Instead she determines to make him a thief (he can even steal a man's pajamas without waking the sleeper who is wearing them—even trickier than stealing the bed, and an even more intimate bed-trick) so that he can gain access to the court, catch the king's eye, and ultimately win his father's throne, and she can win his father.[13]

Often the son bears a striking physical resemblance to his father. The importance of this quality is deeply embedded in Indo-European mythology; in Hesiod's *Works and Days*, the gods reward righteous people with peace, good crops, and the blessing that "their wives give birth to children that resemble their fathers."[14] The factor of physical resemblance operates

---

iii. See chapter 7, p. 200.

iv. See chapter 3, p. 71.

even better when the father is not a thief but a prince. In one tale, the boy "was struck to recognize himself in the face and shape of the prince," and when the prince's father saw the two of them together he said, "Our son and this boy are as if one and the same person!"[15] In another variant, the unknown son publicly pretends to be his father the king, wearing his ornaments, and the king says, "This indeed is not my son. What of that? There is a little like my son's face."[16] In this case the resemblance extends to mind as well as body: the king decides that the boy he knows to be his son is a fool and makes the unknown son sovereign in his place. The son's active role in capturing his unwitting father makes the story a variant of the myth of the boy who seeks his true but unknown father—the Family Romance.[v]

In the Muladeva story, the son plays a far more active role than he does in most variants of the tale of the clever wife, while the ring in that text plays a much less important role than usual. It is as if the boy takes the place of the ring, the other piece of evidence in the tale. The boy's cleverness identifies him as the true son not just of his father the thief but, even more, of his mother the clever wife. She is the riddler and trickster who uses her head, as well as her body, to trap her man, both at the start of their courtship and in its final resolution. She plays an even stronger role in the folk variants than in the Sanskrit text; she teaches her son "how to change his appearance, how to climb ropes, how to steal."[17] Though at the end Muladeva's wife's relatives refer to a stain on the family honor, she knows all along that her honor is clean, despite appearances, just as she knows that she is not a courtesan, despite appearances—or even, perhaps, despite actions (though the Sanskrit text carefully specifies that she turned away all of her customers).[18] Yet the myth in which the woman manipulates her husband by pretending to be a glamorous (and, counterintuitively, chaste) courtesan shades off into darker stories in which a rejected woman (often, but not always, a wife) actually sinks into real and more sordid forms of prostitution and, without her intending any disguise, is so disfigured by her sufferings that her husband does not recognize her when he presents himself as a paying customer.[19]

In other South Asian variants, the rejected wife engages in only slightly more respectable professions: she becomes a street juggler,[20] a dancing girl,[21] an acrobatic dancer,[22] or a rope dancer.[23] Sometimes she steals the

---

v. See chapter 2, p. 40.

man's ring instead of trading for it. Yet Muladeva admits at the end that she is an exception to the general rule of such appearances. The moral that he culls from his story is one of grudging misogyny: not *all* women mis-behave *all* the time. This is also the moral of Scheherazade in the *Arabian Nights*:[24] yes, there is just one good woman, the woman who tells the sto-ries (Scheherazade). The assumption that women are animals in their sexuality[vi] supports this misogyny. A Kashmiri folk variant of this story begins when a man refuses to marry until his family assure him that "all women are not alike"—that some are like trees that give welcome shade, although others are like bitches that bite your heels as you go in and out at the door.[25] Muladeva's wife is of the shade-tree variety.

Thus all three members of Muladeva's nuclear family are tricksters. The "mutual vows" that Muladeva and his wife exchange are not, as in our parlance, marriage vows, but vows to deceive one another. Muladeva's son mockingly calls him "the crown jewel of tricksters," but Muladeva is out-tricked not only by his tricky boy but by his tricky wife (who is described, at one point, as a "trickster courtesan," in two senses—that is, a woman who pretends to be a courtesan, and also a courtesan who tricks people). At various points, Muladeva and his wife see through one another's tricks. She does not, apparently, recognize him when he comes in disguise and lives in her father's house for four months, but she recognizes him on their wedding night. Muladeva fails to recognize her at the crucial meet-ing in Ujjain, simply because he cannot process the fact that his wife—whom he has, after all, only bedded once, and even then did not touch—is a courtesan. No other reason is given. In one variant, he "of course had not recognized her since she was dressed up completely as a juggler's girl."[26] Another simply says, "The husband did not recognize his wife because of her dress and makeup."[27] In the Sanskrit text, he knows that his "courte-san" is pregnant because he sees her nipples darken, a sharply observed, earthy fact that will, with much else, be jettisoned in the European retell-ings. She recognizes him long before he recognizes her, and teaches her son to recognize him when he does not recognize his son. Only at the end does he recognize her, through her deeds and her words: the promise fulfilled.

We never learn her name at all, or her father's or her son's. She is just the Brahmin's daughter. But, significantly, she gives herself a

---

vi. See chapter 1, pp. 10, 19.

name—Sumangala—when she becomes a courtesan. Does this mean that her masquerading identity as a courtesan is her only true independent identity? "Sumangala," however, is not a courtesan's name; it is a married woman's name, or, more precisely, the word you use to bless a married woman: "May you be Sumangala—Well-Favored." So in calling herself that, she is giving Muladeva a clue that she is his wife. Muladeva, of course, has a name, indeed a notorious name, which is all that she gets from the ring in this text, just as Shakuntala gets Dushyanta's name from his ring (though that ring goes on to play a more important role).[28] The Brahmin's daughter doesn't know who she's sleeping with when Muladeva gives her the ring, for she's asleep, unconscious. In other versions, the husband doesn't know who he's sleeping with when he gives his disguised wife the ring; he is, as Muladeva is with "Sumangala," unconscious of her identity.

Other Indian Variants

As in the tale of Shakuntala,[vii] the ring plays little or no role in this earliest Indian version of the tale of the clever wife, but a ring is central to later versions. Muladeva's ring reveals the father's name only to the mother. In other tellings, however, it reveals to the whole world the father's connection with both his wife and his son. Often the ring is flanked by two other pieces of jewelry. Sometimes, before the disguised wife will sleep with her husband, on three separate occasions, over three years, in three different cities, she demands that he give her first his pearl necklace, then his diamond necklace, and finally his ring,[29] or his diamond necklace, signet ring, and breast-ornament,[30] or (on two occasions) his ring and handkerchief,[31] and years later she produces them, along with the grown child (or children). In a Moroccan variant, he gives his disguised wife first his ring, then an anklet, and finally a necklace. Years later, when he is about to marry another woman, the first wife produces three children, each carrying one of the three pieces of jewelry, and each named after the town in which she seduced her husband, the names being regarded as part of the proof, too.[32] Sometimes the proof consists of just the three children named after towns, devoid of jewelry.[33]

---

vii. See chapter 3, p. 69.

Three pieces of jewelry, though with only one child, appear in a South Indian oral tale retold by A. K. Ramanujan, who called it "The Wager":

A king's son came upon a local man's rich daughter; she was utterly beautiful, and he stopped and posed a riddle, but she out-riddled him. He flew into a rage and said, "You don't know who you're talking to. You talked back to me. So I'll marry you and shut you up in my basement. If I don't, I wouldn't be my father's son." She countered, "King's son, I'll marry you then and I'll get your own son to tie you up to the post in the marketplace. If I don't, my breast is no breast." He told his father how she had insulted him, bandying wager for wager, and concluded, "So I must marry her and teach her a lesson." His father tried to reason with him, saying, "That's no good reason to marry anyone." Moreover, the king pointed out, she was not of their caste. But the prince insisted, and the king arranged the marriage. Meanwhile, the prince had an underground basement house built for his bride.

When she came to the palace, the prince didn't even look at her. He sent her to the basement house and shut her up in it. Then he went to another country in search of a new bride, married again, and lived with his new wife quite happily; they had several children. Meanwhile, with the help of her father, the girl escaped from the basement, learned acrobatic dancing and black magic, performed for her husband (who did not recognize her, though again he was struck by her beauty), and allowed him to seduce her. She stayed with him for three nights, and made him give her the ring on his finger, his necklace, and his dagger.

She returned home pregnant, gave birth to a son, and raised him, teaching him all the arts she had learned. One day she told him the story of the two wagers, and the boy asked the pivotal question: "If my father never came here, how did I come about?" And she told him about the acrobatic dancing. The son managed to get into the palace and steal the silver legs off the king's golden bed, as well as every piece of jewelry the queen was wearing from all over her body. He disguised himself as the bailiff's son-in-law and slept with the bailiff's daughter. And then he tricked the king into letting him tie him up in a bundle of dirty clothes. When a crowd gathered, he untied the king, who looked at his captor, amazed, for the young man looked just like him. King and thief,

thief and king, it was hard to tell who was which. Only their ages gave them away.

The young man sent for his mother, who told everyone about the wager and displayed the dagger, the necklace, and the signet ring that had once belonged to the king. The king admitted that she had won the wager. Everyone, needless to say, was happy.[34]

Where the prince swears by his resemblance to his father (a crucial point in many of these stories), she swears by her secondary sexual characteristics, and her beauty. But he marries her to punish her, as usual, despite his father's warning that this is a really bad idea. Like Muladeva's son, the boy brings off a literal bed-trick, but this time he also steals the queen's jewelry (which might have been expected to lead to yet another subplot of identification-by-jewelry, but doesn't) and even throws in a sexual bed-trick (with the bailiff's daughter), to prove that he is not just a thief but a sexual trickster like his mom. And in this version, the boy himself asks the riddle that is usually stated only by the husband and the clever wife: How did you get pregnant—with *me*—if your husband "never came here?" as he delicately words it.

A contemporary Tamil folk telling is so truncated that it works only if the storyteller can assume that the listeners are familiar with the full version, evidence of its wide popularity:

A raja went to a village to find a bride. He asked a woman a riddle, and she asked him another in return; neither could answer the other's riddle. "So the prince said, 'I'm going to marry you and lock you up in prison until I find the answer to your riddle!' To which, she said, 'I'll marry you, but if I don't have your child, without you even knowing about it, then I'm not the woman I think I am.' She made this pledge, but he married her anyway." He locked her up in a stone prison, where he visited her, chewed betel nuts, and enjoyed himself.

But she dug a tunnel and escaped to her parents' house. " 'This stupid raja won't recognise me,' she thought and disguised herself as a dancer, with her father as her teacher. Soon the raja called them to dance in his assembly, and when she danced he was infatuated." She spent one night with him, and in the morning she asked him for his ring and riding whip as souvenirs. She returned to the stone prison via the tunnel, and eventually gave birth to a son, who grew up in his father's house.

One day the boy stole the raja's golden bed right out from under him, and tricked the raja into hiding in a sack. "When the raja's men ... saw the raja's son, they thought he was the raja himself! He was sitting on the raja's horse.... Then the son beat the sack with his riding whip.... But when they opened the sack in the palace, they found the raja, and still they couldn't tell the difference between him and his son. 'Who are you?' they asked the raja's son. 'My mother's the woman in the prison; let her out, and she'll tell you the whole story.' When they brought her from the prison, the raja said, 'How did you give birth to a child?' And she said, 'Well, here's your ring and your riding whip. Remember now? Anyhow, I won the bet.' "[35]

Since neither the man nor the woman can answer the riddles at the start, she is no cleverer than he. And though the raja ostensibly imprisons her to find the answer to the riddle, he makes no effort to do so. It is she who, like Muladeva's wife, makes the impossible vow, which she later refers to as a "bet." Unlike the prisons in other stories, this one does not isolate her at all; the raja visits her there and apparently sleeps with her, which is what seems to be implied by the chewing of betel (an essential part of love-play in Indian literature, like the post-coital cigarette in Western erotic conventions) and the euphemism that he "enjoyed himself." Nevertheless, she disguises herself to get pregnant by him (remarking, cynically, that the raja is too stupid to see through any disguise), just as she does in stories where he has *not* already slept with her, and he is later surprised that she managed to get pregnant, apparently forgetting his own nights with her. It is as if the old pattern of the bed-trick hangs on even when a new twist has made it superfluous. She gets from him, along with his ring, not his horse (as often happens in other variants) but his whip, which her son has—and uses—when he tricks his father, though the son now also has, inexplicably, the horse. Though the raja did not notice that the dancing girl looked an awful lot like his wife, everyone does notice that the bed-thief looks just like the raja. And when the raja finally demands an explanation, she merely shows him the ring (and the whip!) and assumes that he will now remember—what? The night they spent together, or the well-known tale of the Clever Wife?

Who is asking the riddle? Who is testing whom? In the Muladeva story, the wife sets the task herself, and she not only satisfies her own conditions but out-riddles her husband and makes a fool of him. She is the one who turns her back in bed (though he has *told* her that he will abandon her), and in another variant, too, it is she, rather than he, who gets up and sleeps in a separate bed when she realizes that he has tricked her by spying on her disguised as her cook[36] (a common disguise for lovers in these stories).[viii] But usually the man sets the task for his wife, to test her cleverness or to punish her for it.

Her cleverness often inspires her to set up the riddle in revenge. When he vows, "As a punishment for your impertinence—cracking riddles with me!—I shall marry you! But right from that moment I'll throw you into solitary confinement!" she replies. "If indeed you will marry me, then I shall bear you a son without you even knowing it, and I shall make him flog you with a whip!"[37] Or, when he vows, "Someday I will marry you and punish you greatly," she replies, "When I have borne you a son, I will tie you to your horse's leg and have you beaten,"[38] or she vows that she will bear him a son who will tie him in a sack and beat him.[39]

Sometimes the husband challenges his wife, or rejects her, for no apparent reason. In an oral Arabic variant, "When the prince entered the nuptial chamber he did not touch his wife at all, nor spoke even a single word to her, but, on the contrary, distanced himself from her with contempt."[40] In one Indian variant, although there is no initial antipathy between them, and hence no reason for revenge, the husband casually remarks, as he sets out on a business trip, "When I return I expect to find you have built me a grand well; and also, as you are such a clever wife, to see a little son!"[41] (In a Moroccan variant, the well is already there, and he throws her into it.)[42] The unmotivated rejection appears in the opening banter in a Kashmiri version of the tale. When the king of Kashmir meets a beautiful woman deep in the forest, the first words he says to her are, "Ha ha! Certainly! A wife like you, whom after marrying I could put aside here in this jungle!" to which she replies, "Of course, I'd marry somebody like you and get a child; and the boy should marry your daughter!" He sends for her and marries her but then puts her in his harem and ignores her. She tells her mother "that she supposed it was on account of her retort that the king of Kashmir thus treated her."[43] But he had stated his intention to abandon her before she ever said a word.

The core of the story, with the bed-trick and the vindicating ring, appears in an Indian folktale about the god Shiva and his wife the goddess Parvati.

---

viii. Recall the disguised cooks in the Cinderella stories and Solomon stories, in chapter 2, pp. 27 and 45.

Their marriage is celebrated in myth, literature, and ritual throughout the Hindu world. Annual festivals reenact every phase of the marriage, from the courtship through the wedding and even beyond, to the bride's annual return visits to her father's home, celebrated at the festival of Durgapuja in Bengal. But the solemn joy of these celebrations is frequently undercut by acknowledgment of the problems that bedevil even a marriage literally made in heaven. Parvati berates Shiva for his refusal to beget a son as well as for his addiction to marijuana, his cheating at their dice games, his poverty, his infidelity, his refusal to get a job, and other marital shortcomings. Sometimes she deals with Shiva's habitual womanizing (or goddessizing) by masquerading as the object of his desire. In a Bengali story, Parvati disguises herself as a *dom* (low-caste) ferry-woman and gets a diamond ring from her husband, who fails to recognize her.[44]

A Tulu tale, recorded in Karnataka in 1970, begins when Shiva and Parvati quarrel and Parvati leaves in fury. This time she makes a paste of charcoal and water and smears it on her face to make herself black. Then she dresses as a woman of a forest tribe, a Korpalu, a person of very low caste. Shiva approaches her, but she protests:

> "Oh, my! What kind of a way is that to speak to a Korpalu?" "What difference does it make if you are a Korpalu? You are a human being, aren't you? I'm a human being too. Our blood is the same, is it not?" argued Shiva. "What you are saying is not right," answered the woman. "You are a god. I am a Korpalu." Then Shiva and the woman remained in the forest together for two days and three nights.
>
> On the third day, Shiva said, "I'm going now, Korpalu." "If you are going, go," she replied, "but just one thing. If I get pregnant, who will pay for my expenses?" "I will provide for your needs. Here is a golden knife, a silver case for lime, and a silver snuffbox. I also have a golden ring with my seal. Take these things. Use them for your expenses if you get pregnant!" said Shiva. "Now I am going back to my palace, Korpalu." Shiva ran home by one path, while Parvati ran home by another.
>
> When she reached her house, Parvati quickly took a bath and combed her hair. Before she even had a chance to put on her sari, however, Shiva arrived home. She said, "I have the feeling that you had a good time with a forest woman." "No, I didn't," said Shiva. "Didn't you have sex with a Korpalu?" asked Parvati. "When you

left here you took your golden knife, your silver box for lime, and the silver snuff box. Didn't you give those things to the Korpalu?" "I didn't give them to her," said Shiva. "Don't say things like that about me. I didn't do it!" "Don't lie to me!" said Parvati. "A Korpalu came here and gave those things to me!"

"Where did you see her?" asked Shiva. "She came here and gave them to me," repeated Parvati. Then Shiva said, "You have no defects. You were born from truth. Let us be on good terms together."[45]

Parvati gets Shiva's jewelry—including a golden ring with his seal—as a kind of prenatal medical insurance to defray her expenses if she gets pregnant, a practical use for the ring that we have already noted in variants of the Shakuntala story[ix] and that extends the role of jewelry beyond its classic function as identification into the realm of home economics. It is worth noting that Parvati does not mention the golden ring when she catches Shiva out in the end. The ring seems almost an atavism in this story, a convention that has no actual effect. When she masquerades as the Korpalu, she does not ask explicitly for the ring, but she asks for something, and what else would he give her? (In a Himalayan folktale the woman has hardheaded misgivings and explicitly asks for the ring as she says to her departing seducer, "The male of the species is very bad. You will forget me and marry again. Give me your token." And he gives her his ring, with all ten of his names inscribed on it.)[46] Equally down-to-earth is Parvati's inspired lie about how she knows that he gave away the jewelry: she implies that, good housekeeper that she is, she *misses* those items on his person and deduces that he must have given them to some woman. This tale was told by a woman, and a woman's eye for jewelry, and for household inventory, may have put that bit of sharp observation into the story.

Parvati appears to Shiva doubly disguised, as a human and as low-caste. Shiva dismisses both problems, lying by saying that he is a human (he is a god, as she immediately reminds him) and lying in the eyes of Hindu caste law by saying that all human beings are equal when it comes to sex. Parvati thus uses sex and jewelry to deconstruct the power of a husband, the power of a god, and the power of caste.

---

ix. See chapter 3, p. 71.

Tamar and Judah

The Muladeva story is not the oldest of the texts that follow the skeletal plot of the story of the clever wife. The assumption that a ring is proof of sexual consummation is deeply embedded in still older texts, such as the tale of Tamar and Judah in the Hebrew Bible (Genesis 38.12–26, c. eighth century BCE). Tamar fits the criteria of the core definition of a clever wife, for she becomes pregnant as the result of a bed-trick and later, when accused of adultery, identifies the father by his ring. But this version is slightly off-center, for Tamar departs from the pattern on an important point: the man she sleeps with, Judah, is not her husband, and he does not (therefore) explicitly challenge her to become pregnant by him. The central incident could be summarized thus:

> Tamar married Judah's eldest son, Er, but Er died leaving her childless. Under Jewish law the second son, Onan, had to marry his brother's widow, but he refused to give her a child and he died too. Judah then promised her that she could marry his third son, Shelah, when he grew up, but Shelah grew up and Tamar was not married to him. A long time afterward, Judah's wife died, and he went up for the sheep shearing. Then Tamar took off her widow's garments, covered her face with a veil, and sat by the road, where Judah saw her and took her for a harlot because she had covered her face. He gave her his seal, cord, and staff, as temporary pledges, to be redeemed, and he lay with her and she conceived by him. Then she got up, went away, took off her veil, and put on her widow's garments, and he could not find her to redeem his pledges. About three months later, Judah was told, "Tamar your daughter-in-law has played the harlot, and she is with child by harlotry." Judah said, "Take her out and let her be burned." As she was being taken out, she sent word to her father-in-law, "By the man to whom this seal and cord and staff belong, by him am I with child." Judah recognized and said, "She is more in the right than I, for I did not give her to my son Shelah."[47]

Did Judah recognize "her" or "it," Tamar or the ring? The Hebrew text, which omits the direct object of the verb, does not say—perhaps both. The passage about Judah specifies a seal, not a ring, but seal rings occur elsewhere in the Hebrew Bible, and in the third century BCE Greek Septuagint

THAMAR.
Bella THAMAR, luctu posito, velata theristro,
6. *Cum Iuda socero dissimulata coit.*

FIGURE 6.1 Tamar holding Judah's ring (in her left hand) and staff (in her right hand), in an engraving by Hans Collaert, Antwerp, late 1500s.

Source: © The Trustees of the British Museum. All rights reserved.

version of Genesis 38.18, Judah's seal is explicitly said to be a ring: Tamar asks him to give her his *daktylion* (finger ring), his *hormiskon* (necklace or a signet cord), and "the rod that is in your hand." The fact that Judah's seal ring is one of three pieces of identification, like the tokens in so many tales of clever wives, further supports the classification of this tale with them.

Since Judah is not Tamar's husband, his feigned "forgetfulness" comes before the seduction, when he "forgets" to give his son Shelah to Tamar. Afterward he honestly cannot remember her; her veil has done the work of the mystifying ring or potion, or mere darkness.[x] He may also have been drunk; sheep shearing in ancient Israel was apparently followed by a fairly riotous celebration. Judah does not challenge Tamar to become pregnant, but we have seen other husbands of clever wives omit this challenge, and the agenda of the book of Genesis in general, and of this chapter in particular and of Tamar herself, is to continue the line of descent of the Israelites, specifically the perpetuation of the bloodline and the household of King David. And so, like other clever wives, Tamar is determined to become pregnant by hook or by crook. Judah's threat to burn her to death when he thinks she is illicitly pregnant also puts her in the company of the adulteresses, or alleged adulteresses, forced to undergo an ordeal by fire. Like Kalidasa's Shakuntala, Tamar is barely pregnant when she confronts the father of her child. The ring is all the proof she has, in contrast with other versions such as the tale of Muladeva, or the *Mahabharata* version of Shakuntala, where there is a son whose cleverness or resemblance proves the encounter.

Judah unknowingly accepts Tamar as a substitute for the prostitute who is substituting for Judah's dead wife, while Tamar knowingly accepts Judah as a substitute for Shelah (who is already also substituting for his older brothers). But Judah allows himself to be tricked, for he too really wants the child, as well as the sex, though he must insist that she has violated the law. All in all, Tamar qualifies with the other clever wives, but the Hebrew Bible takes the story in different directions, polemical and political, thus deepening our understanding of the meaning of the theme and broadening our range of options for its implications in other aspects of human life.

The biblical text regards the testimony of Judah's ring in Tamar's hands as definitive proof, but that testimony is challenged when the story

---

x. See chapter 3, p. 85, chapter 4, p. 97, and chapter 5, p. 112.

is retold in *The Testament of Judah*[48] (second century BCE) and narrated by Judah himself. He prefaces the tale by insisting that he was drunk when he encountered Tamar in her disguise (as he may have been in the Hebrew Bible, too). Here is the central incident:

> "I went in unto her, and she conceived. And not knowing what she had done I wanted to kill her: but she privately sent the pledges and put me to shame. And when I called her I heard also the secret words that I spoke in my drunkenness while sleeping with her. And I could not kill her, for it was from the Lord. But I said, Perhaps she did it deceitfully, having received the pledge from another woman. . . . And I thought that nobody knew that I had gone in unto her."[49]

As it is narrated in the Bible, Tamar's confrontation with Judah is probably public, though she may have sent him the signs privately. *The Testament of Judah* makes it a private reckoning between a man and a woman. Judah is so drunk that he does not recognize Tamar. He even blurts out secrets that she later throws back in his face. He then recognizes her privately as the woman he had slept with, but denies it publicly because he thinks no one else knows. He suggests that she might have gotten the pledges (and, presumably, the pillow talk) from another (treacherous, colluding) woman. This perfectly logical, reasonable argument (though it's a lie) seems not to have occurred to Judah in other texts, including the Hebrew Bible. Even here, after having thought of effective ways to deny her claim, in the end Judah confesses the truth of his own accord.

Reason (bolstered by cynicism, not unrelated) also creeps into the story of Tamar in Thomas Mann's retelling. When Tamar, in disguise, demands a pledge from Judah and he promises to send her something later, she remarks, "A man says that beforehand. Afterwards he is a different man and remembers not his former word. I must have a pledge."[50] Of course, afterward it is she, not he, who will be a different person.

The Clever Wife in the Decameron

One of the best-known versions of the tale of the clever wife is Shakespeare's *All's Well That Ends Well*, which scholars have traced back through French sources to Boccaccio in the fourteenth century. Both Boccaccio and Shakespeare could have known the story from the biblical story of Tamar and Judah. But Boccaccio could also have learned it from ancient Indian versions of the story of Muladeva, brought from India to Italy through the intermediary of Arabic sources,[51] transmitted through Muslim empires in India and the mediation of Moorish Spanish retellings. We've noted the close association between the text in which the Muladeva story occurs (the *Ocean of the Rivers of Stories*) and the *Arabian Nights*. This process of diffusion, going against the current of political domination, colonized Europe, narratively speaking. Scholars have long noted a "slight resemblance" between Boccaccio's story and the tale of Muladeva's wife.[52] The correspondences between the European texts and the biblical narratives as well as the Sanskrit text are of a general nature, indications not of direct influence but rather of the existence of a wide corpus of stories of which the two ancient texts are a part and into which Boccaccio and Shakespeare may have tapped. But direct links have been traced between Boccaccio and other tales from the *Ocean of the Rivers of Stories*,[53] and such links may also obtain between their versions of tales of the clever wife. The correspondences between Boccaccio and Shakespeare involve proper names (Bertrand, Florence, Roussillon), suggesting a far more direct borrowing.

Boccaccio told the story in his *Decameron*, composed during the great Florentine plague (1349–53):[54]

> The Count of Roussillon had a physician whose daughter, Gillette, fell in love with the Count's only child, Bertrand, an exceedingly handsome and charming young man. When the Count died and left his son (now the Count) in the hands of the king, Bertrand had to go to Paris to see the king, and when Gillette's father died soon after, she longed for an excuse to go to Paris to see Bertrand. Rich and alone, she refused her many suitors, for she could not forget Bertrand. When she learned that the king was suffering from a fistula, she thought that not only would this furnish her with a legitimate occasion of going to Paris, but that, should the king's ailment be such as she believed, she might manage to have Bertrand as her husband.
>
> She took to horse and went to Paris; the king promised that, if she cured him, he would marry her to any husband she would choose (except a member of the royal house). She cured the king and said, "Then, my lord, I have earned Bertrand de Roussillon, whom I began to love even in the days of my childhood and have ever since loved over all." The king deemed it a grave matter to give

him to her; nevertheless, having promised her and unwilling to break his promise, he sent for the Count.

Bertrand, who had seen and recognized Gillette, knowing her to be of a lineage far below his quality, refused (though she seemed to him very fair). Forced to marry her, he went off to the wars in Florence, and she returned to Roussillon, where she managed his estates wonderfully. When she sent for him, he said, "I will return thither to abide with her when she shall have this my ring on her finger and in her arms a son by me begotten." Now the ring in question he held very dear and never parted with it, by reason of a certain virtue which it had been given him to understand that it had.

The Countess (as Gillette was now), pretending to go on a pilgrimage, went to Florence. There she found out that her husband was in love with a certain unmarried woman, and she told the woman's mother her story and bribed her to help her, offering her money that would allow her daughter to marry. Gillette told the mother to send to the man and ask for the ring; and then, she said, "If he sends you the ring, you must give it to me and then send to him to say that your daughter is ready to do his pleasure; then bring him here in secret and privily put me to bed with him in the stead of your daughter. It may be God will vouchsafe me to conceive, and in this way, having his ring on my finger and a child in my arms of him begotten, I shall then regain him and abide with him, as a wife should abide with her husband."

The mother got the ring (although this seemed somewhat grievous to the Count) and adroitly put Gillette to bed with Bertrand, in the place of her own daughter. In these first embracements, most ardently sought by the Count, the lady, by God's pleasure, became with child of two sons, as her delivery in time made manifest. Not once only, but many times, did the gentlewoman gratify the Countess with her husband's embraces, contriving so secretly that never was a word known of the matter, the Count all the while believing himself to have been, not with his wife, but with her whom he loved. Eventually, the Countess gave birth to two male children, most like their father. She presented herself, the boys, and the ring to her husband in public, told him the story, and he from that day forth ever honored her as his bride and his wife and loved and held her dear over all.[55]

Bertrand rejects Gillette because, like the Cruel Knight in the ballad,[xi] he regards her as both lower class and foisted on him against his will. In the end, the identifying factor is the boys' uncanny physical resemblance to their father, as well as their mother's possession of the father's ring. Whereas, in the Muladeva tale, that ring merely reveals to the mother the identity, more precisely the name, of the father, in Boccaccio, as in many of the vernacular variants, it reveals to the father, and to the whole world, the identity of the mother. Its "virtue" (never specified) may well be its ability to reveal the truth, to revive lost memory.

Boccaccio makes the son into the twins who recur in many folk variants[56] as well as the Bible (Tamar gives birth to twin boys). But he also, most significantly, doubles the women. Muladeva's wife (who fakes a pilgrimage, as Boccaccio's heroine does) simply pretends to be a courtesan, but there is no particular courtesan whom she or Tamar replaces, nor do the women in the folktales substitute for other actual women. But in Boccaccio's story there is a particular woman—"a certain unmarried woman"—whom the husband desires, and whom the wife replaces.

The double women remain in a film based upon the Boccaccio version, one of four vignettes in *Decameron Nights* (Hugo Fregonese, 1953). The film is set in Spain, but the clever wife still goes to Florence, and the woman is named not Gillette, as in Boccaccio, but Isabella:[57]

> Isabella de Marco (Joan Fontaine) was a doctor, scorned by the other doctors because she was a woman, but she cured the king and insisted, for her reward, on marrying Bertando, a notorious womanizer. He rejected her and went away, saying that unless she obtained his ring and gave him a son he would never be hers. She said, "How can I when you will not stay with me?" to which he replied, sarcastically, "You're a doctor; work a miracle."
>
> Isabella went to Florence and arranged secretly to replace, in bed, Maria (Joan Collins), a young woman whom Bertando was wooing. He gave the ring to Isabella-as-Maria, and she accidentally lost (in the bed) a blue earring, which he picked up. Then she slipped out of the bedroom and the house. In the morning, Maria was shocked to find Bertando in her bed; she knew nothing of the trick. He tried to give her "back" the earring, thinking it was hers, and she threw

---

xi. See chapter 2, p. 34.

it down. A comedy of misunderstandings ensued, and the people of the house threw Bertando out, believing that Maria had had a change of heart between the night and the morning.

When Bertando returned to Spain and found that Isabella had had a baby, he accused her of infidelity. She showed him the ring, but it meant nothing: "You bought it from Maria," he insisted. She maintained that she had been the woman in the bed in Florence. He laughed and said, "You're a cold fish. You're a doctor dressed as a female. How could a doctor kiss me as Maria did?" Then Isabella became seductive and started to kiss him. As her face came near him, he saw that she was wearing the other blue earring. He was convinced by this and kissed her passionately.

Boccaccio (played by Louis Jordan), who appears as the narrator on the frame of the story, swears that Bertando (also played by Louis Jordan) became a model of fidelity.

In this rather crude, proto-feminist variant, Bertando scorns the professional woman (he will not "stay with" her, the equivalent of other euphemisms such as "cannot stand" her or "never came" there) and makes explicit his belief that such a woman cannot be a satisfying sexual partner. He gives a nice twist to the riddle in his taunt that she might use her medical powers to get pregnant by him, imagining, perhaps, some scenario of stolen sperm and in vitro fertilization. Bertando is not persuaded by the hard evidence of the ring, against which he invokes the commonsense logic ("You bought it from Maria") that we recognize from *The Testament of Judah*. But he is persuaded by the hard evidence of the earring; in the end, the jewelry (enhanced by the soft evidence of the kiss) carries the day.

Shakespeare's Rings III: The Riddle of the Ring

When Shakespeare retells the story, there are two rings.

Shakespeare probably took the basic plot of his story from William Paynter's 1566 compendium, *Palace of Pleasure*, which contained Boccaccio's version of the story.[58] W. W. Lawrence discusses the debt that the play owes to folktales dealing with "the clever wench,"[59] but Howard C. Cole cautions us against following Lawrence's Oriental trail and pooh-poohs any analogue "likely to turn up on the banks of the ancient Ganges."[60] Certainly, old-fashioned tale-tracking, merely pointing out the themes that came from India, *ex oriente lux*, cannot enhance our appreciation of the beauty of Shakespeare's language and thinking, or illuminate his deep soundings into the dark sides of human psychology. But folklorists chasing their tales can explain some of the otherwise puzzling atavisms in the plot and certain perplexing aspects of some of the characters.

All's Well That Ends Well

Let me begin by reminding the reader of the rather complicated role of the two rings in *All's Well*, in a kind of ring-centric CliffsNotes version:

> Helena healed the ailing king and chose Bertram as her reward; the king also gave her a ring, which she always wore. Bertram unwillingly complied with the king's wish; he married Helena but said he would not sleep with her until she presented him with a son and with the ring that he never took off. He went away to Florence and there made an assignation with a young woman named Diana. Helena followed him to Florence and persuaded Diana to allow her, Helena, to get into bed with Bertram in the dark, instead of Diana. They did this, and Bertram did not notice the difference. Helena became pregnant. Before the tryst, Diana had insisted that Bertram give her his ring, and he did so, unwillingly; then Helena, in the night, gave him her ring in return. When Helena eventually confronted him with her pregnancy and the king demanded answers about both rings, Bertram swore he would love her forever.

Scholars call *All's Well That Ends Well* one of Shakespeare's "problem plays," and one of the problems is the conceit that Bertram doesn't realize he's in bed with Helena instead of Diana when Helena takes Diana's place in the dark bedroom. Shakespeare plays with the conventions of non-recognition, depicting Bertram as an "in the dark all cats are gray" kind of guy, but chooses not to challenge the folktale's assumption that he does not recognize his wife.

I have another problem with this particular variant. Why does Helena, a real smart gal, persist in loving the spectacularly inadequate Bertram? The two questions are interrelated: one might ask, why does Helena persist in loving a man who doesn't recognize her in bed? *All's Well That Ends Well* does not end well at all. Helena gets Bertram, but Bertram is no prize and doesn't want her. The folk tradition supplies at least a partial answer: the clever wife wants to get her husband back even though he rejects her; that's the convention, that's the way the story goes.

But this, we may assume, also had a kind of psychological truth for Shakespeare. Women, and men, sometimes stay with people who treat them very badly indeed. Helena continues to want Bertram, even when Diana—who admires Bertram's good looks and bravery—tells Helena (not knowing that she is married to Bertram) how she pities Bertram's wife for being married to a philanderer who detests her. Even at the end, when the king has Bertram cornered, and Helena turns to Bertram and shows him the ring and the letter with his challenge about ring and child, he turns from her to say his very last lines not to her but to the king, and they are, "If she, my liege, can make me know this clearly, / I'll love her dearly, ever, ever dearly" (5.3.314–315), lines that ring as hollow as any in English theater. And instead of spitting in his eye, Helena just says, not to the king but to Bertram, "If it appear not plain and prove untrue, / Deadly divorce step between me and you!" (5.3.316–317). An ominous note on which to begin a marriage.

There are significant differences between the Italian and Shakespearean tellings. Rejecting Boccaccio's innovation of the twins, Shakespeare ends his play while Helena is still pregnant, but he compensated by introducing a second ring.[61] As usual, it is the combination of the ring(s) and the (not yet born) son that fulfills the conditions of the riddle. Helena says to Bertram, when she claims him, "This is done; / Will you be mine, now you are doubly won?" (5.3.311–312). "Doubly" is a pun: he is won in two ways (by child and ring), and by a double (Helena doubling as Diana). "Won" also puns on "one" in a way that invites Bertram to create a unity for himself and her.[62]

Bertram's ring, which he gives to Diana and Diana gives to Helena, ultimately proves who *he* was, the man who impregnated her, while the ring that Helena gives to Diana and Diana gives to Bertram proves who *she* was, the woman in the dark. Where in Boccaccio Bertram's ring had a special "virtue," in Shakespeare Bertram's ring is symbolic of male inheritance. When she contrives to get it from him, Helena advises Diana's mother: "A ring the county wears, / That downward hath succeeded in his house / From son to son, some four or five descents / Since the first father wore it: this ring he holds / In most rich choice" (3.7.22–26). This ring of patrilineal descent is the ring that Diana produces at the end of the play to "prove" (falsely) that Bertram took her virginity.[63] The Countess, Bertram's mother, avers that the ring has been in the family not for four or five generations, as Helena said, but for *six*. She concludes: "This is his wife: / That ring's a thousand proofs" (5.3.198–199).

To win the ring from the reluctant Bertram, Diana equates it with her virginity: "Mine honour's such a ring; / My chastity's the jewel of our house, / Bequeathed down from many ancestors" (4.2.45–47). The ring that is a sign of male succession is balanced by the jewel of the maidenhead[xii] that assures the purity of that male line. Diana's chastity is her "ring"— a symbolic evocation of a chastity ring or chastity belt[xiii]—that can be used in bargaining for Bertram's ring. The maidenhead for which men literally lose their heads in other Shakespeare plays about bed-tricks (such as *Measure for Measure*) here causes a man to lose his ring.

The ring that Helena gives to Diana and Diana gives to Bertram is used in a mock wedding ceremony of exchange. Diana tells Bertram, "On your finger in the night I'll put / Another ring, that what in time proceeds / May token to the future our past deeds" (4.2.61–63). Like other clever wives, Helena anticipates a moment when the ring will be used to unmask what amounts to fraud; but Bertram, as usual, doesn't get the point, doesn't see what the fraud is. The ring will prove that it was Helena who slept with Bertram, that her child is his child. In that sense, the ring that he puts on his finger that night eventually produces his heir. The one meaning that Diana's promise does *not* have is the literal meaning that Bertram may well assume, namely, that Diana will use it to claim him as a husband.[64] Bertram later wears this ring in the presence of the king, who recognizes it as the one that he himself had given to Helena.[65] Bertram, who apparently never noticed it (or anything else) on Helena, repeats his honest belief that "the ring was never hers" (5.3.89), but then he lies about how he got it (he says some *other* woman threw it to him from a window).

The king then recalls a most odd thing that Helena said about her ring, which exactly parallel Bertram's oath concerning *his* ring: "She call'd the saints to surety, / That she would never put it from her finger, / Unless she gave it to yourself in bed, / Where you have never come, or sent it us / Upon her great disaster" (5.3.108–112). The words of this speech echo Bertram's oath: "the ring upon my finger, which never shall come off" (3.2.55–56). The two conditions under which Helena said she would part with the ring collapse into one; the fact that Bertram has apparently "never

---

xii. Recall the identification of rings with women's sexual organs, in chapter 1, p. 10.

xiii. See chapter 1, p. 3.

come" to her bed is itself the "great disaster." Not realizing that it is the fulfillment of the first of Helena's conditions, rather than the second, that explains Bertram's possession of the ring, the king accuses him of having killed her. The unwitting Bertram replies, appropriately enough, with a reference to the first rather than the second condition: "If you shall prove / This ring was ever hers, you shall as easy / Prove that I husbanded her in bed in Florence, / Where she never was." (5.3.124–127). Again, the words exactly echo Helena's oath (itself an echo of Bertram's oath): "unless she gave it to yourself in bed—Where you have never come" (5.3.110–11).

When Bertram has gotten himself into terrible trouble about *Helena's* ring, Diana displays *Bertram's* ring, which he admits having given to her. But then, just when he thinks he's in the clear, Diana blandly suggests, "Send for your ring, I will return it home, / And give me mine again" (5.3.223–224). Bertram says he does not have her ring (Helena's ring). The king then asks Diana to describe it and she identifies it as the ring that is on the king's finger, the ring that the king had given Helena, Helena-as-Diana had given Bertram ("This was it I gave him, being abed" [5.3.228], Diana sweetly lies, though later she tells the truth: "I never gave it him" [5.3.275]), and Bertram has just given the king, in a kind of chain familiar from folktales or Schnitzler's *La Ronde*. At this point, Bertram understandably begins to collapse, and lamely blurts out: "My lord, I do confess, the ring was hers" (5.3.231) (*which* ring? *which* "her"?).

Neely comments on the connection of the two rings "with chastity and sexuality, with betrothal and consummation, and with the commercial flavor of the transactions."[66] Helena's ring also gives her a measure of authenticity; because it is a gift from the king, it gives her a male supporter, indeed a very powerful male supporter, a kind of champion to enter the lists against Bertram. Muladeva's wife *said* that she belonged to the king, though it was not true. In some versions, the king is actually the husband of the clever wife.[67] And in the European retellings, Muladeva's fantasy king becomes a real player in the game, as a kind of father figure.

The connection between the two parents and the two rings is well glossed by Janet Adelman:

"The act by which Helena simultaneously makes Bertram a father and gets his father's ring is, I think, a fantasized replication of the act of parental intercourse by which Bertram himself was bred. Hence the complex logic governing the exchange of rings in the dark: Bertram's father's ring is given unawares to Helena, the

mother's choice, and the ring taken from Helena turns out to have
been the king's. Even here, when poor Bertram thinks that he has
escaped his family, the exchange of rings is in effect between father
and mother; in the last scene the ring-play turns out to have been
a symbolic sexual exchange between surrogate parental figures."[68]

Helena does not triumph independently, but rather with the help of a
powerful father figure, just as the medical skill that gets her Bertram as
her husband in the first place comes from her father. Where Muladeva's
wife uses her *son* as the essential helper, Helena (who does not yet
have a son) finds her male helper in the older generation. Helena's
ring therefore adds weight both to female independence and to female
dependence.

Bertram's ring poses a riddle, as it did in Boccaccio. Bertram writes to
Helena, "When thou canst get the ring upon my finger, which never shall
come off, and show me a child begotten of thy body that I am father to,
then call me husband: but in such a 'then' I write a 'never'" (3.2.55–58).
This riddle (How can you get the ring if it never comes off?) doubles the
more basic riddle: How can you get a child if you never sleep together?
On the surface, Bertram is saying, "I dare you to get this ring I wear," but
John F. Adams points out a deeper meaning: " 'When you can get the ring
upon my finger' means plainly, 'when you shall have sexual relations with
me'; 'which never shall come off' means, in effect, sexual exclusiveness,
or chastity (Bertram's) in marriage."[69] A minor character (the clown) has
already used the metaphor of one person's ring getting on another person's finger to refer to the fact that people are getting into the wrong beds
(2.2.22). Now it will take Helena's bed-trick to get the right ring on the
right finger.[70]

For beneath the riddle of sexless procreation hides the riddle of chastity and sexual passion, signified by the names of the two women: Diana
(Roman goddess of chastity, the Greek Artemis) and Helena (Helen of
Troy, the Greek poster girl for sex, whom the clown invokes when he
speaks of Helena [1.3.69–79]). The associations are the reverse of what we
might expect: the sexy mistress should be named Helena, the chaste wife
Diana. But Bertram is a twisted fellow and requires a twisted bed-trick.
Helena's mission is to combine the two wrongly separated aspects of a
single woman, in this case to bring out the unthreatening nature of the
chaste young mistress to neutralize the overpowering threat of the sexually mature wife.

There is yet another sexual riddle embedded in this play, Helena's riddle, which intercepts and transposes Bertram's.[71] Helena tells the Countess that she hopes for a time when she might be one who "riddle-like lives sweetly where she dies" (1.3.212), that is, who lives "sweetly" (chastely) but also experiences the "little death" of sexual passion.[72] She is addressing the second, deeper level of Bertram's riddle, not the riddle of sexless procreation but the riddle of chaste sexuality, the challenge of uniting Diana (chastity) and Helen (sexual passion).

The "little death" becomes an imagined real death when the paradox of sexless procreation is addressed in a final riddle, and its solution invokes another meaning of dying. Near the end, when it has been falsely announced that Helena is dead, Diana says of Bertram: "He knows himself my bed he hath defil'd; / And at that time he got his wife with child. / Dead though she be, she feels her young one kick. / So there's my riddle: one that's dead is quick" (5.3.299–301). The myth breaks through at this point, reminding us that this is a story not only about philandering men and clever women but about the mystery of dead women giving birth to live children, "quick" having the double sense of "alive" and "pregnant"—that is, having life within you. It is also about the mystery of a woman giving birth to herself, for Helena-as-Diana is not the same woman as Helena-as-Helena: Helena-as-Diana is able to seduce Bertram and demand things from him as Helena-as-Helena never could, and the Helena at the end of play who takes Bertram back is now not merely clever but wise. At the very least, she is wise to Bertram.

Is All Well That Ends Well?

The clever wife gets the child. But is that the happy ending? Does she really get what she wants? I wonder. The usual legal process is for a woman to get a ring and then get a baby; the usual physical process is first sex, then baby. To have the baby but not the ring is, of course, the defining situation of every unwed mother, the fate worse than death that haunted all those Doris Day films.[xiv] The narrative paradox of the clever wife reverses this process, requiring the woman to have a baby (and a ring) in order to get the sex. Of course here too the sex must come first; it merely appears to come second.

---

xiv. See chapter 1, p. 20.

The question of inheritance, which is generally viewed as a male problem —"Give me lots of sons just like me"[xv]—is also a female problem: "Let my children inherit." This is, in fact, the main point of the Shakuntala story[xvi] and other tales in which the woman demands, before she will sleep with a king, not (or not only) his ring but his promise to put her son on the throne (and thereby, incidentally, to give her the status of queen mother). The king does not want to acknowledge the child of the abandoned wife. The clever wife resembles Shakuntala in her concern for the legitimacy of her child (and in the role of that child in getting back her husband), but Shakuntala's weapon is not cleverness but moral justice.

These stories condemn the husband not for sleeping with other women, since philandering is considered the norm, but for not sleeping with his wife, for failing to fulfill his duty to impregnate her. This duty is a matter of law in ancient India—the husband must sleep with his wife during her fertile period[73]—and is implicit in many European texts. These being the stakes, most of the clever wives (and their husbands) can accomplish their ends during a one-night stand: just long enough to beget a child and/or make sure that there was a maidenhead. These are not stories about ongoing relationships, looking forward to a golden anniversary; sometimes he, sometimes she, walks out after the one night. If the wife is willing to settle for a child that her husband acknowledges as his own, with all the rights and privileges thereto, then all may indeed end, more or less, well.[74]

But often the rejected wife wants an erotic partner as well as a baby. Many a clever wife shares with forgotten or betrayed wives the sadness of having a husband who will not sleep with her, though most of the wives in the stories hope to satisfy primarily their desire for a child and only secondarily their desire for a husband's love. She may win his body for a night, long enough to make a child, but some of the stories tell us that she also desires his desire, or even his love. The woman who marries the king of Kashmir comes to him in disguise because, "It happened, however, that she loved him,"[75] and at the end of another Kashmiri variant, the husband capitulates completely and declares, "You are the master, I am the pupil. Forgive my conceit, love me again thoroughly."[76] Even the

xv. See chapter 7, p. 200.

xvi. See chapter 3, p. 69.

husband of the "Fortunate Farmer's Daughter," who threatens to kill her if she does not bring back his ring, ultimately falls in love with her.[xvii]

William Butler Yeats spoke of the desire of the man "which is for the woman" and "the desire of the woman which is for the desire of the man."[77] Does the clever wife's trick achieve the desire, let alone the love? Sometimes, the stories tell us, it does. But if the wife's goal is to win back her husband's heart forever, then it is she who seems self-deceived. She has won her husband's respect for her perseverance and ingenuity, but this is likely to be a temporary, or even Pyrrhic, victory.

Two patterns are at work here: Muladeva's wife is using her husband to get a baby, perhaps even stealing his substance to give her what she wants, while Helena uses the baby to get the husband. The two aspects of the clever wife's goal are reflected in two aspects of European adultery law: "adultery" is a crime because it "adulterates" both the lineage of the child and the wife's affection for the husband. Folklore tends to emphasize the goal of fertility and babies, literature the goal of love; but in some stories of both genres, the two goals are inseparable.

In these stories about the tension between illicit eroticism, on the one hand, and legal marriage and progeny, on the other, circular jewelry expresses the circular paradox of marital sexual rejection. The husband desires both an erotic encounter and a legitimate child, but not always from the same woman. To close the circle his wife must circle back to become the person she knows she is, the person he cannot see until she transforms herself there and back again: his erotic partner. And indeed, it may well be that he does know, subconsciously, that this "other" woman is in fact his own wife, so that he satisfies both of his desires at the same time.

The logical paradox, the catch-22, is for the wife to get the child *before* he loves her. Once she solves that riddle, she wins. But do we accept the idea that the clever wife's husband loves her after she has borne him a male child? That depends very much on the very different cultural and individual expectations of the women in different variants of the tale. In some texts, even, perhaps, in the tale of Muladeva's wife, the husband is, in the end, quite pleased to have such a clever wife, precisely the quality on account of which he rejected her in the beginning. Bertram clearly is not. Shakespeare's Helena, rejected and wronged, must, in the words of Zwi Jagendorf, imitate her "desired rivals, tolerate more or less consciously the

---

xvii. See chapter 2, p. 34.

degradation of being loved for someone else and work a kind of salvation out of an ambiguous sexual encounter."[78] This is also true of Muladeva's wife, even though there is no actual "someone else" in her story. Adelman sounds a wise warning: "Given the status of the bed tricks as tricks and the characters' failure to provide much evidence that they have been transformed by them, our hope [that he will ever love her, let alone love her ever, as Bertram swears] seems frail indeed and the marriages at the end . . . remain equivocal."[79] When Helena speaks of herself as "the shadow of a wife . . . / The name and not the thing" (5.3.306–307), she is expressing the tragedy of every clever wife.

The clever wife must bring into a single focus the often clashing personae of what Freud stereotyped as the Madonna and the whore, or the virgin and the whore—or Diana and Helen. But she must also reconcile the wife and the mistress, not quite the same thing. The wife is undesirable for many of the reasons we have considered, but also, and perhaps primarily, because the husband knows that she is his wife, that he *must* desire her in order to have a child. This is why he rejects her and why he subsequently accepts her only when he thinks she is *not* his wife.[80]

Thomas Hardy brilliantly satirized this quandary of a "fickle husband" in *Far from the Madding Crowd*. As a man of this type put it, "Feeling she's ticketed as my lawful wife, I can't help my heart wandering, do what I will." The narrator described the solution:

> "At last I believe he cured it by making her take off her wedding-ring and calling her by her maiden name as they sat together after the shop was shut, and so 'a would get to fancy she was only his sweetheart, and not married to him at all. And as soon as he could thoroughly fancy he was doing wrong and committing the seventh, 'a got to like her as well as ever, and they lived on a perfect picture of mutel love."[81]

The husband had, in effect, staged his wife's bed-trick, ring and all.

This, too, is a riddle, what Stanley Cavell has called "the riddle of intimacy," the danger that a marriage will disappoint one or both of its partners through "its impotence to domesticate sexuality without discouraging it."[82] And disappointment seeks revenge—first the husband's (in his cruel rejection of his wife) and then the wife's (in her public humiliation of her husband). The tales of clever wives argue that for both the man and the woman, marriage may be the best revenge.

Often the upper-class wife attempts to overcome her husband's paralyzing respect through a change in class (she dresses like a whore) or culture (she dresses like a foreigner). Most of the clever wives' adventures take place away from home, where you leave your context behind. You are yourself only at home, in your surroundings; you go abroad sometimes precisely in order to become someone else. Memory is preserved in a social context and disappears with the loss of context. The clever wife is usually "foreign" not merely in the explicit political sense (she may wear the costume of another culture—Helena goes from Paris to Florence, Muladeva's wife from Pataliputra to Ujjain) but in the psychological sense of alienation or defamiliarization: she makes herself strange to her husband, and hence desirable, no longer the boring legitimate partner, but fresh again. The fantasy of the wife-as-mistress is the Ur-form of the Marabel Morgan "Total Woman" approach to spicing up a marriage (an approach that has, more appropriately, been called the "Totaled Woman"), in which the housewife dresses up for her husband in a sexy negligee (or leather-and-chains, or French maid apron-and-garters).

But, as we have seen, when the wife, rather than the mistress, is of a lower class, that, too, can be the reason for her rejection. Too high or too low, too clever or well connected, or simply not his own free choice, she seems to begin in a no-win situation. Her only way out is to escape from all of these superficial labels and turn her cleverness from a liability into an asset. Becoming someone else, she makes him see who she really is. And by getting his ring, she proves it. The stories pit men's power against women's cleverness. No matter who actually sets the terms of the test, he always has the power, and he always leaves her. But she is always clever enough to trick him into coming back.

7

The Rape of the Clever Wife

Rape and Rejection

The husband of the clever wife suffers from a paradoxical desire: to keep his wife a virgin but also to have legitimate children from her.[1] He refuses to sleep with her and often locks her up so that no one else can either. This seems to accomplish his first goal, keeping her from cuckolding him; but it also blocks his second goal, as it keeps her from getting pregnant by him. And in fact, it doesn't really accomplish the first goal either. The comedy that drives many of the versions we are about to encounter, and that indeed lurks beneath the surface in many of the serious versions, stems from the inadvertent self-cuckolding that the husband achieves. The clever wife must masquerade in order to spring him from his own trap and provide the other half of what he desires. In an Egyptian story, a husband about to remarry sees the three sons he has unknowingly begotten, and thinks, "If I had such lovely children I would never remarry." When their mother proves to him that they are indeed his, the celebration is transformed from a second wedding to a triple circumcision.[2]

The paradox of self-cuckolding often produces such tension that it escalates into violence against a woman the man thinks is not his wife—or, perhaps, a woman he subconsciously knows to be the wife he bitterly resents. Several of the stories we have encountered involve sexual violence, sometimes explicit rape. The "jewels" that Diderot's magic ring caused to talk told the truth about a rape.[i] Dushyanta's seduction of Shakuntala[ii] amounts to a rape, one scholar has argued, because Shakuntala was

---

i. See chapter 1, p. 19.

ii. See chapter 3, p. 69.

"completely innocent until the arrival of the king and therefore highly sus-
ceptible to the king's advances. . . . The tale thus continues the old theme
of rape with a new twist."[3] More blatantly, Yvain rapes the mother of the
future Bishop Kentigern,[iii] and Siegfried rapes Brünnhilde in several versions of that story.[iv] Some scholars consider all of the bed-tricks or sexual
masquerades that clever wives employ a form of rape, because the person
so tricked does not consent to what is really happening.[4]

The husband's refusal to sleep with his clever wife appears to be the
very opposite of rape, but there is a subtle link between the two sexual
extremes that we don't need Freud to untangle. It emerges clearly enough
from aspects of the mythology of Tristan[v] and of Siegfried[vi] that bear re-
examination. When Tristan puts his sword between himself and Isolde,
King Mark reads it as evidence that they have been chaste, though in fact
they are lovers. Tristan has, however, refused to consummate his marriage
with the other Isolde, though there is no sword between them. His use of
the sword is therefore the manipulation of a symbol to conceal the truth.
As for Siegfried, in the *Völsunga Saga*, Ibsen, and Wagner, where Siegfried
most definitely does *not* rape Brünnhilde, he takes his sword and lays it
unsheathed between himself and her when they sleep, and later he swears
by that sword that he never touched her sexually. Rape and sexual rejection
are uneasily intertwined throughout the entire Siegfried corpus.

The sword in the bed—usually said to be a "naked" sword, as if to force
us to confront its sexual symbolism—is a violent image, setting a violent
form of chastity against its even more violent, closely related, polar opposite: rape. The metaphorical sword in the bed is a problem that the rejected
wife must solve; it denies her children as well as sexual pleasure. In the
medieval courtly tradition, the literal sword in the bed appears to be a solution (to the conflict between male bonding and sexual desire for another
man's woman) but it is in fact the symbol of a quandary to which there is
no solution (the conflict between the man's rejection of his wife and desire
for a son).[5]

Moreover, the sword in the bed expresses the same male anxiety that
is at the heart of the episodes of rape. Both rape and the sword in the bed

---

iii. See chapter 2, p. 89.

iv. See chapter 5, p. 113.

v. See chapter 4, p. 101.

vi. See chapter 5, p. 114.

are sexual abuses that objectify women, disregard their feelings, use them as pawns to other ends, and avoid the mutuality and intimacy that are the essence of the ideal relationship between the sexes. The apparent paradox that the sort of man who rejects his clever wife (and often locks her up) is also the sort of man who will rape a woman who is not his wife is a recognizable psychological syndrome. It is well personified in the Victorians, who, on the one hand, would not let a lady expose her ankle in public, or mention legs even when they belonged to pianos, but on the other hand, produced and consumed a staggering quantity of appalling sado-masochistic pornography.[6]

Stories of clever wives that incorporate rape, or attempted rape, or mock rape occur in many cultures, as we have seen. In this chapter we will focus on tales from the ancient Greco-Roman world and from Arabic and Turkish culture. In making explicit the latent theme of sexual violence, these stories are twisted into new patterns, as the storyteller finds it necessary to re-arrange other factors in the story, including chronology, agency, and even gender. Yet all the main themes are still there, like the cards in a shuffled deck: the rejection, the masquerade, the child, and the signet ring.

Menander and Terence

Two Greco-Roman comedies, from the fourth to the second centuries BCE, develop versions of a story that seems to have the makings of a tale of a clever wife. As in the story of Tamar and Judah, there is no explicit challenge or riddle, and the women's roles are reversed: a man rejects his wife until another woman, taking his wife's place, helps him to rediscover his lost ring and his abandoned, unknown son. Everything in the Greco-Roman narratives turns out quite differently from most stories of clever wives,[vii] in part because the assumptions of the Greek and Roman audience are so different from those of India or Elizabethan England. In this world, the introduction of an explicit rape turns the plays into what amount to anti-clever-wife stories or clever-wife stories played out in Looking-Glass Land.

The first play is *The Arbitrators (Epitrepontes)*, by Menander, who lived and wrote in Athens from 342 to 290 BCE; the second is *The Mother-in-Law (Hecyra)*, by Terence (a.k.a. Publius Terentius Afer), a Phoenician born in

---

about 190 BCE in Carthage (North Africa). Terence based his Latin play upon Menander's Greek play,[7] but there are major shifts in the plot.

Let's begin with Menander. His play is known only from fragments, but these amount to more than half of the play and happen to contain the essential ingredients of our story: the masquerade, the baby, and the ring. Here is a summary of just those parts of the plot; the first paragraph summarizes what has happened before the play begins:

While Charisios was on an extended trip away from home, just five months after his marriage to Pamphile, she had given birth to a baby. Pamphile gave the inconvenient baby to her nurse to abandon in the forest. Charisios heard what had happened and, though he loved Pamphile, he left her, moved into the house of his friend Chairestratos next door, and brought in a hetaera (courtesan), Habrotonon. In fact, Charisios had actually fathered Pamphile's baby four months before the wedding, in an act of drunken rape. But neither he nor she had seen the other's face in the dark, so neither of them (nor anyone else) knew who the baby's father was.

As the play opens, Chairestratos's slave brings on an abandoned baby that he has received from a shepherd, together with a necklace and other pieces of jewelry, tokens. The slave gives the baby to his wife, who takes it into their house, while the slave and the shepherd dispute the ownership of the tokens. Onesimos, Charisios's slave, arrives and recognizes one of the tokens as a ring belonging to his master. He takes it but hesitates to show it to Charisios because it identifies him as the father of the abandoned baby. Onesimos knows that Charisios had lost that ring at the night festival of Artemis, a women's festival, when he was drunk. He reasons that Charisios must have raped a girl and lost his ring in the struggle, and she must have taken the ring and, after she gave birth, abandoned the baby: "Find the girl, show her the ring, and you'd have clear proof." But no one knows who the mother is.

Habrotonon, the hetaera, overhears all this. She tells Onesimos that she had been at that same festival of Artemis, and that a very pretty girl, whom she did not know but would recognize if she saw her again, had been raped, returning to the other women sobbing, filthy, her clothes torn to shreds. Still neither Onesimos nor Habrotonon will tell Charisios about all this without more proof. Habrotonon takes the ring and tells Charisios that she herself had gotten it when she was raped at the festival of Artemis. Charisios thus learns, and admits, that he was the father of the baby found with the ring, but thinks that Habrotonon was the mother.

When Habrotonon meets Pamphile she recognizes her as the girl she saw at the festival of Artemis. She tells her that Charisios is the father of the abandoned child, and then she tells Charisios that Pamphile is the mother.[8] Onesimos finally tries to explain to Pamphile's father (who had supervised the arbitration over the baby's tokens) that the child is in fact his daughter's. He begins obliquely, saying only, "At the festival of Artemis, my master grabbed the girl and dragged her away from the dancing. And now they've recognized each other and all is well." The old man says in reply, "What a shocking story! If what you say is true . . ."[9]

And the play breaks off there, unfinished.

Like many clever wives we have encountered, Pamphile becomes pregnant by her husband and is falsely accused of being false. But Menander's play departs from the usual pattern in several respects, all stemming ultimately from a transformation in the chronology: this husband unwittingly sleeps with his (soon to be rejected) wife *before* he marries her. Still, a ring, as usual, ultimately establishes the identity of the husband's shameful (if marriage-saving) rape of his (future) wife, which he had forgotten because his mind was blurred by drink.

The man who first seduces a woman and then marries her is of course a familiar figure. The man who rapes, rather than seduces, his future wife is not so common, and the man who does not *know* that he was the one who raped the woman who was to become his wife is quite a rare bird. The transposition of the sexual encounter back to a moment before the (unconsummated) marriage leads to a major inversion of the agency as it appears in most other versions of the story: it is he, not she, who initiates this encounter, and indeed she is raped and impregnated not only against her will but, like him, without knowledge of the identity of her partner. The double amnesia is produced without any magic ring, just simple darkness and wine.

The ring here, as so often, plays a double role, intended to identify the abandoned child but actually identifying the father. The first role is made much of in the play, which takes its name from the arbitration of the argument over ownership of the jewelry found with the child, jewelry at first variously described not as a ring but as a necklace and ornaments, golden things (Menander 301–309), and, most significantly, tokens (331), literally "things to be known" (*gnorismata*),[10] the Greek word for objects by which a lost child, and his parentage, could be identified. The slave who brings the child onstage remarks, "His mother, wherever she is, gave them to the child to keep until he was grown," and he goes on to cite antecedents in Greek plays, particularly a tragedy in which a goatherd found the twins Neleus and Pelias, and showed them, when they were grown, the "pouch of tokens," which eventually proved that they were kings. And, he adds, "One man avoided marrying his sister through tokens, one found his mother and saved her, a third his brother" (340–343). The first of these examples is a reference to a lost play by Menander, a little self-referential, intertextual joke about incest, which haunts these stories of Family Romances.[viii]

The mother, Pamphile, intended the jewelry to do what it usually does: identify her child to the finder as of noble birth. But by including the ring in the bundle, she unknowingly identified the father as her own husband. The men in arbitration do not notice the ring, but Onesimos does, and describes it in detail: it is a finger ring (*daktylion*), gilt over iron, with a stone carved with a bull or a goat (appropriately macho animals for Charisios), and letters saying that it was made by Kleostratos (388). Onesimos is absolutely certain about the significance of the ring, but Habrotonon is not. First, she doesn't recall whether the woman she had met at the festival had a ring or not, and second, she doesn't think that the ring proves that the owner of the ring was the rapist. For, she points out, "Someone else could have gotten the ring from him as pledge, and then lost it—who knows? Or else he lost it gambling, or gave it up in some transaction—a million things like that can happen when men are drinking" (500–510). This is the reasonable argument that keeps cropping up in these tales of recognition. And, as usual, it proves wrong: the ring really does identify the rapist. At the very end of the play, Onesimos quotes a line from a lost Euripidean tragedy, the *Auge*, in which Heracles rapes Auge at a night festival. She bears a child, and the identity of the father is discovered by means of a ring he had left with her (1125).

Onesimos says, at the end, "And now they've recognized each other and all is well" (1123). As usual, how well it all is depends on one's point of view. The most troublesome point for a contemporary reader is the attitude to the rape. When Habrotonon tells how she plans to get Charisios

---

viii. See chapter 2, p. 40.

to confess, she says she is counting on the fact that he's pretty drunk, but also, "I'll flatter him with the things that girls always say, like, 'Oh how bold and rough you were! How brutally you threw me down, and tore my clothes'" (528–530). It is disquieting to hear that this is a how a man would like to hear a woman react (or pretend to react) to a rape.

Charisios's attitude is only slightly better. When he learns that he is the father of the child, he says, "Look at me, the cad. I myself commit a crime, fathering a bastard child. Yet I felt not a scrap of mercy, showed none to that woman who had the same bad fortune. I'm a heartless brute" (895–900). "That woman" refers to Pamphile, and the "bad fortune" is her conception of a child out of wedlock. Charisios does not yet realize that it is his child, but he believes that he and his wife are victims of the same situation, ignoring the difference between the fact that he raped, apparently quite brutally, the woman he impregnated, while Pamphile, he presumes, either willingly took a lover or was herself raped. Not at all the same thing. And he continues in this vein, now addressing himself: "You slimy scum, you won't tolerate a woman's forced misfortune, though you stumbled in just the same way yourself. And she'll treat you tenderly, while you insult her. You're a crude, heartless brute" (913–920). The self-flagellation is all very well and good, but when Habrotonon tells him, "It's your wife's own child," his first reaction is, "I wish it were" (956). That is, he would be happy to learn that he (rather than someone else) had raped his wife, Pamphile.

This problematic attitude remains in Terence's adaptation of Menander's play, though Terence made some interesting changes. The name of the wife, Pamphile, is turned into the name of the husband, Pamphilus, while the wife, renamed Philumena, never appears on stage at all. Habrotonon's imagined masquerade as the girl Charisios raped (all that is left of the usual wife-as-courtesan bed-trick in the clever-wife pattern) is entirely erased. The wife's father, who played a central role in the Menander play, is replaced by the wife's mother, the (husband's) mother-in-law who gives Terence's play its title. Now the rape takes place just two months before the marriage, and the birth seven months after. And now the telltale ring belongs not to the husband but to the wife.

A summary by Gaius Sulpicius Apollinaris, a contemporary of Terence, supplies the main points of Terence's play:

"Pamphilus married Philumena, whom he had raped earlier, while she was still a virgin, without knowing who she was. A ring of hers, which he had seized from her by force, he gave to his girlfriend, the courtesan Bacchis. Subsequently he set out for Imbros without having consummated his marriage. Philumena, now pregnant, was taken back to her own home by her mother on the pretext of being ill, so that her mother-in-law might not learn of her condition. Pamphilus returned, discovered the birth and kept it secret, but refused to take his wife back. His father blamed the affair with Bacchis for alienating the couple. While Bacchis was defending herself against that charge, Philumena's mother, Myrrina, happened to recognize the ring. Pamphilus took back his wife and his son."[11]

The tension in the play is sustained by rearranging the order of the events that Apollinaris presents chronologically in the summary. Unlike Menander's play, which apparently began with a deity telling the audience of the rape, in Terence's play it is not until the final scene that the audience, as well as the husband, learns who it was that raped Philumena before the play began. Pamphilus does not forget his wife; he forgets that he had slept with her before he ever married her and, as usual, his memory is jogged when he sees her ring.

Apollinaris's summary leaves out Terence's expansion of the emotional development, the reasons Pamphilus first rejected, then loved, and finally accepted his wife. Terence adds all of that. A slave tells us that Pamphilus was in love with Bacchis and only married Philumena out of duty to his father. He came to resent his mistress's unkindness, however, and to pity his wife and finally to love her, finding her more compatible, more like himself, than his mistress was.[12] Pamphilus himself confesses that only after he was parted from his wife did he begin to transfer his affections from his mistress to his wife (Terence 300 ff.).

At that point, instead of going to bed with his wife, Pamphilus learns that apparently someone else has already gone to bed with her. Myrrina—his mother-in-law, Philumena's mother—tells him that Philumena was "assaulted before you married her—we don't know the brute's name."[13] Myrrina assumes that the baby is not his, for she counts the months, and the couple have only been married seven months, during the first two of which he had refused to consummate the marriage. But she offers to pretend that the baby is his (a stunning instance of unwitting self-imitation), merely premature, and she is confident that no one will doubt that he is its "true father." Thus she will protect the reputation of her daughter. But then she offers to expose the baby at once, so that it won't be any trouble to him (380 ff.)—although this would presumably not be necessary if he did in fact agree to pretend to acknowledge the child.

Still Pamphilus refuses to take back his wife, even though he feels the strong pull of their companionship and love. He resolves to stifle that love, as he stifled his love for Bacchis (400 ff.). Privately, he wants to take his wife back, but public opinion forces him to reject her. This is the inversion of the situation of his marriage to her in the first place, publicly required, privately rejected.

Myrrina then tells us that Philumena failed to seize anything from her assaulter by which he could afterward be identified, though he took the ring from her finger (570 ff.). She seems to be citing the folktale; she regrets that her daughter, presumably not so well up on her folklore, did not play her role correctly, failing to grab the piece of incriminating evidence (preferably a ring) that the wife-as-mistress conventionally reveals at the end of the story. Instead, in another reversal of the standard plot, the rapist gets *her* ring.

At this point, the two key women players, Bacchis and Myrrina, meet in order to exonerate Pamphilus, who has been accused of adultery. Pamphilus's father has censured him for spurning his wife not for any known fault in her but rather presumably because he is still sleeping with Bacchis. And so Bacchis is asked to swear to Philumena and her mother that she has not been sleeping with Pamphilus since his marriage, which is the truth (another significant departure from the folk theme, which depends upon the husband's adultery after the marriage).

While Bacchis is giving her testimony, Myrrina just chances to see her ring and recognizes it as Philumena's. Then Bacchis remembers that about nine months ago (!), Pamphilus had come home drunk with that very ring, which he gave to her (Bacchis). He said he had assaulted a girl in the street (he didn't know who she was) and had pulled the ring off in the struggle. Now Bacchis tells the story, revealing that Philumena's child is Pamphilus's own son (810 ff.). The meeting of the two women thus unexpectedly exonerates not the husband but the wife, though this had not been the purpose of the meeting for either of them, since Bacchis knew nothing of the pregnancy and Myrrina knew that it was still a well-kept secret.

Bacchis and Pamphilus rejoice at this discovery. Bacchis takes credit for giving Pamphilus great happiness and many blessings, saving his son, "whom he nearly lost through his own fault," and his wife, with whom he thought he would never live again (810 ff). Pamphilus says, "If this is really true, I'm in heaven, the most fortunate of men, so lucky in love!" (850 ff.). What is *wrong* with this man? Why was he, we might ask, so stupid in the first place as to give his mistress the ring that he had stolen from a woman he raped? In *The Queen of Corinth* (written by Fletcher, Field, and Massinger in 1616 or 1617),[14] a man is falsely accused of rape on the evidence of the victim's ring, which he had, in ignorance, received from the rapist (who had taken it from his victim) and given to his fiancée. He pleads innocent, asking who in his right mind would have raped a woman and given her ring to his fiancée, who was bound to meet the woman since they lived in the same house: "[Who,] all to perpetrate unknowne his Lust, / Would fondly in his Person bring a Ring, / And give it a betroth'd Wife ith' same house / Where the poore injur'd Lady liv', and groan'd?"[15] But this is in essence what Pamphilus does, and boasts about it. Siegfried, too,[ix] gives his wife the ring he had taken from Brünnhilde after either raping her, seducing her, or tricking her (depending on which version of the story you read), and, as usual, the ring "proves" that he did whatever it is that he did. Indeed, we may well ask a variant of Fletcher's question about the men in many of the stories of clever wives: Why, if you don't want to be recognized as an adulterer, give the girl the ring at all?

Cultural context goes some way—though, in my humble opinion, not nearly far enough—in justifying Pamphilus: since rape is an acceptable macho thing in his world, he experiences no guilt when his rape of his wife becomes public knowledge. Pamphilus may have given the ring to Bacchis because he assumed that the woman he raped, a woman of some status, would never meet Bacchis, a courtesan. The expectations set up by the folktale and here overturned are not surprising in Greco-Roman comedy, in which the girl almost always ends up with the man who raped her. Moreover, the rape often happens during a nighttime festival, like the festival of Artemis in which Pamphile comes to grief.[16] And the man who first seduces a woman and then marries her was already so common a literary character in Carthage as to have become a cliché, which Terence himself used in other plays.[17] Henry Thomas Riley remarked that Pamphilus's "adventure with Philumena was by no means an uncommon one. We find similar instances mentioned by Plautus; and violence and debauchery seem almost to have reigned paramount in the streets at night."[18] In what amount to Hellenistic sitcoms there are formulaic

---

ix. See chapter 5, p. 113.

plots and characters, and the formulaic response—"Oh, I'm a daddy!"—is pasted into this particular scene even though it is not really appropriate here. Indeed, Pamphilus is relatively sensitive, compared to the common run of men in these plays. We may see problems in Pamphilus's moral world, but within that social world, he is behaving normally. He may not be a cad as far as his own culture is concerned, but if you ask me, the whole culture is a cad.

Worse than that, Terence's protagonist (I can hardly call him a hero) is delighted to learn that he not only raped his wife (well—his friends would say—he was a bit the worse for the liquor, of course, and boys will be boys) but robbed her (even drunkenness is surely no excuse for *that*, hardly a crime of passion, let alone gentlemanly behavior). Yet he may feel *some* sense of shame, since he takes pains to make sure that no one will know about it: "We needn't breathe a word. I'd rather this weren't like the comedies, where everyone ends by knowing everything"[19] (another nice moment of self-referential intertextuality). And we know that he is capable of some degree of introspection, however small, of pity for his wife and sentimental regard for his own tender feelings. How, then, can he say, "I'm in heaven" (more literally, "I am a god," *deus sum*) and "lucky in love" (literally, "so lucky to be so full of the gifts of Venus," *fortunatior venustatisque adeo plenior*)? Why is he incapable of guilt? It is as if he remembers the rape and robbery only long enough to legitimate his son. He does not remember them long enough to apologize to his wife.

He cannot apologize to her because she is not there. Terence erased her. Menander's Pamphile speaks quite a few lines; Terence's Philumena never says a word. Her name evokes, surely intentionally, that of Philomela, famous in Greek mythology for having been raped by Tereus, who, to silence her, cut out her tongue, and she became a nightingale.[20] The silence of the raped Philumena speaks to us through the myth of Philomela. Philumena is so passive that she has vanished altogether and is not present to evoke Pamphilus's sympathy or ours: she does not appear on the stage at all, is not even listed in the dramatis personae.[21] Where other clever wives have the upper hand because they know the truth of the bed-trick while their husbands do not, Philumena is as much in the dark as he is. She does nothing but give birth to a son, offstage. She does not have to trick her rejecting husband into sleeping with her because he has already done so. Nor, even in what is reported of her, does she do anything to exonerate herself; when she has a child she makes no attempt to make the husband acknowledge his paternity (either at the time when he rejects her or when her pregnancy is first revealed), because she does not know about it. Instead, other women—her mother and her husband's mistress—bring the truth to light, still inadvertently and unknowingly (could we say unconsciously?).

This, too, can be blamed on the cultural context. In Greek plays of the fourth century BCE, and the Latin plays based on them, women can't be clever wives because they can't go out and perform sexual seductions. Older wives, and courtesans, do have agency in Greco-Roman plays—hence the importance of the mother-in-law, and of Bacchis. But Philumena does not play the role of the typical Roman wife; she is the virgo, a different type, the young virgin who is always passive. In the conventions of this theater, such a girl can never appear on stage to talk about her sexual experience; it has to be told in third person. Often she never appears at all. The true agent of the discovery here is really no single person at all (though Bacchis claims credit, and Myrrina actually makes the discovery) but the ring—this time not the husband's, but the wife's. The ring is really the only one in the play who knows the story. In the dark, both husband and wife are fooled, but the ring knows and tells the truth. As Bacchis puts it, "And all this train of discovery was set off by a ring!" (810 ff.).

These two plays, by Terence and Menander, raise a conundrum of chronology. Since their plot lines reverse, in essential ways, the plots of almost all the other recorded variants of the tale of the clever wife, I am inclined to call these differences deviations from the prototype. But since Terence and Menander lived long before the authors of almost every other version of the story—with the notable exception of Genesis 38—it would be more correct to say that those later versions deviate from the earlier Greek and Latin prototype. In that case, the evolution of the tales of clever wives could be said to follow the pattern of the tales of Dushyanta and Siegfried:[x] in the earliest versions, the male protagonist is a terrible cad, but in the later versions his character has been, at least in part, whitewashed. I would, however, prefer to regard the Greek and Latin plays as an entirely different subtype of not-so-clever wives, since the wives play little or no roles in them, and to regard Tamar as the earliest Clever Wife of the primary sort.

---

x. See chapter 5, p. 131.

The Dream Ring

Let us turn now from Greco-Roman cynicism to a far more idealistic and romantic tradition, which enriches the prototype of the clever wife with a different sort of variation, namely, stories about a ring (often from a lover) that is first found in a dream world, or what seems to be a dream world, and is then brought back into waking life. Such stories occur widely in the Indian,[22] Persian, and Arabic traditions, which are connected by the Muslim presence in India from the ninth century CE.

A typical example occurs in a sixteenth-century Indian Sufi romance, in which heavenly nymphs transport a prince to the bedroom of a sleeping princess. She awakes and they fall instantly, completely, in love. Promising eternal love, they exchange rings as signs of their pledge to be true to one another, and then fall asleep and awake in their separate homes; eventually they are reunited.[23] An early instance of this genre occurs in the *Ocean of the River of Stories* (also the source of the Muladeva story),[xi] in the tale of the prince of Malava and the princess of Swan Island:

> A prince of Malava named Shridarshana married a princess named Padmishtha and enjoyed all pleasures with her. A merchant found, on the edge of a tank, an image of the god Ganesha, carved out of a jewel. He gave it to that prince, who, recognizing that it was priceless, set it up in a very splendid manner in a temple, as an act of devotion to the god. Ganesha, pleased, had his servants (*ganas*) bring Shridarshana in his sleep to Anangamanjari, the princess of Hamsa-dvipa ("Swan Island"), who had begged the god for a husband. The *ganas* did as he told them.
>
> The prince and princess woke up and fell in love and told one another their names and lineages and where they lived. They quickly shed the mistaken idea that they were merely dreaming, but they exchanged jewels in order to make certain. And though they were full of desire, and eager to consummate their union, the *ganas* put them to sleep again.
>
> As soon as Shridarshana fell asleep, his desire unsatisfied, they took him and carried him back to his own palace. He awoke and saw himself wearing a woman's ornaments and thought, "What is this? Where is the daughter of the king of Swan Island? And where

---

xi. See chapter 6, p. 139.

is that heavenly room? And why am I here? It cannot be a dream, for here are those ornaments on me; so it must be some trick of fate." While he was engaged in these speculations, his loving wife Padmishtha woke up and questioned him and comforted him, and so he passed the night. On the next day, he appeared wearing the ornaments marked with the name of Anangamanjari. His people tried in vain to find out where Swan Island was, and the prince pined away.

Meanwhile the Princess Anangamanjari woke up and remembered what had taken place in the night, and saw her body adorned with Shridarshana's ornaments. And she thought, "These ornaments prove that I cannot have been deluded by a dream, and they fill me with love for an unattainable object." When her father saw her wearing the ornaments of a man, marked with his name, he called for an envoy, who went to Malava and brought Shridarshana to Swan Island. Shridarshana and Anangamanjari married and returned to Malava, where Shridarshana lived in happiness with his two wives.[24]

The image of Ganesha carved out of a jewel at the start of the story sheds a kind of magic on the other jewels, which make dreams come true. This version insists, again and again, on the role of exchanged jewelry—marked with the wearer's name—as proof of a sexual experience that would otherwise be regarded as a dream.

Dream lovers also meet in the "Story of the Two Viziers"[25] in the *Arabian Nights*, in which two djinns (the Arabic equivalent of the Indian *ganas*) catch sight of a beautiful woman and a beautiful man who are asleep in far distant cities. The djinns (one male and one female) think that (a) each is surpassingly beautiful (the male djinn admires the woman, and the female djinn, the man), and (b) they look very much alike. The djinns bring the lovers together for one night and then part them, leaving them to find one another again. Unlike Shridarshana and Padmishtha, these lovers consummate their love on the first night, and this time there is no ring. Instead there is an elaborate series of tests by which the hero proves that he was in bed with the woman: the taste of the pomegranate he cooks;[xii] the reconstruction of an entire room, with all of his clothes,

---

xii. Recall the role of cooked food as an identifying sign, in chapter 2, p. 47.

that he recognizes; the extraordinary sight of a hunchback upside down in a latrine; and so forth. The number and detail of these proofs of identity bear impressive testimony to the power of the signet rings that, in so many other stories, accomplish the same goal, either with or without magic.

The dream ring lives on in the American cinema. In the film of *Peter Ibbetson* (1935, Henry Hathaway), based upon a novel by George du Maurier (1891), Peter and the woman he loves are separated, but they meet in their dreams. When he questions the reality of her presence in a dream, she says, still within the dream, "I *am* here. . . . Do you see this ring? Is it real? If I promise to send it to you tomorrow, then will you believe? Unless I'm really here now, I couldn't promise to send it to you. You'll get this ring tomorrow." The next day, she sends him the ring; when he sees it, he says, "It's real," and the man who brought it says, "Of course it's real. It's a ring." But Peter counters, "It looks like a ring. But it isn't. It's the walls of a world." As in the Arabic tradition, the hard evidence of the ring validates the soft evidence of the dream.

How Budur Almost Raped Her Husband Qamar

The tale of Budur and Qamar-al-Zaman, which takes the theme of the dream ring in new directions, is part of the oldest core of the *Arabian Nights*.[26] It is retold in numerous versions of that much-retold text,[27] in Europe as well as Asia. George Eliot, in *Daniel Deronda* (1876),[xiii] likens her hero, Daniel, to "Camaralzaman" and his beloved Mirah to "Queen Budoor," on several occasions.[28] Unlike "The Story of the Two Viziers,"[29] this story is *not*, in fact, about a dream meeting. Although the characters in it think they have dreamed it, they do actually (magically) meet. In this it is closer to the Indian tale of the prince of Malava. Moreover, in this story, the woman is the one who does the raping, or, rather, stages a homosexual rape of her husband. The rings play different, though still essential, roles:

> King Shahraman had a handsome son named Qamar al-Zaman. The King wanted his son to marry, but Qamar insisted, "Father, I have no wish to marry, nor am I inclined to women, for I have read tales of their guile and heard verses on their cunning." When

---

xiii. See chapter 9, p. 230.

he remained adamant, his father had him imprisoned in a tower. Meanwhile, the beautiful Princess Budur, the daughter of the king of the Interior Islands of China, had said, "I have no wish to marry, for I am a sovereign princess who rules over men, and I do not wish any man to rule over me." Her father imprisoned her in a tower. Two djinns brought Budur to Qamar's tower in her sleep, to determine which was the more beautiful. They laid her beside the young man. They looked very much alike, as if they were brother and sister.

First the jinns awakened Qamar, who was stunned by Budur's beauty and desired to make love to her. He undressed her but could not awaken her, for the djinns kept her asleep. He wondered if this was the woman his father wanted him to marry, or if his father had sent the woman to test the sincerity of his resolve. He therefore refrained from touching her, but as a souvenir, he took from her little finger a valuable ring and placed it on his own little finger. The ring was inscribed with a verse that began and ended thus: "Do not think that I have forgotten your vows. . . . By God, I will remain with you always." Then he turned his back to her and went to sleep.

The djinns then awakened Budur, who assumed that Qamar was the man her father had wanted her to marry. She, in turn, tried to awaken him to make love, but again the djinns kept him asleep. When she saw her ring on his little finger she cried out, "I love you, and you love me, but you turn away from me out of coquetry. You came to me while I was asleep, and I do not know what you did to me, but I will not take my ring from your finger." Then she took his ring from his finger and put it on her own and kissed his mouth and hands and every spot on his body, even his penis. She took him in her arms and embraced him, but felt ashamed of her own desire, and fell asleep.

The djinns returned Budur to China. At dawn, when Budur and Qamar awoke alone, each remembered the other and saw the ring, but each was told that no one had been there in the night. After three years, Budur's stepbrother entered the harem disguised as a woman. He spoke to Budur and promised to help her find her prince. He brought Qamar to the kingdom of Budur's father, and Qamar sent Budur a letter, enclosing her ring. They met and were married; they made love, and slept in each other's arms until the morning.

Then Qamar persuaded Budur to return with him to his father in his own country. One day on the journey Qamar came upon Budur asleep; desiring her, he began to remove her pants, whereupon he discovered a blood-red jewel that she had kept tied to the ribbon of her pants and hidden in her most precious part. He took the jewel outside to look at it in the light, and a bird carried it off. Qamar followed the bird and did not return. Budur awoke to find that he had gone and had taken the jewel, without knowing its secret power. Fearing that her servants would make bold with her if they knew her husband was gone, Budur put on some of Qamar's clothes and a turban like his, veiled the lower part of her face, and departed. No one discovered her identity, for she resembled Qamar so much that everyone took her for him.

In this guise she journeyed to the City of Ebony, where the king said to her, "I have not been blessed with a son, but I have one daughter, whose face and body resemble yours in beauty and grace. Will you be willing to live in my country? I will marry you to my daughter and give you the kingdom." Budur-as-Qamar agreed to this, but when she failed to consummate the marriage, the princess, Hayat al-Nufus, said, "I fear for you from the king, for he has resolved that if you don't take my virginity and consummate the marriage tonight, he will depose you and banish you from his country; he may even become more enraged and kill you." Budur-as-Qamar revealed that she was a woman, and Hayat said, "I will not divulge your secret." She took a chicken, slaughtered it and smeared herself with its blood. Then she took off her pants, and cried out. The women of her family went in to her, and her waiting women let out trilling cries of joy.

After some time, Qamar found the jewel that was the cause of his separation from his wife. He hid it in a cask of gold on a ship that was to take him to the City of Ebony, but the ship sailed without him. When it landed, Budur-as-Qamar, now king of the Ebony Islands, found the jewel. Through it she discovered Qamar's whereabouts and sent her men to capture him and bring him to her. When Qamar arrived, Budur-as-Qamar said to him, "I love you for your surpassing beauty and grace, and if you grant me my desire, I will grant you more favors, make you more prosperous, and appoint you vizier, just as the people made me king, in spite of my youth." When Qamar heard this, he felt embarrassed and blushed until his cheeks seemed on fire, and he said, "I have no need of favors that lead to sin."

Budur-as-Qamar kept arguing with him, reciting many obscene verses about men who prefer anal sex (with boys or with women) to full frontal sex with women. At last Qamar became convinced that there was no escape from compliance with the king's will. He said, "O King of the age, if you must do it, promise me that you will do it to me only once." He opened his trousers, feeling extremely embarrassed and shedding tears in fear. Budur-as-Qamar smiled, took him with her to bed, and said, "After tonight, you will experience nothing offensive again." Then she bent over him, kissing and embracing him and wrapping her leg around his. When Qamar discovered that she lacked male genitals, he said to himself, "Perhaps this king is a hermaphrodite, being neither male nor female." So he said to her, "Your majesty, you don't seem to have a tool like other men. What then moved you to carry on like this?" When Budur-as-Qamar heard this, she laughed until she fell on her back, and she said, "O my darling, how quickly you have forgotten the nights we spent together!" Then she revealed herself to him, and he recognized her as his wife Budur. So he embraced her and she embraced him, and he kissed her and she kissed him, and they made love. Then he began to remonstrate with her, asking, "What made you treat me like this tonight?" She replied, "Do not reproach me, for I only did it in jest, to increase the pleasure and joy."

Qamar married Hayat al-Nufus, and Budur, who was not jealous, willingly became her maidservant and co-wife. Qamar ruled his people well and lived with his wives in happiness and delight and fidelity and cheerfulness, spending one night with each in turn. Eventually Budur returned to her father's kingdom, and her son ruled there, while Hayat's son ruled on the throne of her father, and Qamar al-Zaman went back and ruled his father's kingdom.[30]

Only a few elements of the story of Budur and Qamar can be mapped onto the outline of the clever wife theme. These could be summarized as follows: Qamar vows never to marry. He encounters Budur while she is asleep, gives her his ring and takes hers. He leaves without consummating their union. Searching for her, he sends her a letter, enclosing her ring. He marries her, but again leaves her. Budur disguises herself as a king and seduces Qamar, who does not recognize her in her disguised form. At last she reveals herself to him and he welcomes her. She bears him a son who becomes king of her country.

The husband's refusal to sleep with his wife, in the folktale, appears here first in the form of Qamar's refusal to marry any woman at all and then in the episode in which he abandons Budur when he steals her jewel. It is also echoed in his violent resistance to sleeping with her when he thinks she is a man. The riddles of the folktale appear here in the riddling verses that Budur-as-Qamar recites to Qamar, verses that are simultaneously obscene, misogynistic, homophobic, and blasphemous.[31] And the ring that identifies the impregnator in other stories here appears both as the rings with which the lovers persuade others of the reality of their encounter and as the ring with which Qamar identifies himself to Budur as her husband. The son is not, as he usually is, the pivot of the first part of the story, with its riddles and rings, but he does appear at the end of this tale.[32]

The Arabian story can no more be reduced to this set of themes than Mozart's Twelve Variations on the tune of the French folk song "Ah vous dirai-je, Maman" can be reduced to the jingle known in English as "Twinkle Twinkle Little Star." These narrative bones are grotesquely bare, but other details of the Arabian text flesh them out in interesting ways and tie up some loose ends that otherwise seem to play no significant role in the story as we have it.

Budur and Qamar exchange two rings in a mock wedding ceremony, but neither ring is intentionally given: on the contrary, each of the lovers takes the ring from the hand of a sleeping partner who cannot give it freely. In one version of the story,[33] Qamar puts one of his own rings on Budur's finger when he takes her ring; she does not take his ring from him, nor does her ring have an inscription.[34] Departing slightly from the conventional roles of rings as proof that the lovers have slept together, the rings in the tale of Budur and Qamar, like the jewelry in the tale of Shridarshana and Anangamanjari, prove only that they have met and fallen in love, but that is enough.

First, Qamar uses Budur's ring to persuade his father that he really did spend the night with Budur. Significantly, he likens the ring's power of proof to that of a blood-stained sword as proof of a killing, and says, "How could all this be a lie, when the matter of the ring is true? Were it not for the ring, I would have thought that it was a dream. This is her ring on my little finger at this moment. Look at the ring, your majesty, and see how valuable it is." The fact that the ring is valuable is part of the proof: the dream woman was a princess.[xiv] Later, Budur's ring, sent with a letter, is what makes her recognize Qamar after their first separation and before their marriage. In the version of the story in *The Arabian Nights' Entertainment* (the first English translation, in 1706), the letter says: "He presumes to present you with his ring, as a token of his passion; and, in exchange, would be proud to receive yours, which he encloses in this billet. If you will condescend to return it, as a reciprocal assurance of your love, he will reckon himself the happiest of all lovers."[35]

Qamar's ring is equally useful to Budur. It convinces her that she didn't dream their encounter, and it convinces her stepbrother, too. When he hears that Qamar had exchanged rings with his dream woman, he puts two and two together. But Budur never uses Qamar's ring to convince anyone else, and so she is locked up in the harem as a madwoman, until her stepbrother rescues her. In the *Arabian Nights' Entertainment*, Budur does attempt to use the ring to persuade her father, but in vain: " 'But that your majesty may no longer doubt whether I have seen this cavalier, whether he has lain with me, whether I have caressed him, . . . see, if you please this ring.' She then reached forth her hand, and shewed the king a man's ring on her finger. The king did not know what to make of all this; but as he had confined her for mad, so now he began to think her more mad than ever."[36] And so he still locks her up as a madwoman. In both texts, the ring always works as hard evidence when the man invokes it, but not always when the woman does.

As in several European medieval romances,[xv] the ring is inscribed with the foreknowledge that it will be given to someone who may abandon, betray, and/or forget the giver. ("Do not think that I have forgotten your vows, no matter how long your cruel disdain lasts.") And this is precisely what happens when the role of the ring(s) is taken up by the "blood-red jewel" that is hidden in Budur's genitals and acts as a metaphor for them,[xvi] a "metonymy of sex."[37] But what of the writing on the jewel? *The Arabian Nights' Entertainment* tells us that this talisman was a kind of Chinese horoscope, a scheme of Budur's nativity, drawn from the constellations of heaven, which her mother had made for her as a charm that would keep her from any harm as long as she had it about her.[38] It was a carnelian

---

xiv. Recall the ring's similar proof of royalty in the tale of Ratnavali, in chapter 3, p. 66.

xv. See chapter 4, p. 91.

xvi. See chapter 1, p. 10.

engraved with unknown figures and characters, which would function to identify her. Andras Hamori has this to say about it:

> "The indecipherable jewel snatched from the hero by a predatory creature might be an image of anxiety about sexual possession, of a worry (justified by later events) much like Gratiano's about Nerissa's ring.[xvii] Or, the failure to read the inscription on this intimate jewel might be seen as an encoding of fears of inadequacy. ('He does not know its secret,' says Budur). Anxiety about the very nature of sexual passion would fit too: like magic, sexuality threatens to cut across the order of things, and sexual magic is like the magic of rings and lamps in being detachable from the rest of the personality."[39]

We will return to this theme of sexual anxiety at the close of this chapter. Here let us just remark that in his ignorance of the power of the jewel/ ring he takes from the sleeping Budur, Qamar resembles Siegfried,[xviii] who does not know the power of the ring that he takes from Brünnhilde, sometimes in her sleep, sometimes after raping her.

In several Arabic texts, what is hidden in Budur's pants is not just a jewel but a ring set with a blood-red jewel.[40] The widely distributed theme of a ring of identity that is lost and then found in a fish (reuniting separated lovers)[xix] is here conflated with the also common theme in which a bird mistakes a ruby for flesh and carries it off, causing the separation of lovers who are reunited when the ruby is found in the craw of the bird.[41] These myths convey the sense of the unbelievable, unlikely good luck of finding a jewel in an animal; the odds of finding a jewel in a bird may not be quite so astronomical as those of finding a ring in a fish, but close. The jewel in the tale of Budur, however transformed, still bears most of the weight of the proof of identity that it has in the plot of the tale of the clever wife. The skeleton plot of the clever wife thus provides a framework that reveals Budur as the heroine of the story.

Budur breaks out of the initial conventional situation of amazing physical identity with her lover to become a most unconventional woman, and someone quite different from him in every way—more active, more

---

xvii. See chapter 4, pp. 107–109.

xviii. See chapter 5, p. 111.

xix. See chapter 2, p. 25.

powerful, more deceptive. Yet she can only accomplish her goal of union with him by pretending to be him, using her cleverness to play upon the convention of their identical beauty. And in the course of her maneuvers, she threatens to rape him. To do this, she cross-dresses.

As jewelry is often strongly gendered, the exchange of rings (and other things) amounts to a kind of minor cross-dressing, which may have inspired the more extensive cross-dressing in tales like that of Budur and Qamar. The connection between cross-dressing and rings that identify disguised women is widespread; we have seen it in *The Merchant of Venice*.[xx] In a Jewish story from the Persian oral tradition, a woman who cross-dresses uses a ring to find the husband whose father has appeared to her in a dream and given her the ring.[42] A number of clever wives cross-dress[43] and are not recognized. In an Indian variant, in which the woman cross-dressed as a man in order to travel safely, and later disguised herself as a cowherd's daughter, "The husband was attracted by her beauty, but did not recognize her, and proposed marriage";[44] and when another woman cross-dressed, her husband was "thoroughly ignorant of her real character, although he had constantly seen her at *darbar*, and had often heard her speak."[45] Budur has been compared with the Greek mythic princess Kainis, who is raped and obtains the boon of being transformed into a man, in order to be invulnerable.[46]

Unlike most cross-dressing wives, Budur does not bother to change back into a woman before she seduces her husband, which results in the strange case of the woman who threatened her own husband with homosexual rape. Budur may well blame Qamar for having left her (and robbed her: she comments, blandly, "It seems that he has taken the jewel and gone") as well as for turning his back to her in bed on their first encounter. Qamar's initial rejection of Budur leaves her with the suspicion that he might have raped her in her sleep: "You came to me while I was asleep, and I do not know what you did to me."

Budur both loves and hates Qamar. Her unexpressed (repressed?) resentment for being rejected, twice, may best explain her quite evident sadistic pleasure in tormenting Qamar when he thinks she is the king. She plays the trick on her husband in order to exert power over him as he had exerted power over her, to put him in danger of being raped just as his absence had put her in danger of being raped. Her own rather lame excuse

---

xx. See chapter 4, p. 107.

("Do not reproach me, for I only did it in jest, to increase the pleasure and joy") explains nothing but the trickster's pleasure in manipulating others and wielding power over them by virtue of the trickster's knowledge and the victim's ignorance.[47] The closeted sexual motives seem to me to make the best sense of this twisted story. Budur's initial refusal to marry at all is, like Brünnhilde's, the female equivalent of the male sword-in-the-bed theme. A wife in drag actually rapes her husband in another variant of the tale in which there is "a parodized sodomy which the woman carries out in the guise of a physician with a radish, and thus emasculates the man and dominates him."[48]

Rape and rejection appear together in yet another form near the end of this story. For when each of the two women has borne and raised a son, each woman falls in love with the other's son, propositions him, is rejected, and accuses the boy of rape. Qamar believes the women at first and orders the boys killed, but they are spared and prove their innocence with the help of the fathers of Budur and Qamar. We know this as the "Potiphar's wife" scenario in the Hebrew Bible (Genesis 39), and the Greek myth of Phaedra, in which rejection is reprocessed as rape. It is yet another example of the combination of these two sexual scenarios that appear to be polar opposites. The tale of Qamar and Budur conflates the two sexual extremes in two different ways: first, a mock rape as a revenge for rejection (Budur-as-Qamar with Qamar), and then the accusation of rape made in revenge for rejection (the two queens' calumny against the two sons).

When Budur-as-Qamar teased Qamar about forgetting how she was in bed, she laughed "until she fell on her back," precisely the sexual position for a woman that the obscene poems explicitly rejected (advising the women to turn over on their stomachs) and that therefore may be an invitation for sex in the missionary position. The little touches of revenge in Budur's trick are bitter. In their first encounter, she had touched his penis and felt ashamed; now she gets him to touch what he thinks is her penis, and enjoys his confusion when it is not there. Her revenge extends into the last part of the story, when she almost makes him destroy his son (by the other wife) by claiming that the boy had raped her.

One of the obscene verses that Budur-as-Qamar recites to Qamar implies that one reason that Budur-as-Qamar does not sleep with women is that s/he does not want to have children. He chooses to sleep with men, writes the poet, because they do not menstruate or bear children; he does not wish to overpopulate the world with brats.[49] A legitimate son is,

however, the raison d'être of the more typical clever wife, and Budur does
have a son, though for a while he is a problem rather than a solution. The
blithe assertion that Qamar "lived with his wives in happiness and delight
and fidelity and cheerfulness, spending one night with each in turn,"
evokes the Middle-Eastern tradition that goes awry in the Hebrew Bible, in
the story of Rachel and Leah, and fares little better here, where the "fidelity
and cheerfulness" is certainly short-lived. The fact that the solution to all
of this transvestism and quasi-incest is to send the women home to live
with their fathers might give a Freudian pause, but Qamar, too, ends up
in his father's realm, and it was in order to return to his father that Qamar
left Budur in the first place. Here I think the return to the fathers indicates
little more than one more example of the virulent misogyny (and in this
case the literal patriarchy) of the story.

The Vizier's Daughter

A clever wife cross-dresses in a story that has no rape but does develop, in
extraordinary detail, a kind of sexual violence that may provide an explanation for the sexual violence in other versions of the tale that we have
considered. In this Turkish variant, collected by a German anthropologist
in the late nineteenth century, the woman has no name except a generic
patronymic; as Muladeva's wife was just the Brahmin's daughter, this
woman is the Vizier's daughter. We can recognize her as a clever wife
through the motifs of the seal ring, the riddle, the cleverness, and the masquerade of the rejected wife:

> A certain prince had a Vizier, who was the father of a twelve-year-
> old daughter. Hearing the maiden's cleverness praised, the prince
> called the Vizier to him and propounded a riddle, which the Vizier
> was to answer within three days or lose his head: What is a kid at ten
> years, a fox at twenty, a wolf at thirty, a tiger at forty, a halter at fifty,
> and "halted" at sixty? After three days had passed, and the Vizier
> could find no answer, his daughter gave him the solution: a human
> child, frisky as a kid at ten, sly as a fox at twenty, brave as a wolf at
> thirty, strong as a tiger at forty, lazy and slothful as a horse in a hal-
> ter at fifty, and at sixty, "halted," unable to do any work at all. When
> the prince discovered that the Vizier's daughter had given him the
> answer, he said, "If that is the case, the maiden will do for my wife,
> and I will hold her above all my forty wives." She demanded that,

before they were married, the prince should bring her a white elephant and a man without sorrow.

The elephant was procured from another prince within a year, but for three years the prince searched in vain for a man without sorrow. Finally he came upon a ruler who drank wine in the midst of his assembled people, laughing and joking. When the prince asked this king if he was, as he appeared to be, a man without sorrow, the king invited him to come home with him. There the prince saw the king's very beautiful wife, and beside her a foul, black giant[50] and two children. When the woman saw the king, she said, "What are you doing here?" and boxed his ears and drove him out of the house. Then the king explained: "This woman is my wife, and the giant is my slave. When I took some medicine during an illness, I lost my virility and could not satisfy my wife, and so every day she begged me to set her free to take another man. I told her not to leave me, since I was the King and would lose face if the people learned of this, but to find a handsome young man and live with him. And so she lives with this giant and bore him two children, and kisses him whenever he comes near her, but kicks me out. No one has greater sorrow than I."

The prince returned home and called the Vizier and said, "I have found no man without sorrow in all the world, but even so, give me your daughter." The prince then married the Vizier's daughter, but did not live with her. Instead, he went off hunting, announcing that he would be gone for nine years. As he left, he gave his wife an empty chest, sealed with his seal, and he commanded her to fill it with gold and silver without opening it, and he gave her a mare that, he commanded, must give birth to a foal that was just like his black stallion. He also told his wife that she must bear a child, instruct him well, and send the child to him, mounted upon the foal. Then he rode off on his stallion, taking his seal.

After he had been gone three days, the wife attired herself like a prince, dressed up four hundred maidens like men, and rode out after her husband. She pitched her tent near the place where he was staying, thus attracting his attention. Hospitalities were exchanged, but the prince did not recognize his wife in disguise. The prince proposed that they should play "Dame" (checkers), and after a while the wife-as-prince proposed that they play for a stake. So each wagered his horse, saddle, trappings, and seal. The wife-as-prince won, and retiring to her tent with the seal, she let the black stallion cover the mare. Opening the chest, she filled it with gold and silver and re-sealed it with her husband's seal. She then sent the stallion, trappings, and seal back to the prince. The next evening, the wife-as-prince proposed that they play for a woman. She purposely lost, and told the prince that she would send him a beautiful female slave. Retiring to her tent, she then assumed that disguise, and came back to her husband. He was aroused by the wife-as-slave-girl and lay that night with her. Then they drank spirits, and the prince became drunk. The wife-as-slave-girl gave the prince a box on the ear. Angry and drunken, he chased the wife-as-slave-girl away from his tent. She collected her retinue and returned home. After nine months, nine days and nine hours, she bore a son, and the black mare bore a foal. She instructed the son well, and had him tutored by a mullah from the age of five.

At the end of the nine years, the prince returned. The Vizier's daughter sent her son to meet his father, riding on the black horse. The prince was told that the boy was his son, born of the Vizier's daughter. At first he was angry, thinking that the child was not his own. Then his wife showed him the chest, told him that the horse on which the boy was riding was the issue of her mare and his own horse, and that he had fathered the boy during the night he had spent with her when she was disguised as a slave-girl; she related the whole story. The prince was overjoyed at what she had done. Because she was exceedingly clever and well taught, he exalted her above all his other wives. After he had lived with her for many days, he finally died.[51]

The king's seal on the treasure is probably a seal ring. At the very least, it plays the role usually played by the seal ring: to stamp and identify the person who slept with the woman. The (gold) sealing ring is conflated with the sealed box of gold as a symbol of virginity, like the sealed trunk that is the symbol of Imogen's chastity in *Cymbeline*.[xxi]

Here, something has gotten into that trunk, though it remains sealed, a metaphor for the womb and for the surface of a woman that the true lover must penetrate. This is precisely what her husband cannot do: he fails to recognize his wife either when she is de-sexualized (as a boy) or

---

xxi. See chapter 4, p. 106.

hyper-sexualized (as a slave girl). The male costume may also account for the unusual aggression and agency of the woman in this version of the story: it gives her the courage to challenge the men.

The riddle that the prince poses for the Vizier is about the decline of human life. It is answered by a second riddle, which the Vizier's daughter sets for the prince in return, on the same general subject—the inevitability of sorrow. This second riddle turns out to have two answers, one of which is also about decline, now sexual decline, the tale of the impotent king. And this raises the issue of sexual performance.

Though the prince searches in vain for a man without sorrow (a variant of the old Buddhist parable of the impossible task given to a woman who prays for medicine that will bring back her dead child—find a house in which there has been no death),[52] what he finds instead is the reason for the man's sorrow: his wife has taken a lover. The prince learns this lesson so well that he rejects his own wife, who reappears in disguise and boxes his ears just as the wife of the impotent king had boxed his. But in the end the prince comes to realize the half-full optimism of Muladeva's story:[xxii] there is at least *one* woman without evil, or, as the prince puts it here, one "exceedingly clever and well-taught" woman, the exception to the rule. This is the male view, of course, the dominant view of the storyteller.

But we may also find women's voices in male texts,[53] and the woman's voice here tells another story: as in the tale of Muladeva's wife, the husband, in the end, is proud of his clever wife. A feminist twist in this tale is apparent in the unusual feature that the wife of the king cannot be satisfied or impregnated by her husband, not because he rejects her (as the husband of the clever wife does) but because he himself cannot perform. Unlike the clever wife, who jumps through hoops to win the privilege of her husband's sexual favors, the wife of the impotent king simply takes up with another man she fancies, a common-sense move that short-circuits the entire conventional scheme of the folktale. The storyteller may not approve of it, but he includes it, thus perhaps inadvertently allowing a fifth column of proto-feminism to slip into his story.

Why do none of the clever wives, including the one in this very story, the Vizier's daughter, think of this simple but elegant solution to the problem of the rejecting husband—go and get pregnant by another man? Because of the double problem of inheritance and inherited characteristics. There has to be proof that the husband is the father of his son.

---

xxii. See chapter 6, p. 144.

The proofs in this story are multiple (or over-determined, as Freud would have said). The sealed treasure is backed up by the more significant double evidence of the foal and the human child, part of the Indo-European corpus of stories of a queen and a mare who give birth to male offspring simultaneously.[54] (In one Norse variant, the mare foals simultaneously with a woman who had cross-dressed to get pregnant.)[55] The birth of the child of the Vizier's daughter is flanked by two other birth-stories, of the foal and of the illegitimate children of the impotent king. These two supplemental births are also bound together by the motif of black skin: the main protagonists are presumably fair-skinned, but the stallion and mare as well as the lover of the impotent king's wife are black. And the illegitimate children of the black lover? Are they, too, black, like the stallion's foal? Blackness in the foal serves as proof that it was sired by the king's stallion; presumably the children fathered by the black lover are also black. The black children of white wives (or the reverse, in the case of Persinna, the Ethiopian queen)[xxiii] cause terrible problems in many myths,[56] and that may explain why more women didn't take the uppity queen's route: there is great danger in attempting to foist off non-resembling children as legitimate heirs to the throne. (Recall the king's fear that he will lose face before his people, evidence that there is some force of convention holding his authority in place.) Most wives of men who may have been impotent or simply unsatisfactory wouldn't have wanted to risk having other men father children who might be rejected.

The main proof of the paternity of the clever wife's child, however, is not just the existence of a horse and a sealed treasure but words: the clever wife tells him the story, and he knows she is right. Her story takes the place of his seal ring as the final arbiter. "And then she told the whole story, in front of everyone," says the tale of Muladeva's wife.[xxiv] Though the Vizier's daughter does not act as willfully as does the wife of the impotent king, she has a power (or, if you prefer, agency) that is extreme and complete.

The story lives on. Monia Hejaiej recorded a variant, still entitled "The Vizier's Daughter," in early 1990:[57]

The Vizier's daughter, 'Aysha, out-riddled the king to save her father's life. When the king asked for her hand in marriage, she

---

xxiii. See chapter 2, p. 40.

xxiv. See chapter 6, p. 141.

guessed that he was motivated by anger because she had embarrassed him and forced him to spare her father. She told her father,
"I don't think he really wants to marry me. I can see what he's up
to. He wants to take his revenge . . . and now he wants to kill me."
Still she agreed to marry him, but took the precaution, in advance,
of having a secret tunnel built between her father's home and the
palace. The king and 'Aysha married, but immediately he locked
her up in a small cell. When, months later, he went off on a trip
to Sfax, she said, "I have a sister there who is very like me. Give
her my love." She then escaped through the tunnel, dressed as a
man, and arrived in Sfax before him. Dressed again as a beautiful
woman, she tricked him (and her father the Vizier, who did not
recognize her, either), slept with him, and asked him to give her
something as proof that he had spent the night with her. He gave
her, on three successive visits, over three years, his royal armband
with his seal, his royal chain of office with his seal engraved on it,
and, finally, his royal ring with his seal engraved on it. On each
occasion she slept with him and nine months later gave birth to
a son.

One day, news reached 'Aysha that the king was going to marry
his cousin. She found out when the bride's trousseau ceremony was
to be held, dressed each of her children in one of the three pieces
of royal insignia, and sent them there to mess things up. If asked,
they were to say that it was their father's house and they had a right
to make a mess in it. And so they broke the bride's new plates and
glasses and used the embroidered silk cushions as horses, and said,
"It is our father's house and we have every right to do as we please."
The bride's mother, horrified, summoned the king, who recognized
his ring, armband, and chain of office. He realized that 'Aysha had
outsmarted him again; the ceremony became 'Aysha's postponed
wedding celebration.[58]

The riddle of the unbegotten child is here, as so often, implied rather than
spelled out: The day after the wedding, the king shuts 'Aysha up in a small
cell and asks her, "What makes a woman beautiful?" "Her children," she
replies, and he walks out, cursing her never to have any joy of children.
At that point the woman narrator says: "Her marriage was unconsummated, so how could she have children?" The children then save their
mother not through any extraordinary skill (like thieving) or even by their

resemblance to their father, but simply by behaving like children, naughty, spoiled children at that: they break up the place. The actual proof then comes not through the child(ren) but through the ring.

The naughty children are a touch that a narrator who was a mother may well have contributed, and the voice of the woman narrator of this version is strong, adding details not found in other versions told by narrators who are male or of unknown gender. Now the Vizier's daughter has a name, 'Aysha, and each time she gives birth, "The baby crawled, toddled, held to the wall and walked. In real life a child grows in a year or two, but just in a couple of words in a tale." As in other Muslim variants, each child is put in the care of a mullah, or of "a tutor who was entrusted with his religious education and general knowledge," but this time he is also, first, put in the care of a wet nurse. 'Aysha serves meals on a Louis Quinze dinner service, and the woman who hopes to marry the king has in her trousseau another Louis Quinze dinner service as well as a couscous steamer, embroidered bedsheets (cross stitch, Nabel stitch, appliqué, fleurs-de-lys, etc.), and other charming domestic details characteristic of women's stories.[59]

But there are also original insights that are not necessarily gender-linked. The storyteller remarks that the first time 'Aysha seduced her husband while disguised as another woman, "He went to sleep with the woman. After all, she was legally his wife." This is, of course, part of the charm of the tale of the clever wife—the husband gets to have all the fun of committing adultery without actually breaking the law—but few texts bother to spell it out. This text also interjects reason at three critical points. First, it accounts for the "strange" woman's uncanny resemblance to 'Aysha by creating an imaginary sister and letting family resemblance explain the doubling. Second, it has 'Aysha explicitly ask not just for jewelry but for proof—why? Why is he not suspicious of this request? Or, rather, why, in all the other versions, does he give the jewelry to her without being asked? Just payment for a night's services? Why not cash, or at least a woman's jewelry, not a man's ring? And, third, 'Aysha asks not just for his jewelry but for his royal insignia, as proof that her lover was the king. These details retrospectively inspire us to ask similar reasonable questions about all the other versions that gloss over these practical matters. We will return to these questions.[xxv]

Most interesting of all is what is *not* in this version, the dog that doesn't bark,[60] another use for intertextuality. 'Aysha cross-dresses as a man, but she never encounters her husband in this form, as Budur does. Even in the nineteenth-century version of the tale of the Vizier's daughter, the encounter that the wife-as-prince has with her husband is merely an asexual prelude to the sexual encounter that she has as slave girl. Why does the storyteller put in the cross-dressing and then drop it? It is not such an essential traditional element of the plot that she could not leave it out, though it is popular enough to slip in uninvited, as it were. What is 'Aysha's motivation for cross-dressing? Perhaps just to travel in safety, the explicit reason given in several other variants. But, just as this variant inspires us to ask questions of other variants, so, too, other variants, such as the tale of Budur and Qamar, where the sexual encounter takes place while she is still cross-dressed, shed intertextual light on the atavistic, truncated episode of cross-dressing in the tale of the Vizier's daughter.

Parental Imprinting and Uncertain Fathers

The tale of the Vizier's daughter raises the issue of sexual deficiency. In other tales of clever wives that we have considered, too, the sexual rejection that the wives experience as the back of the man in bed or the empty pillow is also a dramatic expression of his sexual deficiency. The juxtaposition of rejection and rape in the Greco-Roman and Arabic tales that we have just considered reveals the sexual ambivalence of the man (and, in the case of Budur, the woman) who perpetrates the rape. Performance anxiety is often relieved by a subordinate woman with no legal connection, a woman of lower class (or caste, in the Indian examples) or another culture, the woman the clever wife often pretends to be. In such an encounter, the ring bears witness to the man's performance and the woman's pleasure.

If we consider the fear of inability to perform or of sexual deficiency as an ingredient in male rejection we may gain new insights into the relevance of the signet ring in these stories. For to the man's fear of deficiency we must now add his uncertainty about the paternity of his son. When the husband in one South Indian variant that we have considered declares that he will shut his wife up, he says, "If I don't, I wouldn't be my father's son." It is surely significant that the scene in the *Ramayana* where Rama sends Sita away forever comes right after the moment when, shortly after he has brought her back from the island where the ogre Ravana has kept her captive for many years,[xxvi] he learns that she is pregnant.[61] Is he worried that Ravana is the father? In Nina Paley's contemporary retelling, *Sita Sings the Blues*, the Indian commentators on the soundtrack say, "Is Ravana the father?" And we see Rama looking at Sita's womb and seeing a little Ravana in it.

"No one knows who your father is," the children taunt the son of Muladeva;[xxvii] and that is the heart of the matter. Muladeva doesn't know who the father of his son is, either. The men in these stories are desperate to find proof that they are in fact the fathers of the children that their wives bear, and with good reason: they believe that their own survival depends upon it. A Sanskrit text from perhaps as early as the eighth century BCE expresses the belief that the father actually is reborn as his son:

> The father enters his wife; he becomes an embryo inside her, who is now his mother. In her he becomes new again and is born in the tenth month. And so the wife is called wife (*jaya*) because he is born (*jayate*) again in her.[62]

When the Indian lawmaker Manu repeats this over a thousand years later, he adds: "The wife brings forth a son who is just like the man with whom she makes love; that is why he should guard his wife zealously, in order to keep his progeny pure."[63] The crucial resemblance is here directly dependent upon both the wife's love and the husband's ability to keep her away from other men.

The father thus reproduces himself the way a stamp might imprint a coin, and indeed the metaphor of coinage is often used to refer to a false woman.[xxviii] Thus in Shakespeare's *The Winter's Tale*,[xxix] the lethally jealous Leontes says to the son of Polixenes (the man he wrongly suspects of fathering his, Leontes's, child), "Your mother was most true to wedlock, prince, / For she did print your royal father off, / Conceiving you" (5.1.124–125). The related metaphor of the signet ring imprinting the unique signature of a man lies at the heart of the story of the clever wife.

---

xxvi. See chapter 3, p. 63.

xxvii. See chapter 6, p. 140.

xxviii. See chapter 1, p. 4.

xxix. See chapter 2, p. 52.

Paternal nervousness is often expressed through the metaphor of stamp-ing the embryo with the father's seal. This is yet another meaning of the seal ring. Aristotle is, as so often, the original culprit: he and his followers believed that the father, with his semen, stamps the female matter (made from menstrual flow) to produce his image in the fetus. From these active male and passive female elements, the fetus is shaped just as "a ball comes into being from the wax and the form."[64] As Lorraine Daston summarizes this theory,

> "If all goes well, the offspring is a perfect copy of the father, the male form having flawlessly imprinted itself on the soft female matter. . . . In the ideal case, the male semen imprints the soft female matter with the form of the father as a seal imprints wax (or, in a variant on the theme, as a coin is stamped with the likeness of the sover-eign). Not coincidentally, Aristotle invoked the very same metaphor of a seal imprinting wax to describe how normal, veridical perception worked: the sense impression was transported through the body by a form, the 'species,' imprinted on the vaporous animal spirits that fed heart and brain, 'in the way in which a piece of wax takes the imprint of a signet-ring.' "[65]

As Daston neatly puts it, "signet rings mimic the fantasy of authenticity in both perception and conception."[66]

The belief that the father lives on in the son only if that son is a true copy of him is the driving force behind the paranoia of paternal insecu-rity, well captured by the Latin legal phrase, *pater incertus* ("the father is uncertain"), or the variant, *pater semper incertus* ("the father is always uncertain"), often coupled with the phrase *mater semper certa est* ("the mother is always certain").[67] It is usually interpreted to mean that the father is "uncertain" in the sense of "unknowable, impossible to ascer-tain," but it also has the overtones of "uncertain" in the sense of "nervous, full of doubt," a meaning highly relevant to our corpus of narratives. In our day, it is nicely translated by the South Chicago saying, "Mama's baby, papa's maybe."[68] The stories of clever wives pit male fears about legitimacy, about corrupted paternity, against women's knowledge about sexuality.

We have noted the recurrent statement, in the tales of clever wives, that the son uncannily resembles his father. As Shakuntala puts it, "The son born from his wife is like a man's face in a mirror. . . . your other self, your reflection seen in a clear pond."[xxx] The son is, in a sense, what Saint Augustine called a "worsened resemblance,"[69] a second-rate copy, while the mother is, in this model, either invisible, or implicated in this copying process through the stigmatizing of resemblance itself as the "mother of falseness," or, finally, vindicated in her chastity by the "proof" that her son was not fathered by some man other than her husband. The visual criterion is essential in this pre-DNA world, in which paternity is difficult if not impossible to establish; the husband imprints his image on his child even as his identity is imprinted on his signet ring. And the need to be reassured of that stamp of approval fuels the father's paranoia.

The plot thickened when[70] it came to be widely believed that the image of what a pregnant woman saw or even imagined, and in particular whatever frightened her,[71] would stamp itself upon the embryo she was carrying and leave a mark on the child. Thus a woman who thought of her lover while being impregnated by her husband might give birth to a child that looked like the lover. This "maternal impression" or "maternal imprinting," as it was sometimes called, did grant some power to the woman in the fashioning of a child, a real improvement over the earlier view that she was simply a receptacle for the all-powerful semen. But it also led to the false accusation of some innocent women whose children did not happen to resemble their fathers closely enough for patriarchal comfort. A famous victim of this sort of thinking was the black Ethiopian queen Persinna,[xxxi] who conceived a white child because she had gazed, during the act of conception, on a picture of Andromeda.[72] (Greek artistic convention generally represented Andromeda with white skin.) Apparently the maternal imagination is still alive and well today in the field of in vitro fertilization, though transferred from sight to sound; one German doctor who does the in vitro fertilization under a microscope is absolutely convinced that if she plays Wagner while doing it the resulting test tube babies will become musical geniuses.[73]

The theory of maternal imprinting must also have kept many adulteresses from being accused and punished. After all, if a man's child is the spitting image of his best friend, there is a more logical explanation than maternal imprinting. But then it was argued that a woman who knew this would think of her husband while in the arms of her lover, in order to

---

xxx. See chapter 3, p. 70.

xxxi. See chapter 2, p. 40.

conceal her crime, by imprinting the love child with her husband's features, and this backlash cast suspicions upon faithful women whose children did in fact resemble their husbands.[74] Sometimes you cannot win.

Perhaps texts that seem, in the end, to value the woman's cleverness reflect a cultural suspicion that intelligence, like complexion, can be inherited, even from the distaff side, perhaps even by maternal imprinting, so that in a world of dangerous court intrigues it's a good idea for the dynasty to find a really smart wife for the king. Perhaps the other sort of text, in which the clever woman is never truly loved, is either ignorant of these genetic factors or (as was the case in most of our texts) assumes that the father alone, not the mother, hands on his characteristics to the child.[75]

A topsy-turvy version of the rejected impregnated wife appears in the English Renaissance drama *The Hollander* (1636), in which a man refuses to sleep with his wife not because he rejects her but because he is insanely jealous of her; he wants to have proof that if she becomes pregnant, she has betrayed him.[76] A similar but even more drastic solution to the torment of paternal uncertainty is recorded in an anecdote told by Poggio Bracciolini (1380–1459):

> A man from Gubbio, called Giovanni, was fearfully jealous of his wife and did not know by what means he could positively assure himself that she was not deceiving him with other men. Finally he hit upon a plan worthy of a jealous man; he castrated himself, saying: "Now, if my wife should become with child, I will be convinced that she has committed adultery."[77]

Far-fetched though the tales of clever wives may be, they are, at least, an improvement on this scenario.

The ghost of this mythology hovers over these stories of clever wives, which regard the father's signet ring as proof of paternity, against all logic, because the father in the stories (often telling the stories) wants something hard, like a piece of jewelry (which, after all, can get lost but not so easily broken as a heart), to prove what can in fact never be proven: that the child is his own. Even though shamed, he is happy to have the son, and to have seen his wife prove her fidelity; he accepts the lie that "the ring proves it's your kid" because he so dearly wants to believe that it's his kid.

One might hope that DNA would lay this ghost to rest at last, but alas, no. DNA can offer proof of paternity and is resorted to by a surprisingly high number of nervous men, many of whom turn out to have good cause to be nervous. One such DNA test proved that a woman who had twins had slept with two guys within a week, and one twin belonged to one and the other to the other. An obstetrician-gynecologist at a Manhattan hospital, quoted in the *New York Times*, called this a case of "superfecundation" (in this case heteropaternal superfecundation), and the *Times* remarked that it was "a rare phenomenon classically illustrated in medical textbooks with a black baby and a white baby who are twins."[78] The vivid contrast between black and white skin is evidently as useful to medical examples of suspicious paternity as it has been traditionally for the mythological parallels.

But we have come to learn that even DNA is a far from certain method of identification, and in any case, a DNA test cannot prove chastity or fidelity, or cure sexual jealousy. It might simply prove that the particular child in question was (or was not, as the case may be) fathered by the man who paid for the test.[79] Who knows, your wife may have been thinking about your DNA when she slept with some other guy, and imprinted the genes with it. As Robert Pippin has put it,

> "It is as if, apart from false biology, there is no real history. The 'proofs' are as much a tangle as the oral pledges; the evidence of the ring is always ironic, as if sexual life travels in this little sealed capsule through historical time. Romantic/sexual love is an archetypal domain of deep, fundamental uncertainty. The vulnerability is greater than any other human domain, the need for proof correspondingly the highest and the frailest."[80]

It is far more difficult to prove chastity than to establish paternity. There is no scientific proof of chastity. The evidence of a signet ring, however flimsy, is probably as good as it gets.

8

The Affair of the Diamond Necklace

IN PREVIOUS CHAPTERS of this book, rings have occupied the center ring. But as we move into modern Europe and America, in the final three chapters, we'll enlarge our scope to include jewelry more generally, particularly necklaces, simply because some of the best jewelry stories from this period happen to be about necklaces. Indeed, even in many folktales of the genres we have already discussed, the telltale piece is not a finger ring but some other circular jewelry—a bracelet, an anklet,[i] a necklace, or even a nose-ring.[1] Sometimes the ring is combined with a watch and chain, a foot-bracelet and chain, or a girdle and crown.[2] In a sense, bracelets and necklaces, even tiaras, are just bigger rings, all working by the same encircling logic. But necklaces are taken off more often than rings. They are designed to please someone's eye other than the wearer's, and because they are larger, they are often showier and more costly. All of this makes a difference in the narratives. In this chapter we will dip into recorded history, unique and datable events, to consider a great eighteenth-century scandal involving a diamond necklace. But we will find ourselves dragged back, inexorably, into the realm of myth.

Marie Antoinette and the Scene in the Bower

The "Affair of the Diamond Necklace" (sometimes called "The Affair of the Necklace" or "The Queen's Necklace") is the name given by historians to a scandal that raised French hatred of Marie Antoinette to a fever pitch, an episode that they regard as so important that one would presumably not

---

i. See chapter 3, p. 63.

confuse it with any of the many other affairs of other (diamond) necklaces (or other queens). Thomas Carlyle wrote, "Among the host of miserable mistakes and crimes that preceded the French Revolution, exciting hostile public opinion and intense hatred of the monarchy and existing institutions, the affair of the Diamond Necklace is prominent.... The odium of

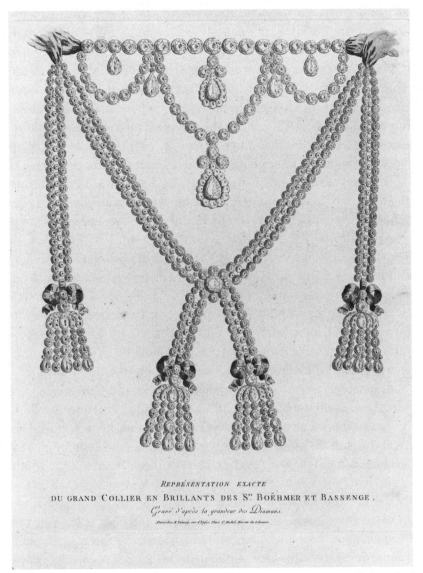

REPRÉSENTATION EXACTE
DU GRAND COLLIER EN BRILLANTS DES S⁹ BOËHMER ET BASSENGE.
Gravé d'après la grandeur des Diamans.

FIGURE 8.1 The diamond necklace that Cardinal Rohan bought and thought he had given to Marie Antoinette.

Source: © The Trustees of the British Museum. All rights reserved.

the 'Diamond Necklace' imbittered all [the Queen's] future life, and followed her to the very steps of the guillotine."[3] Napoleon is said to have said
(on St. Helena),[4] "The Queen's death must be dated from the Diamond
Necklace Trial." All but one of the lawyers in the trial went on to take part
in the revolution.[5]

It all began in 1772, when Louis XV commissioned, for his mistress
Madame du Barry, a diamond necklace said to be the most expensive
(and, according to some, the ugliest) ever seen, an oversized ornament
of the type sometimes called a *rivière*, which "flowed" like a river down
from the neck. Others called it a "necklace of slavery" (*collier d'esclavage*).[6]
It boasted 647 flawless, well-matched diamonds, a total of 2,800 carats.[7]
Carlyle describes it as having one string of seventeen diamonds, "as large
almost as filberts" (five to eight carats; others said that some were the size
of thrushes' eggs)[8] and then three strings of "pear-shaped, multiple star-
shaped, or clustering amorphous" diamonds, and then more strings, and
"a very Queen of Diamonds [eleven carats], on the bosom."[9] Two streamers
hung down the back, to counterbalance the weight of the necklace which
might otherwise make the wearer topple forward[10]—as, indeed, Marie did
in the end.

But in 1774, before the jewelers, the Paris firm of Boehmer and Bassenge,
could finish the necklace, Louis XV died. The jewelers tried unsuccessfully to sell this "dinosaur of rococo jewelry"[11] to the new king, Louis XVI,
as a present for his wife Marie Antoinette, on the occasion of the long-
awaited birth of their first child, on October 22, 1781. But she refused
it. She did not want it known that she had indulged in such an extravagance at a time when France was involved in a war—the American War
of Independence—and arming a fleet. In Alexandre Dumas's novel
about these events, which we will soon consider, the queen tells the
king to use the money to buy a battleship instead; he agrees and says
he will christen the ship, "The Queen's Necklace." It is sometimes said
that Marie did not want a necklace that had been intended for another
woman, let alone a courtesan, let alone a courtesan whom she particularly disliked (du Barry), but this is unlikely; for the queen had already
purchased from Boehmer a pair of diamond earrings, each with three
enormous pear-shaped diamonds, that had likewise been intended for
Madame du Barry.[12] It is also said that she seldom wore necklaces at all,
let alone a "shoulder-cracking" necklace like the one in question, "since
they detracted from her neck's sinuous grace."[13] In any case, she did not
buy this necklace.

Then, in 1784, a woman who called herself Jeanne de Saint-Rémy de Valois (let's just call her Jeanne), and who claimed descent from a bastard son of Henry II, played a very clever and very dirty trick on the queen and on Cardinal Louis René Édouard de Rohan, bishop of Strasbourg. (Carlyle calls it "a colossal and daring project of fraud.")[14] Now, the cardinal was a very wealthy fifty-year-old man with a reputation as a womanizer;[15] this "dissolute, gullible, aristocratic" man[16] had served, from 1772 to 1774, as French ambassador to Vienna, where he had incurred the displeasure of the Empress Maria Theresa, Marie Antoinette's mother. Recalled to France from Vienna, the cardinal then further angered Marie Antoinette herself, allegedly by slandering Maria Theresa at a party at Madame du Barry's house.[17] Banished from the court at Versailles, the cardinal was anxious to ingratiate himself with the queen.

Jeanne managed to finagle her way into the fringes of the French court and bruited it about that she had the confidence of the queen. She persuaded the cardinal that she would intercede with Marie Antoinette on his behalf. She had her lover, Rétaux de Villette, forge affectionate letters from the queen to the cardinal, to which the cardinal ardently replied (through Jeanne, who of course never delivered his notes).

Now, Jeanne's husband Nicholas (who called himself Comte LaMotte, making her Comtesse LaMotte, sometimes called Lamotte or de la Motte) had encountered a prostitute, Marie-Nicole Le Guay (who also used the name of Le Guay de Signy),[18] in the usual way that one encounters prostitutes. He had noticed that she bore a striking resemblance to Marie Antoinette ("in figure and profile," as Carlyle puts it).[19] Born in 1761, she was seven years younger than the queen. Jeanne soon made her acquaintance and called her the Baroness d'Oliva, a near anagram of her own name, Valois. Let's call her Nicole.

Jeanne persuaded Nicole to participate in what she represented as a little joke for the amusement of the queen: on August 11, 1784, Jeanne told the cardinal that she had arranged an assignation for him with the queen. It was to take place that evening in a secluded bower of the garden at Versailles, sometimes known as the Bower of Venus (*Bosquet de Venus*), because there were plans to set up a statue to Venus there. (The statue was never made, and the bower was later called the Queen's Bower, "in memory of this particular night.")[20] That moonless night in the Bower, the cardinal met Nicole, who was dressed like the queen. She gave him a rose and said, "You know what this means." Immediately they were interrupted and the phantom woman fled. The cardinal was left alone with his rose and his fantasies, believing that he had met with the queen.

On January 29, 1785, Jeanne went in for the kill. She persuaded the cardinal that Marie Antoinette wished to purchase the diamond necklace and wanted him to act as her secret emissary, because she did not want it known that she had indulged in such an extravagance. Rétaux forged documents from the queen, agreeing to the price and the method of payment. Jeanne then gave these documents to the cardinal, who conveyed them to the jewelers. The cardinal pledged his own credit to pay for the necklace in installments, and he made a substantial down payment. On February 1, 1785, the jewelers delivered the necklace to him. He took it to Jeanne's house and handed it over to a man he believed to be the queen's valet. It was, however, Rétaux, who, together with Comte LaMotte, took the necklace to London and Amsterdam, where it was broken up and sold. The jeweler Regnier set some of the larger diamonds as rings that Jeanne, with her customary sangfroid, wore in public.[21]

Meanwhile, to his great confusion and consternation, the cardinal had still not been invited to Versailles, nor had he, or the jewelers, seen the queen wearing the necklace. Jean Plaidy imagines how Jeanne might have reassured the cardinal on that point: "She dare not wear it. . . . The necklace could not possibly be unnoticed, and the King is still against her buying more jewels. Sometimes she puts it on in private."[22] This is precisely the problem we will see faced in nineteenth-century fiction by adulterous married women who have accepted expensive gifts from men other than their husbands: how to wear such jewelry in public.[ii]

On July 30, 1785, when the jewelers demanded the next installment from the cardinal, he told them he was acting for the queen. When they went to the queen for payment,[23] she of course told them that she had not negotiated to buy the necklace and had had nothing to do with the cardinal. King Louis XVI, in what is generally regarded as an act of great stupidity, decided not to hush up the affair. On August 15, Assumption Day, almost exactly a year after the meeting in the Bower of Venus, the king summoned the cardinal and asked him to explain it all. When the cardinal displayed the letters signed "Marie Antoinette de France," he was mocked for not knowing, as an ambassador and a prince of France, that royalty never use surnames.[24]

---

ii. See chapter 9, p. 237.

What became of the diamonds? Jonathan Beckman's guess is as good as any: "Diamonds are hardy things, and history does not scar them. Somewhere, anonymously, in a Swiss safe or around a neck, reconfigured into earrings or brooches or a mortuary statuette of a beloved Doberman, they sit, unperturbed by the anguish they caused."[25]

The Official Trial

The king imprisoned the cardinal in the Bastille. Three days later he sent Jeanne there as well. A trial took place, over nine months, in which many of the facts emerged, as well as many fictions. On April 24, 1786, Jeanne admitted disguising Nicole as the queen in the Bower of Venus to fool the cardinal, but only to take revenge on him when he persisted in pleading with her to intercede with the queen.[26] Jeanne testified in court that she was the cardinal's mistress,[27] which he passionately denied.

No one at the trial ever accused the queen of having received the necklace. Jeanne maintained that the cardinal had had it sold and presumably pocketed the cash.[28] But it was the scene in the Bower, and that alone, as King Louis XVI argued, "in which the dignity and virtue of the Queen were outraged."[29] "The real issue," as Sarah Maza puts it, was this: "Should the cardinal be charged with 'criminal presumption' and 'lèse majesté' for believing that the queen would stoop to dealing with the likes of Mme de la Motte and to assigning a nocturnal rendez-vous"?[30] After all, his defense was based on his fervent belief that that the queen was the sort of woman who would meet a lover at midnight in the Bower of Venus.[31] Or should he be acquitted, "on the implicit grounds that such behavior on the part of Marie Antoinette was not at all implausible?"[32] Put differently, the cardinal's crime was the theft not of a necklace but of the royal name,[33] of the queen's honor.[34]

The responsibility for the scene in the Bower was much disputed. Jeanne insisted that the idea of deceiving the cardinal in this way originated with the queen herself, that she knew who had been chosen to impersonate her, where the interview was to take place, and so forth, and that the queen had not only put the rose into Nicole's hand to give to the cardinal but was actually present, concealed, at the Bower. Jeanne even asserted that "the Cardinal de Rohan was also privy to the trick played upon himself, and connived at the deceit in order to humour her majesty."[35] She told the story in many different ways.

The court did not believe any of them. On May 31, 1786, the cardinal was acquitted of the charge of having fraudulently acquired the necklace, though he was stripped of all his offices and exiled to the abbey of La Chaise-Dieu in Auvergne. Nicole Le Guay was acquitted too. She claimed that she had not understood that she was impersonating the queen ("She was really stupid," Jeanne later said of her),[36] and her lawyer argued that she could not have thought that she was impersonating the queen since Jeanne told her that the queen would be present.[37] As Antal Szerb put it, "People were shocked by Nicole's innocence, for who could be more innocent than an innocent courtesan?"[38] Louis-Pierre Manuel Charpentier, in his *Bastille Unveiled* (*La Bastille devoilée*, Paris, 1789), said of Nicole, "Never was so much simplicity and depravity seen in the same person."[39] Besides, while Nicole was in prison she gave birth to a charming baby boy, whom her boyfriend gladly acknowledged as his. Rétaux was banished. LaMotte was condemned to the galleys for life, but he was out of reach by that time and never served his sentence.

Jeanne, however, was sentenced to be flogged and branded (with a "V" on each shoulder, for *"voleuse,* thief") and imprisoned for life in the Salpêtrière prison in Paris. On June 21, 1786, her sentence was carried out, but on June 5, 1787, she escaped from prison—allegedly dressed as a man,[40] and with the help of a kindly nun[41]—and went to England, where she lived comfortably and published her memoirs, vilifying Marie Antoinette. On August 23, 1791, after a bad fall (incurred when she was fleeing from the bailiffs), Jeanne died.[42] She was thirty-five years old.

Trial by Libel

Despite the evidence at the trial, and its final ruling, the crowd still believed that the queen had somehow connived with the cardinal to buy the necklace and had used Jeanne as a scapegoat,[43] or that he had given the necklace to the queen. As Beckman puts it, "A stolen necklace was an apt symbol for the lost virtue of Marie Antoinette, orbited by rumours of infidelity."[44] It was also widely believed that the cardinal was the queen's lover, or Jeanne's, or both.[45] And most people believed that no matter who had bought and sold the necklace, at the very least the cardinal had in fact slept with Nicole, thinking she was the queen.[46] The accusation that the cardinal (and/or Jeanne) was the queen's lover lends another layer of meaning to "the *affair* of the necklace."

Public opinion, writes Simon Schama, transformed Marie Antoinette "from innocent victim to vindictive harpy."[47] He continues: "The phobic hysterias gathering about her, even before the plot was hatched, meant that she would be suspected of collusion, of luring others to their doom in the service of her insatiable appetite."[48] Pamphlets ("little books," *libelle*, source of the English word "libel") had flooded the city all during the trial and long after, proclaiming that the cardinal and Nicole "had spent the night together after the scene in the Bower, the cardinal in the belief that he held the queen in his arms."[49] As one journal of the time put it, "In granting her favours to the Cardinal the d'Oliva made him believe, with both their heads on the same pillow, that she was the queen herself."[50] It was but the work of a moment to claim that the cardinal had not been deceived in this belief, or to hedge, suggesting "that Rohan was or aspired to become one of the queen's paramours." One of the *libelles* intimated that the queen was "infected with disease from sleeping with a dissolute cardinal,"[51] and that all the women in the case were Rohan's lovers. Or, on the other hand, the pamphlets spread rumors that the queen's "sexual tastes ran more to women, which of course explained the mysterious link between the queen and her debauched 'cousin' Jeanne de Valois,"[52] who figured "prominently among the queen's many female lovers."[53] A cartoon from c. 1791 depicts the queen striding over Jeanne's head, with the diamond necklace falling on Jeanne from between her legs.[54] Beckman (who visualizes an anal rather than genital source for the necklace) describes the cartoon well (reproduced on the following page):

"An anonymous print of the time shows Marie Antoinette floating out of the Tuileries with her family clinging on to her. A necklace descends from the enormous balloon-like canopy of her dress, like a rope of glittering turds. Jeanne, her decolletage revealing almost everything, hangs on to the lowered diamonds with Rohan by her side. It offers an eccentric version of the much-chewed-over theme of royal extravagance—the queen shitting diamonds in her hurry to escape—and a telling instance of historical compression: the Affair is the original cause of the queen's incarceration—Marie Antoinette can never escape it, just as she fails to escape the palace. The necklace will always haul her down."[55]

FIGURE 8.2 A cartoon from c. 1791, artist unknown, depicting the diamond neck-lace falling on Jeanne from between Marie Antoinette's legs.
Source: Artist unknown/© RMN-Grand Palais/Bibliotheque Nationale Paris

This is an extraordinarily explicit incarnation of the metaphor of jewels as female sexual organs.[iii]

The pamphlets also reported that Comte LaMotte was now in Turkey, where he had been circumcised and made a pasha,[56] and wore a turban.[57] The rumors, the grubby insinuations of the pornographic press,[58] and the notorious trial added fuel to the already smoldering mythology of Marie Antoinette's extravagance and wantonness, convincing people, as Maza puts it, "that female powers of deceit were indeed corrupting the monarchy."[59] So close was the association between scheming women and incriminating jewelry, by the eighteenth century, that although Marie Antoinette had had no knowledge whatsoever of the diamond necklace, or of the doings of the cardinal, she was besmirched, in the public mind, with the guilt and promiscuity of two other women, the cunning Jeanne and the naïve (or perhaps not so naïve) Nicole.

The final libel of the period was published in May of 1789, just as the French Revolution began. It was Jeanne's memoirs, of which 1,500 copies were at once smuggled into France; more were to follow, perhaps 10,000

---

iii. See chapter 1, p. 10.

altogether. In her version of the story, the queen and the cardinal were lovers, and the queen asked Jeanne to get Nicole to masquerade as her in the bower so that she could watch how the cardinal behaved when he thought he was with her. He negotiated to buy the necklace, and the queen told Jeanne to forge her signature.[60] And so on. "Not true, of course," as one text characterized the *libelle* version of the affair, "but when everyone believes a lie, it might as well be the truth."[61]

Alexandre Dumas

Many of the subsequent fictional and semi-fictional tellings of the Affair of the Diamond Necklace follow not the historical record but the rather different story that Dumas told in *The Queen's Necklace* (*Le collier de la reine*) in 1849, right after the French Revolution of 1848.

Dumas picks up the accusation made by the *libelle*—that the cardinal did sleep with the woman he met in the Bower of Venus—as well as the accusations made by Jeanne, namely, that the queen wanted the necklace and negotiated with the cardinal for it. In Dumas's version of the story, the allegation that the queen was present in the Bower is more important, as it was in the mind of the public (and of the king), than the allegation that she bought, or received, the diamond necklace. And for Dumas, both accusations are true in spirit though not in the flesh: the cardinal thinks, wrongly, that he has slept with the queen, and the queen thinks, wrongly, that she can have the necklace.

Dumas's Marie meets personally with the cardinal on several occasions and asks him to negotiate secretly to buy the necklace for her; she mistakenly believes that she will be able to get the funds to pay for it. Dumas's Jeanne—who is actually in Marie Antoinette's confidence, which makes her betrayal all the more damnable—facilitates all of these meetings. The cardinal brings the necklace to the queen. But when she realizes that she will not have the money to pay for it after all, Marie tells Jeanne to return the necklace to the jewelers and get a receipt. She says, "This necklace brought with it cares and fears; diamonds cannot compensate for these.... One may humiliate one's self for a person one loves, to save a living creatures, were it only a dog; but only to keep some sparkling stones—never, countess; take it away."[62] So much for the queen's lust for the diamonds. Jeanne does indeed take it away—but not to the jewelers ... and from here the fate of the necklace in Dumas follows much the same course as it did in history.

As for the love affair, the night tryst in the Bower of Venus is the key to the whole story for Dumas, who makes it into a consummated bed-trick: the cardinal actually goes to bed with the prostitute that he mistakes for the queen. But it happens rather differently this time: the cardinal (rather than Comte LaMotte) meets Nicole (here called Oliva Legay; let's call her Oliva) at a masked ball and talks flirtatiously with her; when her mask slips for a moment, he thinks he recognizes the queen and makes sly (and to Oliva incomprehensible) German references to Schoenbrunn, Marie's palace in Vienna. Jeanne observes this and realizes that the cardinal is in love with the queen. Several other people say that they saw the queen at the ball, and the rumor reaches the ears of the queen, who denies it; she was with the king that night, as he affirms. But now she knows that she has a double.

Jeanne arranges the tryst in the Bower of Venus, proposing to Oliva that since she is "so terribly bored, . . . we should have some amusement with that officer who is rather mad, and in love with the Queen, whom you resemble a little; and endeavor to persuade him that it was the Queen he was walking with."[63] At the trial, "Oliva asserted vehemently her own innocent participation in what she believed to be a joke, played on a gentleman unknown to her."[64] This time the cardinal gives Oliva the rose, and kisses her hand. Once they are alone together inside the bower, as Jeanne says to Oliva later, "It seems you did not stop here."[65] Moreover, Jeanne continues, "As you are not the Queen, and have taken her name, and in her name have committed a folly of this kind, that is unfortunately treason."

In order to prevent the cardinal from discovering his error by confronting the real queen, Jeanne warns him that he and the queen have been seen together in the park, and if the king finds out, it's the Bastille. The cardinal, growing impatient and jealous, asks Jeanne for proof that the queen is, as Jeanne has told him, pining for him just as he is for her. She retorts, "Proofs! Are you in your senses, Monseigneur, to ask a woman for proofs of her own infidelity?" and he replies, "I am not speaking of proofs for a lawsuit, Countess, only a token of love."[66]

Dumas's plot is now thickened by the introduction of a subplot: a man named Olivier de Charny is in love with the queen and she with him, though neither has revealed their love to the other. Olivier sees Oliva with the cardinal in the Bower and mistakes her for the queen. The queen protests her innocence and argues, "I have already been injured through the resemblance to me of some woman, I know not who, but who is like her unhappy queen."[67] She goes into the park with Olivier that night, to see if they can find the girl, but no one appears there. They, however, are seen together, and now people testify that they saw her in the Bower with the cardinal, both on the occasion when Oliva (whom they mistook for Marie) was there with the cardinal and on the occasion when Marie was there with Olivier (whom they mistook for the cardinal). Everyone, including the cardinal, thinks that the queen slept with the cardinal. Olivier's doubts are increased by widespread rumors that the cardinal must be the queen's lover, because he bought her such an expensive necklace.[68]

To prove her innocence, Marie summons the cardinal and hides Olivier in her bedroom so that he can hear their conversation. But of course the cardinal, instead of confirming that he never met her anywhere at night, as she expects, tries to remind her of their "sweet but perfidious love" in the Bower, and, by implication, later in bed. She throws him out, and although (or because?) Olivier still believes that the cardinal had been her lover, he falls at her feet and declares his love for her. The king suddenly enters and finds them that way. To save the day, Marie pretends that Olivier is asking her to intercede for him with her lady in waiting.[69] Finally Oliva is brought to the queen, dressed in one of the queen's favorite costumes.[70] But this time Olivier is not there to see Oliva and to realize that the queen had told the truth.

Nor is the cardinal there. "Ah!" cries the queen; "in this woman, doubtless, lies all his error." And indeed, "when Oliva was shown to the Cardinal the blow was dreadful. He saw at last how infamously he had been played upon."[71] The queen continued to be played upon. Jeanne "confessed that she had deceived the Cardinal, but declared that it was done with the consent of the Queen, who watched and enjoyed the scene, hidden behind the trees. To this story she kept; the Queen could never disprove it, and there were plenty of people willing to believe it true."[72] And this persisted even though the queen had published accurate reports about the nocturnal meetings. The mistaken identity plagued the queen even in the trial, where, when Oliva testified, "Many people trembled at seeing this living image of the Queen sitting there as a criminal."[73]

Thus, in Dumas's novel, both the cardinal and Marie lust in their hearts, and neither achieves his or her desire (though, for a while, the cardinal thinks he has). The jewelry is a false proof of identity: it seems to prove that the cardinal was the queen's lover. The identical double is a better, truer proof: Nicole's existence proves that the queen was not the one who was the cardinal's lover. Dumas turns this part of the story into a recognition comedy, and indeed the recognition does acquit the queen of both of the false accusations (adultery and fraud), but it cannot free her from the tragic consequences of the deception. The assumption that, if someone gave a woman a valuable necklace, he must have slept with her, would continue to plague women for centuries to come.

The affair of the diamond necklaces is one of those moments in history that, as the film director Max Ophüls put it, "take on the flavor of an old ballad."[74] The fictionalized versions of the story, in novels[75] and films,[76] are not even as lurid as the "historical" sources of the pamphlets. In the 1938 film *Marie Antoinette* (with a script by Donald Odgen Stewart, among others, including F. Scott Fitzgerald), Norma Shearer is Marie and the ever villainous Henry Daniell is LaMotte (with Jeanne reduced to a bit part). The film adds two significant jewelry episodes. Before the episode that concerns us, Marie appears wearing a large, but not spectacular, diamond necklace. She wagers the necklace in a bet that she can get the newly arrived Swedish Count Axel Fersen (Tyrone Power) to go to a party with her. He refuses and, when he discovers that she has gambled away the necklace, scolds her.[iv] On the next day, the Austrian emissary remarks that her mother is angry at her because of her extravagance, and mentions "a necklace costing 200,000 livres." Marie laughs and says, "Which I lost tonight on a wager." And then the film adds a ring: after Count Fersen has become her lover, she gives him a large, domed signet ring, which he sends to her when he comes to rescue her as the Revolution begins.[v] She gives it back to him when he visits her in prison and he gazes at it on his finger as she goes to the guillotine. It is the last thing we see before the camera pans up to the sky, presumably to heaven.

The rest of the film sticks fairly closely to the historical record. Rohan is duped by Jeanne, as usual, though with a significant twist: in the scene in the Bower, instead of receiving a rose from the woman he takes to be the queen, Rohan actually hands her the necklace in a box, saying, "Your majesty, the commission with which you honored me. . . . Dare I hope that the past will be forgiven?" to which she replies, with Pythian ambiguity, "You may hope." When he is later called before the king (Robert Morley) and queen, and insists, in her presence, that he had placed the necklace in her hands, she indignantly replies, "I haven't addressed a word to you in eight years. How could you possibly believe that I would employ

---

iv. An episode that may have been borrowed from *Daniel Deronda*; see chapter 9, p. 230.

v. An episode that may have been borrowed from the medieval tale of Tristan; see chapter 4, p. 99.

you as a go-between to buy a necklace behind my husband's back? Your presumption is criminal." When Rohan is exonerated, she realizes that she is doomed. The Duc d'Orléans (Joseph Schildkraut) says to the king, "Take care, Louis, that that necklace doesn't twist around your fat neck and choke it."[77]

Fact and Fiction

Even before Dumas wrote his fictionalized version of the affair, an aura of fiction hung heavily about the true story and helped to generate the actual events. The fabulously expensive diamond necklace was real enough— indeed, the diamonds were the only real things in the whole affair. But even they were theatrical; that sort of necklace, the *rivière*, that hung low over the bosom, was "much associated with actresses in the Palais Royal, who might not blush to show off the generosity of their benefactors."[78] In 1787, a French magazine published a joke about a *rivière*; when one person noted how very low such a "river" poured over "the *décolletage* of a con- spicuous courtesan," another replied, "That's because it's returning to its source."[79] Simon Schama, who retells this anecdote, remarks, "Jokes about sex and jewelry were nothing new."

Nicole's lawyer, Jean Blondel, used theatrical terms (scene, play, rep- resent, character) and depicted Jeanne as writing the script and keeping her actors, "literally as well as figuratively," in the dark: "A scene that was imagined, ordered, directed by Mme de La Motte was performed by night in one of the garden walks."[80] Jeanne was the producer and director, and the audience consisted of no one but the cardinal. And there was even hocus-pocus involved: the slippery Count Cagliostro, a notorious magician and all-around charlatan, was implicated with the cardinal in intricate but inconsequential ways; he testified in the trial, and was exonerated.

The whole story sounds like one of the tales that fill this book: it begins when a man (Louis XV) plans to give a necklace not to his wife but to his mistress; then a low-born, promiscuous woman substitutes in the dark for a virtuous queen, with a man from whom she gets a fabulous piece of jewelry. Jeanne must have heard such stories, and they may have inspired her to stage the scene in the Bower of Venus. Marie Antoinette was inno- cent, but then so were the women, including queens, in so many of our stories, accused by smoking pieces of jewelry that they eventually turned to their own defense. Rose Bertin, Marie Antoinette's dressmaker, called the scene in the arbor "a story that would barely be credible in a bad novel."

It reminded her of La Fontaine's fable, "Le Magnifique,"[81] based on a story by Boccaccio, in which a young woman closely watched by her husband can signal her love to her young lover only by silently dropping a rose to the ground. The plot also echoes that of Shakespeare's *Twelfth Night*: a court clown who believes that a noblewoman is in love with him falls for a forged letter and is tricked in a garden. But it was closest to *opera buffa*, with "a complicated plot, disguises and mistaken identities, purloined letters, elegant settings, and luscious female characters. It had all the elegant shallowness of a light (and late) rococo comedy."[82] Indeed, as we will see, it may even have been inspired by such a comedy.

Many, of the very many people who wrote about this incident, have noticed how intrinsically mythological it was. Imbert de Saint-Amand writes of the affair of the necklace, "It is a sort of romance ... as full of incident as a play; a tragicomedy designed to pique and amuse the malevolence of the public."[83] Szerb compares it to a medieval legend about necklaces planted as false evidence[84] and notes that Nicole's lawyer, in her defense, "tapped the same vein of sentimentality we find in *Manon Lescaut* and the later *La Dame aux Camélias*."[85] Beckman summarizes the situation: "Above all, this is such an improbable story—one which, were it offered up in a novel, would be condemned for violating the laws of plausibility."[86]

Thomas Carlyle, in Beckman's words, "saw a romance more wondrous than a poet could ever compose, which broke through the crust of everyday life to partake in our Universal History."[87] And so Carlyle presents the "small Romance of the *Diamond Necklace*, ... no brainweb of mine, or of any other foolish man's; but a fraction of that mystic 'spirit-woven web,' from the 'Loom of Time.' "[88] Who was the author of this romance? None other than Jeanne, "the Female Dramatist who, for eighteen long months, can exhibit the beautifullest Fata-morgana to a plush Cardinal, wide awake, with fifty years on his head; and so lap him in her scenic illusion that he never doubts but it is all firm earth, and the pasteboard Coulisse-trees are producing Hesperides apples.... Could Madame de Lamotte, then, have written a *Hamlet*?"[89] And so the cardinal was caught in the "Lamottic Circean theatrical establishment,"[90] and even after the necklace was lost forever, "in the Lamotte Theatre, so different from our common Pasteboard one, the Play goes on, even when the Machinist has left it."[91] Indeed, it is not only theater, but myth. Carlyle calls the cardinal "Ixion de Rohan,"[92] after the Greek mortal who lusted for the goddess Hera and was tricked into mating with a cloud in Hera's shape.

Theater and myth continued to nourish a great deal of fiction that called itself fiction, when Dumas and others wrote stories about Jeanne and Nicole and the queen and the necklace. As Maza remarks, "The story of the necklace so resembled a novel that it also rapidly produced fictional spin-offs in the form of (mostly invented) biographies of the main characters."[93] It's as if the story always existed as fiction, and just touched down briefly in history for a few years before going back to being a story. Tragic history as it repeats itself becomes not farce (as Marx said it did)[94] but grand opera and pulp fiction.

The fictional background might have affected not only the trick that Jeanne engineered but the way in which Rohan fell for it, according to Beckman:

> "Rohan was easily beguiled by Jeanne because the assignation in the *bosquet* tallied with the fables he told himself: it confirmed his own seductive prowess, but it also cast him as the hero of a romantic adventure. What seems to us and seemed to his contemporaries incredible—that he believed he had met the queen under these circumstances—was swallowed smoothly in the thrill of self-dramatisation. The story being written for him meshed with the one he believed he was writing for himself. . . . You are never more unwittingly in peril than when you think you're the author of your own fate but are in fact a character in someone else's plot."[95]

And fiction certainly affected the way that history remembered it. The lawyers' melodramatic trial briefs were heavily influenced by Diderot's famous fairy tale,[96] "The Indiscreet Jewels."[vi]

Beaumarchais and The Marriage of Figaro

But the legal briefs were even more influenced by Pierre-Auguste Caron de Beaumarchais. Indeed, the historian Jules Michelet (1798–1874) believed the fabricated story about the queen watching Rohan kneel before d'Oliva, "though the only evidence he could adduce in his favour was Marie Antoinette's fondness for performing plays by Beaumarchais."[97]

---

vi. See chapter 1, p. 18.

Already in the nineteenth century, Imbert de Saint-Amand suggested that in creating the scene in the bower, Jeanne might have been inspired by the final scene of Beaumarchais's play, *The Marriage of Figaro* (which had premiered on April 27 of that year),[98] a scene in which in "the nocturnal confusion under the shadows,"[99] one woman masquerades as another. Saint-Amand suggests that the actual events of the affair of the diamond necklace presented "a plot more strange and improbable than even Beaumarchais could have invented."[100] A character in Dumas's novel, *The Queen's Necklace*, also mentions Beaumarchais's new play, *The Marriage of Figaro*, and the scene in Dumas's novel in which the queen hides Olivier in the closet, and the king later comes in and finds them together, is surely stolen right from the play, in which the countess hides the young page Cherubino in a closet, and the count comes in, and so forth.

The historical connections are even closer than the casual literary borrowings. Jeanne took Nicole to see a performance of the Beaumarchais play,[101] and Marie Antoinette herself played the part of Rosina when Rossini's opera, *The Barber of Seville* (based on the first play in the Beaumarchais trilogy of which *The Marriage of Figaro* was the second) was staged at the Trianon on August 19, 1785, four days after the cardinal was arrested.[102] It was during the rehearsals for that performance that news of the affair of the necklace had first reached the queen.

A diamond ring, rather than a necklace, plays a strangely truncated, atavistic role in *The Marriage of Figaro*, both in the Beaumarchais play and in Lorenzo Da Ponte's libretto for Mozart's opera (1786), which follows the play very closely. In the episode of the play that concerns us,[103] Count Almaviva attempts to seduce Susanna, the maid of his wife the Countess Rosina, and offers to pay her for sleeping with him, in fulfillment of the nobleman's traditional right to deflower brides. Then:

> In response to Count Almaviva's insistence that Susanna grant him a rendezvous in the pine grove, his wife decided to stand in for her maid. Lamenting the loss of her youth and of Almaviva's love, Rosina expressed her hope that she would win him back with this trick. She dictated a letter to Almaviva, ostensibly from Susanna, agreeing to meet him in the grove that night.
>
> At the appointed time, Rosina and Susanna entered the grove, each disguised in the other's clothes. Almaviva wooed Rosina-as-Susanna, and he gave her a diamond ring as a token of his love.

Then he said, "Let us conceal ourselves in here." "In the dark, my lord?" asked Rosina-as-Susanna. "That's what I want; you know I don't want to go there to read," he replied. Rosina-as-Susanna fled. Figaro (Almaviva's valet and Susanna's fiancé) arrived and realized what was happening. He and Susanna-as-Rosina recognized the count's voice and pretended to make love. Almaviva, searching for Rosina-as-Susanna, found them and believed he had caught Figaro and Rosina together. He gathered witnesses, accused Susanna-as-Rosina, and refused to forgive her, but his vengeance was cut short by the arrival of the real countess in her own clothes. He humbly apologized to her, and she forgave him. She gave the diamond ring to Susanna.

The diamond ring does not fulfill its conventional function of revealing the identity of a disguised lover. Almaviva intends to use it to give the lie to the purely monetary aspect of the sordid transaction between himself and Susanna. He spells out the meaning of the ring: "Here is the gold I promised for the purchase of . . . the delicate moment you are going to accord me. But, because the grace with which you accord it is beyond price, I add to it this brilliant to wear for love of me."[104] (In the opera, he says, "Besides your dowry, my dearest, Take this jewel too, Which a lover gives you As token of his love.") Since, however, the woman to whom he gives the ring is not, as he thinks, Susanna, but Rosina-as-Susanna, it promises to function like the ring that the rejecting husband gives to the clever wife in disguise:[vii] Rosina can play it as her trump card at the end. But she never does. All that happens—in Beaumarchais—is that Rosina gives the diamond ring to Susanna at the end. In the opera, the ring never reappears after Almaviva has given it to Rosina-as-Susanna, and never provides any evidence of the masquerade.

The ring seems to be left over from some formulaic requirements of the folktale on which the play is based, and some productions attempt to bring it back in a final reappearance. In the final scene of the 1993 Theatre du Châtelet production of the Mozart opera, Rosina gave the ring back to Almaviva, rather than to Susanna, and that is what made him ask her to forgive him. But the ring is superfluous here, since the final recognition

---

vii. See chapter 6, p. 137.

is just a straightforward identification of people: while Almaviva is refusing to forgive Susanna-as-Rosina, the real Rosina comes out of the place
where he had just tried to seduce Rosina-as-Susanna, and he sees the two
women together, in a sense, cross-dressed. Instantly the classic moment of
recognition washes over him and he crumples to his knees and begs her
forgiveness. Nobody bothers to ask questions about jewelry.

The Ghosts of Versailles

John Corigliano's 1991 opera *The Ghosts of Versailles* (with a libretto by
William M. Hoffman) ambitiously combines the plot of the Beaumarchais/
Da Ponte *Marriage of Figaro* and the plot of the Affair of the Diamond
Necklace, plus that of the third and final play of Da Ponte's "Figaro" trilogy,
The Guilty Mother (*La Mère Coupable*). Perhaps inspired by the knowledge
that Marie Antoinette herself had actually performed the part of Rosina,
Corigliano brought the two women together in his work, substituting
Marie Antoinette's diamond necklace for Susanna/Rosina's diamond ring.

Corigliano constructed an opera-within-an-opera: in the outer frame,
in history, Marie Antoinette is dead, and the ghost of Beaumarchais is in
love with her ghost. Beaumarchais's ghost announces that he has written
an opera, which (like *The Guilty Mother*) takes place years after the end of
The Marriage of Figaro, in the autumn of 1793, during the Reign of Terror.
Rosina and Susanna have grown old and moved from Spain to France,
where Marie Antoinette is in prison awaiting her execution (which took
place on October 16, 1793). Beaumarchais says that by the power of his
art, the words and music of this opera-within-the-opera, he can change
the course of history and rescue Marie from her death in the French
Revolution. He explains that in the opera-within-the-opera, Almaviva, now
the Spanish ambassador to France, and a close friend of the queen, will
sell her diamond necklace to the British ambassador for a million pounds
and use the money to spirit the queen away to London and then to the
New World.

But Figaro disobeys Beaumarchais's script, for he regards the queen
as an arrogant traitor. He steals the necklace from Almaviva, intending
to sell it and use the money to help the Almavivas escape to freedom.
Beaumarchais himself now enters the opera as a character and demands
the necklace, but Figaro refuses. In desperation, Beaumarchais tells

Figaro, "You are my fantasy!" and drags him out of the opera-within-the opera into the historical scene of Marie's trial. Beaumarchais plays the Public Prosecutor and charges Marie with "squandering enormous sums for your pleasures and intrigues," a reference to the Affair of the Necklace. Figaro now realizes how unfair the trial is, resolves to help Marie, and returns to the opera-within-the-opera.

However, just as Beaumarchais is about to release Marie from prison, outside the opera Marie's ghost tells his ghost that she does not want to change history. He protests—"Almaviva brings her to London. The Revolution fails! A new age dawns!"—but she insists, "I had to stay, Beaumarchais, and I had to die." She tells Beaumarchais that she loves him and wishes to remain a ghost with him throughout eternity. As the historical Marie is beheaded and the Almavivas sail off in a balloon heading for the New World, Beaumarchais's ghost places the diamond necklace around the neck of Marie Antoinette's ghost and kisses her hand.

The necklace is at the heart of this two-layered plot. At the start, the ghost of Beaumarchais tells the ghost of Marie: "With your necklace I shall change your past. I shall show you history as it should have been. I'll make you live again." He borrows the necklace in order to work its magic upon the past, first by creating the opera, then by using the necklace to finance the escape. He succeeds with the first step, conjuring forth the opera as he chants, "Diamonds! I see diamonds," but Marie stops him before he can complete the second step. Does he fail because she refuses to be saved, or because the magic of jewelry has its limits, or because no one can change history? All three, I think.

Asimov's Norby and the Queen's Necklace

Norby and the Queen's Necklace is a book for children that Isaac Asimov wrote, together with his wife Janet Asimov,[105] in 1986, five years before *The Ghosts of Versailles*. It shares with that opera the hope of going back into the past to save Marie Antoinette. This time the mechanism is not art but science, not opera but a futuristic technology of time travel, the sci-fi equivalent of memory. For the ring now picks up again some of the magic powers it had in the medieval romances[viii] and in some fairy tales, the

---

viii. See chapter 4, p. 87.

mythical power to cloud memory but also the scientific power to transport people through time and space. Here's the plot:

> The Metropolitan Museum of Art has an exact paste replica of the Queen's diamond necklace; though of "enormous historical value" it is "only junk," which the jewelers, Boehmer and Bossenge, had made to show to possible buyers of the real necklace. Because the real necklace was "stolen, broken up, and the individual stones gone," the paste replica is "the only physical reminder" of the famous necklace. When a girl named Albany, playing the part of Marie Antoinette in a skit at the Museum, puts on the fake necklace and fastens it, she and her friends are transported back in time, to February 1, 1785, the day the necklace was delivered to Cardinal de Rohan. They land in Boehmer's shop and accidentally knock the real necklace out of his hand. Albany picks it up and suddenly vanishes with it as well as the fake necklace. Boehmer calls the police and the other children are thrown into the Bastille. Eventually they and Albany escape and, traveling forward in time, arrive back at the Museum.

While they're cooling their heels in the Bastille, the children discover that the museum's replica of the necklace was actually a replica of the replica, which some alien had invented to use as a time-travel device; it worked only when someone put it on and fastened it. The original replica (which had remained in the jeweler's shop) was made of fake silver and fake diamonds; the replica of the replica was made of extra-terrestrial plastic. This plastic necklace had recently been found in the trunk of the descendants of some Frenchman who had emigrated to England and then to America (perhaps Comte LaMotte?).

When the children had broken into the past, they had taken the real diamonds from the jeweler's shop, preventing the necklace from ever reaching the thieves. They reason that "if there was no affair of the Queen's necklace, Marie Antoinette wouldn't have been blamed for it. Maybe there would never have been a Revolution." Or, "even if the Revolution took place, it might have been less violent. . . . No Reign of Terror."[106] For, "History says that Napoleon said it was the *necklace* that changed things, increasing the public dislike of the royal family, especially hatred of the Queen and her favorites, making the Revolution inevitable."[107] At first, the children prefer the altered version of history, but then they realize that despite the Reign of Terror, the French Revolution was a Good Thing; and in any case, this alternative history has to be erased. And so they escape from the Bastille. Like Corligliano's Beaumarchais, the children fail to save Marie Antoinette. In each case the necklace is both the culprit in history and the hope of redemption from history. But in both cases, it fails. All that is left is yet another story.

9

The Slut Assumption in the Nineteenth and Twentieth Centuries

IN LATE NINETEENTH-CENTURY stories, a woman's acceptance of jewelry given by a man with no official right to her proves that she is unchaste and/or immoral; inexpensive necklaces from good men are sharply contrasted with expensive necklaces from bad men. Jewelry now has become the enemy, no longer the savior. Guy de Maupassant (1885), Henry James (1889), and Somerset Maugham (1925) added to this base, which women novelists had created, elaborating on the tension between real necklaces obtained in immoral ways and fake necklaces obtained in moral ways. Why these reversals of values at this time?

It is perhaps not a coincidence that this last group of stories by men arises at a time when women were agitating for their rights. The stories may also reflect class anxiety: a recurring theme in late nineteenth-century French novels is the shop girl who now dresses so well that she can pass herself off as a lady. Recall that in Shaw's *Pygmalion* (1916, reincarnated in *My Fair Lady*, 1956), Henry Higgins boasts that he'll be able to pass off the guttersnipe Eliza as a duchess or even a get her a job in a nice shop, for which the standards would be still higher.[1] Here, as so often, the real thing is not so good as the fake.

The big question in these cases is, as usual, How did the woman get the jewelry? But now there is also another question: Is the jewelry real? And the two are directly connected. The assumption in these texts is that if a woman is seen wearing fake jewelry, she may well have bought it herself. But if she sports a new piece of valuable jewelry, she must have gotten it by sleeping not (like the clever wives)[i] with her authenticating husband

---

i. See chapter 6, p. 137.

but with an illicit paramour. Let us call this the slut assumption. It was explicitly applied to Marie Antoinette, in the eighteenth century,[ii] and continued to plague women ever after. A character in Mae West's play *Night after Night* (1932) looks at Mae West's diamonds and exclaims, "Goodness! What lovely diamonds!" to which she replies, "Goodness had nothing to do with it" (a line that West used as the title of her 1953 autobiography). Years later, Elizabeth Taylor remarked, "How many young women get a set of rubies just for doing something wholesome like swimming laps?"[2] (Taylor, however, did get a Cartier necklace, bracelet, and earrings from her then husband Mike Todd for swimming laps in their pool in 1957.) "You don't get $137 million in gems by marching in feminist parades," Larry McMurtry said of Taylor.[3]

Chains in Mansfield Park

The slut assumption, alive and well in the twentieth century, was taken up in novels early in the nineteenth century. Two necklaces stand for two moral worlds in Jane Austen's *Mansfield Park* (1814). The impoverished Fanny Price, in love with the virtuous Edmund Bertram, is wooed by the wealthy but irresponsible Henry Crawford. What Austen calls "the almost solitary ornament in [Fanny's] possession" was an amber cross that her brother William had brought her from Sicily, though he had not been able to afford to buy her a chain for it. As Fanny was dressing for a ball, Henry's sister Mary Crawford casually offered to give Fanny one of her own necklaces for her cross; it was "of gold, prettily worked." Fanny resisted—she had just wanted a plain chain—but Mary put the necklace on her. Only then did Mary mention that she had received the necklace from Henry. Astonished and confused, Fanny took the necklace off. Mary chided her:

> " 'Do you think Henry will claim the necklace as mine, and fancy you did not come honestly by it? or are you imagining he would be too much flattered by seeing round your lovely throat an ornament which his money purchased three years ago, before he knew there was such a throat in the world? or perhaps'—looking archly—'you suspect a confederacy between us, and that what I am now doing is with his knowledge and at his desire?' "

---

ii. See chapter 8, p. 218.

Fanny gave in and accepted "this doubtful good of a necklace."

When she returned home, she met Edmund, who also gave her a chain for the cross, "a plain gold chain, perfectly simple and neat," given "as a token of the love of one of your oldest friends." And Fanny replied, "This is the only ornament I have ever had a desire to possess." She confessed to him that she wanted to return the other necklace, but he persuaded her to wear it to the ball, and to keep his chain for another occasion. She found, however, to her joy, that William's cross would not fit on the necklace from Mary (ultimately, from Henry), but fit perfectly on Edmund's chain:

> "Having, with delightful feelings, joined the chain and the cross—those memorials of the two most beloved of her heart, those dearest tokens so formed for each other by everything real and imaginary—and put them round her neck, and seen and felt how full of William and Edmund they were, she was able, without an effort to resolve on wearing Miss Crawford's necklace too."

One could not hope for a more exquisite description of the emotions stirred by jewelry, the one associated with two good men (her brother and her beloved—or, rather, three, for the cross, of course, is also associated with Jesus) and the other with two not-so-good siblings, Mary and Henry. Clearly Fanny felt that in being tricked into accepting a gift of jewelry from Henry she had been tricked into accepting him as a suitor. (The trick did not succeed: she married Edmund.)

Jewry and Jewelry in Daniel Deronda

Two necklaces, one of inexpensive stones from a good man, one of diamonds from an evil man, are the key to George Eliot's *Daniel Deronda* (1876). The necklaces, which play an essential part in the moral redemption of Gwendolen Harleth, act as "emotional stimulants."[4]

The "Memorial" Turquoise Necklace

Deronda first met Gwendolen when he saw her pawning a necklace to cover her gambling losses. He redeemed it and sent it (back) to her. The necklace, with three large, fine turquoises, was already laden with human meaning: the turquoises "had belonged to a chain once her father's: but she had never known her father; and the necklace was in all respects the ornament she could most conveniently part with." Later, when she and her mother were suddenly impoverished and selling what they could, they agreed not to sell the necklace. Not much else of value was left for Gwendolen to keep, her stepfather having carried off her mother's jewelry and disposed of it. But this turquoise necklace from her father, a man who had never been there for her, was redeemed by Daniel Deronda, a man who was to be there for her throughout the great crisis of her life and to redeem her as well. In replacing her turquoise necklace, Daniel also replaced her lost father and became the voice of her conscience, her (parental) superego.

The necklace had meaning for Daniel, too. On several occasions he thought about "the little affair of the necklace" and finally admitted to himself that he was fighting against an "impetuous determining impulse . . . to carry out to the last the rescue he had begun in that monitory redemption of the necklace." When Gwendolen eventually married, her husband, a rather horrid and controlling man named Henleigh Mallinger Grandcourt, sensed the value that Gwendolen placed on the "memorial" necklace, and on an occasion when she was wearing it as a bracelet he confronted her with it: "I suppose there is some understanding between you and Deronda about that thing you have on your wrist."

The "Poisoned" Diamond Necklace

The other necklace, the diamond necklace, both reflected and intensified the dark side of Gwendolen, who was torn between her better self, represented by the turquoise necklace, and her lower self, represented by the diamonds.

The diamond necklace was a gift from her husband. Now, Grandcourt had given his mother's diamonds, worth "some thousands," to his long-time mistress, Lydia Glasher. When he had suggested that the diamonds would be safer in a bank, Lydia had refused, saying, "If you ever marry another woman I will give them up to her: are you going to marry another woman?" And at that time, he had no such intention. But then Grandcourt began to court Gwendolen.

One day a woman who was "unmistakably a lady, and one who must have been exceedingly handsome," accompanied by two children, accosted Gwendolen and said:

"My name is Lydia Glasher. Mr. Grandcourt ought not to marry any one but me. I left my husband and child for him nine years ago.

Those two children are his, and we have two others—girls—who are older. My husband is dead now, and Mr. Grandcourt ought to marry me. He ought to make that boy his heir."

The two women's eyes met, and Gwendolen said proudly, "I will not interfere with your wishes."

But she did: she so desperately needed money that she married Grandcourt, making all sorts of excuses to persuade herself that she had every right to break her promise to Lydia. Grandcourt now wanted to recover the diamonds that he had promised to Gwendolen, and so he went to see Lydia. While they spoke, "the stagnant thought in Grandcourt's mind all the while was of his own infatuation in having given her those diamonds." Lydia assured him that she would keep her promise to give the jewels to his wife: "If you will tell me where you are going on the wedding-day I will take care that the diamonds shall be delivered to her without scandal."

And so, on her wedding day, Gwendolen received a packet, with a letter:

"These diamonds, which were once given with ardent love to Lydia Glasher, she passes on to you. You have broken your word to her, that you might possess what was hers. . . . You have chosen to injure me and my children. He had meant to marry me. . . . Shall you like to stand before your husband with these diamonds on you, and these words of mine in his thoughts and yours?"

Gwendolen threw the letter into the fire. The casket fell on the floor and the diamonds rolled out. "They were like so many women petrified white." This is a wonderfully chilling image of the woman who has sold herself for diamonds and has become frozen into them. Grandcourt, too, "felt sure that Lydia had enclosed something with the diamonds, and that this something, whatever it was, had at once created in Gwendolen a new repulsion for him and a reason for not daring to manifest it." And Gwendolen vowed to herself never to wear those diamonds: "They had horrible words clinging and crawling about them, as from some bad dream, whose images lingered on the perturbed sense." By accepting the diamond necklace she had sold herself to Grandcourt and knowingly destroyed Lydia.

But one evening Grandcourt insisted that she put on the diamonds. He took them out of the jewel box and put them on her, and she thought, "Doubtless he had been used to fasten them on some one else. . . . What a privilege this is, to have robbed another woman of!" When Deronda met her again, Gwendolen was wearing the "poisoned" diamonds: "The words of the bad dream crawled about the diamonds still, but only for her: to others they were brilliants that suited her perfectly."

The "Memorable" Ring of Lost Fathers

Just as Lydia brought out the evil side of Gwendolen, so the "good" woman, the Jewess Mirah Lapidoth, became part of Gwendolen's redemption, when, after Grandcourt's death, Gwendolen, inspired and tutored by Deronda, dedicated herself to a life of service to others. Mirah too is associated with diamonds, not the necklace but Daniel's diamond ring. In a subplot we will not explore here, Daniel saved Mirah's life and they fell in love. Daniel attempted to find Mirah's family and discovered that people who might be related to her owned a pawnshop. He contrived to gain entrance into their circle by saying that he wished to pawn "a fine diamond ring." Right from the start, the ring helped him find Mirah's family.

A classic ring of recognition, the diamond ring had been given to Daniel by the man who held the secret of his birth and the identity of his unknown parents. Daniel had been adopted and raised by Sir Hugo Mallinger (Grandcourt's uncle), and he thought he might be Sir Hugo's illegitimate son. But then he received a letter from a woman who asked him to come to her in Italy. She wrote, "Bring with you the diamond ring that Sir Hugo gave you. I shall like to see it again. Your unknown mother." Daniel traveled to Italy to meet her, and she told him that the ring he was wearing was his father's. That is how he learned that he was not Sir Hugo's son at all, but the child of Jewish parents. The ring had found Daniel's family.

Now that he knew he was Jewish, Deronda felt free to marry Mirah. When he returned to England and visited Mirah's family, he took off his "heavy ring" as he entered the house, and put it on a small table, saying, "I have been wearing my memorable ring ever since I came home. . . . But I am such a Sybarite that I constantly put it off as a burden when I am doing anything." This ring, like Gwendolen's "memorial" turquoise necklace, which reminded her of Deronda, was "memorable" in the sense that it awakened memories of Deronda's father. But Daniel now finds that memory a burden, and casts off the ring—which falls into the hands of another father who functions as a human abyss, Mirah's abusive father, Lapidoth.

Lapidoth had almost destroyed Mirah years ago, and now he had come back into her happy life, threatening to destroy it again by extorting money. On this occasion, he entered the house unseen just as Deronda cast off the ring. Lapidoth saw it and took it, calculating that he would not go to prison for stealing it, for his children would never prosecute him for taking it. He disappeared, presumably forever, never to plague them again. And so, just as a necklace led Daniel to replace Gwendolen's lost father, the ring from Daniel's lost father finally lost Mirah's unwanted father. This is a recognition tragicomedy, with a vengeance.

Guy de Maupassant and Henry James

In many stories, fake diamonds pretend to be real. But in a string of European stories, real jewels pretend to be fake, in order to protect the "reality"—that is to say, the good name, the chastity—of the women who wear them.

In Guy de Maupassant's story, "The Necklace" ("La Parure," 1885), a beautiful woman named Mathilde borrowed a diamond necklace from her rich friend, Madame Forrestier, to enhance her beauty at a ball. She lost the necklace, and she and her husband borrowed 36,000 francs to buy an identical replacement, which she returned to the owner without telling her of the substitution. Madame Forrestier did not notice any difference. For the next ten years, Mathilde and her husband slaved to repay the money they had borrowed. The hard labor ruined her beauty and her life. Many years later, Mathilde confessed to Madame Forrestier what she had done, whereupon Madame Forrestier told her that the necklace she had borrowed was a fake, worth only 500 francs. (When Jay Reid Gould adapted the story for his one-act play, in 1969, he had Madame Forrestier remark to Mathilde, with hard-headed French, or perhaps American, logic, "Who would lend someone a real necklace? We keep it safe under lock and key.")

Neither of the women could tell the difference between the real thing and the fake: Mathilde mistook the fake for real, and Madame Forrestier the real for the fake. Thus the necklace imitated itself; real diamonds stood in for the fakes that had stood in for the real diamonds. And in parallel to the shift from a real necklace to a fake necklace, the one real thing that Mathilde possessed—her beauty—was destroyed by the jewelry, by the need to work so long and hard to repay the debt.

De Maupassant had also written, a year earlier (in 1884), another story about a real necklace that pretended to be a fake ("Les Bijoux," often translated as "The Fake Jewels," though "bijoux" here may also carry overtones of the French slang for the female genitals).[iii] It is the story of a married woman who had an uncanny knack for stretching the meager household budget to procure luxuries, including a great deal of fake jewelry. After her death, her husband was shocked to discover that her supposedly fake jewelry was real. The shock came from his assumption (the slut assumption) that if the jewels were real they must have been received "for services rendered," and that his wife therefore must have been false. But he got over the shock, cheerfully sold the jewelry, and lived the rest of his life in luxury, with a second, virtuous wife (who, we may assume, did not wear expensive jewelry).

This was a basic theme on which other authors could dance their own original variations. Henry James, in 1899, darkened the tone in his story "Paste," changing the diamonds to pearls and adding further psychological nuance:

> Arthur Prime had inherited the estate of his father, who, as a widowed cleric, a vicar, had married an obscure actress several years older than himself; now both of them were dead. Arthur offered his stepmother's fake jewels, stage jewels, to her niece Charlotte, a governess. Most of the jewels, much lighter than the material they imitated, were "too dreadfully good to be true ... flagrant tinsel and glass, they looked strangely vulgar ... shameless pinchbeck." And, like everyone else, Charlotte believed that her aunt had had no valuable jewelry to speak of. But the necklace of pearls, as big as filberts, was surprisingly heavy, and she commented on this to Arthur: "Are you very sure they're not really worth something?" He replied, brusquely, "If they had been worth anything to speak of, she would long ago have sold them." Besides, how could she ever have come by them? How, indeed.
>
> Charlotte accepted all the jewels, including the pearls, and thought nothing of them until a woman of the world and an entertainer, Mrs. Guy, saw the pearls and insisted that they were, in fact,

---

iii. See chapter 1, p. 13.

real; indeed, the lusterless pearls came to life as she handled them. Now persuaded that they were real, Charlotte felt that she ought not to keep them. Mrs. Guy suggested that she sell them, but Charlotte determined to return them to Arthur. Furious at what this implied about his stepmother, Arthur insisted, "They're rotten paste," and said he intended to take them to Bond Street to have them appraised. He subsequently wrote to Charlotte that she had insulted her aunt; that the experts had determined that he was right and pronounced them utter paste; and that he had smashed them. But when she next met Mrs. Guy, Charlotte was astonished to see that she was wearing the pearls, now fully alive and glowing. Mrs. Guy said she had recognized them in a Bond Street window and bargained for them. But Charlotte wondered if Mrs. Guy hadn't actually just gotten them from Arthur.[5]

And that final thought implies, I think, that Arthur, who had been so horrified by the suggestion that his stepmother might have received jewelry for sexual favors, might have given the pearls to Mrs. Guy—"a woman of the world"—in precisely such a transaction. Charlotte suspects that both Arthur and Mrs. Guy are lying. But the reader does not know for certain whether Arthur sold the pearls to a Bond Street shop himself (whence Mrs. Guy bought them) or gave them to her directly.

The subtleties of imitation surface in several conversations. Charlotte grants, "Pearls are so easily imitated," but Arthur snaps back, "That's just what—to a person who knows—they're not. These have no luster, no play." He thinks he's an expert, just as he thinks he is the stepson of an irreproachable woman. To prove that he is right (on both counts), and Charlotte wrong, he goes to another expert—or, rather, says that he does and in any case lies about what that expert reported.

The true expert is the mysterious Mrs. Guy, about whose pedigree James tells us not a word. "Don't you *know* about pearls?" she says to Charlotte, and when Charlotte asks her if she is sure they are real, she replies, "Sure? For what kind of an idiot, my dear, do you take me?" Mrs. Guy awakens the pearls, brings them to life out of their long sleep, as if they were enchanted women in a fairy tale, awakened by a touch, by a kiss. Only when they are on Mrs. Guy's neck does Charlotte finally see that "the ambiguous objects" might pass for real pearls. Unlike diamonds, pearls are made by animals and are therefore fragile, changeable, and subject to life and death. They had been put to sleep by the woman referred to only as "the late Mrs. Prime," the retired actress, who was by definition of a class and respectability far below that of a vicar, and who "had mixed them in her reliquary with false things in order to put curiosity and detection off the scent." That is to say, she hid them in plain sight, where they could masquerade as fakes.

W. Somerset Maugham and China Seas

W. Somerset Maugham (1874–1965) bridges the nineteenth and twentieth centuries. His story, "Mr. Know-All," published in 1925, shares the nineteenth-century slut assumption that underlies the de Maupassant and James stories. And just as George Eliot used the theme of good and bad jewelry to tell a story about Jews (and good and bad women), Maugham uses it to talk about anti-Semitism (and a good-and-bad woman).

The narrator seems to be anti-Semitic; the story begins, "I was prepared to dislike Max Kelada even before I knew him." Max Kelada is a Semite or Levantine from some vague Middle Eastern land who pretends to be English. The narrator, who is forced to room with him on a trans-Atlantic voyage, regards him as a fake gentleman:

> "King George has many strange subjects. Mr. Kelada was short and of sturdy build, clean-shaven and dark-skinned, with a fleshy hooked nose and very large, lustrous and liquid eyes. His long black hair was sleek and curly. He spoke with a fluency in which there was nothing English and his gestures were exuberant. I felt pretty sure that a closer inspection of that British passport would have betrayed the fact that Mr. Kelada was born under a bluer sky than is generally seen in England."

Max Kelada is an obnoxious and self-promoting nuisance. Everyone calls him Mr. Know-All. One night at dinner with a Mr. Ramsay and his wife— "a very pretty little thing" who has been alone in New York for a year during her husband's absence in Japan—Mr. Kelada comments on Mrs. Ramsay's handsome pearl necklace. When Ramsay remarks, "I didn't buy it myself, of course. I'd be interested to know how much you think it cost," Kelada estimates $30,000. Then: "Ramsay smiled grimly. 'You'll be surprised to learn that Mrs. Ramsay bought that string at a department store the day before we left New York, for eighteen dollars.'"

Kelada insists that the pearls are real (wild or natural, and expensive), and Ramsay bets him $100 that they are imitations (either cultured or completely artificial, and cheap). Over Mrs. Ramsay's protests, Kelada examines the pearls with a magnifying glass he has in his pocket. Then:

> "A smile of triumph spread over his smooth and swarthy face. He handed back the chain. He was about to speak. Suddenly he caught sight of Mrs. Ramsay's face. It was so white that she looked as though she were about to faint. She was staring at him with wide and terrified eyes. They held a desperate appeal; it was so clear that I wondered why her husband did not see it. Mr. Kelada stopped with his mouth open. He flushed deeply. You could almost see the effort he was making over himself. 'I was mistaken,' he said. 'It's a very good imitation, but of course as soon as I looked through my glass I saw that it wasn't real. I think eighteen dollars is just about as much as the damn thing's worth.' He took out his pocket book and from it a hundred dollar bill. He handed it to Ramsay without a word. 'Perhaps that'll teach you not to be so cocksure another time, my young friend,' said Ramsay as he took the note. I noticed that Max Kelada's hands were trembling. The story spread over the ship as stories do, and he had to put up with a good deal of chaff that evening. It was a fine joke that Mr. Know-All had been caught out. But Mrs. Ramsay retired to her state-room with a headache."

The next morning, an envelope arrives in Kelada's stateroom, containing nothing but a hundred-dollar bill. The narrator asks him, "Were the pearls real?" and Kelada replies, "If I had a pretty little wife, I shouldn't let her spend a year in New York while I stayed at Kobe." And the story ends: "At that moment I did not entirely dislike Mr. Kelada. He reached out for his pocket book and carefully put in it the hundred-dollar note."[6]

By faking an opinion that the real pearls are false, Kelada simultaneously saves the woman's reputation and ruins his own. He behaves like a real gentleman; he shows that he himself is as real as he secretly knows the pearls to be. But nobody—with the exception of the narrator and you, gentle reader—knows this. They all go on believing that the pearls and Mr. Know-All are fakes, and the woman real.

A film was made of this story in 1950.[7] The basic plot is unchanged, though there is a great deal of additional dialogue involving Mr. Know-All, who does not seem particularly Jewish (perhaps it was not possible to treat anti-Semitism so lightly after World War II) but, though played by the entirely British Nigel Patrick, is definitely not English (as he claims to be). He is more generically Middle-European, perhaps Hungarian, and hilariously objectionable and self-promoting. The other characters are all exaggeratedly English. But the main changes serve to spell out, as obvious as a ten-foot neon sign, what is more subtly implied in the written text: that Mrs. Ramsay is in real trouble if her husband finds out that her pearls are real.

Max Kelada makes a pass at Mrs. Ramsay, and offers her a star sapphire. She says, "My husband is a very jealous man; please go away." And we see this jealousy acted out when Mr. and Mrs. Ramsay are alone in their cabin. He tells her that he feared, while he was away, that she would meet someone she liked better. Then:

"SHE: If I had, what would you have done?
HE: I would have killed him. And you.
SHE: Oh dear, I'd better watch my step, hadn't I?
HE: You certainly had."

Equally unsubtle is the emphasis on the reality or fakeness of the gorgeous, five-strand pearl necklace that she puts on when dressing for dinner. Her husband remarks that they are new, and look very expensive. He comments, "I don't know how you do it on what I give you." She insists that she picked them up for only eight pounds in a shop in Oxford Street. "Well, nobody would ever know," he assures her. Back in the lounge, there's a long discussion about the difference between natural ("real"), expensive pearls and cultured ("fake" or "imitation"), cheap pearls. Max says, "An expert can always tell the difference. And I'm an expert. I'm in the trade. All I don't know about pearls isn't worth knowing. They'll never make a cultured pearl that an expert like me can't tell with half an eye. Take my word for it, Mrs. Ramsay. . . . Those pearls are the goods. Not only are they real, but they're as fine for their size as any I've ever seen." Ramsay bets him ten pounds that they are fakes. Kelada examines the necklace with his back to the others, but in a mirror he sees Mrs. Ramsay's face, silently pleading. After a long moment, he says simply, "I was mistaken. They're imitation." Everyone laughs and Ramsay, yet again hammering home the theme of the slut assumption, remarks, "If they hadn't been, I would have had a serious talk with my wife." Against the general laughter, Kelada just says, "Never mind; we all make mistakes," and pays up. In the final scene, after the envelope with the ten pound note has been delivered, the room-mate/narrator smiles and turns what had been a question in the short story into a statement: "The pearls were real, then." And he calls Max, affectionately, "Mr. Know-all." Kelada simply replies, "Call me Max."

Fifteen years before the 1950 film, a more convoluted variation on the Maugham story (unattributed)[8] appeared in a subplot of the film *China Seas* (1935, Tay Garnett),[9] which put one more twist on the pearl necklace that flickers between real and fake:

As he boards a ship, Romanoff (played by the all-purpose slimy alien Akim Tamiroff) is looking at a man's ring, saying, "Not bad, for a synthetic stone." Soon he encounters Mr. Timmons, a short, fat, nervous man, and his good-looking wife; she is wearing a pearl necklace. Later, in the ship's lounge, Romanoff says to Mrs. Timmons, "You'd better take care of these pearls in case of piracy." Mrs. Timmons: "Why? They're artificial; they're not worth anything." Timmons: "Twelve and a half bucks. Quite a bargain, I'd say." Romanoff: "Where did you get them, Mr. Timmons?" Timmons: "Why she picked them up . . ." Mrs. Timmons interrupts: "I bought them myself, in Tokyo." Romanoff: "Well, you know, it's not always easy to tell the real from . . ." He sees her eyes, pleading and terrified, and continues: "I'm sure you didn't pay *too* much for them." Timmons: "Bet your sweet life she didn't. That little woman gets her money's worth every time, eh, Poopsie?" Later, alone with her, Romanoff asks, quietly, "Where did you *really* get those pearls?" She says, "You won't tell Wilbur, will you?" and he replies, "Twelve and a half bucks to Wilbur," winks and clicks his tongue. Still later, implicitly threatening to reveal the truth about the pearls to her husband, he forces her to kiss him (with a fade-out suggesting, under the Hayes Code, that she will sleep with him).

When Chinese pirates board the ship, she hides the pearls down the front of her dress. Seeing this, her husband becomes suspicious again: "Sweetheart, those pearls, they're not worth anything. . ." She: "I don't want to lose them." He: "There's something funny about those pearls; I'm going to have them appraised when we get to Singapore." She: "Oh, Wilbur, don't be insane." But the pirates, too, think they must be real, and grab them. As both Romanoff and Timmons watch intently, the head pirate bites them to test them. He spits them out and throws them down, whereupon Timmons says, cheerfully, "I'm sorry, Poopsie. Looks like that guy did the appraising!" and she looks daggers at Romanoff.

We are left to surmise that Romanoff was telling the truth at the beginning when he said they were fakes, and that the pirate was right to spit them out. In this new twist, the fake pearls first pretended (in the hands of her lover) to be real and then pretended (in her own hands) to be fakes. Both Romanoff and the lover who had given them to her in the first place had lied by implying that they were real—Romanoff additionally lying when he implied that he had lied for her in saying they were fakes (as Max Kelada had actually done in Maugham's story). We may also assume that, like that earlier lover, Romanoff slept with her. (All of this frames the main story, in which Jean Harlow plays a prostitute who seems to be no good but in the end turns out to be true and real.)

Maugham's genuineness is also at stake in the Max Kelada story: Is he really an anti-Semite himself, or just writing about one? Is he the narrator? Does he approve of the narrator? Does the narrator cease to be an anti-Semite at the end? And is the whole story of Kelada, like that of the clever wife,[iv] a narrative of resistance, the ethnic underdog fighting back, siding with the woman (also an underdog) against the Christian man, her husband? Is Max Kelada sympathetic to Mrs. Ramsay because the terror that he sees in her eyes is something that he knows about as a Jew?

Maugham later (1943) wrote "A String of Beads,"[10] a satire on his own Max Kelada story. At a dinner party, a governess was asked to stand in for a fashionable woman who had canceled at the last minute. Another guest at the dinner, an expert on jewels, insisted that the string of pearls the governess was wearing was genuine, worth fifty thousand pounds. She strenuously protested that she had paid only fifteen shillings for them. Eventually the truth emerged: the governess had taken her own, fake pearls to be mended and the jeweler had given her back, by mistake, someone else's real pearls. The mistake was detected, the necklaces exchanged, and the governess received a reward, which she used to set herself up as a demi-mondaine in Paris (presumably now able to get her own real jewelry from rich lovers). As the governess had substituted for a "real" member of high society, so real pearls had substituted for her fake ones.

---

iv. See chapter 6, p. 137.

The story is told to Maugham by a person who claims to have been present at the party and who remarks, "We all laughed. It was of course absurd.
We've all heard of wives palming off on their husbands as false a string of
pearls that was real and expensive. That story is as old as the hills.'" And
Maugham, retelling the vignette, continues: "'Thank you,' I said, thinking
of a little narrative of my own." Maugham is making fun of his own earlier
story in conscious self-parody. His remark here, in 1943, that "that story is
as old as the hills," is one that he returns to in introducing the film of "Mr.
Know All" in 1950. He says, "I believe it's a story of my own invention, but
I wouldn't like to go into the witness box in a court of law and take my oath
on it. I think I might venture to make use of a phrase of Dr Johnson's and
say that if a story is good it is unlikely to be new, and if it's new it's unlikely
to be good. I've come too late to a world too old." One couldn't ask for a better definition of narrative intertextuality; the world of stories is always much
older than the narrator.

Twentieth-Century Films

Intertextuality comes into its prime in Hollywood, which is ruled by the
maxim of stealing from the best (as the saying, variously attributed [often to
Milton Berle], goes; it, too, was constantly stolen). Like all effective myths,[v]
popular films recycle again and again the themes that have done well at the
box office.[11] Throughout the second half of the twentieth century, in America
and Britain, the big studios in Hollywood and Pinewood used rings and
necklaces much as they had been used in myths for hundreds of years, as
proof of identity and fidelity (or infidelity, as the case may be). But some of
the studios put new twists into the old necklaces.

Random Harvest

Two necklaces embody the remembering and forgetting of true love in the
film of *Random Harvest* (Mervyn LeRoy, 1942)[12] in ways that are strikingly
parallel to the double necklaces in *Mansfield Park* and *Daniel Deronda*.
Like so many clever wives,[vi] the heroine of *Random Harvest* pretends to be
someone else and in that guise receives jewelry from her husband, who

---

v. See chapter 11, p. 301.

vi. See chapter 6, p. 137.

does not recognize her. But this bed-trick is not consummated for many years, and there is no child. Here's the plot:

A shell-shocked World War I veteran (Ronald Colman) has lost his memory of everything before the war, including his name. He takes the name of Smith. He falls in love, on Armistice Day, with a music hall star named Margaret Hanson (Greer Garson). He calls her by her stage name of Paula; she calls him Smithy. They marry and live in the country, but one day he goes to Liverpool and there is hit by a car; he remembers that he is Charles Rainier, a wealthy man, and he goes home to his estate. He forgets Paula and all else that happened since the Armistice and the accident.

Years later, they meet again. She has resumed her name of Margaret Hanson, but he does not recognize her; she is part of the forgotten period of his life. Eventually they marry, but the marriage remains unconsummated, as he is still tied to the memory of some woman he knows he loved but cannot precisely remember—Paula. After many years, he finally recognizes that Margaret is Paula.

Smithy had given Paula an inexpensive necklace of beads that were, he said, the color of her eyes (blue). Later, Charles gave Margaret a diamond necklace with a magnificent emerald that had belonged to the Empress Marie Louise. That night he came into her bedroom to find her weeping over the old necklace of blue beads, which she had chanced to find when she went to put away her new diamond and emerald necklace. He asked if the beads had been a gift, and she told him, "He said they were the color of my eyes. They are, aren't they?" And when he asked her if she was sorry she had married him, she laughed and said of course not, for how else would she ever have gotten to wear an emerald that belonged to an empress?

Smithy/Charles gives her one necklace in each life, something he apparently likes to do, one of several character traits that survive his loss of memory. Each necklace has colored stones, blue for Smithy, green for Charles, the same necklace but not the same necklace, just as he is the same man but not the same man. She hopes that the clue of the blue necklace will trigger his memory, but he is merely jealous of the other man who gave it to her. She says, "They're just cheap little beads." Looking at his emerald necklace, he responds, "But they have a value for you that this has not." The cheap beads are real because they were given in love; she never wears them, only holds them, for she does not get to keep the love that they represent. The precious emerald necklace is fake, hollow, because it is given as a reward for services *not* rendered, a kind of apology necklace[vii] to compensate her for his inability to allow himself to love her, his rejection of her. (When he proposes to her he says, "You need have no fear that I would make any emotional demands on you. I have only sincere friendship to offer, I won't ask any more from you." This is a British euphemism for the sword in the bed.)[viii] But the emerald necklace is the one she wears, the one that connects her with the hollow remnant of her love. Though she seems to pick up the blue beads by accident as she puts away the emerald, Freud has taught us that there are no accidents: she picks up the blue beads now because the emerald reminded her of them.

The jewelry never does revive Charles's memory; it simply torments the memory of Margaret, the clever wife. The sense that there ought to be a telltale ring in *Random Harvest* persists to this day, as a 2003 posting on the Internet demonstrates. It says, in its entirety: "Did I miss something or did Ronald Coleman [sic]/Smithy not have a wedding ring when he went to Liverpool and was hit by the car?"

Vertigo *(and* Gaslight*)*

In George Cukor's version of *Gaslight* (1944), a film somewhat reminiscent of Henry James's story, "Paste," an actress makes real jewels act the part of fake jewels. A king who was the actress's lover had given her four fabulous, priceless jewels, once part of a crown. She sewed them onto her costume along with a lot of fake jewels and wore them on stage, hidden in plain sight. No one in the audience knew what they were, except the man who had given them to her, watching her from the royal box. There was even a painting of her wearing the costume with the jewels—yet another remove from reality.[13] The actress was murdered by a man (Charles Boyer) who failed to find the jewels in the house at that time. He then married the actress's niece (Ingrid Bergman), who had inherited the house, so that he could continue searching there for the jewels. He also used jewelry to "gaslight" her,[14] that is, to make her believe that she was going mad: he hid the brooch he had given her and made her think she lost it, but when she

---

vii. See chapter 10, p. 271.

viii. See chapter 7, p. 171.

found the brooch, she realized that she was sane after all. That was a vital clue of recognition—a recognition of hate, not love—provided by jewelry.

Vertigo (Alfred Hitchcock, 1958)[15] borrows several of these themes (making the woman, rather than the man, the murderous doubler) while also replicating some of the structure of *Random Harvest*. (Hitchcock, too, stole from the best, including himself, and was often stolen from.) A man called Scottie meets a woman twice, first under one name ("Madeleine," a blond) and then under another (Judy, a brunette). Only near the very end of the film do we learn that the real Madeleine's husband had hired Judy to impersonate her:

> Madeleine's husband, Gavin, hired Scottie (James Stewart) to tail his wife. Scottie followed "Madeleine" (Kim Novak) to a museum and observed her staring, for hours on end, at a portrait[16] of a woman wearing a fabulous necklace. Gavin told Scottie that the woman in the painting, Carlotta, was Madeleine's ancestor, that Madeleine had inherited the necklace and that she had recently begun to put it on and stare at herself in the mirror wearing it. Scottie and "Madeleine" became lovers. Scottie thought he saw "Madeleine" fall from a tower, but in fact, Madeleine was pushed to her death.

FIGURE 9.1 The portrait of Carlotta, by John Ferren, from Alfred Hitchcock's *Vertigo*.

Source: *Vertigo* (1958) © Universal Studios

Some time later, Scottie met Judy (Kim Novak), who was the spitting image of "Madeleine," though her hair was a different color and worn in a different style. Judy adamantly denied that she was "Madeleine." Scottie persuaded her to change her look (back) to look exactly like "Madeleine" (again) and one day they became lovers. That evening, dressing to go out, Judy asked Scottie to fasten her necklace. Looking over her shoulder as she looked at herself in the mirror, he recognized the necklace that Carlotta (in the painting) had worn. He realized that Judy was in fact "Madeleine"; or, more precisely, that "Madeleine" had been Judy in disguise.

Judy is made over to become "Madeleine," who presumably looks like the Madeleine who is to be murdered, a woman we never see. We (and Scottie) are told that Madeleine wears the necklace in imitation of her ancestor, Carlotta, whom we do see in the portrait, with the necklace. Scottie's ex-fiancée Midge (Barbara Bel Geddes), the "good girl," who is a painter, copies the painting as a joke, replacing Carlotta's face with her own. Scottie is not amused. The mythical necklace therefore travels down through four generations (and more): from Carlotta (seen wearing it in the portrait), to the murdered Madeleine (alleged to wear the necklace), to "Madeleine" (never seen with it), to Midge (wearing it in her portrait), to Judy (seen wearing it). Eventually the necklace supplies the vital proof of identity, making real Scottie's false memory of "Madeleine."

When Scottie tells Judy how he had finally realized the impersonation, he concludes, "The necklace, ... that was a slip. I remembered the necklace." Scottie reasons that Gavin must have given it to her in partial payment for her part in the masquerade, and as a lover's memento. The necklace is the sharply focused thing, when everything else is as blurry and out of focus as Doris Day's close-ups, shot through gauze and Vaseline. The necklace awakens Scottie because it is the classical mythological clue, the piece of jewelry that unmagics the amnesiac or bewitched lover, and surely if ever a man was bewitched, it's Scottie.

But Judy is bewitched too. Why else does she make the "slip" of wearing the necklace? Perhaps because, as Scottie tells her, she is careless and sentimental, qualities that she allows to override her hard-headed knowledge that it is insane to keep a souvenir of a murder. (Just as it is insane to keep a souvenir of a rape, though a lot of guys do that, too.)[ix] But also because, especially now that they have become lovers (again), she's tired of the masquerade and tired of waiting for him to figure it out. She wants to blow up the masquerade so that he'll love her as she really is. And so she gives him a great big clue. The circle of the jewelry is echoed in the spinning vortexes of the famous opening credits, in the circles of "Madeleine"'s hair-do, and in the circular tree rings of the crosscut redwoods they see together. It's echoed in the spinning circles of the room when they kiss. And it is there in the circular plot, where in the second half Scottie circles back to do again all the things he did in the first half.

In *The Living and the Dead,* the novel on which *Vertigo* is based, we learn more about the necklace, which is made of amber, capturing the ancient past (as in "flies in amber"). Madeleine is a prostitute who is tricking the man for the money and meets him twice as two different women, both named Madeleine. He is fascinated by what the first Madeleine tells him about her necklace:

> "When her mother died, she naturally inherited a lot of family things, including some jewelry and ornaments that had come down from her great-grandmother, among them an amber necklace. And these beads seem to have a special meaning for her. She's always fiddling with them and gazing at them with . . . with a sort of nostalgia. . . . I once caught her with the picture propped up beside a mirror—she had the amber necklace on and was trying to do her hair like the woman in the portrait."[17]

When he was with the second Madeleine, he found the necklace where she'd hidden it: "His fingers came in contact with something which intrigued him—some oval beads, a necklace. Yes, it was a necklace. He took it to the window and held it up in the pale glaucous light which filtered through the frosted glass. The amber beads glowed faintly golden. His hands began to tremble. There was no room for doubt." It was the necklace of the first Madeleine's great-grandmother.[18] Still, the second Madeleine denied that she was the first Madeleine, and he was almost persuaded. But then:

> "All the same, there's that necklace. . . . Why don't you wear it?"
> "Because I don't like it. I've told you so already." "Or was it because you were afraid I might recognize it?" "No."

---

ix. See chapter 5, p. 113, and chapter 7, p. 179.

He rejects her lie about where she got the necklace: "That was possible, of course ... no, it wasn't. Such a coincidence was inconceivable."[19] He rejects the argument from coincidence—and the duplicitous woman. Like Scottie, he finally uses the necklace to break out of the enchantment.

The Earrings of Madame de . . .

The problem faced by the female protagonist of Max Ophüls's *The Earrings of Madame de . . .* (1953)[20] is the reverse of that of the married women portrayed by de Maupassant and James and Maugham: she must account for a gift of diamonds not from a lover but from her husband, a gift that she discards in her indifference to him and rediscovers in her passion for her lover. She does not lie to her husband about jewelry she has received from her lover; she lies to her lover about jewelry given her by her husband. The chain reaction of lies she generates demonstrates that while to lie to a husband is normal, to lie to a lover (about lies you told to your husband) is unforgivable treachery.

The prelude to the film tells us that nothing would have marred the happy, uneventful life of the Countess Louise de . . . had it not been for the jewelry. And it does seem so:

> To raise cash for her extravagances, the Countess Louise (Danielle Darrieux) sells a valuable pair of heart-shaped diamond earrings back to the jeweler from whom her husband, the Count, General André de . . . (Charles Boyer), had bought them. (That was the first financial transaction; hers now is the second.) When the jeweler asks, "What will you tell your husband?" she smiles and tells him not to worry; she'll think of something. And indeed, she manages it quite well: at the opera, she tells her husband she lost the earrings. He believes her, and searches everywhere.[21] The jeweler, frightened by a newspaper article alleging the theft of the earrings, tells the general that his wife had sold them to him; the general buys them back (the third financial transaction) and gives them to his mistress, whom he is sending away to Constantinople. When she arrives there, she tells the customs officer that they are "a gift from a man who loved me." Later the mistress sells them (the fourth transaction) and Baron Fabrizio

Donati, the Italian ambassador to France (Vittorio de Sico), buys them (the fifth transaction).

Baron Donati, returning from Constantinople to Paris, meets the Countess Louise briefly at another customs shed, another border. Through a series of encounters, they fall in love. They meet only in public, but the general suspects them. Louise travels to Italy by herself. Donati brings the earrings to her there and presents them, saying, "They could have been made for you," as indeed they were. Back in Paris, Louise pretends to find the earrings again in her closet, among her gloves. She thinks she has fooled her husband, and so she wears them in public, but of course he knows she never lost them and realizes that she must have gotten them from Donati. He takes the earrings from her, summons Donati, shows him the earrings, and says, "Constantinople?" to which Donati replies, "Yes." The general then tells him the true story, concluding, "I want you to take these jewels to my jeweler and tell him to charge them to me."[22]

Donati confronts Louise. He asks her what she had told her husband that made it possible for her to wear the earrings in public; she concocts a series of desperate lies that she claims to have told (she had gotten the earrings from a rich aunt who detests her husband; she had gotten them from her mother). Now she is telling her lover lies about the lies she told her husband. But Donati, who knows the truth, tells her that he will never see her again. He takes the earrings to the jeweler (transaction #6), who presumably pays him for them; and the general buys them back from the jeweler (#7, the third time the general has bought them).

The general gives the earrings back to Louise, but when he sees how much she loves them, he immediately takes them back and makes her give them to a poor relative, her niece, who has just had a baby. The niece says, "I hope you too will have such a happy event soon"; but Louise is barren. The niece then sells the earrings back to the same jeweler (transaction #8),[23] and the jeweler offers them to the general (#9a), noting that this would be the fourth time the general has bought them ("It's our usual business"). But this time the general refuses, saying, "Don't bother me with those stupid jewels." Now Louise sees them in the jeweler's window and buys them back again (#9b), selling all of her other jewelry to pay for them.

When the general looks in her room and says, "I don't see your diamond cross or your emeralds," she shows him the earrings and says, "I sold them for these." Now he apologizes to her for his own indiscretions, but challenges Donati to a duel. She takes the jewels to the church and offers them to the Virgin, praying that Donati will not die, insisting, truthfully, that they never slept together; it was all just in their minds. Donati is killed in the duel and Louise dies of a broken heart. The jewels remain in the church, with a note indicating that they are the gift of Madame de . . .

Louise tries to justify having the earrings (more precisely, wearing them) by pretending to find them again, and she might have gotten away with it, had the frightened jeweler not told all to the general at the beginning. When she buys them back for the last time, she promises the jeweler, "I won't wear them; and in fact I'll have to hide them." She keeps her word, but her husband finds out the truth not by seeing the earrings but by *not* seeing all her other jewelry; the earrings have become a negative force, a subtraction.

When Donati gives her the diamond earrings, he asks her, as the jeweler had asked, but with a twist, "How will you wear them?" And when she brushes this off, as she had the jeweler's question, he adds, "How is it that your husband allows you to accept such a gift?" This question reveals the same slut assumption that underlies the nineteenth-century stories: expensive jewelry betrays a woman's infidelity. (It works on the general, too. Seeing his wife wearing the earrings, he rightly concludes that Donati has given them to her because they are lovers.) But then, why did Donati give them to her? Did he expect her to wear them only when she was alone, the way people who steal famous works of art can only contemplate them behind locked doors?[x] To answer Donati, Louise concocts her first lie to him, lying about the lie she will actually tell the general: "I'll tell him a distant aunt left them to me; that's our little lie." But no; it's just *her* little lie, not *theirs*. And that is her undoing. Donati rejects her, not because she lied to her husband but because she lied to him, Donati, about the lie she was going to tell her husband. That is when he says he

---

x. This was Jean Plaidy's interpretation of Jeanne de la Motte's suggestion about Marie Antoinette and the diamond necklace: "Sometimes she puts it on in private." See chapter 8, p. 210.

can no longer believe in her. He leaves her before she finally confesses the truth, that the earrings were a wedding present from her husband. It is only when the general learns that Louise had lied to Donati, too, that he realizes she is in love with him.

Louise's attitude to the earrings is the barometer of her changing capacity for true love. After all, the diamonds are hearts—"hearts made of diamonds," *coeurs en diamants*. At the start, she hesitates to sell them, recalling that her husband had given them to her at their wedding, as a symbol of his love, but then she realizes that she loves all her other jewelry more, a sad comment on the marriage. She comes to value the earrings only when they are the gift of a man other than her husband. She croons to them, "Poor earrings, you had to go all the way to Constantinople before you could come back to me." After Donati leaves her, and she buys the earrings back, they become a fetish to her; she has them in the place of the lover she has lost. When the general discovers what she has given up to have them (all the things she would not part with at the start of the film) and sees how happy she is to have them, how she caresses them and kisses them as if they were her lover, he realizes how deeply she is in love with Donati. He says to her, in anger, "You're trying to turn the regret of lost love [*chagrin*] into mementos [*souvenirs*]." The earrings tell him the truth. By this time the language of the earrings has been thoroughly glossed and is patent to all parties to the transactions. The general, who hated to see her so happy because of another man, hates even more to see her so unhappy on account of the same man, and he determines to kill Donati.

When Donati bought the earrings, he loved no one. He bought them in the joyful expectation that he would find some woman to give them to; we get the impression that he has done this often before. And he uses the earrings to get to meet Louise: when he first catches sight of her in the customs shed, and wants to remain there to talk with her, he asks the customs man to lie, to pretend to be querying him about the earrings, though as a diplomat he is exempt from customs inspections. But that's his only lie, and though, like her lies, it is about the earrings, it has no real relevance to her, since he tells it before he knows her or loves her. At one point, he tells her, "Our happiness is only superficially superficial."[24] It seems to be fake, because they only meet in public, and waltz in ballrooms, but never make love; nevertheless, it is real. Thus he remains a man of honor, not actually lying to her husband. She, of course, lies constantly to everyone, about the earrings and about love.

The ultimate transaction of Louise's earrings is religious. In the beginning of the film, her prayer book falls to the floor when she's looking for something to sell, and she remarks casually, "I've never needed it much." She breezes into the church and gives only four centimes for a candle, as she prays that the jeweler will agree to buy the earrings. And her prayer is answered. But in the end, she really does pray, and promises her earrings to the Virgin Mary in the vain hope of saving Donati's life in the duel. This time her prayers are not answered: her lover dies, but the Virgin keeps the earrings.

Thus the earrings circle back to Louise, even as they have circled back, again and again, to the jeweler. Like Polycrates with his ring,[xi] the jeweler can't get rid of them. The circulation of the earrings is visually reflected in the endless turning and turning of the waltz, as the camera circles around the couple in love.[25] The cycle of financial/sexual transactions is very like the cycle of sexual transactions in Arthur Schnitzler's play *La Ronde* (1897, filmed by Max Ophüls in 1950). A bracelet tracks the sexual circle in "Ring around the Rosy," a variant of *La Ronde* (plus *The Earrings of Madame de ...*) that is the second of three ballet episodes in a film (*Invitation to the Dance*) made by Gene Kelly in 1956, just three years after *The Earrings of Madame de ...*:

> A man gives his wife a beautiful bracelet; she gives it to an artist (Igor Youskevitch) who gives it to his model, who gives it to a suitor, who gives it to a femme fatale, who gives it to a crooner, who gives it to a hat-check girl (Diana Adams). But when the hat-check girl's lover, a Marine (Gene Kelly), sees the bracelet, he assumes she has been unfaithful, yanks it from her wrist, and leaves. Later, the drunken Marine gives it to a streetwalker (Tamara Toumanova). She walks past a hotel, where the original husband spots the bracelet on her wrist, buys it, and returns home, joyously greeted by his wife.

Significantly, Kelly gave to the only character that he himself danced (the Marine)[26] the explicit pantomime of the emotional significance of the gift

---

xi. See chapter 2, p. 30.

of the bracelet implicit in *all* of the encounters: the Marine assumes that his girl has gotten it by sleeping with someone else.

The *New Yorker*, in 2011, ran a delightful short piece entitled "Girls' Best Friend,"[27] that I, at least, see as an *homage à* Max Ophüls. It began with an anecdote identified as "company legend, . . . related over the phone by a Van Cleef executive," and said to have taken place in Paris, sometime in the 1950s:

> A woman walked into Van Cleef and Arpels and coveted an expensive diamond necklace, worth perhaps four hundred thousand francs. She told the jeweler that she would return with her husband: "Tell him the price is half that. I promise I'll pay in full." The next day, she came in with her husband, pretended to fall in love with the necklace for the first time, and got him to buy it for two hundred thousand francs. Later, she returned the necklace and, still later, came in with her lover. Same routine, and the lover paid the remaining two hundred thousand francs. Everyone was happy.

A now elderly Van Cleef staff member, hearing this anecdote, remarked, "I've heard stories like that. . . . You know, that was pure gossip." But the *New Yorker* wisely commented, "Reality can sometimes merge with fantasy when it comes to jewels." Paris in the 1950s is just when and where *The Earrings of Madame de* . . . was playing to rave reviews. I wonder if the clever lady who brought her husband and lover into Van Cleef and Arpels[28]—or the person who started the "gossip," not to mention the Van Cleef staff member who had "heard stories"—had seen the film. Unlike the Countess Louise, however, the *New Yorker* lady has cleverly worked things so that she can wear her diamond necklace both with her husband and with her lover, and each of them thinks both that the diamonds are real (which they are) and that the woman is faithful to him alone (which she is not).

Real Jewelry and False Women

The tales of fake jewelry intersect so often with the mythology of sexual deception in marriage because the necklaces and earrings in these stories function as evidence of adultery, in contrast with the rings in other stories that symbolize true love, and/or marriage. The protagonists of these stories are primarily concerned about the chastity of the women, and therefore not so much about the genuineness of their jewelry as its provenance. But the questionable authenticity of pieces of circular jewelry ambiguates their ability to authenticate the identity of the women who wear them.

Jewelry, like a woman, is always suspected of being false. The clever wives,[xii] after all, succeeded in their tasks by becoming fake courtesans (or fake rope dancers, or even fake kings) and, in effect, fake wives. Both women and their jewelry may be replaced by imitations, doubles or forgeries; the women masquerade as other women and are unmasked; the genuine jewels are replaced by identical fakes. The jewelry in *Random Harvest* and *Vertigo* and *The Earrings of Madame de . . .* is real, but the women are not.

The traditional assumption is that the fake is inferior to the real. Lorelei Lee, a "professional lady" in Anita Loos's novel *Gentlemen Prefer Blondes* (1925),[xiii] remarks of "paste" diamond jewelry. " 'Paste' is the name of the word a girl ought to do to a gentleman that handed her one.' "[29] For the "professional lady," fake jewelry is a sign of false love. In the 1958 film musical, *Gigi* (based on a 1944 novella by Colette), a young girl (Leslie Caron) is tutored in the art of a courtesan, which includes the ability to identify fine jewels. Her aunt, herself an old courtesan, expresses her scorn for a woman who is wearing "dipped" black pearls, that is, fake pearls, that her lover had given her: the woman does not know that they are fakes and therefore does not know that her lover is cooling. In this case, the fake jewel that pretends to be real is a sign that the man is a fake, his love a fake.

This simple equation was affirmed in a story that made the supplementary point, namely, that a real jewel that pretends to be fake is a sign that a man's love is true. Elizabeth Taylor[xiv] told this story about her husband, Mike Todd. A pair of inexpensive, paste "diamond" earrings in the window of a boutique in Paris caught her eye and she bought them. Taylor later wrote:

---

xii. See chapter 6, p. 137.

xiii. See chapter 10, p. 265.

xiv. We will return to Liz Taylor's diamonds in chapter 10, pp. 276, 281.

"A couple of months later we were back in New York, and I went to put on those earrings. . . . I opened the box, and the earrings looked all polished up, and I put them on. But there was something different about how they fit. And I said, 'Mike, there's something wrong with my earrings. They're not quite the same.' Well, he just chuckled and told me he'd taken the paste ones and had them made up with real diamonds!"[30]

But most of the nineteenth-century stories of necklaces we've seen turn this simple logic (fake jewelry = false love) on its head, and argue that if the jewelry is real, true, the woman is false—that is, untrue to her husband. If, on the other hand, she can prove that the jewelry is a fake, she remains authentic. (In modern variants, a woman can also authenticate herself by proving that she bought the jewelry herself.)[xv] In Alfred Hitchcock's 1955 film *To Catch a Thief*, Grace Kelly assumes that Cary Grant, a notorious cat burglar, wants to steal the fabulous diamond necklace she is wearing. "You know as well as I do that this necklace is an imitation," he says. To which she replies, "I'm not."

The paradoxical judgment that the fake may be more valuable than the real has become quite trendy in twentieth- and twenty-first-century postmodernism. And jewelry, fake or real, is often a key to this inversion. Anthony Hope's novel *The Prisoner of Zenda* (1894) was often adapted for stage and screen. In John Cromwell's film version with Ronald Colman (1937), the drunken king gives his ring (presumably with the royal seal) to the better man who will stand in for him as his double. But the double gives his own ring to Flavia, the woman they both love, and Flavia, who at first believes that this is the king's ring and that the double is the true king, continues to wear the ring when she discovers that he is not the true king, but realizes that he is her true love (and that, therefore, the fake ring is the true ring, for her).

The fake was often superior, certainly more useful, than the real. Formulas for making imitation gemstones had been part of alchemy from ancient times, but they came into their own in the eighteenth century, when Christopher Pinchbeck compounded a brass alloy (still called "pinchbeck" in his honor) that could pass for gold, so that ordinary people could wear "golden" jewelry; his son Edward Pinchbeck perfected a way of

---

xv. See chapter 10, p. 288.

making paste stones that looked like diamonds. Rich people, too, openly made use of these fakes, "for convenience and in the interest of preserving one's authentic jewels . . . without on the one hand risk of loss or, on the other, revealing that one had been obliged to relinquish one's material wealth."[31]

Lorelei Lee, in *Gentlemen Prefer Blondes*, commented on the use of fake jewelry for security:

> "The gentleman at the jewelry store said that quite a lot of famous girls in Paris had imitations of all their jewelry and they put the jewelry in the safe and they really wore the imitations, so they could wear it and have a good time. But I told him I thought that any girl who was a lady would not even think of having such a good time that she did not remember to hang on to her jewelry."[32]

But jewelry, like a woman (or a man), can also pretend to be what it is. Wealthy women in New York City used to wear copies of their diamonds, like the women in Lorelei Lee's Paris, in fear of being mugged; but after a while, when this practice became well known, many of them once again wore their real diamonds, trusting that would-be muggers would take them for fakes. One woman who owned a lot of valuable diamond jewelry had copies made of all her major pieces. When she went to a gala affair, where rich people might be expected to be present, she wore the copies. But when she went out in her jeans, casually, she wore the real jewelry, because no one would think they were real.[33] And there are other ways in which fake jewelry (or something that proclaims itself to be fake jewelry) is more useful than the real thing; a sign seen in the window of a jewelry store in Vancouver proclaimed: "All display rings are replicas with no cash value."[34] Presumably this would discourage thieves from smashing the window.

A close parallel to this sort of thinking was recently reported by the *New York Times* in an article entitled "Real Fur, Masquerading as Faux." It began, "The problem was that the faux fur was, in fact, real fur. That's right: it was faux faux fur." Apparently several retailers were federally prosecuted for marketing real fur (rabbit, raccoon, and, possibly, dyed mink) as fake fur. As the *Times* commented, "On the face of it, the real-for-fake switch might not seem to make business sense." But in fact, because many people have ethical objections to the killing of animals for fur (or social misgivings about being caught wearing it anywhere but at the opera), they prefer faux fur, and so the sellers mislabel the furs in order to reach a wider market. "The lines between real and fake have gotten really blurry," said Dan Mathews, a senior vice president with People for the Ethical Treatment of Animals. And the *Times* concludes, scratching its head, "Mislabeling real fur—inexpensive rabbit as luxurious mink, say— is an old game. But mislabeling real fur as fake fur is relatively new."[35] Mislabeling real jewelry as fake jewelry, on the other hand, is as old as the hills.

10

Are Diamonds a Woman's Best Friend?

The Symbolic Baggage of Baguettes

The diamond engagement ring is the epitome of "bling," a word that the *Oxford English Dictionary* glosses as "(a piece of) ostentatious jewellery. Hence: wealth; conspicuous consumption." "Conspicuous consumption" is a term that Thorstein Veblen coined in 1899 (in *The Theory of the Leisure Class*) to describe people who buy expensive items to display their wealth and income rather than to cover their real needs. A "bling ring," as in the title of Sofia Coppola's 2013 film, is both a band of jewel thieves and an ostentatiously expensive jeweled ring. Both definitions of the bling ring are evoked by De Beers Consolidated Mines, Ltd., which has, since the nineteenth century, dominated and controlled the diamond industry—both mining and trading, operating mines of all kinds (open-pit, underground, large-scale alluvial, coastal and deep sea) all over the world. For in the twentieth century De Beers invented a new mythology of the engagement ring, the success of which allowed them to elevate the price of diamonds to a dizzying height that amounts to highway robbery. That this new myth—that a diamond ring was an essential part of an engagement—took off as it did was due in large part to the momentum it stole from the pervasive mythology that connects rings with sex and/or love.

Myths generally look back to a blurry, unknowable past, but from time to time you can see a myth taking shape right before your eyes. Such is the case with the myth that you have to have a diamond ring when you become engaged to be married, a dogma that has been called "an urgent mythology."[1] Many people take it for granted now, but it is really a most peculiar idea. Tom Zoellner reports that he asked the villagers who worked in the diamond mines in Africa "if they knew how their diamonds would eventually be used when they left Africa. They answered no, they had no idea. 'In America,' I said, 'it is traditional for a man to give a woman a diamond when he asks her to marry him,' and this set off a round of laughter. They had never heard of such a thing. It was ridiculous to think of. I was asked . . . if I was joking."[2]

The essential diamond engagement ring is a new myth. But "new" myths always ride piggyback on old myths, and the engagement ring myth draws upon the more general mythologies of jewelry that have buoyed up the stories in this book. Zoellner remarks of the first advertisements for diamond engagement rings, "There is not a hint of anything being cutting-edge or trendy or modern. There was instead an overt expectation that the reader was *of course* going to play the game just as his ancestors had (even though they probably hadn't)."[3] As J. Courtney Sullivan describes De Beers's task, "Not only were they to impress upon average women and men—especially the men!—that diamonds were now an imperative for marriage, they were to make it seem as though it had always been that way."[4]

Making it "seem as though it had always been that way" is the job description of a myth, as Mircea Eliade pointed out long ago: the myth that happens now must make us believe that it has happened already *in illo tempore*, "in that [ancient] time."[5] And so De Beers didn't have to invent the myth from scratch; they could hitch their wagon to the old stories about women and their jewelry. Moreover, diamonds, being devoid of any particular shape or color, can fit into anyone's myth. They are, as Zoellner puts it, "nothing more than an empty cage for our dreams."[6]

An article in the *Economist* in 1997, entitled, "The Diamond Business: Glass with Attitude," noted that De Beers, from their headquarters on Charterhouse Street in London, were selling not just gems, "but symbols, myths, magic. As worldwide dealer in enchanting illusions, Disney has nothing on De Beers."[7] Moreover, the *Economist* declared:

> "Vanity, greed, envy, desire, even love: the diamond barons could scarcely appeal to more common human instincts. . . . The diamond myth lives in a world a bit outside of logic, outside of ordinary economics: a world where there are still a few talismanic substances whose magic rubs off on the bearer. Thus do the sorcerers of Charterhouse Street concoct glamour from carbon, and fool us all."[8]

De Beers added to the inherited mythology of the ring of love the simple codicil that it had to have a diamond. But that rider trailed a long narrative train, for diamonds have a mythology of their own, beyond their place in the more general mythology of jewelry. Philip Roth beautifully captured this mythology in the words of a Jewish merchant who sold diamond wedding and engagement rings:

> "It's a big deal for working people to buy a diamond, ... no matter how small. The wife can wear it for the beauty and she can wear it for the status. And when she does, this guy is not just a plumber—he's a man with a wife with a diamond. His wife owns something that is imperishable. Because beyond the beauty and the status and the value, the diamond is imperishable. A piece of the earth that is imperishable, and a mere mortal is wearing it on her hand!"[9]

Everyone knows that diamonds are hard, therefore indestructible and permanent, and colorless, therefore honest ("transparent") and pure. Or are they? Let's consider first hardness, then purity.

Diamonds, whose name comes from a Greek word for "unbreakable" (*adamas*), are indeed hard, the hardest of all material substances; they can scratch anything else. In sixteenth-century Italy, gems engraved and set in signet rings were valued because, unlike gold and precious metals, stones could not be liquefied; their power therefore was believed to be unchanging, permanent.[10] In ancient and medieval India, the hardness of diamonds made them a fairly obvious symbol not of love but of virility, and these "militaristic/masculinist connotations"[11] help to explain why Maharajahs "often *owned* diamonds for symbolic reasons," though they rarely wore them as jewelry.[12]

But in the hands of De Beers, the meaning of the hardness of diamonds underwent a significant change, to stand for the hoped-for durability and permanence of marriage. Unlike flesh and memory, and above all unlike love, diamonds do not seem to be subject to time. In the twentieth century, ads proclaimed: "May your marriage last as long as your diamond."[13] A man buying an engagement ring joked about what a cubic zirconia would say about their union: "A diamond is a 10 on the Mohs scale," he said, referring to the scale of mineral hardness. "C.Z. is an eight. What am I saying—our relationship is only strong as about an eight out of 10?"[14] During World War II, the diamond that a soldier's fiancée wore was said to give protection against her soldier's infidelity abroad; according to the ads, "Through all their wartime parting, this shining symbol, their engagement diamond, so close to her, by him so well remembered, inspires an inward courage that disdains all doubt and fear."[15] In other words, your GI would stay away from French prostitutes.

But the durability of diamonds was also contrasted with the transience of the human body (and, perhaps, of the sort of love inspired by the body). The lyricist Leo Robin contrasted the changeless qualities of diamonds with the inevitable changes that would overcome the women who wore them:

> Men grow cold / As girls grow old, / And we all lose our charms in the end. / But square cut or pear shape, / These rocks don't lose their shape / . . . Time rolls on, / And youth is gone, / And you can't straighten up when you bend. / But stiff back / Or stiff knees, / You stand straight at Tiffany's.

(In an earlier, unpublished version, Robin had promised more: "But stiff back / Or stiff knees / They cure you at Tiffneys.")[16] Diamonds outlast youth, outlast a human lifetime—and, by implication, outlast love.

But nothing is unchanging, not even diamonds, let alone love. There is an old German legend about a magic ring set with a diamond: "Should the woman wearing this ring prove unfaithful in love, the gold turned to dross, and the diamond became glass."[17] In other stories, a ring may break in two, or the color of the stone may change, if the giver proves untrue. And indeed, diamonds, though hard, are not indestructible; they are very brittle, more brittle than jade, easy to crack with a moderate tap of a hammer.[18] Diamonds burn, too, if the flame is hot enough. Diamonds are not permanent after all. Besides, even the big ones are pretty small, compared with, say, a Porsche or even a pearl necklace. You can as easily lose a diamond ring as any other ring[i] (and it is more likely to be stolen). So much for hardness, indestructibility, and permanence.

Perhaps we can do better with purity. The symbolism is fairly transparent, like the diamond itself. The function of a diamond "is to display the matrimonial promise, which must be clear and unambiguous."[19] George

---

i. See chapters 2 through 7.

Buchanan (1500–1582) wrote a Latin poem comparing the hardness and purity of the diamond to those same qualities of his heart:

> This gem behold, the emblem of my heart
> From which my cousin's image ne'er shall part;
> Clear in its lustre, spotless does it shine,
> 'Tis clear and spotless as this heart of mine.
> What though the stone a greater hardness wears,
> Superior firmness still the figure bears.[20]

The last line (*Quamvis dura magis, non magis firma*) is more literally rendered as, "And though less hard, it's no less firm." So firmness, rather than the diamond's special hardness, is the quality of love, though purity is also essential. The ring in this poem was a gimmel-ring ("twins ring"),[ii] two diamonds joining together to form a heart, of which Queen Elizabeth I is said to have kept one half and given the other to her cousin Mary, Queen of Scots (whom she later beheaded—so much for lasting love).

Thus the hardness of diamonds and the purity of a loving heart can be mutually exclusive.[21] Moreover, diamonds are frequently colored and often flawed; that's why people pay experts to tell them how good their diamond is. And they are easily faked, more easily than rubies or pearls, constantly imitated by "paste";[iii] hence, again, the need for experts. So much for purity.

Who Said, "Forever"? Anita Loos, Leo Robin, De Beers, and N. W. Ayer

The alleged durability and permanence of diamonds was used by De Beers to engineer the transformation of diamonds into the most important of all gemstones. To appreciate the nature of this achievement, we need to take a brief look at their history.

From the beginning of the Common Era to early modern times, most diamonds came from shallow pits near the Krishna River in Golconda, in what is now Hyderabad, in India.[22] But then, in 1725, a major source of diamonds was found in Brazil; in 1860 the great diamond mines in

---

ii. See Preface, p. xvi.

iii. See chapter 9, pp. 235, 254, 256.

Africa were discovered;[23] and in 1888 Cecil Rhodes, with Rothschild funding, founded De Beers. (Indian diamond merchants said that Brazilian diamonds were inferior, so people used to ship Brazilian diamonds to India and sell them—often to people in Brazil—as Indian diamonds.[24] Look again at the double-back track of the diamond earrings in that Max Ophüls film.)[iv]

Long after Brazil, and then Africa, had taken over from India the major part of the diamond trade, the mythology, as usual, trailed behind. Orientalism continued to color novels, films, and legends about big diamonds that carried fiendish curses. The Koh-i-Noor was a 186-carat diamond (later cut to a mere 108 carats) the shape and size of a small hen's egg. It had belonged to a series of Indian rulers, including the Mughal Emperor Babur, before the British stole it in 1850 and made it quite literally the jewel in the crown of Queen Victoria. Indian legend alleged that it would bring bad luck to any man who wore it, and from Victoria on, no male ruler has worn it—an interesting sidelight on women's right to own jewelry. (A much-cited but unverifiable "Indian text" warns: "He who owns this diamond will own the world, but will also know all its misfortunes. Only God, or a woman, can wear it with impunity.")[25] The 45.52-carat blue Hope diamond (named after one of its many owners, Henry Phillip Hope) was originally said to have been stolen from an unspecified Hindu idol, but "in subsequent accounts, specific, suspect gods and divine figures—Rama, Sita, Shiva, Vishnu, Kali, and even the Buddha, have been named."[26] (There are also many stories about a curse on the Hope diamond that supposedly brought death to several of its owners.) The Eye of Brahma (a 67.5-carat black diamond, also called the Black Orlov) was said to have been stolen from a temple in Pondicherry, in South India, and was blamed for the mysterious deaths of several of its owners. The "moonstone" in Wilkie Collins's 1868 novel of that name is a large diamond said to have been taken from the forehead of the Hindu god Shiva in the temple of Somnath, "Lord of the Moon," on the western shore of Gujarat, India, and tracked to England by servants of the god Vishnu (not Shiva, but never mind; in the dark of British Orientalism, all Hindu gods look alike); several people in the novel died, under the requisite "mysterious circumstances," before the gem was returned to India. And so the Orientalist mythology of cursed diamonds continued

---

iv. See chapter 9, p. 248.

to grow. Anita Loos, in her 1925 novel *Gentlemen Prefer Blondes*, makes fun of this mythology when she has Lorelei Lee remark, on being told that the Russian Crown jewels were unlucky, that she still meant to buy them, and if she found out that they were in fact unlucky, "I could toss them over my left shoulder into the Hudson river some night when there was a new moon, and it would take away the curse."[27] (The cursed diamond also appears in a joke about a beautiful blonde wearing a ring with an enormous diamond that, she said, was called the Krupnick diamond, and came with the Krupnick curse—Krupnick.)

We have seen the role that diamond necklaces played in the affairs of Marie Antoinette[v] and in various stories by George Eliot, Guy de Maupassant, and others.[vi] As for rings, the tradition of diamond engagement rings is attested among kings and the upper classes from at least 1475, the date of a miniature in the Vatican library that depicts Hymen, god of marriage, wearing a tunic on which diamond rings are painted, standing before an altar on which "a huge diamond ring binds together a pair of flaming torches as a symbol of fidelity."[28] In 1477, Austria's Archduke Maximilian gave a diamond engagement ring to his fiancée, Marie of Burgundy. In 1655, Samuel Pepys married and gave his wife (to whom he was famously unfaithful) a diamond ring.[29] In 1829, Prince Albert gave Queen Victoria a ring with a large heart-shaped diamond surrounded by smaller diamonds forming two hands.[30]

But diamonds first became fashionable among the middle class in America only in the 1890s,[31] just when the discovery of diamonds in South Africa led to a glut, making diamonds very cheap to buy, and when Thorstein Veblen wrote his *Theory of the Leisure Class*. By then, diamonds were no longer trophies for royalty only but were available for the fast-growing tribe of American *nouveaux riches*.[32] In 1892, Sears was selling diamond rings through the Roebuck mail-order catalogue for as little as $5.75 each (about $150 today).[33]

By the early decades of the twentieth century, rings, with or without diamonds, became common symbols of engagement to be married.[34] But it was not until the end of the Depression years, in 1939, that the big marketing push for diamond engagement rings began.[35] That is when Harry Oppenheimer of De Beers hired the N. W. Ayer advertising agency

---

v. See chapter 8, p. 206.

vi. See chapter 9, p. 234.

to boost diamond sales.[36] Oppenheimer's idea was to turn diamonds into "an essential middle-class accessory, a statement of aspiration to luxury, yet within the reach of bourgeois pockets."[37] People had other things on their minds besides diamonds from 1939 to 1945, but the advertising campaign became spectacularly successful after World War II, in 1948. Why then? Well, there was a lot of money around at the end of the war, and there were also a number of cross-ethnic marriages in which the bride and groom might expect very different sorts of wedding gifts. Diamonds stepped neatly into the breach as the modern version of bride-price, the inverse of a dowry. As Robert N. Proctor puts it, in his furious and often hilarious diatribe against the diamond cartel:

> "In an urban society you cannot really give a pig or a cow as bride-price; a *new kind of social currency* was needed to ease the transition, to cement the exchange.[38] ... Diamonds did for jewelry what MacDonald's did for the evening meal; the diamond became a kind of gemstone Big-Mac, albeit an expensive one."[39]

But the main reason diamond rings took off like a rocket at that time, over and above the social and economic factors, was the brilliant Ayer/De Beers campaign. As Proctor (who has a world-famous collection of agates) bitterly put it, "Diamonds are expensive because they are *plentiful* and *ugly*; agates are cheap because they are *rare* and *beautiful*."[40] How did De Beers turn this ugly duckling into a financial swan? Oppenheimer concentrated on planting in the public imagination the belief that diamonds were an essential part of any romantic rite of passage, first engagements, then weddings, and, later, anniversaries,[41] simultaneously transforming gemstone tastes and engagement finances.[42]

The key to the Ayer campaign was the phrase, "A diamond is forever," which Mary Frances Gerety, a copywriter for Ayer, came up with in 1948. The phrase can be traced back to a line in Anita Loos's 1925 novel, *Gentlemen Prefer Blondes*: "Kissing your hand may make you feel very good but a diamond and sapphire bracelet lasts forever."[43] The De Beers copywriter may well have read the Loos book before coming up with her motto.[44] Two women, in that case, are responsible for this epoch-making exaltation of a diamond.

Loos's book was made into a stage musical that opened on December 8, 1949 (music by Jule Styne, lyrics by Leo Robin), with Carol Channing as Lorelei Lee. Leo Robin had worked on the script in 1939, and again in 1942.

The miracle of love

A girl's joy, flowering like a rose, is radiant and full in the
lovely miracle of love awakening. And for her a star,
blazing bright as her dreams, will recall this moment always.
Her engagement diamond, fair spark of eternity,
reflects the light of her happiness in changeless splendor,
and treasures its tender message of love until the end of time.

Remember, color, cutting and clarity,
as well as carat weight, contribute to
a diamond's beauty and value.
A trusted jeweler is your best advisor.
Extended payments can usually be arranged.

a diamond is forever

De Beers Consolidated Mines, Ltd.

FIGURE 10.1 An advertisement with the De Beers motto, "A Diamond Is Forever."
Source: © The Advertising Archives/Alamy.

In the final version, he transformed the Loos line into the song line,[45] "A
kiss on the hand may be quite continental, / but diamonds are a girl's best
friend." (Over the previous decade, he had left a number of rejected lines
for this song on bits of paper. One, in the Orientalist tradition, was: "When
you are left with no amour / It's nice to have a Koh-i-noor.")[46] Significantly,
both Gerety and Robin jettisoned Loos's sapphires and concentrated on
the diamonds; and Robin, but not Gerety, also jettisoned "forever."

For the girls Robin had in mind weren't interested in the sort of thing that "lasts forever" (such as an idealized marriage: the song also contains the line, "That's when those louses / Go back to their spouses"). He substituted for "lasts forever" a phrase that became one of the most famous lines in the history of show business (more famous, even, than Mary Gerety's "forever" line), the title of the song Robin himself regarded as "the National Anthem for the Women of America"[47] and that is surely one of the great American jewelry myths: diamonds are a girl's best friend. As Alex Gottlieb, an old friend of Leo Robin and Jule Styne, remarked, "Leo's alteration of the line's emphasis is a big one, even though he may not have been aware of the change. The joke is not merely that diamonds are better than money, because they last, unlike men; that goes without saying. . . . They are friends, best friends."[48]

But that discarded "forever," which had been built into diamond mythology for centuries (the quality of lasting that "goes without saying"), is precisely what Mary Frances Gerety picked up in the tagline, "A Diamond Is Forever." The *Economist* article ("The Diamond Business: Glass with Attitude") included the subtitle, "Forever, for now"[49] and glossed the implications well: "That clever marketing slogan . . . sells two dreams in one: that diamonds bring eternal love and romance, and that diamonds never lose their value."[50] (Diamonds were also supposed to be classic and timeless, eternal in practical terms, "a consumer good without the distraction of fashion changes.")[51] Proctor remarks that "diamonds are of course forever"[52] in several ways, including being " 'forever yours' if you try to sell them";[53] you can't get back even half of what you paid for them. (Of course, that does make a diamond a realistic symbol for some marriages.) In the Smithsonian book about the Hope diamond (which now resides in the Smithsonian's collection), the last line is, "the Hope, more than the rest of us, will likely be here forever"[54] (as in, "Hope springs eternal"?)[55]

In addition to that "forever," the Gerety revision of the Loos phrase made a counterintuitive (from the standpoint of marketing) move from "diamonds" to "a diamond," a transition from plural to singular that brought the symbolism of purity back into the equation and made the diamond legitimate, authoritative, socially authentic. Recall the distinction between the married woman authenticated by her one man, one ring, and the courtesan authenticated by her many lovers, many jewels.[vii] And

---

vii. See chapter 1, p. 20.

remember what happened to the respectable married women who crossed the line by accepting real jewelry from more than one man.[viii] The Ayer/ De Beers ads promised to protect married women from that danger, from that promiscuous mythology. By changing "Diamonds are" to "A diamond is," moving from bad girls to a good girl, they moved from show business to big business.

The women that the ads were aimed at didn't want to be courtesans; they wanted true love. Ayer/De Beers nailed the "I love you forever" mythology to a single diamond: purity and permanence, purity instead of promiscuity, permanence instead of a series of conquests. A single big diamond (weigh the love in carats) from a prince charming who is yours alone, rather than a miscellaneous pile of smaller, lesser, colored gemstones from a stable of guys whose names you can't remember.

But eventually Ayer/De Beers also cashed in on the "girl's best friend" line, as well as on its show business allure. Built into Leo Robin's diamond song in *Gentlemen Prefer Blondes* were a number of what we would now call product placements; Lorelei Lee sings, "Tiffany! Cartier! Black Starr! Frost Gornham! Talk to me, Harry Winston, tell me all about it." Anita Loos said that for the opening night party Carol Channing "came wearing a special real diamond tiara from Van Cleef and Arpels which came accompanied by two security guards who had to dance with her all night." Anita Loos herself gave "a special token from Tiffany's" to Leo Robin's blond showgirl wife.[56]

How did the diamond merchants get in on opening night? Well, at the tryouts of *Gentlemen Prefer Blondes* in Philadelphia, the "diamonds" number had stopped the show for long minutes of wild applause. Word of the show's success, and perhaps of the prominence of diamonds in it, had reached New York by opening night and may well have inspired Van Cleef and Arpels to lend Ms. Channing what Lorelei Lee would have called "expensive jew-els" (to rhyme with "du-els").

De Beers had had no financial interest in the show before opening night.[57] After the show's great success, however, the diamond men rode in on the coattails of the bad girls mythology, beginning with the 1953 film version of *Gentlemen* (directed by Howard Hawks), with Marilyn Monroe as Lorelei wearing gobs of real diamonds,[58] including a 26-carat canary diamond around her neck.[59] (False women and fake jewelry[ix] were joined

viii. See chapter 9, p. 234.

ix. See chapter 9, p. 253.

FIGURE 10.2 Marilyn Monroe wearing diamonds in a publicity still.
Source: © INTERFOTO/Alamy

in a single metaphor when Ruth Dubonnet, commenting on the casting of Marilyn Monroe in the role that Carol Channing had made her own on stage, said, "It is like seeing a zircon up against a diamond.")[60]

This then became part of a more general outreach to movie studios by diamond merchants, encouraging screenwriters to write plots about diamonds and lending diamonds to stars to wear in films such as *To Catch a Thief* (Alfred Hitchcock, 1953) and *The Pink Panther* (Blake Edwards, 1963). Ayer paid Margaret Ettinger, a Hollywood press agent, $425 a month to get popular magazines to publish photos of stars like Merle Oberon wearing diamonds.[61]

A fine example of the pervasive success of the Ayer campaign is the career of *Breakfast at Tiffany's*, Truman Capote's 1958 novel. Capote described Holly Golightly, the heroine of his novel, as an "American geisha." He wanted Marilyn Monroe to play Holly in the 1961 Blake Edwards film, in which Holly's habit of taking money from the men she slept with was tactfully glossed over, but Monroe refused, allegedly because she didn't want the call-girl image (though Holly was no naughtier, surely, than Lorelei Lee). The film, starring Audrey Hepburn as Holly, pokes fun at the engagement ring scenario when Holly and her boyfriend (George Peppard) try, in vain, to get Tiffany's to engrave a Cracker-Jack ring.

The bad-girl association (together with the telltale use of the plural of "diamonds") snuck back in, in the title of *Diamonds Are Forever* (Guy Hamilton, 1971), the sixth and last film with Sean Connery as James Bond. In the 1956 Ian Fleming book on which the film is based, Bond muses that the eyes of a corpse "spoke to him and said, 'Mister. Nothing is forever except what you did to me,'" and later Bond says, "They [the eyes of the corpse] had been wrong. Death is forever. But so are diamonds."[62] With the plural, in the film, came the Wrong Sort of woman with her many lovers, definitely evoked in the sexy title song (with lyrics by Don Black, music by John Barry), sung by sassy, brassy Shirley Bassey:

> Diamonds are forever / They are all I need to please me / They can
>   stimulate and tease me / They won't leave in the night, / I've
>   no fear that they might / desert me.
> Diamonds are forever / Hold one up, and then caress it / Touch it,
>   stroke it and undress it / I can see every part, / Nothing hides
>   in the heart / To hurt me.

The diamonds here are men—more precisely, men's (family) "jewels"— their virile hardness now spelled out, and their moral transparency seen as a promise of fidelity—the perfect lovers, though far too multiple to be the perfect husband. One line in the song even manages to dwell upon the "lust" in "luster": "Sparkling round my little finger / Unlike men, the diamonds linger. / Diamonds never lie to me / For when love's gone they'll luster on."

De Beers, too, could treat diamonds as male, to send another message, loud and clear, to men: "Diamonds will help you seduce." Sexy diamond ads bragged (or warned) that "Her bliss—and his worth as a man—are dependent on his ability to whip out the stone."[63] "Whip out" is a particularly neat bit of suggestion, I think.

But the mythology of diamonds generally assimilated them to the women whose best friends they were, rather than to their lovers. As John

Beckman rhapsodizes: "In the flare of the diamond, one meets the lure of the dangerous, enigmatic female."[64] "How," asks Zoellner, "could diamonds simultaneously represent fidelity *and* sexual liberation, tradition *and* the Age of Aquarius?"[65] Easy; one of the great virtues of myths is that they can work both sides of the street,[66] reversing the moral force while maintaining the appeal of the same tried-and-true structural elements.[x] After the sexual revolution of the 1960s, De Beers decided that it was OK for diamonds to be sexy.

The Divorce Ring and the Apology Ring

Eventually De Beers realized that they had painted themselves into a kind of marketing corner with their "one love, one big diamond" campaign, since it might discourage people from buying more than one diamond (though one could always hope for divorce and remarriage, a new love and a new ring). But that did not stop them. In the 1980s they invented the "eternity ring," not just one diamond but a whole band of them, to celebrate the tenth wedding anniversary, and the "remarriage ring," marking the twenty-fifth anniversary,[67] a ring that would, we were told, "Show her you would marry her all over again."[68]

The next logical step was, of course, the divorce ring. Actually, George Frederick Kunz had anticipated this possibility in 1917:

"It seems that in view of the great number of divorces now granted we might well introduce the custom of giving 'divorce rings,' [which] might be differentiated from the old-fashioned wedding-ring by substituting the inscription ABC *from* DEF for ABC *and* DEF. A novel idea in divorce-rings is reported from Chicago, where a fashionable divorcee had her wedding-ring made smaller so that she could wear it on the little finger of her left hand as a divorce-ring.... Perhaps in some cases this wearing of the wedding-ring, even in a modified form, after a divorce, might be intended to indicate that the old love had not wholly vanished, and that some day those who had been put asunder could be rejoined, as occasionally happens now-a-days."[69]

---

x. See chapter 11, p. 301.

But this "repurposing," of course, was not what De Beers had in mind; no, a *new* ring—this one, too, with a diamond, of course—was required to mark the divorce.

Almost a century after Kunz's musings on the divorce ring, a journalist asked, "Will 'divorce rings' catch on?" and conjured up a rather different scenario from Kunz's: "Imagine: a man bent on one knee, gazing up into the eyes of a teary-eyed woman. He takes out a velvet jewelry box, opens it, and she gasps. Inside is a diamond ring in the shape of a broken heart. 'Darling . . . will you divorce me?' "[70] Such a ring, "rather than a symbol of eternal love and commitment, [is] a symbol of 'things didn't quite work out.'" One divorce ring advertised on the Internet has a diamond bursting out of a golden broken heart, "as if casting off a shell or cocoon"; another consists of a golden heart, jaggedly shattered, with a diamond-studded spear plunged down between the two halves.[71]

Closely related to the divorce ring is the apology ring, which might also be called the anti-divorce ring (or, if it fails to work, the ante-divorce ring), as it is given in an attempt to head-off a divorce after an exposed, or suspected, infidelity. Ayer/De Beers actually started planning such a ring in 1966–67, according to an N. W. Ayer Annual report to De Beers in that year: "There are many reasons why men decide to give their wives diamond jewelry. When a man is truly motivated by warm sentiment, he likes to feel reassured and encouraged. When his reasons are less than lofty, he likes to give himself a lofty rationale."[72] "Less than lofty" is a slimy way to allude to infidelity. If the infidelity is still secret, the plan may backfire: the sudden presentation of an expensive piece of jewelry may make her suspicious. "What did he do to make him give me this ring?" nicely turns the tables on the slut assumption.[xi]

The apology ring given *after* an infidelity has been discovered is something else again. Kobe Bryant bought his wife Vanessa a fabulous ring after he was booked on suspicion of raping another woman. As one report commented,

> "If diamonds are a girl's best friend, perhaps Vanessa Bryant will find solace in hers as she works through her divorce from husband Kobe Bryant. The mom of two filed for divorce in Los Angeles on Friday—though the fate of her $4 million diamond sparkler, a

---

xi. See chapter 9, p. 228.

gift from her soon-to-be-ex, is to be determined. Kobe purchased the ring for Vanessa in July of 2003, three days after prosecution declared he'd be charged with the rape of a 19-year-old employee at a Colorado resort where he'd stayed. Dubbed the 'apology ring'— though PEOPLE reported that the basketball star had commissioned the bauble two weeks before charges were announced—it's an 8-carat purple diamond set in a glimmering band."[73]

Kobe was certainly not the first guilty husband whose "less than lofty" motives inspired him to present his long-suffering wife with a piece of expensive jewelry as a kind of bribe or booby prize. When Philip Roth finished his novel *Deception*, in 1990, his then wife, the actress Claire Bloom, found in the manuscript a chapter describing in bleakly unflattering terms the protagonist's wife Claire, an actress. "She was still shaking with rage when he came home, much earlier than usual, bringing an extravagant gift, a gold ring in the shape of a snake with an emerald head bought from Bulgari on Fifth Avenue." (Was the snake a symbol of the loss of their Eden? Or an unconscious confession of his own reptility?) She threatened him with legal action if he did not remove her name; he agreed. "Then," she said, in 1996, "I accepted his guilt offering. I wear it to this day." But she had divorced him in 1995.[74] The engraved bracelet that Prince Charles gave to Camilla Parker Bowles two days before he married Diana, on July 29, 1981,[75] surely served as a ring of apology—not to the wife, in this case, but to the mistress. A bouquet of roses used to be standard issue for this problem before the De Beers inflation struck.

And now they are trying to sell us "Mangagement Rings." Jewelers tried, as early as 1926, to sell the idea of engagement rings for men, with ads featuring "photos of a man's left hand, a cigarette resting between the first two fingers and a large rock flashing on the fourth. The rings even had ultra-macho names: the Pilot, the Stag, the Master." But the idea didn't catch on, proving "unable to overcome the ingrained femininity of the symbol."[76] It needed the kind of manipulation of "the symbol" (including its masculinization) that DeBeers/Ayers achieved two decades later.

One journalist asked, "Is this some gimmick by the jewelry industry to get you to spend more? Is it some ploy by feminists to brand men with engagement rings, too?" A "gimmick by the jewelry industry" seems to me precisely what this is. But in defense of the second option, Kunz foresaw, in 1917, the feminist possibilities of the mangagement ring: "Perhaps the objection of the extreme advocates of 'woman's rights' might be satisfied by the introduction of an exchange of rings both at engagements and marriages."[77] And one rationale for such an exchange was suggested by a spokesman for the jewelry industry: "The idea that the man will also wear an engagement ring gives relationships a new sense of equality."[78] To understand why a mangagement ring is unlikely to be a "ploy by feminists," to advance "women's rights" in our day, or bring "a new sense of equality," however, we must first take into account the anti-myth of diamonds and then consider the twenty-first-century woman's resistance to the mythology of diamonds.

The Anti-Myth: Diabolical Diamonds

For every myth there's an anti-myth,[79] and the dark sides of diamonds keep surfacing, despite all the attempts by the diamond cartel to cover them up. We have already seen examples of the anti-myth of evil diamonds in *Daniel Deronda* and in the nineteenth-century French and English stories about diamond necklaces,[xii] as well as in the mythology of large Oriental diamonds carrying diabolical Oriental curses, but especially in the mythology of greedy, seductive women.

The anti-diamond myth was frequently evoked by texts with religious agendas, for Christianity has always been distrustful of jewelry (except, naturally, as worn by the princes of the Church).[xiii] The Puritans under the Commonwealth in England tried to abolish wedding rings because of their association with bishops, but people insisted on having them.[80] Mephistopheles in Goethe's *Faust, Part I* (1806) tempts Gretchen with a box of jewels, and in Jacques Offenbach's 1881 opera, *The Tales of Hoffmann* (with a libretto based on stories by E. T. A. Hoffmann), the devil incarnate uses a huge diamond to entice Giulietta to help him steal Hoffmann's soul. He sings an aria about a scintillating diamond that catches a woman as a hunter catches a lark:

> Sparkle, diamond, fascinate, draw her,
> The lark or the woman, to this conquering bait. . . .
> One leaves her life there,
> The other loses her soul.[81]

---

xii. See chapter 9, pp. 230, 234.

xiii. Recall the Pope's ring in chapter 2, p. 41.

Giulietta says she was seduced by the diamond; she steals Hoffman's reflection for the devil, and dies. Offenbach had died before he had completed the opera, and among the many versions of the libretto that others later composed, one interpolates a bit of Orientalist dialogue before this aria. When the devil shows her the diamond, he says, "It was one of the eyes of the god Brahma. I had it brought from India, a true talisman, a souvenir for all women. It is worth millions."[82]

Diamonds sometimes challenged, rather than enhanced, the promise of permanence in a wedding ring. According to Thomas Fuller (a seventeenth-century English churchman), "Marriage with a diamond ring foreshadowed evil, because the interruption of the circle augured that the reciprocal regard of the spouse might not be perpetual."[83] In the nineteenth-century, a man named Dr. Drennan gave his wife a ring, sans diamond, accompanied by this poem with a strongly negative view of diamonds:

> Emblem of happiness! Not bought nor sold;
> Accept this modest ring of virgin gold.
> Love, in this small, but perfect, circle trace;
> And duty, in its soft but strict embrace.
> Plain, precious, pure, as best becomes the wife;
> Yet firm to bear the frequent rubs of life.
> Connubial life distains a fragile toy,
> Which rust can tarnish and a touch destroy;
> Nor much admires what courts the general gaze,
> The dazzling diamond's meretricious blaze
> That hides, with glare, the anguish of a heart,
> By nature hard, but polished bright by art.[84]

The positive words for gold and marriage—"virgin," "perfect," "duty," "plain, precious, pure," "firm"—are contrasted with negative words evocative of non-gold, diamonds, and a bad marriage—"fragile," "rust," "meretricious," "hides," "glare," and "art."

"The anguish of a heart" is part of another sort of anti-diamond narrative, not religious and fictional but political and historical, and all too real. The Mughal emperor Babur, when he owned the Koh-i-Noor, is said to have remarked that it was worth the value of two and a half days' food[85] for all the people in the world. And indeed, many people have starved, and died in other ways, too, for diamonds. Zoellner, who called his book about diamonds *The Heartless Stone: A Journey through the World of Diamonds, Deceit, and Desire*, documented the heartlessness in the conditions under which diamonds are produced and have been produced throughout modern history. In a fictionalized version of the life of Mary Frances Gerety, a woman who refuses to marry bites her lip to keep from saying, when her friends are making such a fuss over their diamond wedding rings, "You realize these stupid things have fueled entire brutal regimes in Africa, right? They're shiny little death pellets. Let's be honest."[86] Diamonds have been mined in Africa under conditions of appalling human suffering and abuse of human rights,[87] not to mention the so-called blood diamonds (also called "conflict diamonds" or "war diamonds") mined in countries at war to finance invading armies or warlords. And "All," as Lord Randolph Churchill said when he visited the South African diamond mines in the 1890s, "for the vanity of woman"[88]—and of man, though Churchill somehow left that out.

But this book is not about the human suffering that surrounds the production of diamonds; important as it is, it is not the only thing worth saying about diamonds. We cannot do justice to these human tragedies in this book, which merely concerns the mythology of women and their jewelry. But we can acknowledge the hideous truth of the situation before going on to consider the way that the mythology of those diamonds caused far less serious hardships among engaged couples in Europe and America. Elizabeth Taylor devised an ingenious rationalization for keeping the 33-carat Krupp diamond, which was tainted with moral evil over and above the moral evil of African mining, having been owned by Vera Krupp, of the famous German munitions family that was responsible for the deaths of millions of Jews. "When it came up for auction in the late 1960s," said Ms. Taylor, "I thought how perfect it would be if a nice Jewish girl like me were to own it."[89] Somehow I don't think that works so well for diamonds in general. But you mustn't forget about those men in the mines; they are always there, in every diamond that you ever wear.

Expensive diamond engagement rings could take the joy out of the wedding (or even the marriage) of those who could not come up with the money,[90] and they impoverished others who did manage to scrape it together. The rule was, and still is, that a man should spend three months' salary on an engagement ring.[91] The Ayer/De Beers advertising was "enforced by a process of shaming used occasionally even today by diamond mongers: 'Spend less and the relatives will talk; spend more and the relatives will rave.'"[92] And it worked: few people in the United States owned a diamond engagement ring early in the century, but by 1950 about

50 percent of all brides would receive one, and by 1960, nearly 80 per-cent.[93] As early as 1949, an article in *Commonweal* lamented "couples' desire for expensive rings, the larger the better, to manifest love," and one in *Mademoiselle* in 1990, entitled, "Rock Me: A Girl and Her Ring," quoted a girl who said, "The minute you get engaged these days . . . everyone asks, 'Where's the ring? Where's the diamond?' If you don't have one, they look at you like you're lying about the engagement."[94]

Rebecca Okrent captured the subtle influence of diamond ring mythology in an autobiographical piece (entitled "Ring Cycle") that she wrote in 2007, about a wedding ring she lost in a pond and miraculously found again.[xiv] At first she resisted the myth, but in the end even she succumbed to it:

> "When my husband and I decided to marry he'd already handed down the family's heirloom ring to an earlier wife. I'd only entertained an objective, hanker-free appreciation of the jewels in Tiffany's win-dows, so it made sense that before our wedding we went to the dia-mond district to buy two diamondless bands. . . . I gardened, cooked and never missed having to place my non-existent gems in a soap dish before plunging my hands into bread dough or compost. . . . Later, this seemed too cheap and easy and what, I wondered, might that signify? My gold band seemed more slave ring than proper sig-nifier of our life together. I spent a therapeutic hour analyzing my wish for flashier adornment before boldly directing my husband to a certain jeweler and a particular ring. It didn't change my life, but it acknowledged our marriage more lavishly."[95]

The siren song of "more lavishly" and "flashier adornment" as a "proper signifier of our life together," in contrast with the "too cheap . . . slave ring," drowned out the voice of reason.

But not all of the blame for the "shaming" can be laid at the feet of Ayer/De Beers. We noted that the taste for diamonds began in the late nineteenth century, but even before that the custom of plain gold wedding rings had become a hardship for some. As Charles Edwards wrote in 1855:

> "The use of the ring has become so common in England that poor people will not believe the marriage to be good without one; and

---

xiv. See chapter 2, p. 25.

the notion also is that it must be of gold. At Worcester (England) on one occasion, the parties were so poor that they used a brass ring. The bride's friends indignantly protested that the ring ought to have been of gold; and the acting officer was threatened with indictment for permitting the use of such base metal. In another case of humble marriage, the bridegroom announced that a ring was not necessary. The woman entreated to have one. The super-intendent of the poor took part with the woman and represented how the absence of it would expose her to insult; and he, kindly, hesitated to proceed with the marriage until a ring was produced. The man yielded at last and obtained one. The woman's gratitude brought tears into her eyes."[96]

Even without Ayer/De Beers, public pressure often made poor people spend more than they could or should on wedding rings.

But some people found ways to resist the myth. Saint Augustine asked priests to perform weddings without rings for those who could not afford them.[97] James Remington McCarthy noted that according to custom in Ireland, a marriage was not legal without the use of a gold ring, as great an imposition on most Irish farmers as a diamond was for most New Yorkers. But,

> "at a certain town in the southeast of Ireland someone is said to have kept a few gold wedding rings for hire, and when parties who were too poor to purchase a ring of the necessary precious metal were about to be married, they obtained the loan of one, and paid a small fee for the same, the ring being returned to the owner imme-diately after the ceremony."[98]

Sometimes such couples could borrow the jewelry from their friends, for nothing. The heroine of Guy de Maupassant's "The Necklace" ruined her life paying for diamonds she had borrowed and lost.[xv] But borrow-ing jewelry was quite common among the upper classes at that time. In eighteenth-century European society, jewels were "regularly borrowed or hired. Nor was there any ignominy connected to this—on the contrary." Hugh Walpole in 1742 told how the Princess of Saxe Gotha attended a

---

xv. See chapter 9, p. 234.

masked ball wearing diamonds worth £40,000, which the merchant lent her for nothing, "only desiring that she would tell whose they were," a scenario reminiscent of Carol Channing in all those Van Cleef & Arpels diamonds. For such people, money was not the point; the fun of wearing someone else's gorgeous jewelry was the point. Thus, Lady Jane Harrington, famous both for her great wealth and for her sense of fashion, borrowed jewelry from actresses.[99] Apparently, some lower-class people, for whom money very definitely *was* the point, might borrow wedding rings in the same way.

Americans nowadays can use a very similar subterfuge. An article that wisely advises, "Brides: Steal His Heart, but Borrow the Jewelry," reports that a number of hotels now let brides borrow quite expensive jewelry (which the hotels apparently stock for this purpose) as long as they are married in the hotel.[100] The "Inside Weddings" website, under the heading of "Something Borrowed," noted this and suggested that "you can feel just as confident walking down the aisle as your favorite superstar strutting the red carpet by borrowing show-stopping jewels." But embedded in this promise is, of course, the assumption, the threat, that without the "show-stopping jewels" of "a superstar" (note that theatrical metaphor), you would not be confident at your own wedding.

Take Back Your Ring: The Legal View

Another factor that worked in De Beers's favor was a shift in legal attitudes regarding the property that a woman could take away from a broken engagement, attitudes that swayed back and forth in the strong winds of the bi-polar mythology of women's sexual natures. The predatory women whose best friends were diamonds were from about 1920 known as "gold diggers," a term that the *OED* glosses, in the singular, as "a girl who attaches herself to a man merely for gain; *slang* (orig. U. S.)." At first, the term was not particularly pejorative; a series of Busby Berkeley films were entitled *Gold-Diggers of 1933, 1935, 1937*, and so on. But Lorelei Lee in the Loos book is a much more brutal gold digger than she is in the later musical; she gets a rich man to propose to her in writing, planning to behave so extravagantly that "if he should change his mind, and desert a girl, . . . then it would only be right if a girl should sue him for breach of promise"[101] (this being, as we will soon see, one of the defining legal acts of a gold digger). Loos's Lorelei even traffics in fake diamonds: when a man gives her a diamond tiara, but later decides that he should give it to his wife, she gets a shop in Paris to make an imitation, which she palms off on the man's wife, while she keeps the real thing (for a while . . .).[102] Many of these women were digging for diamonds rather than gold.

But this image of the gold digger was for a while challenged by a very different view of women's sexuality. On November 24, 1950, less than a year after *Gentlemen Prefer Blondes* opened on Broadway, and while it was still standing-room-only (it ran for 740 performances), *Guys and Dolls* (music and lyrics by Frank Loesser) premiered, with a song whose lyrics seemed to contradict the worldview of Lorelei Lee. Adelaide, a sexy show-girl, sings:

> "Take back your mink, / Take back your pearls. / What made you
>   think/ That I was one of those girls?"
> (Or, in the immortal accent of Vivian Blaine, as Adelaide:)
> "Take back your mink, / Take back your poils. / What made you
>   think / That I was one of them goils?"

Adelaide is arguing that she is *not* a gold digger. To prove it, as the song continues she pantomimes a superficial strip—only to take off, presumably to return, the jewelry and gifts that she fears her boyfriend intended as down payment for services to be rendered. She is insisting that she is the other sort of girl, the sort who gets married and gets the other kind of jewelry. In her signature number, "Adelaide's Lament," she complains, "Just from waiting around for that plain little band of gold / A person can develop a cold," and she pities the single woman who suffers "from a lack of community property." So the poils are no longer the spoils; that "plain little band of gold," and the legal right to the community property that goes with it, are what she's after now.

The gold digger's game had changed, and we can chart its change in American history. The sort of woman we call a gold digger was known as a type in England and Europe for centuries before this term was coined. We recognize her in Gwendolen in *Daniel Deronda* (1876)[xvi] and in Lizzie Greystock in *The Eustace Diamonds* (1871). Indeed, most of the women in the stories in this book are gold diggers of one sort or another, determined to get men to give them either legitimizing or illegitimizing jewelry. But

---

xvi. See chapter 9, p. 230.

much legal ink flowed in the twentieth century in an attempt to distinguish between the different ways in which the gold digger "attaches herself" to her man (before, during, after, or without marriage) and to decide under what circumstances she did and did not have to return the poils.

In an earlier, more innocent age, in the nineteenth century, both fictional and legal texts had concerned themselves with "nice" women, of the one-diamond ilk, whom they regarded as fragile, needing to be protected from men who promised unique devotion but really were only After One Thing. And so there were "heart-balm" laws, allowing women to claim damages (presumably with "heartless stones" serving as balm for a wounded heart) if men seduced them with a promise of marriage and then reneged on the promise after the sexual fact. (Men could also sue under these laws, but seldom did; the double standard worked here in women's favor.) Since jewelry has sentimental value over and above its cash equivalent, vindictive divorcing couples (and contentious siblings) often attach great sentiment to the jewelry they bicker about, clearly equating jewelry with (lost) love. But, as Lorraine Daston has observed, "the logic of repairing broken hearts with cash or a diamond ring can be traced right back to medieval *Wehrgeld* customs (paying monetary compensation to the family of a victim of violence, including murder) or for that matter, much Sharia law (wronged wives are also paid off in court)."[103] And as Linda Kerber points out (in "Why Diamonds Really Are a Girl's Best Friend: Another American Narrative"), new laws in the nineteenth century made diamonds the only friend a woman still had in cases of breach of promise.[104]

In a more romantic vein, well into the twentieth century women continued to keep their rings as the sentimental salvage from the shipwreck of their great loves. In 1988, when Ava Gardner, aged sixty-five, two years before her death, was running out of money, she decided to write a memoir, because, as she told the biographer Peter Evans, "I'm broke, honey. I either write the book or sell the jewels. And I'm kinda sentimental about the jewels."[105] So was Elizabeth Taylor, who understood well the relationship between rings and lost lovers. In 1969, her husband Richard Burton gave her, with much fanfare, much jewelry, including the pear-shaped 69-carat "Taylor-Burton" diamond (which was called the "Cartier Diamond" until Burton bought it, for $1.1 million).[106] But Burton left her, in 1978, for another woman. After expressing her regret, Taylor concluded, philosophically, "At least I got to keep the ring."[107]

FIGURE 10.3 Elizabeth Taylor and Richard Burton in Budapest in 1973. She is wearing the 69-carat "Taylor-Burton" diamond.

Source: Photo by © Norman Parkinson Ltd./courtesy Norman Parkinson Archive/Corbis/ Corbis via Getty Images.

But by then the courts had moved in a different direction. After the turn of the century, as women fought to get the vote and became more aggressively visible in public, calls for equal treatment of the sexes led many state legislatures and high courts to revisit the laws that favored the woman in a broken engagement. This shift in the wind led, in 1935, to a number of laws that limited the damages to which a woman was entitled when an engagement failed to lead to a marriage. The new legislation was quite notorious at the time. Jilted brides, who had once been awarded tidy sums, now encountered courts reluctant to enforce breach of promise laws. Now, "the once-common and oft-successful female plaintiffs disappeared from the case reports, replaced by theretofore virtually unknown, and suddenly successful, male plaintiffs."[108] Equality does have its price.

Another factor behind the change in legislation was a new belief in the non-commodifiability of love and marriage, an argument that trying to measure lost love with money (as the heart-balm laws did) was "ridiculous, impossible, and wrongful." This attitude, rooted in old-fashioned ideas of "pure, romantic, nonmaterialist love," muddied what were previously crystal clear waters in breach-of-contract law.[109]

But the change was also sometimes seen as a response to the rise not merely of suffragettes or romantics, but of gold diggers: "women falsely proclaiming an engagement, or exchanging marital vows just to extract funds from the prospective husband."[110] Twentieth-century courts turned their attention from wronged women—innocent, seduced, and abandoned—to wrong women, the rapacious gold diggers, the many-diamonds type, who led men on, milked them dry, and then ditched them, keeping the ring (and other spoils). The tricky, cunning woman that these courts conjured up is the reincarnation of our old friend the clever wife,[xvii] but where the clever wife usually succeeded in getting the ring and the man, this temptress did not want the man and now, if the guy had a good lawyer, did not get to keep the ring. Marcia Pointon tells a heavy joke about one such woman, which is also a comment on the link between jewelry and memory:[xviii]

> "Following the demise of her wealthy husband, a widow goes to have lunch with a friend. The latter sympathetically and tactfully enquires about the widow's situation. 'He left me really well provided for,' is the reply; 'the only thing he asked for himself was that I spend half a million dollars on a memorial stone.' Holding out her ring finger, she concludes: 'And here it is!' "[111]

The pejorative term, "fortune hunters," which originally (from 1689 to 1870)[112] had been applied exclusively to men (hunting for women with rich dowries), was now extended to women.

But as we have seen, gold diggers and fortune hunters had been around for quite a while. The new anti-gold-digger (or, as it was often called, anti-heart-balm) legislation was therefore a response not to the rise of these predatory women but to a shift in attitudes to them, a shift in the mythology of women. In contrast to nineteenth-century heart-balm legislation, designed to protect vulnerable women from "naturally dominating male

---

xvii. See chapter 6, p. 137.

xviii. See chapter 3, p. 85.

influence" and from "duplicitous men attempting to get sex," the twenti-eth-century anti-heart-balm laws were designed to protect "love-blinded" men from "duplicitous women attempting to get material goods."[113] All in all, a woman could no longer count on a big settlement if she was jilted.

But then, in yet another mythological move, the courts began to make an exception for engagement rings. This was in part because rings are the most common engagement gifts, usually given only because of the engage-ment (unlike other gifts such as cars or fur coats, which might be birthday or holiday presents), but in part because of their unique symbolism. The legal scholar Rita Tushnet suggests, "Perhaps a general intuition that women needed some security against men who promised, seduced, and then aban-doned them led women to look for symbols such as rings."[114] It is striking that even the lawyer Tushnet regards "*symbols* such as rings," in addition to their material value, as a source of a jilted woman's security. Legal arguments about the special symbolic value of rings drew upon much of the mythology that we have traced heretofore. "The triumph of diamonds has to be understood in terms of their symbolic functions," says Proctor,[115] and Tushnet agrees:

> "The justifications for the ring (and the rules of etiquette governing its return) focus on the symbolism involved. . . . If the woman's loss of virginity is to be compensated, she should always keep the ring. The fault rule itself represented a new relationship between love and property in which the jilted lover could retain or reclaim the material symbol of the lost love. Sexual relations, loss of status or future prospects, and other consequences of a broken engagement have been eliminated from consideration."[116]

Under the new laws, therefore, a woman could keep her "material sym-bol" if she were jilted, just as she could have done under the old heart-balm laws (before the gold digger backlash), even though she was now no longer allowed to sue a jilting bridegroom for anything more than a ring, and even if she was the jilter rather than the jiltee and thus vulnerable to prosecution by him under the anti-heart-balm laws. The rule was, "The ring belongs to the bride."

The diamond ring sometimes had the added advantage of circumvent-ing litigation entirely. As Kerber puts it:

> "In the nineteenth and early twentieth centuries, valuable jewels came to carry an additional value when given as an engagement

present. The jilted fiancée no longer needed to face the humiliation of soothing her aching heart with money awarded to her in a breach of promise lawsuit: she got to keep the diamonds."[117]

Thus diamonds became valuable to women as insurance both inside and outside the courtroom.

De Beers hired Ayer and began their big push in 1939, the very year when the anti-heart-balm legislation hit fever pitch and engagement rings—now more desirable than ever as a source of property that could withstand a subsequent legal challenge—became "common symbols of impending marriage."[118] The anti-heart-balm legislation further inspired Ayer/De Beers and accounts in large part for the spectacular success of their campaign.

Eventually, shifts in both legal doctrine and popular custom required the return of engagement rings. When Elizabeth Taylor broke off her engagement to Dennis Stein, in 1985, she later recalled, "Naturally, I returned the engagement ring to my fiancé."[119] "Naturally"? After all the legal switches and switchbacks, after all the massive economic changes, the old mythology was still right back there at square one: "Take back your ring." But another, more realistic solution was soon to rescue women from this quandary.

Hard Values

The desire to get rid of the ring not (or not merely) because you are legally required to do so but because you now hate the guy who gave it to you was noted by the columnist Judith Martin ("Miss Manners"), who argued, in 1996, that since an engagement ring is a symbol, although the fiancée should return it after a breakup, "she would still be treating it symbolically if she ran over it with her van, melted it down, or threw it off a mountain."[120] The right of a "wronged" woman to throw away her engagement ring was defended in an act of the British Parliament designed, according to one scholar, "to preserve the right of the wronged woman to throw the ring into the river rather than return it to her former fiancé."[121] (The Parliament did not, apparently, take into account the possibility that the ring might be returned by a fish.)[xix]

---

xix. See chapter 2, p. 25.

But, as Tushnet points out, symbolism and materialism can work together as well as in conflict:

> "The ring is a powerful symbol in large part because people do care about market value.... Rings were not just symbols; they were tangible economic commitments, and they gained significance as other economic incidents of marriage were in flux.... The ring may have been perceived as a symbol originally, but its objective monetary value becomes critical when the engagement ends."[122]

And as another lawyer commented, "The whole problem people have [with this issue] is talking about the symbol of the ring.... But when you're talking about a \$20,000 ring you don't just say 'you can keep this as a souvenir.' "[123] On the other hand, a ring given by a man who then jilted you might have unexpected practical uses; in an article in *Mademoiselle* in 1995, entitled, "Diamonds Aren't Forever," one woman declared, speaking of such a ring, "I did, for a short time, consider turning it into a bullet."[124] The compromise between symbolism and materialism is also evident when couples buy the ring together, cheerfully discussing the price, blowing out of the water the old romantic stereotype of a man surprising his beloved with a ring.[125] Now the acid test for the symbolic power of the ring is whether the ring, retained by the jilted lover, is hocked for cash.

Ultimately, Taylor did *not* always "keep the ring" that Burton had given her; after she and Burton divorced in 1978, for the second time, she sold the Taylor-Burton diamond for \$5 million, using the proceeds to build a hospital in Botswana.[126] According to one report, "She seemed unattached to the jewel, saying only, 'It was very large and very heavy.... Anyway, I hadn't worn it in ages.' "[127] She also sold several other jewels that Burton had given her, including an emerald ring (sold in 2002 for \$80,000). But she did keep the 33-carat Krupp diamond all her life; it was sold (for \$8,800,000) a few months after her death in March 2011.[128] So much for heart balm.

One jewelry ad that told the story of Liz Taylor's sale of her jewels from Burton advised, "If you have jewelry from an old relationship, the easiest way to make a clean break is putting those items on consignment!"[129] After all the twentieth-century heart-searching about whether a woman should or should not give back the ring, twenty-first-century women have often decided to *sell* the ring—and the rest of the jewelry—when the husband or boyfriend becomes history (or, if you prefer, myth). There is now a website called exboyfriendjewelry.com that advises women to

"BUY, SELL, TRADE AND BLOG ABOUT THE BREAKUP!

Pawn shops are icky.... Consignment shops are even worse.... So, what's a girl like you to do? You have all that jewelry sitting around that you loved so hard to get (that sounded dirty, but you know what we mean) and will never wear again.... Welcome to **EXBOYFRIENDJEWELRY.COM**—a site where you can buy/sell/trade and blog about all of those little painful reminders in your jewelry box that make you wonder 'what did I ever see in him?' You set your own price. You get it off your chest and out of your sight. Just because you don't want it, doesn't mean somebody else isn't dying for it. Everyone's a winner! Maybe you love him, maybe you never want to speak to him again, but either way, you're ready to move on and make a little rent money in the process.... Here's the story, you don't want it and he can't have it back."[130]

Blasting away all that boring legalese, this hard-nosed website tells it like it is.

The decision to sell the ring given to you by a guy who turned out to be a cad is vividly justified in Nora Ephron's semi-fictionalized tale of her divorce from Carl Bernstein in her novel, *Heartburn*.[131] The protagonist's husband, Mark, had given her a diamond ring when their son was born. When an attempted robbery in the subway damaged the ring, she took it to the jeweler, Leo, from whom Mark had always bought all his jewelry, including that ring. She chatted with Leo while he fixed it:

> "He said did I know the diamond in the ring was a perfect stone. I said Mark had told me that. He said it wasn't the kind of diamond I'd ever have trouble selling if I ever wanted to—he had told Mark he'd be glad to buy it back for what Mark had paid for it. I said I was glad to hear that. He asked me how I liked the necklace. The necklace, I said. Leo looked up, and the loupe dropped from his eye. 'I must be thinking of another customer,' he said. 'No you're not,' I said.... The diamond caught the afternoon sun and made a rainbow on the wall of the store."

She realized that her husband had bought the necklace for the mistress she had suspected him of having. She told the jeweler, "I love the ring, but it really doesn't go with my life. . . . and if you've got a ring you can't wear on the subway, what's the point of having it?" He gave her a check for $15,000. "I realized I had just been given the means to walk out of my marriage." So, once again, jewelry as incriminating evidence (in this case, a necklace) reveals the man's betrayal, while jewelry as portable property[xx] (in this case, a ring) comes to the rescue of the betrayed woman.

The Rebellion of Twenty-First-Century Women

Almost a century ago, women began to revolt against wedding rings and engagement rings, as Kunz reported in 1917:

> "In England, it is said that a movement has been initiated to abolish the use of the wedding-ring, possibly in some sense as a war measure, to constitute a slight check on the use of gold for ornamental purposes. It is, however, conjectured that its real source is rather to be sought in the general movement for the complete independence of women, the wedding-ring being looked upon by some extremists as an antiquated badge of slavery. It is hardly probable that such a movement will meet with any considerable measure of success, for the idea that the ring is a symbol of faith has become too deeply rooted in the popular mind to warrant the rejection of the time-honored usage."[132]

Time has proven Kunz right; most women do indeed still insist on their wedding and engagement rings.

But some twenty-first-century women have rebelled against the De Beers mythology, and moved to free themselves from the power that men have exerted over them through jewelry. They rebel in various ways: not only by (a) selling their diamond rings but by (b) buying their own diamond jewelry, or (c) buying themselves something other than diamonds, or (d) buying costume jewelry instead of the Real Thing, or (e) forswearing jewelry altogether, or, for many women, (f) never giving a damn for jewelry in the first place. Only option (b) still plays into De Beers's hands, but it, too, can serve feminist ends.

---

xx. See chapter 11, p. 96.

A woman prefers to buy her own diamond ring in one of the subplots of the first film of *Sex and the City* (Michael Patrick King, 2008):[133]

An actress named Blair Elkin is selling, at auction at Christie's, all the jewelry she had received from her billionaire boyfriend before he kicked her out on the street. Elkin is now getting "the ultimate breakup revenge: an embarrassing and very public auction of all the jewelry he had given her when they were happy." Samantha (Kim Cattrall) wants to buy a two-finger diamond cocktail ring in the shape of a gardenia; when she saw it in the catalogue she told her boyfriend, Smith, "This flower ring is the essence of me, one of a kind, filled with fire." At the auction, she remarks, "I deserve this. I work hard. Sex with only one man for I don't know how long." She bids furiously on the ring but is outbid by someone who buys the ring, via phone, for $55,000. Later, Smith (wearing nothing but bulging underpants and coming on to her) gives her the ring, and she realizes that he was the one on the phone at the auction. She tries to explain to him that she wanted to buy it for herself, but he insists on giving it to her. She hedges: "Well, just to be clear, this is a ring with diamonds. . . . It's not a diamond ring, right?" "Yeah." "Well, in that case, I love it." And they go to bed together.

But some time later, talking to a woman friend about the way that she always thinks of Smith's needs before her own, she looks at her ring and says, "Even this ring. I wanted to buy this for myself. That meant something to me. To be able to do that. Then, he buys it for me. . . . Now, every time I look down at it, I see him. Not me." Eventually, when she leaves him, she looks at the gardenia ring on her finger and starts to take it off, but then she tells him, sadly, affectionately, "No. I'm keeping this. Every time I look down at it, I want to think of you."

Several conflicting ideas about jewelry are packed into this tiny, fragmented vignette, beginning with one incident taken from the life of an actual public figure. "Blair Elkin" is a near-anagram for the name of the film actress Ellen Barkin, who in 2006 had auctioned off at Christie's the jewelry that her husband, Ronald Perelman, had given her. The *New York Times* called it "a symbolic and literal purging of the union" and quoted Ms. Barkin as saying, "These are just not memories I want to wear out every day." "Take Back Your Pearls" (a line from Adelaide's song, "Take

Back Your Mink") was the *Times'* caption for one of the photographs in the story,[134] but of course Barkin did *not* tell her ex-husband to take them back; she sold them.

So, in the *Sex and the City* story, Blair Elkin is selling the jewelry that she presumably received in love and now is disposing of in hate. Samantha wants her ring to have no connection with love at all; she wants it to symbolize herself as an individual, not a partner; yet she says she has earned it not only through her individual effort (she will be spending her "hard-earned money") but also through her fidelity to a single partner. She is therefore playing a double game. Her boyfriend ruins her dream of independence by sweet-talking, and sex-talking, her into accepting the ring from him. All she can do to reaffirm her independence is insist that it is *not* a "diamond ring," an engagement ring, and that she is therefore still at least technically a single woman. In the end, she leaves him to become single altogether, though now that she is free of him she values the ring in a new way, as a memory of him that takes his place. Presumably the many viewers who buy reproductions of Samantha's two-finger cocktail ring available from several online merchants are women buying them for themselves—but perhaps not.

As the movement for women to buy their own jewelry gained momentum, De Beers tried to sleep with the enemy by advertising, in 2012, a ring, generally featuring stones of less than 2 carats, that women were encouraged to buy for themselves. The implicit message of these ads is "that women don't necessarily need a man to buy them diamonds, and that female empowerment is only one purchase away."[135] An ad in *Vanity Fair* aimed at married women declared, "Your left hand celebrates the day you were married. Your right hand celebrates the day you were born." Another ad cut to the chase: "Your left hand says 'We.' Your right hand says 'Me.'" (A brand of diamonds marketed in India to women rather than men was called *Asmi*,[136] which means "I am," in Sanskrit.) A spokeswoman for De Beers said that the right hand ring was designed "to create a 'cultural imperative.'"[137]

A more political ad, with echoes of the suffragettes' battle to win the vote for women, ran like this: "Your left hand believes in shining armor. Your right hand thinks knights are for fairy tales. Your left hand says, 'I love you.' Your right hand says, 'I love me, too.' Women of the world, raise your right hand. The diamond right hand ring. View more at adiamondis-forever.com."[138] Cunningly expressing the same sort of ambivalence that Samantha confessed to, De Beers assures women that they can have their ring and eat it too. Indeed, Zoellner suggests that the "Right Hand Ring" ads are aimed primarily at "single women seeking a bit of *Sex and the City* glamour."[139]

De Beers used a similar ploy in a vain attempt to make diamonds replace gold in the Indian imaginary. In Bollywood, when Sushmita Sen, a former Miss Universe and the star of *Main Hoon Na (I Will Be There,* Farah Khan, 2004), was seen wearing a 22-carat solitaire ring, people started speculating about a possible engagement—surely some man had given her the ring, but who? Sushmita insisted that she had bought the ring for herself: "I don't need a man in my life to have diamonds. I can own them myself."[140] Yet one can detect a bit of slippage in a remark that she made (invoking the De Beers line) on another occasion when asked about that ring: "A diamond is forever. My most famous rock, a massive ring that I gifted myself a while ago[,] gently stated, 'Either beat the size of my stone or match the size of my heart.'"[141] Presumably, if he did "beat the size of her stone," he would own her.

Other diamond merchants have tried in vain to duplicate De Beers's marketing bonanza. The Jared jewelry company in 2010 produced numerous commercials trying to convince the buying public that "He went to Jared!" should be a woman's joyous exclamation meaning, "He proposed marriage to me!"[142] But the company stopped the ads when the slogan failed to catch on, except to inspire some good satirical Internet videos, of which my favorite is, "He went to Jamal," in which a young man complains bitterly that Jared expected him to cough up three months' salary for a diamond ring; instead he buys a big red plastic ring from Jamal, a sleazy guy who flashes jewelry on the inside of his coat, in the parking lot of Jared's. "She couldn't tell the difference," he insists.

Many women are finding their way out of the tyranny of diamonds. As Proctor optimistically remarks, "Diamond rings were popular in an era of sexual inequality. . . . In a more egalitarian society, and especially one with a less rigid sense of ornamental aesthetics, the diamond fashion may lose some of its appeal."[143] The spectacular boom in diamond engagement rings that De Beers engineered in Japan starting in 1966 suddenly ended at the end of the twentieth century; the bubble burst.[144] If the Japanese could break the spell (admittedly under very different cultural and economic conditions), why can't we? Tiffany's is still doing good business, better than ever, using the same tried-and-true mythology: "Fall in Love," exhorted a Tiffany's ad in 2013. But many women are raising their left hands without diamonds on them. As Sarah Maza put it, "Diamonds are a girl's best friend and, if a considerable body of imaginative literature is to be believed, a kind of poison."[145] Diamonds are, as one critic archly remarked, "a cartel's best friend."[146] Sean Connery, as James Bond, in the film *Diamonds Are Forever*, mused, "I suppose they've replaced dogs as a girl's best friend." Diamonds may once have been a *girl's* best friend, but they are no longer always a *woman's* best friend.

The Ties That Bind

Women who buy their own jewelry are swimming upstream against the still operative assumption that your jewelry proves that some man, your husband or your lover, owns you. To buy your own jewelry is therefore to say, "Nobody owns me." But does it also say, "Nobody loves me"? That fear seems to be addressed in another sort of jewelry that would make any card-carrying feminist weep: "love bangles" marketed by Cartier and other firms, bracelets that come with a key for the man to lock onto the woman's wrist and then wear on a chain or key ring, with a screw that he screws shut using a screwdriver that he wears on a chain. Shades of "The Story of O"![xxi] These are, alas, very popular, and selling well, setting the feminist movement back about five centuries.

Another discouraging modern trend is one in which not husbands but fathers use rings as symbolic chastity belts to shackle the sexuality of their women. Some Christian fathers now give their daughters silver purity rings (recall the "purity" of diamonds; this is apparently a less expensive kind of purity), also called chastity rings, promise rings, or abstinence rings. A Mississippi jeweler made a ring for his thirteen-year-old daughter with two sapphires representing his watchful eyes, guarding her virginity until the day she marries.[147] The custom has both incestuous overtones (as in the Cinderella stories in which fathers give their daughters wedding rings)[xxii] and religious resonances (as in the nuns' rings that marry them to Christ).[xxiii]

The practice originated in the United States in the 1990s among Christian-affiliated sexual abstinence groups, where wearing a silver purity ring is typically accompanied by a religious vow to practice abstinence

---

xxi. See chapter 1, p. 3.

xxii. See chapter 1, p. 45.

xxiii. See chapter 1, p. 11.

until marriage. The Silver Ring Thing (a subsidiary of a Pennsylvania evangelical church), True Love Waits, and Wanting an Individual to Trust are prominent among a number of organizations that distribute purity rings. Evangelical Christians host chastity balls [*sic!*] to which young girls go, often with their daddies. Yet, though more than one in eight American adolescents has made a virginity pledge, less than 12 percent of that 8 percent keep their vows until marriage.[148] Moreover, many of them use what might be termed the Bill Clinton floating definition of sex, which allows for a malleable and ingenious variety of sexual actions[149] without violating the wording of the pledge.[150] And, finally, many of the teenagers in these programs just take off the ring when they want to abstain from abstinence, and then put it back on,[151] conveniently losing it for a while just like so many of the men in the long mythology of magic rings.[xxiv] Sex, if not love, will always find a way—out of a promise, even the promise embodied in a ring.

---

xxiv. See chapter 3, p. 74, and chapter 4, p. 87.

II

Two Conclusions, on Money and Myth

I Money: The Lap of Luxury

What is the conceptual thread on which we can string these gems of stories? There are several, of course, and I laid out half a dozen of them in the Introduction.[i] But I wish to focus here on one so obvious that I haven't really talked about it directly, and that is the eternal triangle of jewelry, sex, and money. Most of the stories we have seen are about the interaction between jewelry and, on the one hand, sex and gender (or, if you prefer, sex and women) and, on the other hand, money and power. These stories remind us why the word "luxury" meant "lust/lasciviousness" before it came to mean "opulence/extravagance," and why Luxury, "usefully compress[ing] together opulence and libido,"[1] is the patron goddess of jewelry, giving a double meaning to the phrase "the lap of luxury." There's a lot of talk about love in these tales, but they are really all about lucre, about payment for services rendered. They are not True Love Stories. The clever wives[ii] are not primarily after love; they are trying to secure their sons' inheritances. And though it's not at all clear what different cultures mean by "love," they seem generally to agree on the meanings of sex and money.

Men—male jewelers, male buyers—exchange jewelry in much the same way that, as Claude Lévi-Strauss taught us to see, men exchange women to cement alliances between men.[2] Fathers give their daughters

i. See Introduction, p. xx.

ii. See chapter 6, p. 137, and chapter 7, p. 170.

away to sons-in-law in marriage ceremonies, often in exchange for a bride-price (the reverse of a dowry). The ancient Indian lawmaker Manu railed against this: "No learned father should take a bride-price for his daughter, no matter how small, for a man who, out of greed, exacts a bride-price would be selling his child like a pimp. . . . No matter how great or small the price, the sale amounts to prostitution."[3]

And men who have controlled both the production and the sale of jewelry have also generated much of its mythology. We have seen how the mythology created by the De Beers corporation in Amsterdam bamboozled several generations of Americans into buying diamond engagement rings they could not afford.[iii] The jeweler is the obvious pivot of all the transactions in Max Ophüls's 1953 film, *The Earrings of Madame de,*[iv] but jewelers are there, behind the scenes, in every story involving jewelry. The exaggerated number of transactions in that film merely makes blatant, and tragicomic, what is always present, usually hidden, in all of these tales: jewelry is money, and constantly changes hands, circulating just like money, or sex. Jewelry worn by a woman is a way for a man to broadcast to another man his ownership both of wealth and of the woman. The necklace that the general and Donati give to Louise in *The Earrings of Madame de* is part of a transaction between the two men that ends in a duel.

Courtesans are generally even more aware of the value of jewelry than wives are. Since 1860, the Paris restaurant Lapérouse has been noted for its "private salons," frequently used by courtesans of the period. When the women were paid, in diamonds, for services rendered, they would scratch the mirrors in the private rooms to make sure that the diamonds were real. Those scratches are still visible in the salons to this day.[4]

Direct connections between rings and financial considerations about women are quite ancient. Sometimes the seal or signet on the ancient Greek or Roman betrothal ring featured a key to signify that the woman was to have the right of sealing up the household goods. According to Clement of Alexandria, the ring was not a mere ornament; the seal signified not a woman's right but her duty to preserve her husband's goods and to care for the house.[5] George Frederick Kunz sees a vestige of this right, or duty, in a possible overtone of the words of the old Anglican marriage ceremony: "With all my worldly goods I thee endow."[6]

---

iii. See chapter 10, p. 262.

iv. See chapter 9, p. 248.

The woman herself often became the most visible of a man's worldly goods, and if he went one step further and draped her with precious jewels, she herself, as the jewel in the crown of his possessions, became an even more vivid display of his personal wealth. The singer Margaret Whiting spoke of "small men who felt inadequate and had to wear a beautiful blond girl on their arm, like a jewel, so everyone would know they were real men."[7] We speak nowadays of a "trophy wife"—a young, very pretty wife of a much older, very rich man—but the metaphor can work in both directions: if she is what used to be called a "gold digger,"[v] then he is *her* trophy, as well as her bankroll.

As the texts in this book testify, for many centuries in many parts of the world, jewelry has been the only property that most women have been allowed to own. Jewelry gives a woman a degree of financial and political independence. "She has nothing but the jewels she stands up in," a catty woman says of a penniless English widow in the film *Up at the Villa* (Philip Haas, 2000), based on the book by W. Somerset Maugham. Jewelry was for women what James C. Scott has taught us to call a weapon of the weak:[8] often women's jewelry was all they could use to defend themselves against men who denied them the ownership of land and permanent property. Jewelry has all the advantages of what Wemmick, in Dickens's *Great Expectations* (1861), called "portable property," and advised Pip to "get hold of." It has often been all that a woman could take with her if she was divorced or if she divorced her husband; it is the key to her freedom. Jewelry is both portable and fungible. Until recently, if a woman wanted to leave her husband, few legal or economic sanctions were available to her. But she was usually allowed to keep the jewelry that she had brought into the marriage (as part of her dowry), and sometimes also the jewelry that she had been given by her husband, and this bought her some degree of independence. In early America, "the jewelry a woman had been given was the last asset that the probate officers could touch, the last asset vulnerable to being seized as payment for her late husband's debts."[9] Outside the law, too, a woman in desperation could simply take her jewelry and run off into the night, taking her chances.

Divorce laws varied enormously from culture to culture, however, and what a woman could keep under certain circumstances in one country in a certain period was by no means guaranteed to her in another time

---

v. See chapter 10, p. 279.

and place. The legal scholar Manu stated the conditions under which a woman in ancient India could or could not keep her jewelry (her inheritance) when she wanted to part from her husband: "If she transgresses against a husband who is infatuated, a drunk, or ill, he may deprive her of her jewelry and personal property and desert her for three months. But if she hates him because he is insane, impotent, sterile, or suffering from a disease caused by his evil, she should not be deserted or deprived of her inheritance."[10] This is just about as good as it gets for women in that time and place.

Dowries in India were sometimes more of a curse than a blessing. Even today, Indian women are murdered for their dowries. In nineteenth-century India, particularly in Bengal, where widows were allowed to inherit their husbands' property, such widows were sometimes encouraged (or forced) to become satis by burning themselves on their husbands' funeral pyres. A sati was usually made to distribute her jewelry before ascending the funeral pyre or to wear it, in which case her relatives would later retrieve the gold from the embers.[11] Nowadays, Indian widows often keep their jewelry but are not allowed to wear it. Families try to prevent the widow from remarrying so that the jewelry will remain in the family.

In parts of India the picture is brighter; a mother may give jewelry to her daughter, passing by the men altogether, though the money is often regarded as belonging to the family, not to the individual woman. And women have control of their jewelry nowadays in Saudi Arabia and the Gulf States. There, jewelry is "a sign of wealth, security, and status, . . . a wearable investment."[12] Women receive jewelry as part of the bride-price or marriage price (*mahr*) and as gifts from their husbands throughout the marriage, and they keep all of it in divorce.[13] A woman who uses her jewelry as a fluid asset is not necessarily acting selfishly, let alone against her husband's interests. Those armfuls of gold bracelets that women wear in so many Hindu and Islamic regions are often the family's venture capital, regularly pawned for cash needed for business investments and (if all goes well) later redeemed. Islamic pawnshops are the equivalent of banks, and though good Muslims aren't supposed to charge interest, they can charge "storage fees" for gold, almost always in the form of jewelry.[14] In the Christian world, too, Crédit Municipale in France is nicknamed the widows' bank because women strapped for funds can bring in their jewelry and get loans against it (pawn it, in effect).[15] Tibetan nomadic women wear all their jewelry—often all the family's portable wealth, usually extremely heavy—all the time, to keep it safe, as they're always moving about, sleeping in tents, and there are no safe deposit boxes. They have Tibetan mastiffs to protect them.[16] It has been well remarked that jewelry is the world's oldest and most beautiful form of banking.[17] Women have found various ways to use jewelry to negotiate between the carat[18] of sexual bargaining power and the stick of financial dependency.

II Myth: Recognition, Rings, Reason, and Rationality

Let's shift our focus now from the social context of the jewelry myths to the texts that arise from that context. Many of these tales were borrowed by one culture from another, or diffused from a common source. But the very fact that these stories, and not others, were able to travel, like certain wines, and to be told again and again in such different contexts indicates that they are in a very real sense at home in several cultures, however much they may be differently inflected and take on different meanings in each new context.[19]

Why do so many people tell these same stories again and again? Why do these mythic structures have such a stranglehold on the human imagination? More particularly, why do people keep telling stories that fly so blatantly in the face of logic and reason, even when logical concerns are explicitly raised in the course of the stories themselves?

We will look for answers to these questions both inside and outside the narrative frame. We saw, in the story of Marie Antoinette's diamond necklace, how a moment of history came out of myth in the eighteenth century and went back into it.[vi] And we saw how in the twentieth century an advertising campaign about women and their diamonds created myths of the same genre as those that recur throughout the fictional sources.[vii] Robert Pippin has commented insightfully on the persistence of the central motifs:

> "Romantic/sexual love is an archetypal domain of deep, fundamental uncertainty. The vulnerability is greater than any other human domain, the need for proof correspondingly the highest and the frailest. The "proofs" are as much a tangle as the oral pledges. The

---

vi. See chapter 8, p. 206.

vii. See chapter 10, p. 262.

ring evidence is always ironic, double or triple edged, as if sexual life travels in this little sealed capsule through historical time. Post feminism, we still have *Sex and the City*;[viii] not only has nothing changed from Indian mythology/folklore to Shakespeare's *All's Well*,[ix] nothing, not even DNA,[x] has changed since then."[20]

What is it that makes people, in the world as well as on the page, swallow such myths and allow themselves to be fooled by them?

The Recognition of Myth and the Myth of Recognition

A myth can be defined as a story believed by many people over a long period, despite persistent evidence that it is not factually true.[21] Mythic narratives survive because, while the basic plot may remain intact, the point of the plot, even its moral and its relationship to forms of skepticism, reason, or cultural constructions of "common sense," may be changed, even reversed, to suit the changing assumptions of different times and different places.[22] Myths endure precisely because people keep changing them into something that serves their present needs.

What literary critics call the recognition narrative, the ultimate revelation of the identity of someone who has been in disguise for much of the story, is a myth in my sense of the word. What is experienced by the characters inside a recognition story is also experienced by the reader or hearer, outside the frame of the story. As the story unfolds, we see through the disguise of the new superficial details—now the princess has become a chambermaid, the palace a cattle ranch—to realize that it is, in fact, our old friend the disguised heroine or the forgetful husband. When the victim of the masquerade finally recognizes the masquerader ("Oh, it's my wife!"), the reader or listener of the story recognizes the plot ("Oh, it's a recognition story!").

Beaumarchais's *Marriage of Figaro*[xi] mocks the cliché of the recognition scene when (in Act III) the valet Figaro remarks, in the presence of the woman (Marcellina) who is about to force him to marry her, that he

---

viii. See chapter 10, p. 289.

ix. See chapter 6, p. 159.

x. See chapter 7, pp. 204–205.

xi. See chapter 8, p. 221.

has been searching for his lost parents for years, that rich shawls and jewels (!) found on him as an infant identify him as noble, and that his parents had taken the precaution of marking a unique scar (a spatula) on his right arm. At this everyone realizes that Marcellina is Figaro's mother (and has narrowly averted incest).[xii] "His mother!" one character after another cries out. Mozart's librettist, da Ponti, stretches it out to six repetitions at one point—"Sua madre?" "Sua madre!" "Sua madre?" and so on. Johann Strauss's comic opera *Die Fledermaus* culminates in a classic recognition scene, after which someone rushes in, looks around, and says, "Oh dear, I see they've already played the recognition scene!"[23]

The moment when two apparently different characters are revealed to be two aspects of one person brings with it the same satisfaction as the moment when the last piece of the jigsaw puzzle—or the last line connecting the dots—slips in to reveal the total image, or when, in a piece of music, the essential final sequence of chords comes to resolution. This always/already expected finale accounts, in Terence Cave's opinion, "both for the extraordinary popularity of recognition scenes in all types of literature and for the contempt and suspicion" with which cultural critics commonly regard them.[24]

The tales in the first seven chapters of this book, with their rings in fish, forgetful knights, and clever wives, are all recognition stories in which a ring is a vital clue. The stories about Marie Antoinette in chapter 8 are about a different sort of recognition—the mis-recognition of the queen in the masquerade in the Bower of Venus. In chapter 9, jewelry supplies the evidence for the recognition of the woman in the film *Vertigo*; it is also a more subtle clue to the recognition of a woman's character, her identity in a broader sense, in many nineteenth-century stories. And men and women in chapter 10 parade their diamonds, in the spirit of conspicuous consumption, in order to be recognized not as individuals but as people of a certain type and status: "I am a man who can afford expensive diamonds"; "I am a woman whose husband loves her enough to buy her expensive diamonds."

If we classify the corpus of recognition narratives as a family (in the phylogenetic sense), the narrative of recognition by means of a ring is a genus, and recognition of your own disguised wife or husband by means of a ring is a species. On each of these levels, there seems to be a limit to

---

xii. See chapter 2, p. 43.

the number of basic plots that a storyteller can use, increasingly limited as the plot becomes increasingly specific.[25] Stith Thompson captured most of them in his multivolume index to all the folktale motifs; they are numerous, but not infinite. Alexander Goldenweiser's "principle of limited possibilities" explains what he calls "dependent convergences."[26] If we apply his theory of cultures to narratives, it suggests that the constraints of the traditional narrative repertoire must somehow accommodate the constantly changing needs of the narrative community.

Repetition and Originality

The variants of a myth recorded in different texts build a potentially infinite number of stories by rearranging a finite number of mythic themes. Lévi-Strauss compared the process of recycling these inherited mythic themes to bricolage, the work of the French handyman (the *bricoleur*), the rag-and-bones man who makes new things out of broken pieces of the old, using one leg of a broken chair to replace a missing leg on another chair. The myth-maker's toolbox consists of fragments of old stories that can be recycled in new stories. Each culture chooses the scraps that it wants to keep; audiences as well as storytellers know them. Some, such as the ring narrative, have proved more recyclable than others.

For some critics, such repetitions are a literary flaw. In "A String of Beads,"[xiii] Maugham expresses concern that if a story is recycled often enough, like a woman passing from lover to lover, it is likely to be taken as false even if it is true. Similarly, in Shakespeare's *The Winter's Tale*,[xiv] someone remarks, "This news, which is called true, is so like an old tale, that the verity of it is in strong suspicion" (5.2.28-30). Cave argues that the recognition narrative is a knee-jerk, hackneyed repetition or reuse of a plot element, a cliché: "The sense of cliché is the sense of being cheated, of being brought to a moment of fullness only to find that it is empty."[27] This sense of being cheated is indeed what is experienced by the people inside the story: the person the protagonist thought he was, or was with, turns out, at the moment of fullness, to be empty of the desired identity.

But the sense of being cheated is not, I think, what is experienced by the reader of or listener to a recognition story, outside the frame of the

---

xiii. See chapter 9, p. 241.

xiv. See chapter 1, p. 52.

story. Unlike literary critics and cultural snobs (who, Cave admits, are the main people who accuse recognition narratives of fraudulence),[28] the common or garden variety reader or listener does not feel defrauded by a plot that he recognizes. Unlike our reaction to most repeated anecdotes or the narration of other people's dreams, we do not think, "O lord, not again," when we encounter a familiar mythic text. The voice of myth is meant to be predictable. The audience has an expectation of what the story should say, and the storyteller imitates that paradigm, fulfills that expectation. The audience takes pleasure in predicting what will happen and satisfaction in seeing it happen, rather than in being surprised or shocked. And it is precisely the known quantity of the clichéd plot (plus its intrinsic appeal: clichés endure because they represent truths) that makes it ultimately not empty but filling, the comfort food of narratives. As Marina Warner says of the end of the *Arabian Nights*, "This conclusion, in all its preposterous, cruel unlikelihood, accords of course with the fairytale conventions [and] still has the power to work its charm of release and contentment on the reader."[29]

Originality is therefore not an essential ingredient of a good myth (as Maugham ultimately pointed out in defending his own reuse of a good story in the film of "Mr. Know All").[xv] In the hands of traditional storytellers, originality is a medicine to be taken on an "as needed" basis only. In a world without copyrighting, plagiarism has no legal repercussions—and indeed no meaning. Retellings of old stories are "covers," as contemporary musicians call their own renditions of other musicians' songs. Great myths serve storytellers as the Pieta or the Madonna and Child served medieval European sculptors and painters, as a classic shared theme that challenges the artist to use it as a foil for individual originality—for tellers of myths can, in fact, be highly original, as long as they also take pains to touch all the bases that their audiences expect. They learn from other storytellers, not necessarily in a formal teacher-student relationship, but just by following them around (in an oral tradition) or reading them (in a literary tradition). They claim to tell the very same stories, as they heard them and learned them and as they themselves have always already told them, but they change them with every retelling, just as Claude Monet painted haystacks, and the Houses of Parliament, over and over again, but never the same. Artistry rather than context explains the way the cliché

---

xv. See chapter 9, p. 237.

comes alive. In addition to variation in plot, originality expresses itself in the music, intonation, and other aspects of an oral performance, and the drawing out of character, setting, and subplots in a literary rendition, as well as the skill of the wording. The self-propagating trope relies on the inventiveness of storytellers.

In both literary and oral transmission, new versions do not replace old ones but rather exist side by side, at least for a time but potentially forever.[30] Each time we hear a new presentation of the myth, it carries with it the complex cumulative memories of all the other times we heard it, flashing us back to the people we were then—a young child in our parents' home, or in love for the first time, or in the throes of a dilemma. Many such myths also connect us to all the other people who have said those words, heard those words, throughout the history of our families and wider communities. (To return to the musical analogy, as we hear Louis Armstrong sing "Mack the Knife," we sense Lotte Lenya singing, in German, behind him.) And every time we hear the words adds, like the layers of a pearl, to our deeper feelings about that text. Myths snowball as they roll through a culture.

The film *Big Fish*[xvi] begins by presenting the hardheaded view of repetition. When the father insists that "everyone loves" his story of the fish and the ring, the son says, "No, dad, they don't. And I don't love that story, not any more, not after a thousand times. I know every punch line, I can tell them as well as you can." But finally the son recants entirely, and the film ends with him saying:

> "Have you ever heard a joke so many times you've forgotten why it's funny. But you hear it again and suddenly it's new; you remember why you loved it in the first place. A man tells his stories so many times that he becomes the stories. They live on after him and in that way he becomes immortal."

It's the repetition that produces the immortality.

The Colluding Audience

Audiences also pretend not to know, not to see through the paper-thin masquerades. The audience's/reader's knowledge of the plot, of the true

---

xvi. See chapter 2, p. 27.

identity of the masquerader, sometimes seems to leak into the minds of some of the characters, who have a sense of the realistic truth even when they are apparently under the power of the mythic illusion. The myth persists because of the collusion of storytellers and audiences in its preservation. Neither the audience nor the storyteller has complete control of the story; it is an act of mutual creation.

Myths are like what George Orwell called "good bad" poems (epitomized by those of Rudyard Kipling): when you hear them you think how trite, how obvious, but they stick in your mind, and then when something happens to you like that, as it will, you remember the story, and you like it better than you did when you first heard it.[31] And so you recognize the myth in your life, yet another layer in the palimpsest of recognition, and the stories keep coming back, like the rings thrown into the ocean. The recognition myths are therefore not only about the events that they narrate but also about themselves, about the recognition of the presence of myths in human lives. Sometimes they are even self-conscious about it, as when, in Terence's *The Mother-in-Law*,[xvii] someone remarks, "I hope this won't be a comedy, where everyone learns everything in the end." So too, near the end of *The Winter's Tale*,[xviii] speaking of Hermione, who is presumed dead, Paulina says, "That she is living, / Were it but told you, should be hooted at / Like an old tale: but it appears she lives" (5.3.115–227).

The joys of repetition are especially characteristic of movies, a main source of our contemporary mythology.[xix] So it is that every Christmas season we listen, again and again, to *A Christmas Carol*, and watch, each year, the different film actors playing Scrooge (Reginald Owen, 1938; Alastair Sim, 1951; George C. Scott, 1984; etc.). Horkheimer and Adorno wrote, in 1947, of the culture industry's standard plot lines that are rarely reversed except to reinforce existing conventions; a popular movie requires a set of stock narratives from which the audience draws in order to make predictions about the plot's outcome, which ensure humor if thwarted and satisfaction when fulfilled.[32] Americans so notoriously love to recycle film plots again and again that when Alan Bennett made his

---

xvii. See chapter 7, p. 176.

xviii. See chapter 2, p. 52.

xix. See chapter 9, p. 242.

1991 play into a film in 1994, he changed the title to avoid confusion. As he wrote:

> "The title of the stage play is *The Madness of George III* and of the film, *The Madness of King George*. This was a marketing decision: the American backers somewhat shamefacedly explained that the audience might think, seeing *The Madness of George III*, that they had missed out on *The Madness of George* and *The Madness of George II*. A survey had apparently shown that there were many movie-goers who came away from Kenneth Branagh's film of *Henry V* wishing they had seen its four predecessors. Where this leaves *The Third Man* (or *The Second Mrs Tanqueray*) I'm not sure."[33]

And so it is with stories about rings of recognition; we like to listen to "Clever Wife II," and III, and IV.

Sometimes, however, it is the divergence from the expected plot that delights the audience, especially if they can see it coming. (This is true more of written variants—in which we, as scholars and students, may identify and appreciate such clever twists—than of oral presentations, though it works well in the theater and cinema.) As Warner has noted:

> "Much pleasure for the reader arises when, like the protagonist or other character, the story takes an unexpected turn and springs a different denouement. Or when, as in some cases, the reader succeeds in foreseeing the end result of the characters' action when they fail to do so. In these ways, the story ties up its subjects and its audience in crafty knots and self-mirroring devices."[34]

Conventional plotlines may swerve off course to lead us on to the assimilation of new stories, from our own culture or from others, as familiar themes come to be combined with less familiar ones. Just as the prince, in the old story, follows the deer until he finds himself in another part of the forest, *una selva oscura* (as Shakespeare and Dante, respectively, called it), so the storyteller lures the reader or listener from one story to another, from the familiar territory of the recognized general plot ("Oh, I know this story, it's the one about the prince chasing the deer") to the terra incognita of the new version with its unique details—the deer is chasing the prince, or the prince becomes the deer or turns out to be the deer in disguise.

The Ring to the Rescue

When men within the stories use rings to salve their consciences, or to wriggle out of tight spots,[xx] storytellers are using rings to save the story. Storytellers often find themselves caught between a rock and a hard place, between an inherited, traditional story that they are holding onto like a monkey with a banana in his fist, and a new cage of ethics that traps the monkey's paw (cum banana) within it. At such a moment, a ready-to-hand narrative theme may be invoked as a key to unlock the cage. When a storyteller has painted herself into a corner, she reaches for something to fix the story she has inherited, to adapt it to her own purposes. Sinking into the moral quagmire produced when one moral standard collides with another that follows but does not quite supplant it, such as the tension between the siren song of adultery and the monogamous wax poured into the married couple's ears, the storyteller reaches for a life-saving narrative. And a narrative device like the smoking ring or ring ex machina is always readily available to do the job.

If the author cannot change what happened, the plot, she may at least be able to change the balance of power of knowledge in the plot: who knew what, and when (as we often ask about corrupt politicians). The ring of forgetfulness, balanced by the ring of memory, produces and obscures knowledge at will, shifting the balance of power as well as the responsibility. As the folklorist W. R. Shedden Ralston remarked, "The recognition by means of a ring is, as everyone knows, one of the commonest contrivances for bringing a story of adventure to a close."[35] Less charitably, A. S. Byatt has a woman who writes stories for children ask a museum curator to suggest an object around which a story can be made, "something that's *always been missing*—with a story attached to it, naturally—and that can be made to have magic properties, an amulet, a mirror that shows that past and the future, that kind of thing. . . . Not a ring. There are so many tales about rings."[36]

Sexing Texts

Most of these stories appear in texts that were written by men. Yet women are storytellers too, as we have seen even among the earlier tales and still more in modern folk renditions (such as the tale of the Korpalu

---

xx. See chapter 3, p. 69, through chapter 5, p. 136.

woman[xxi] or Monia Hejaiej's 1990 variant of "The Vizier's Daughter").[xxii]
Two women, Anita Loos and Mary Gerety, were indirectly and directly
responsible for the famous line, "A diamond is forever," though the line
was marketed by men.[xxiii] Even texts that male scribes recorded often tell
stories that they heard from mothers or nurses, the sources of so many
"old wives' tales."[37] But though we can occasionally note a different tone in
stories whose tellers have been identified as female, by and large the same
sexist cultural rationale pervades the culture of both men and women
and, consciously or unconsciously, constrains the stories of narrators of
both genders.

Why do men tell these stories when they show men up to be such
cads? Because they reflect the rationality of their time and place, in which
such behavior was considered normal (or macho, or virile, or honorable,
or what you will).[xxiv] And because, as we have seen, the old myths live
on, often patched up a bit, even when new ethical norms make them an
embarrassment. And because there is something in the stories that reas-
sures men about things that are important to them, such as the paternity
of their children.[xxv] Such stories often encode repressive social agendas;
the tales of clever wives enforce the view that it is the job of women to
remain faithful to their husbands no matter how badly, how unreasonably,
they are treated, and they let men off the hook by pretending to redress
the balance of power, as if to say, "I'm not a bully; she can defend herself
by her wiles."[38]On the other hand, we may ask why women tell stories
that depict them as promiscuous tricksters. Perhaps because they are also
depicted as cleverer than the men, and (usually) only *apparently* promiscuous. It might also be argued that it is in the interest of women to see men
depicted as cads and in the interest of men to see women depicted as promiscuous tricksters. Viewed that way, it's a win-win situation.

The connection between jewelry, women, and deception is an enduring
one. Our stories accuse jewelry and women of faking it in various ways;
fake jewelry is mirrored in the deceptions, the lies, the women pretending
to be other women. But considerations of the changing social contexts of

---

xxi. See chapter 6, p. 150.

xxii. See chapter 7, p. 196.

xxiii. See chapter 10, p. 265.

xxiv. See chapter 7, p. 179.

xxv. See chapter 7, p. 200.

these stories shift our focus back to the outer level of the narrative frame, where the narrator uses the ring to obscure the fact that the *men* were faking it when they said that they had not slept with the women or that they had forgotten that they had slept with the women. The cross-cultural corpus of stories about fake jewelry reveals how male narrators fake it (with the audience's collusion): how they cast moral aspersions on one of the few sources of women's independence, their jewelry; how they maintain the illusion that if you can get someone's ring you can prove that he slept with you, or that he did not really abandon you but was merely helplessly bewitched into temporarily forgetting you; or that if you can prove that a woman has real jewelry that her husband did not give her, you can prove that she was unfaithful to him. The gender myths mesh nicely: the slut assumption[xxvi] (if the woman has the ring, she slept with some guy) balances the paternity fear[xxvii] (if she has your ring, you must be the father of her kid).

Here is where the cross-cultural distribution of this theme is so impressive. It shows us how often narrators have tricked their audiences into believing what they so deeply want to believe: that a little thing like a ring can bring justice to the asymmetrical power relations that have controlled female sexuality for most of human history. It shows us how widespread is the desire to project the responsibility for sexual rejection or betrayal onto an external force like a gold ring.

Reason and Rationality

So welcome is the alibi of the ring—both to the man in the story and to the (usually male) storyteller—that it is often accepted as a valid excuse even when it violates both reason and rationality. My distinction between these terms draws upon Lorraine Daston's formulation of the difference between reason, in the sense of freely working things out by your individual intelligence, and rationality, in the sense of playing by strict and consistent rules.[39] Reason in this context is often synonymous with logic as well as with what Enlightenment cultures construe as common sense (though common sense is always culturally configured, and means different things

---

xxvi. See chapter 9, p. 228.

xxvii. See chapter 7, p. 200.

in different cultures). Rationality, by contrast, might be someone else's rules, the culture's rules, not yours.

Myths in general discourage reason but depend upon rationality. As Lévi-Strauss has shown, the myths of each culture may ignore logic but they are usually entirely rational in the Dastonian sense of following the often complex rules that underlie that culture's formulation of meaning.[40] The ring myths veer back and forth between reason and rationality like a drunken driver weaving back and forth across the center line of a road. Let's consider the role first of reason and then of rationality in myths of rings of recognition.

The Ring Runs Rings around Reason

Knowing that these stories are myths makes it easier to understand why no one objects to the violations of reason, either in hearing the stories or in deciding to spend $10,000 on a diamond engagement ring instead of a down payment on a condo. As the *Economist* noted, "The diamond myth lives in a world a bit outside of logic."[41] Myths disdain reason almost by definition, at least by my partial definition of a myth as a narrative capable of ignoring evidence. Myths as a whole are unreasonable not merely from the standpoint of Enlightenment types standing outside the culture but even for the people who make the myths, people who are perfectly capable of noticing that human beings cannot fly and who can also see the logical flaws in the use of a ring as proof text. Such stories demand that the reader or listener suspend the sense not only of what is physically possible but of what is logical, overlooking easily available explanations for certain events in favor of the extremely unlikely explanation that the traditional story offers.

For example, where other forms of concealment may operate in more realistic texts, rings of invisibility up the ante in more fantastic stories. Herodotus (c. 485–420 BCE) tells the tale of King Candaules, who, having made the mistake of falling in love with his own wife, urged his friend Gyges to hide behind the bedroom door to see how beautiful she was[42] (as, in the *Nibelungenlied*, King Gunther hides, watching his friend Siegfried deflower his wife).[xxviii] When Plato (427–347 BCE) retold the story,[43] he substituted for the entirely realistic device of the bedroom door a magical ring

---

xxviii. See chapter 5, p. 116.

of invisibility. So, too, in early versions of the Siegfried myth, Siegfried merely changes into Gunther's clothes to impersonate him; in later versions, he uses first a magic cloak and then a magic helmet. Reason gave way to mythology, as it generally does in the development of stories in which a magic ring is inserted into later retellings of the tale.

Adam Gopnik has spoken well of the special pleading that we allow narratives about rings (even though he is talking about the *other* sort of rings, Tolkienian rings of power):[xxix]

> "Certain kinds of truths are convincing only in a narrative. The idea, for instance, that the ring of power should be given to two undersized amateurs to throw into a volcano at the very center of the enemy's camp makes sound and sober sense, of a kind, in Tolkien; but you would never expect to find it as a premise at the Middle Earth Military Academy. Anyone watching Hamlet will find his behavior completely understandable . . . though any critic thinking about it afterward will reflect that this behavior is a little nuts."[44]

A narrative that makes perfectly good sense as a trope should not be discounted on dreary old empirical grounds. Conventional recognition narratives are not at all like World War II spy flicks, in which agents carefully learn accents, make sure to wear the right shoelaces, and so forth, knowing that if they make a tiny slip, the Gestapo will catch them. The myths are playing a different game.

The signet ring is the only kind of ring that is a certain sign of identity, with the bearer's name or emblem on it. And even the signet ring is not proof of what the bearer had *done*; someone else might have stolen it, sold it, and so forth, and worn it to commit the act in question, or indeed *not* to commit the act in question. That such arguments from reason were always available to storytellers and audiences is easily demonstrated by a number of stories we have seen in which someone does question how, after all, a ring can prove that someone did or did not commit an act of sexual infidelity. Reason often pipes up to argue against the "proof"; reason says, "Look for the ring where you lost it"; reason says, "Lots of people have rings like that," or "You stole the ring," or "That's not my ring"—in other words, "The ring lies." Habrotonon, for instance,[xxx] resists the evidence of the ring on grounds that "a million things" might have made a man lose a ring in ways other than the occasion of a rape. 'Aysha[xxxi] pretends to have an identical twin sister in order to provide a reasonable explanation for the success of her masquerade. In Jay Reid Gould's version of the de Maupassant story of the necklace, someone sensibly remarks, "Who would lend someone a real necklace? We keep it safe under lock and key."[xxxii]

The unreasonable "proof" of circular jewelry is sometimes either forgotten at the end of the story, leaving atavistic traces in the text (as in the *Marriage of Figaro*),[xxxiii] or, though kept in the plot, is pushed aside to make way for more logical proofs of identity, as in *The Lady of the Jeweled Necklace*.[xxxiv] In one of the short French fragments of the tale of Tristan and Isolde,[xxxv] when Tristan objects that Isolde did not recognize him until she saw the telltale ring of green jasper, she replies "We are surrounded by treachery. . . . Neither the mention of your past life, nor the sound of your voice, not even this very ring, proved anything to me, for all these might have been the evil tricks of a sorcerer. Nevertheless I yield myself at the sight of this ring; did I not swear, as soon as I should see it again, at the risk of my life to always do what you bade me, be it wisdom or folly?"[45] In other words, she really did not trust the ring, but merely kept her promise to act as if she trusted it. Thus occasionally reason, even about rings, makes people act in unreasonable ways.

Warner has argued that fairy tales, a subset of myths, "face two ways, towards a past realm of belief on one side and towards a sceptical present on the other."[46] I want to take this a bit further and argue that they also face a skeptical past. When, at the end of Shakespeare's *The Winter's Tale*,[xxxvi] the lost child is found, a gentleman remarks, "The Oracle is fulfilled, the king's daughter is found, such a deal of wonder is broken out within this hour, that ballad-makers cannot be able to express it" (5.2.23–26). In

---

xxx. See chapter 7, p. 175.

xxxi. See chapter 7, p. 198.

xxxii. See chapter 9, p. 234.

xxxiii. See chapter 8, p. 223.

xxxiv. See chapter 3, p. 66.

xxxv. See chapter 4, p. 99.

xxxvi. See chapter 2, p. 52.

answer to the question, "Has the King found his heir?" another gentleman speaks:

> "Most true, if ever truth were pregnant by circumstance: that which you hear you'll swear you see, there is such unity in the proofs. The mantle of Queen Hermione's, her jewel about the neck of it, the letters of Antigonus found with it, which they know to be his character; the majesty of the creature in resemblance of the mother, the affection of nobleness which nature shows above her breeding, and many other evidences proclaim her, with all certainty, to be the king's daughter." (5.2.31–40)

The "unity in the proofs," not just "her jewel about the neck of it," is the voice of reason. Despite the fantasy of the romance, the whole pile of proofs is needed, to supplement the proof offered by the jewel—though it all goes to show that the jewel was, in fact, telling the truth, and the old tale was true. The same combination of arguments pops up just a few lines later, when Antigonus (the one who exited "pursued by a bear") is identified by his ring, though the man who tells this remarks, "Like an old tale still, which will have matter to rehearse, though credit be asleep and not an ear open" (5.2.62).

Reason challenges the ring-proof in a tale told by an Irish woman and retold by the poet William Butler Yeats. It seems that a girl whom the fairies had taken years ago is eventually returned to her parents. Her father thinks she is long dead and he does not recognize her. She says, "Stop, dear father, till you look at this ring on my finger. Look at your name and mine engraved on it." "It certainly is my daughter's ring; but I do not know how you came by it. I fear in no honest way." She calls her mother and says, "You have all forgotten me; but look at this mole on my neck. Surely, mother, you know me now?" "Yes, yes," says the mother, "my Gracie had a mole on her neck like that . . ." and all is well.[47] The mother reasons that a mole cannot be stolen or faked as the father fears a ring might be.

The unreasonable recognition by rings is balanced by the equally unreasonable non-recognition of people in disguise. Sometimes a reasoned explanation is given for the success of such deceptions. In a fantastical story in the *Mahabharata* (which does not involve a ring), this sort of non-recognition is justified by a boon that the god Dharma grants to his son, King Yudhishthira.[48] Yudhishthira tells Dharma that he and his brothers have been forced to go into exile in disguise and will lose their kingdom if they are recognized. He asks the god to promise that they will not be recognized, and the god agrees. This boon justifies the shallowness of the disguises that the king and his brothers subsequently adopt, parodies of their well-known characters. Magical though it is, the god's promise does interject a reasonable, if not realistic, explanation of how they got away with such obvious and playful masquerades.

The Hindu god's explicit boon is implicit in every recognition plot in every culture: no matter how poor your masquerade is, no one will recognize you. Similarly, the ring as evidence would never stand up in court, but it either jogs the forgetful husband's memory, if he really has forgotten, or jogs his conscience, if he is lying, so that he confesses. The clever wife is like a sharp courtroom lawyer, tap-dancing with material that she knows would not actually be admitted as evidence. Is it possible that all of the clever wife folktales are satires on the dumb idea that you could prove paternity with a ring? And is Shakespeare's *All's Well That Ends Well*[xxxvii] a satire on it too? Is *The Testament of Judah* a satire on Genesis 38?[xxxviii] I wonder.

One reasonable argument that challenges the "proof" of the ring is the argument from coincidence: maybe two unrelated people just happen to have the same ring (or the same name, or the same face). But the idea of coincidence itself flies in the face of reason, and can be challenged. In *The Lady of the Jeweled Necklace*,[xxxix] someone helpfully explains the "resemblance" of two people who are actually the same person by reference to coincidence, using a word (*ghunakshara*) that literally designates an alphabet letter eaten into a page by a bookworm, rather like our quantum metaphor of a monkey randomly typing out the complete works of Shakespeare.[49] The coincidences of resemblance point us toward another sort of coincidence, the coincidence of the masquerading self with the undisguised self,[50] of the clever wife with the make-believe prostitute. This high-wire act, the self flying through the masquerade to catch the outstretched hands of some other self, must be performed without any net but the narrative chain-mail made up of rings. And that chain-mail is what preserves these illogical stories even in cultures where the more logical likelihood has been acknowledged.

---

xxxvii. See chapter 6, p. 159.

xxxviii. See chapter 6, p. 155.

xxxix. See chapter 3, p. 66.

Myths revel in the violation of reason. Lewis Carroll's White Queen, perhaps quoting Tertullian ("Credo quia impossibile [I believe it because it is impossible]"), chides Alice when she says she can't believe impossible things, and advises her to practice: "When I was your age, I always did it for half-an-hour a day. Why, sometimes I've believed as many as six impossible things before breakfast." In the heat of the myth, cold reason has no more chance than a snowball in hell.

Rationing Rationality

Reason in myths is often sacrificed on the altar of rationality. Against the forces of reason, the power of the myth depends upon the human habit of making individual logic yield to the rationality of the group, often embodied in convention or "tradition" (as Tevye celebrates it in *Fiddler on the Roof*). What Joe Campbell used to call "the power of myth" in an individual (as in, "find your own bliss") is not really your own myth at all but someone else's myth putting you in their power, overlaid upon and obscuring your own individual desires and your own intellectual power to poke holes in the official party line. The conflict then comes down to the tension between what individual intelligence can work out (reason) and what the culture as a whole expects everyone to accept (rationality).[51]

I am not using myth in the sense of political or religious totalitarian mythmaking, something you are not *allowed* to question, or are burned at the stake for questioning.[52] I am speaking of narratives that are self-consciously alert to their human origins, narratives that you might question but do not, because there is something intrinsic in the story that you don't want to give up.

In the *Testament of Judah*,[xl] Judah, faced with the "proof" of the ring, argues, quite reasonably, that Tamar might have bought it from the woman he thought he gave it to (and slept with), but he still decides to accept her child as his. The rationality of the myth—the need for the descendants of Judah to be fruitful and multiply—overcomes the reason of the myth (which knows that the ring cannot prove that Judah is the father of Tamar's child). So too, men in several of our stories give a woman a ring that they obtained in the course of raping another woman.[xli] Why were they, we

---

xl. See chapter 6, p. 155.

xli. See chapter 7, p. 179.

ask, so stupid, so unreasonable as to do this? The rationale of the story demands it.

The Triumph of Myth over Reason

Naïvete and cynicism often endure side by side, sometimes even within a single text; the women in the stories naïvely assume that their rings will be adequate proofs of their innocence; sometimes they are, but sometimes they are not. Both possibilities are acknowledged in the Hellenistic novel, the *Ethiopika*,[xlii] when Persinna's daughter says, of the telltale jewelry, "These tokens are tokens to those who know them or who exposed them with me; but to those who know them not, or cannot recognize them all, they are mere unmeaning keepsakes or, perchance, necklaces that involve their holders in suspicion of theft and brigandage."[53]

The ring story survives because, despite the distortions that it often inflicts upon reason, it also fulfills more positive functions. One is the salvaging of the sense of a moral world. When it comes to saving our moral sense of balance, we would rather suspend the laws of both nature and culture than endure ethical discomfort.[54] Perhaps we can be truly moral only in a world where magic is there to bail us out. When our inherited narratives become immoral in the light of changing ideas,[xliii] a ring ex machina, however illogical, may be the only solution.[55] Rebalancing the world in a moral sense mitigates the asymmetrical relations between rich, lecherous men and poor, vulnerable women.[56] Stories don't change society, of course, but they can compensate for hard realities in the soft realm of the senses, and they can help us imagine the sort of world that we might someday actually take steps to achieve. Myths express hopes; that's what the happy ending is all about. They depict injustice "in order to declare it need not continue."[57] Angela Carter called this "heroic optimism."[58] Myths work against not the unreasonable but the immoral; they repair the immoral universe and give us hope that we might make it more moral.

These narratives work on us at a very deep level in a way that is hard to resist. The myth persists because of its intrinsic value for the individual, over and above its value for the rationale of the culture. Freud's concept of denial shows us some of the factors that often trump reason: people see

---

xlii. See chapter 2, p. 40.

xliii. See chapter 5, p. 131.

not only what fits with the view of the world that supports their lives but also what they want to see, for their personal emotional needs. The belief that love will last forever, and that your special ring is proof of this, is spectacularly counterfactual but not counterintuitive. It is entirely intuitive, it is what we want to believe, it is what our deepest intuitions grab hold of instead of reason, and it is what the mythology feeds on.

Romantic infatuation comes up against hard facts, legal challenges, and scientific proofs, and it wins with one hand tied behind its back. The mythic ring straddles the line between reason and rationality and confuses the issue, for it is a piece of solid evidence but it is invoked to support the claims of irrational romanticism. As even the hard-bitten Tom Zoellner writes of the ring he gave to the first girl he loved, "I still believed—despite all my skepticism—that an engagement ring did carry some kind of mystical charge, even though logic said otherwise."[59] The ring conjures up deep-seated ideas about jewelry and women and desire and deceit that continue to hold us in their thrall, no matter how much we learn that blatantly contradicts our gut feelings or even the song that our culture is singing at the moment. And so the myth carries the day; the ring rings true.

Notes

PREFACE

1. The building still exists, now called the Hotel Polonia, but it ceased to belong to my (Jewish) family in the 1930s.
2. The rings are also called *claddagh* rings, from the Irish village of Claddagh, in Galway, where such rings were made, or *fede* rings, from the Italian phrase *mani in fede* ("hands [joined] in fidelity").
3. Rings with clasped hands date from Roman times.
4. I am grateful to Cynthia Read and Richard Secare for the Italian American version of this prayer.

INTRODUCTION

1. Tolkien also wrote, before he ever wrote about a Hobbit, a verse translation of the *Völsunga Saga*, a great Norse story of women and rings (see chapter 5). J. R. R. Tolkien, and Christopher Tolkien, *The Legend of Sigurd and Gudrun.*
2. Robert Benchley, "Opera Synopses," 68.

CHAPTER 1

1. Diana Scarisbrick, *Rings: Jewelry of Power, Love and Loyalty*, 59.
2. Scarisbrick, *Rings*, 61.
3. John Boswell, *Same-Sex Unions in Premodern Europe*, 215.
4. Personal communication from Lorraine Daston, August 2010, based on a lecture by University of Tübingen Professor Nicholas J. Conard (paleolithic archaeology) on recent Neanderthal findings; in the August 2010 Natur/Kultur Symposium organized by Professor Christiane Nüsslein-Vollhard. See in addition N. J. Conard and M. Malina, "Schmuck und vielleicht auch Musik am Vogelherd

bei Niederstotzingen-Stetten ob Lontal," Kreis Heidenheim. *Archäologische Ausgrabungen Baden-Württemberg* 2005, 21–5.

5. This ad ran in the *New Yorker*, July 7, 2003.

6. A. T. Hatto, trans., *Nibelungenlied*, 373, citing the *Atlakvida*.

7. Charles Edwards, *The History and Poetry of Finger-Rings*, 205, citing Henry Swinburne (1551–1624), "A Treatise of Spousals, or Matrimonial Contracts" (posthumously, 1686), Sect. 15.

8. Edwards, *The History and Poetry of Finger-Rings*.

9. Bangle sellers, at least in South India, are notorious for being, like jewelers throughout India, allowed into women's quarters

10. John Hinton Knowles, *Folk-tales of Kashmir*, 126–136.

11. R. H. Stoddard, introduction to Edwards, *The History and Poetry of Finger-Rings*, iv, citing *Dr. Palmer's Poetry of Courtship and Compliment*, 1868.

12. Pauline Réage, *Story of O*, 50 and 165.

13. Wendy Doniger, *The Implied Spider*, 95–108.

14. Sharon Spencer, "Beyond Therapy: The Enduring Love of Anais Nin for Otto Rank," 101.

15. Personal communication from Father David Tracy, July 2003.

16. *Oxford English Dictionary*, citing A. Robertson, *Nuggets* (1894), 175.

17. George Frederick Kunz, *Rings for the Finger*, 327.

18. James Remington McCarthy, *Rings through the Ages: An Informal History*, 90.

19. Heinrich Zimmer, *The King and the Corpse*, 71.

20. Edwards, *The History and Poetry of Finger-Rings*, 158.

21. See Wendy Doniger, *The Bedtrick*.

22. Summarized from the temple web site http://www.agrohasheelamatamandir. com/brif_story_seelamata.html. See also further discussion of this myth in Lawrence A. Babb, *Alchemies of Violence*, 205–206. Thanks to Paul Courtright for this text.

23. A similar story was told in Russia about an evil general who tried to smear the reputation of an innocent girl, though in this case he used her own ring, not his:

> A king fell in love with a merchant's orphaned daughter, but a "spiteful and envious" general claimed to have slept with her. To defend his sister, her brother said, "If the general is not lying, let him get my sister's ring from her and find out what is her secret mark." The general bribed a woman who found out about the girl's secret mark (a golden hair under her left arm) and stole her ring. When the general showed the ring to the king, he imprisoned the brother and sent for the girl. She wept, and her tears become diamonds; she knitted a golden glove and studded it with the diamonds; then she went to the king and told him that the general had stolen the other glove. The general was forced to admit that he had never seen the girl before, nor been in her house; the king released the brother, executed the general, and married the girl. Afanasiev, *Russian Fairy Tales*, 415–418, "The Merchant's Daughter and the Slanderer."

24. Kunz, *Rings for the Finger*, 186.

25. Kunz, *Rings for the Finger*, 188.

26. The passage about Judah does not specify a ring, just a seal, but seal rings occur elsewhere in the Hebrew Bible: the ring in the book of Daniel, 6.17, is probably a signet, as is the one in Genesis 41.42 (the Pharoah's ring). The ring in the book of Esther, which is taken off Haman's hand, is definitely a signet. King Xerxes gives his ring-mounted-seal to his prime minister Haman, which gives Haman unrivaled power, because whatever is sealed with the king's ring cannot be returned or replied to or undone.

27. Alter, *The Art of Biblical Narrative*, 9.

28. Terence Cave, *Recognitions*; see also Wendy Doniger, *The Woman Who Pretended to Be Who She Was*.

29. Lilliana Leopardi, "Ludovico Dolce's Treatise on Precious Gems."

30. Leopardi, "Ludovico Dolce's Treatise," 72–73.

31. "She Wears My Ring" (words and music by Boudleaux and Felice Bryant).

32. Carlo Ginzburg, "Morelli, Freud and Sherlock Holmes," 5–36.

33. Walter Gregor, *The Folklore of North East Scotland*, 26.

34. Kunz, *Rings for the Finger*, 194, citing Macrobius, *Saturnalia*, lib. VII, cap. 13.

35. Edwards, *The History and Poetry of Finger-Rings*, 47 and 206.

36. Patrick K. Ford, *The Mabinogi*, 168–169, 177.

37. In this convoluted story, Beatrice's father has forced her to marry Alonzo, though she loves Alsemero; she persuades the ugly DeFlores, who loves her though she cannot bear even to look at him, to murder Alonzo. He does so and then, when he cannot remove the diamond ring from Alonzo's finger, cuts off the whole finger to use as proof of what he has done; he presents Beatrice with her dead lover's finger, still wearing the ring, and says, "I've a token for you." Later, when Beatrice, having slept with DeFlores, marries Alsemero, on the wedding night she gets her maid to substitute for her in order to provide the required maidenhead. The "emblem" of the finger with the ring is true evidence of a crime; the "emblem" of the faked virginity is false evidence of innocence. Thomas Middleton, *The Changeling*, act 3, scene 2, lines 20–24, p. 374; act 3, scene 4, line 28, p. 384.

38. "A gentleman while hunting was suddenly attacked by a savage wolf of monstrous size ... and ... contrived to cut off one of its fore-paws. This trophy he placed in his pocket, and made the rest of his way homewards in safety. On the road he met a friend, to whom he exhibited a bleeding paw, or, rather a woman's hand, upon which was a wedding-ring. His wife's ring was at once recognised by the other. His suspicions aroused, he immediately went in search of his wife, who was found sitting by the fire in the kitchen, her arm hidden beneath her apron, when the husband, seizing her by the arm, found his terrible suspicions verified. The bleeding stump was there, evidently just fresh from the wound. She was given into custody, and in the event was burned at Riom, in the presence of

thousands of spectators." Howard Williams, *Superstitions of Witchcraft*, 179. As the woman is unmasked, her animal paw becomes a human hand—the organ that we humans develop when we cease to go on all fours like animals. But it's the ring, the work of human hands, that gives her away.

39. John Fiske, *Myths and Mythmakers*, 91, cites "a parallel case of a cat-woman, in Thorpe's *Northern Mythology*, II, 26." Cf. also Robert Darnton, *The Great Cat Massacre*, 92–93.

40. *Yogavasishtha* 6.1.85–108; Doniger O'Flaherty, *Dreams, Illusion*, 280–281.

41. *Mahabharata* 3.284.

42. Personal communication from Joyce Burkhalter Flueckiger, January 2, 2014.

43. *Ramayana* 5.34.2–3.

44. Cited in *Ramayana*, trans. Robert P. Goldman et al., vol. 5, 446.

45. Carolyn Walker Bynum, *Holy Feast and Holy Fast*, 201, 210. They were sometimes called "Bride Mystics." A red circle with a red lozenge in the center was said to have appeared and disappeared on the finger of Catherine de Ricci (who died in 1589); Bynum, 391.

46. Judith C. Brown, *Immodest Acts*, 92.

47. Brown, *Immodest Acts*, 107.

48. Brown, *Immodest Acts*, 146.

49. Brown, *Immodest Acts*, 113.

50. Brown, *Immodest Acts*, 174–175.

51. Ovid, *Amores*, translation by Anthony S. Kline, Book II, Elegy XV: The Ring. The Latin of the last lines is: sed, puto, te nuda mea membra libidine surgent, et peragam partes anulus ille viri.

52. Eric Partridge, *Shakespeare's Bawdry*, 175.

53. David Bevington, *The Complete Works of Shakespeare*, 181.

54. Florentina Badalanova, *Folkoren Erotikon*, vol. I, 97ff., especially fn. 45, citing Russian erotic folk tales collected and published by A. N. Afanasiev.

55. Badalanova, *Folkoren Erotikon*, 98, citing A. N. Afanasiev, "Poeticheskie vozzreniia slavian na prirodu," Vol. 1, 467.

56. "The Enchanted Ring," cited by Dundes, "The Psychoanalytic Study of the Grimms' Tales," 51.

57. Judith Bruskin Diner, *The One Hundred New Tales*, 26–31; the Third Tale, by Monsieur de La Roche. A diamond ring plays a part in another tale of adultery in this collection (#62): A man sleeps with a married woman while her husband is on watch and, without realizing it, loses his diamond ring in her bed. That same night another man sleeps with her and finds the ring and takes it. The two meet, and the first claims the ring from the second, who refuses to give it to him. Eventually they happen to meet the husband and tell him the story, presumably not mentioning the name of the woman, and the husband decides that the ring is *his*.

58. Poggio #133. In *Poggii Facetiae*.

59. Antoine de la Sale [also Salle], *Les cents nouvelles nouvelles*, chapter 11.

60. And where de la Sale's protagonist offered a candle to the demonic figure below the feet of Saint Michael and was rewarded by the vision of the devil in his dream, Hans Carvel is visited by the devil unbidden. Rabelais's Friar John tells the tale to Panurge, promising that "if you follow my advice, your wife will not make a cuckold of you, without your knowledge and consent."

61. François Rabelais, *Gargantua and Pantagruel*, book 3, chapter 28, 185. It continues: "The devil disappeared. Overjoyed, Hans Carvel awoke, to find his middle finger encircled by his wife's what-do-you-call-it. . . . When his wife felt it, she drew back her buttocks as though to say: 'Oh, no! yes! oh! stop! that's not what you should put there!' . . . Was this not an infallible insurance against cuckoldry? Believe me, Panurge, you should follow his example. Never fail to have your wife's circlet tight about your middle finger."

62. De la Sale had said that the husband's finger was "bien avant ou derrière de sa femme bouté."

63. A contemporary French translation simply says: "Il se trouva que le bon homme avait le doigt où vous savez."

64. A translation that seems to be in the public domain, as it is widely circulated in various texts without the name of the translator, goes like this:

> One night, when company he'd had to dine,
> And pretty well was fill'd with gen'rous wine,
> Hans dreamed, as near his wife he snoring lay,
> The devil came his compliments to pay,
> And having on his finger put a ring,
> Said he, friend Hans, I know thou feel'st a sting;
> Thy trouble's great: I pity much thy case;
> Let but this ring, howe'er, thy finger grace,
> And while 'tis there I'll answer with my head,
> THAT ne'er shall happen which is now thy dread:
> Hans, quite delighted, forced his finger through;
> You drunken beast, cried Bab, what would you do?
> To love's devoirs quite lost, you take no care,
> And now have thrust your finger God knows where!

http://www.poetry-archive.com/p/hans_carvel.html#lQXCqS8UZ1AlK0Ma.99

65. It continues:

> HANS took the ring with Joy extreme;
> (All this was only in a Dream)
> And thrusting it beyond his Joint,
> 'Tis done, He cry'd: I've gain'd my Point.
> What Point, said She, You ugly Beast?
> You neither give Me Joy nor Rest:
> 'Tis done. — What's done, You drunken Bear?
> You've thrust your Finger G-d knows where!

66. Sigmund Freud and D. E. Oppenheim, *Dreams in Folklore*, "The Ring of Fidelity," p. 61. Reprinted in Alan Dundes, "The Psychoanalytic Study of the Grimms' Tales," 51. "A man jealous of his wife had a dream in which a demon appeared. The demon promised him a foolproof way of ensuring his wife's remaining faithful. 'Take this ring,' instructed the demon, 'and wear it on your finger with care. As long as you wear it, your wife cannot lie with any other man without your knowledge.' As the man awoke, excited with joy, he felt that he was pushing his finger into the vulva of his wife."

67. Fit enim, ut quae vigilantes versamus animo, in somniis saepius occurrant.

68. *Arthashastra* 14.3.1; *Kamasutra* 5.6.25–26.

69. Sigmund Freud, "Medusa's Head"; Wendy Doniger, *Splitting the Difference*, 107–110.

70. Aram Vartanian, "Preface" to Diderot, vol. 3, p. 11.

71. Vartanian, vol. 3, p. 11, citing Nocrion, *Conte Allobroge* (1747).

72. Diderot's story is well known in France; Réné Magritte made a pastel called "Les Bijoux Indiscrets," which depicts a woman's naked forearm, palm down, with a face growing on the back of the arm just above the wrist: eyes and lips are closed, and there is no jewelry anywhere in sight.

73. Kunz, *Rings for the Finger*, 122. Lucian attributes this lie to Eurates.

74. Denis Diderot, "Les bijoux indiscrets," 354.

75. The wife of the hero of a modern Hindi variant of the *Mahabharata* insists that he leave such a ring behind, as the usual surety, when he abandons her and his son; but the ring has the power of instant transportation, and so, when he undertakes a major journey now without it, he loses twelve years doing it on foot. Narrated in the Himalayas by Bacan Singh in 1986; translated by William Sax, *Dancing the Self*, 69–70.

76. Diderot, "Les bijoux indiscrets," 415.

77. Diderot, "Les bijoux indiscrets," 427–428.

78. Diderot, "Les bijoux indiscrets," 437.

79. With apologies to the play by that name, by Eve Ensler.

80. Chantal Thomas, "Introduction" to Diderot, "Les bijoux indiscrets," 339.

81. Thomas, "Introduction" to Diderot, "Les bijoux indiscrets," 335.

82. Michel Foucault, *History of Sexuality*, vol. 1, 77 and 79.

83. A woman friend of mine, a university professor, knew a woman who ran and owned a beauty salon. When the salon owner saw a very large diamond on a ring that my friend's husband had given her, she asked, "How many blow jobs did you have to give him to get that?"

84. Edwards, *The History and Poetry of Finger-Rings*, 213, citing *Hone's Table Book*.

85. In Mary De Morgan, *The Necklace of Princess Fiorimonde and Other Stories*.

86. Lyrics by Alan Jay Lerner.

87. "Glitter and Be Gay" by Richard Wilbur, from *Collected Poems: 1943–2004*. © Harcourt, Inc. Reprinted with permission.

88. Isak Dinesen, "The Roads Round Pisa," 166–167.

89. "Baubles, Bangles and Beads." From *Kismet*, musical, lyrics by Robert Wright and George Forrest (to music by Alexander Borodin).

CHAPTER 2

1. Stith Thompson, *Motif-Index of Folk Literature*, B548.2.1. B548.2.1. *Fish recovers ring from sea*. *Type 554; *BP II 19ff.; I 440a, III 61a. He cites: "Wunsche (A.) *Die Sage vom Ring des Polykrates in der Weltliteratur* (Beilage zur Allgemeinen Zeitung, 1893, Nos. 179, 180, 185, 188); Chauvin V 17; KCoehler-Bolte II 209; Clouston Tales I 398ff.; Saintyves Essais de folklore biblique 402. Irish myth: Cross; Italian Novella: Rotunda; Greek: Fox 101; Spanish: Boggs FFC XC 69 No. 515; Jewish: Neuman; India: Thompson-Balys [The Oral Tales of India]. Cf. L412.1. Woman casts ring into sea. Thompson-Balys note on p. 77, 'recover lost magic ring from fish,' ASSAM HILLS. Kuki: Shaw 119. B548.2. Fish recovers ring from sea.-ASSAM HILLS. Kuki: Shaw 119.-CENT.INDIA. Venkataswami Ind. Antiq."

2. Johannes Künzig, "Der im Fischbauch Wiedergefundene Ring," 96.

3. e e cummings, "maggie and milly and molly and may" (went down to the beach/ to play one day). From *The Complete Poems: 1904–1962*.

4. Édouard Chavannes, *Cinq cents contes*, I, 389–390, Number 188. From the *Tripitika* 191.7, p. 22. My translation from the French. The three sages are Maudgalyayana, Aniruddha, and Mahakasyapa.

5. Jeffrey Gantz, *Early Irish Myths and Sagas*, 119–124.

6. Gantz, *Early Irish Myths*, 114.

7. In 1905, Gustav Mahler set several of these poems, including the "Rhine Legend," to music for soprano or baritone and orchestra.

8. Achim von Arnim and Clemens Brentano, *Des Knaben Wunderhorn*, "Rheinlegendchen."

> So soll ich denn grasen am Neckar, am Rhein,
> So werf ich mein goldenes Ringlein hinein.
> Es fließet im Neckar und fließet im Rhein,
> Soll schwimmen hinunter ins Meer tief hinein.
> Und schwimmt es, das Ringlein, so frißt es ein Fisch!
> Das Fischlein tät kommen auf's König sein Tisch!
> Der König tät fragen, wem's Ringlein sollt sein?
> Da tät mein Schatz sagen: das Ringlein g'hört mein.
> Mein Schätzlein tät springen bergauf und bergein,
> Tät mir wiedrum bringen das Goldringlein mein!
> Kannst grasen am Neckar, kannst grasen am Rhein,
> Wirf du mir nur immer dein Ringlein hinein!

9. Louis Ginzberg, *The Legends of the Jews*, s. v. Solomon.

10. Richard Burton, *Supplementary Nights*, vol. iii, p. 72, note.

11. William Jones, *Finger-ring Lore: Historical, Legendary, Anecdotal*, 92.
12. In the King James translation. In the Revised Standard Version, it's pretty much the same, though less eloquent: "He would speak of animals, and birds, and reptiles, and fish."
13. Rudyard Kipling, "The Butterfly That Stamped":
    There was never a Queen like Balkis,/From here to the wide world's end; /But Balkis talked to a butterfly/As you would talk to a friend.//There was never a King like Solomon/Not since the world began;/But Solomon talked to a butterfly/As a man would talk to a man.//She was Queen of Sabea—/And he was Asia's Lord—/But they both of 'em talked to butterflies/When they took their walks abroad!
14. Konrad Lorenz, *King Solomon's Ring*, xi.
15. George Frederick Kunz, *Rings for the Finger*, 288, citing Giovanni B. Rampolli, "Annales Musulmani," vol. viii, Milano, 1824, p. 544 ff.
16. Richard Burton, *Supplementary Nights*, vol. iii, p. 72, note.
17. Ginzberg, *Legends of the Jews*, s. v. Solomon.
18. Ginzberg, *Legends of the Jews*, s. v. Solomon.
19. Stith Thompson took this tale as paradigmatic of a motif, "Polycrates' ring," N 211.1 (also H 94.2).
20. *History* of Herodotus, trans. Grene, 3.40–43; Pliny also tells the story, *Natural History*, 37.2.4.
21. James Remington McCarthy, *Rings through the Ages*, 9.
22. See also Künzig, "Der im Fischbauch," 95; "Jocelin's Life of St. Kentigern," cited by Jones, *Finger-ring Lore*, 99; Pierre Saintyves, "L'anneau de Polycrate," 366, citing Ch. Louandre, *L'Epopée des animaux*, in *Revue des Deux-Mondes*, 1854, p. 319, and Montalembert, *Les moines d'Occident*, Paris, 1868; A. Maury, *Croyances et Légendes du Moyennes Ages*, 1896, p. 377, note 2.
23. More precisely, they date from the time of Bishop Wishert, who lived under Edward II of England (1302–1327).
24. She is sometimes said to be the Queen of Cadzow, sometimes Queen Langoureth of Strathclyde.
25. CatholicCulture.Org. www.catholicculture.org/culture/liturgicalyear/calendar/day.cfm?id=13. The whole story may be confused with an almost identical one concerning King Maelgwn of Gwynedd and Saint Asaph. Queen Nest, the beautiful wife of Maelgwn, King of Wales, wore on her finger a ring handed down over generations by queens of the North. It fell from her finger while she was bathing in the River Elwy. Bishop Asaph calmed the angry king and served them with a locally caught salmon, in which they found the ring.
26. Kunz, *Rings for the Finger*, 215.
27. Cynthia Whidden Green, trans. *The Life of Kentigern*. Chapter xxxvi—"In what manner the Saint wondrously restored to the Queen a ring that had been improperly given away by Queen, and cast into the river Clyde by the King himself."

28. Trial by ordeal was abolished in 1215, in response to arguments that an ordeal was a temptation of God, forcing his hand. But ordeals kept occurring, and in the sixteenth century the Church reversed its position and allowed them, in response to arguments that all martyrdom stories are ordeals: if the martyr gives in, he is not a genuine martyr.

29. Jones, *Finger-ring Lore*, 100, cites the title variously as "The Cruel Knight and the Fortunate Farmer's Daughter," "The Cruel Knight, or the Fortunate Farmer's Daughter," and "The Fish and the Ring, or the Cruel Knight, and the Fortunate Farmer's Daughter." In an appendix on pp. 510–515, Jones reproduces the ballad and says that it was a reprint for William Robinson, Esq., 1843.

30. Thomas Moule, *The Heraldry of Fish*, 127. The story was attributed to Miss Elton of Stratford, but it is, as Pierre Saintyves drily remarks, "evidently a lot older than the lady." Saintyves, "L'anneau de Polycrate," 367.

31. C. J. Davison Ingledew, *The Ballads and Songs of Yorkshire*, 193–202. Cf. also Saintyves, "L'anneau de Polycrate," 367.

32. Saintyves, "L'anneau de Polycrate," 367.

33. Water ordeals were often used in Europe to determine whether or not a woman was a witch: if she floated, or did not drown when submerged for a long period of time ("if the water rejected her"), she was guilty—and, of course, if she did drown, she was innocent but dead (as in "the operation was a success but the patient died"), a no-win situation if ever there was one.

34. Künzig, "Der im Fischbauch," 100, citing Kristensen, *Danske Sagn*, IV, p. 211, Number 707.

35. In the ancient Indian epic *Mahabharata*, a king out hunting, longing for his wife far away, ejaculates and gives the seed, wrapped in a leaf, to a bird, with instructions to carry it to his wife. The bird, attacked by another bird, drops the seed into a river where it is swallowed by a fish (actually, a nymph cursed to become a fish). A fisherman catches the fish and in her belly finds twins: the boy is King Matsya (King Fish), and the girl is Satyavati, the mother of the great sage Vyasa, author of the *Mahabharata* and father of the two patriarchs of the warring families (*Mahabharata* 1.57).

36. *Brahmavaivarta Purana, Krishnajanmakhanda* 115.67–80.

37. *Vishnu Purana* 5.27.1–31; cf. *Bhagavata Purana* 10.55.1–12; *Harivamsa* 99.1–49. Cf. Wendy Doniger, *Dreams, Illusion*, 99–100.

38. Stuart Blackburn, *Moral Fictions: Tamil Folktales in Oral Tradition*. Tale 43: The Fish-Boy and His Wife, 138–143.

39. See Doniger, *The Bedtrick*, 105–139.

40. *The Fairy Tales of Madame d'Aulnoy*, 295

41. Tom Peete Cross, "The Celtic Origin of the Lay of Yonec," 468.

42. Cross, "The Celtic Origin of the Lay of Yonec," 466.

43. See Wendy Doniger, "The Symbolism of Black and White Babies in the Myth of Maternal Impression."

44. Heliodorus, *Ethiopika*, 4.8; J. R. Morgan, in Reardon, *Collected Ancient Greek Novels*, 433, citing Achilles Tatius 3.7 and Philostratos, *Imagines* 1.29.

45. A painting, showing the striking resemblance between Andromeda and Persinna's daughter, is offered as additional proof of the truth of the story.

46. Otto Rank, *The Myth of the Birth of the Hero*. Oscar Wilde's *The Importance of Being Earnest* is a Family Romance, in which the combination of a typed manuscript and a handbag takes the place of the identifying ring.

47. Sigmund Freud, "Family Romances."

48. But there is a magic necklace embedded in the story of Oedipus. It seems that Hephaestus, to punish Aphrodite for her infidelity with Ares, made a necklace of beautifully wrought gold; some say it was in the shape of two serpents whose mouths formed the clasp. He gave it to Harmonia, the daughter of the adulterous couple; it gave anyone who wore it the gift of eternal youth and beauty but would also bring disaster to her. *Statius, Thebaid* 2. 265 ff. Nonnus, in *Dionysiaca* 5. 135 ff., says nothing of the curse, but describes the necklace as made by Hephaestus for Aphrodite, when Eros was born. Harmonia was turned into a serpent, and a series of other women who wore it suffered other horrible fates, including Oedipus's mother Iocasta, whose preternatural youth made Oedipus believe she was too young to be his mother.

49. Hartmann drew on an older anonymous French text. Hartmann's text was, in turn, the source of Thomas Mann's novel *Der Erwählte* (literally *The Chosen One*, but usually translated as *The Holy Sinner*) in 1951.

50. Kunz, *Rings for the Finger*, 262. "The design on the seal depicts St. Peter seated in a bark and holding a net in each hand, the name of the reigning pope being inscribed above. The ring takes its name from the words of Christ ... (Mark i, 17) to ... both Simon (Peter) and his brother Andrew: 'Come ye after me, and I will make you to become fishers of men.'"

51. "The Story of Kuberadatta and Kuberadattā from the *Dharmabhyudayamahaka-vya*," trans. Phyllis Granoff. From Don S. Lopez, ed., *Religions of India in Practice*, 415–417.

52. Yousef Idris, "House of Flesh."

53. Joseph Campbell, *The Hero with a Thousand Faces*.

54. This happens in the Indian tale of Hanchi; A. K. Ramanujan, "Hanchi: An Indian Cinderella." It also happens in a Russian variant, in which the dying mother gives the ring to her *son*, and charges him to marry the woman whose finger it fits; W. R. Shedden Ralston, "Cinderella," 41–42.

55. Occasionally it is a necklace. In the film *Maid in Manhattan* (Wayne Wang, 2002), the identifying clue that Jennifer Lopez keeps on her person back in her real job after wearing it at the ball is a necklace, more precisely a Harry Winston diamond wreath; she has promised not to take it off until she returns it to the shop from which she borrowed it.

56. Ralston ("Cinderella," 41–42) has collected a number of examples of Cinderella stories involving rings. Cf. also the American story of Catskin (Isabel G. Carter, "Mountain White Folklore," 361–363).

57. Alan Dundes calls the shoe-ring alternation "a fine illustration of what has been termed the symbolic equivalence of allomotifs." Alan Dundes, "The Psychoanalytic Study," 60.

58. Thus, in a Sicilian version of Part 1, the heroine's dying mother obtains a promise from her husband that he will marry again only with a maiden whose finger her ring would fit; eventually, after a long search, her daughter finds the ring and tries it on; it fits exactly, condemning her to marry her father. The tale is called "Betta Pilusa." Ralston, "Cinderella," 41–42.

59. Alan Dundes, "To Love My Father All," 236.

60. Ritual echoes of this myth may be seen in the King Cakes of Mardi Gras, where the coin that decides the next king of Mardi Gras is baked into one of the little cakes; and in the Greek Orthodox New Year's ritual of the *vassilopita*, "King's Pie" or "St. Basil's Bread," in which a coin is baked into a loaf of bread, bringing good luck to the one whose slice has the coin.

61. Marcel Proust, *À la recherche du temps perdu* (1871–1922).

62. Lady Eveline Camilla Gurdon, "The Suffolk 'King Lear.' Cap o' Rushes." "Told by an old servant to the writer when a child."

63. Leonard W. Roberts, *South from Hell-fer-Sartin*, 70–72, #18, "The Princess in the Donkey Skin."

64. Arthur Huff Fauset, "Negro Folk Tales from the South," 243–245.

65. John Hinton Knowles, *Folk-tales of Kashmir*, 126–136.

66. "A folktale related by Altaf Husen, and literally translated by Mirza Bahmud Beg." In William Crooke, ed., *North Indian Notes and Queries*, 11–13.

67. Stuart Blackburn, *Moral Fictions*, Tale 48, from Sakkottai: "The Magic Ring," 155–158.

68. Jones, *Finger-ring Lore*, 98–99.

69. *Cape Cod Today*, July 19, 2013, "Cape Cod National Seashore Releases White Shark Safety Tips," by Maggie Kulbokas. One tip: "Limit splashing and do not wear shiny jewelry."

70. Personal research by the author, March 31, 2011. The guide said they saw this happen to as many as six people in one week.

71. Charles Edwards, *The History and Poetry of Finger-Rings*, 59, citing *London Gent's Magazine*, January, 1765, p. 210.

72. Lane Degregory, "A Message from Roger," *St. Petersburg Times*, St. Petersburg, Florida, July 10, 2003, p. 1.A.

73. National Public Radio. Morning Edition, Bob Edwards, July 11, 2003.

74. Denise Levertov, "Wedding Ring," from *Life in the Forest*.

75. Janette Bright and Gillian Clark, *An Introduction to the Tokens at the Foundling Museum*.

76. Bright and Clark, *An Introduction*, 9.

77. Bright and Clark, *An Introduction*, 13.
78. Bright and Clark, *An Introduction*, 9.
79. http://londonhistorians.files.wordpress.com/2012/10/20055375b.jpg. © The Foundling Museum, London.
80. Bright and Clark, *An Introduction*, 18.
81. Bright and Clark, *An Introduction*.
82. Charles Dickens returned to this theme in *Little Dorritt*, where a foundling girl is actually named Tatti Coram, after the founder of the hospital.
83. Charles Dickens, *Oliver Twist*, chapter 1.
84. Charles Dickens, *Oliver Twist*, chapter 38.
85. Charles Dickens, *Oliver Twist*, chapter 24.
86. Charles Dickens, *Oliver Twist*, chapter 51.
87. http://londonhistorians.files.wordpress.com/2012/10/20055375b.jpg. © The Foundling Museum, London.
88. "Foundling Tokens: For Surrendered Children, a Final Tie to Family." By Rebecca Onion. http://www.slate.com/blogs/the_vault/2013/05/02/foundling_tokens_left_with_surrendered_children_at_english_foundling_hospital.html. May 2, 2013.

CHAPTER 3

1. Tom Zoellner, *The Heartless Stone*, 292.
2. See Wendy Doniger, *The Implied Spider*, for an argument to justify this approach.
3. Charles Edwards, *The History and Poetry of Finger-Rings*, 17.
4. Romila Thapar, *Sakuntala*, 54.
5. Visakhadatta's *Mudrarakshasa*.
6. *Kamasutra* 4.2.63.
7. *Kamasutra* 5.6.19, with Yashodhara's commentary.
8. *Kamasutra* book 6.
9. *The Tale of an Anklet: An Epic of South India (The Cilappatikaram of Ilanko Atikal)*.
10. Kannaki then tears off her left breast, sets the city on fire with it, curses the city, dies, and becomes a great goddess. But that is another story.
11. *Ramayana* 3.40–42.
12. *Ramayana* 3.50.27–31.
13. *Ramayana* 3.52.1–3.
14. *Ramayana* 5.33.35–41.
15. *Ramayana* 4.6.9–19; the last verses are omitted by the Princeton edition.
16. *Ramayana* 5.9.2.
17. *Ramayana* 5.13.18–20.
18. *Ramayana* 6.64.171–172.

19. *Ramayana* 5.13.18–20. When he sees her again, later, she is again said to be without her splendid ornaments (*Ramayana* 5.15.21).

20. *Ramayana* 5.13.37.

21. *Ramayana* 5.13.38–42.

22. In *The Journey to the West* (trans. Anthony C. Yu), volume 3, chapters 68–71, pp. 292–297, the princess in captivity is said to wear "neither pins nor bracelets." But the messenger has had the foresight to obtain from her husband "a pair of gold bracelets.... As these were some of her favorite things, they are still kept in a jewel box." When she first saw the messenger and started to throw him out, he "took out the treasure bracelets and presented them with both hands, saying, 'If you don't believe me, take a good look at these objects.' The moment she saw them, the lady began to weep."

23. *Kamasutra* 4.1.42. When he is away on a journey, she wears only jewelry that has religious meaning and power.

24. *Ramayana* 5.34.2–3.

25. *Ramayana* 5.13.39.

26. *Ramayana* 5.34.2–3.

27. *Ramayana* 5.34.2–3, cited in the Goldman translation, vol. 5, p. 446.

28. *Ramayana* 5.36.12ff, 5.38.3,17–19; repeated at 5.63.18–21 when Hanuman tells it to Rama; at *Ramayana* 5.64, Rama speaks at great length about the jewel. The episode is repeated a number of times, always including both Rama's ring and Sita's hair ornament; it is clearly a crucial episode.

29. *Ramayana* 5.1.

30. *Mayiliravanan*; see Wendy Doniger, *Dreams, Illusion*, 95–96.

31. A. K. Ramanujan, *Folktales from India*, 55–56.

32. Harsha's *Ratnavali* and *Priyadarshika*, trans. Wendy Doniger, *The Lady of the Jewel Necklace and The Lady Who Shows Her Love.*

33. *Ratnavali* 4.125.

34. *Ratnavali* 4.19 ff. Here I follow the alternative reading (*ayusmati ratnavali, tvam idrsim avastham gatasi*).

35. *Shatapatha Brahmana* 1.8.1.1–6; Doniger, *Hindu Myths*, 179–184.

36. *Brihadaranyaka Upanishad* 4.3.18.

37. The *Mahabharata* actually calls him Duhshanta, but to avoid confusion I have used Kalidasa's better-known spelling for both versions.

38. It is known as a *gandharva* marriage because the only witnesses are the Gandharvas—demigods, who preside over fertility and music, are related, etymologically, to the Centaurs, and are husbands of the celestial nymphs (Apsarases).

39. *Mahabharata* 1.64–69.

40. *Mahabharata* 1.94.

41. *Ramayana* 2.9.42–47, 10–12, 16.

42. *Mahabharata* 1.68.18, 636* (1.69.41 in the Southern recension).

43. *manasy antardh'yata* (*Mahabharata* 1.68.17/635*) in the Southern recension.

44. Wendy Doniger, *Splitting the Difference*, 79–80; Wendy Doniger, *The Woman Who Pretended to Be Who She Was.*

45. The Jatakas are composed in Pali, a branch of the Indo-Aryan language group that includes Sanskrit, and were not codified until as late as the fifth century CE. The verses are regarded as canonical, and the prose as mere commentary, much later.

46. *Katthaharijataka*, #7 in *Jataka Stories.*

47. *Uddalakajataka*, #487 in *Jataka Stories.*

48. A story from the Tibetan *Kah-gyur*, translated by William Ralston Shedden Ralston (translating Anton Schiefner), *Tibetan Tales Derived from Indian Sources*, 91–92.

49. Kalidasa may also have known the story of Polycrates's ring (Romila Thapar, *Sakuntala*, 56), type A of the ring-in-fish story, though he uses type B (the Solomon type).

50. Robert P. Goldman, "Karma, Guilt, and Buried Memories," 423.

51. Doniger O'Flaherty, *Karma and Rebirth in Classical Indian Traditions.*

52. Goldman, "Karma, Guilt, and Buried Memories," 421.

53. Thapar, *Sakuntala*, 54.

54. Thapar, *Sakuntala*, 54.

55. Thapar goes so far as to suggest that Shakuntala herself is a celestial nymph; *Sakuntala*, 41.

56. *Mahabharata* 1.69.1–4.

57. *Ramayana* 6.103–106. See Wendy Doniger, *The Hindus*, 224–232.

58. Barbara Fass Leavy, *In Search of the Swan Maiden*; Doniger, *Splitting the Difference.*

59. Clifford Geertz uses this story as a metaphor for the imaginative work of the anthropologist: "For me at least … anthropology, ethnographical anthropology, is like that: trying to reconstruct elusive, rather ethereal, and by now wholly departed elephants from the footprints they have left on my mind." Clifford Geertz, *After the Fact*, 167.

60. Rabindranath Tagore, "Sakuntala, Its Inner Meaning," v–xiii.

61. Thapar, *Sakuntala*, 54, 59, 60. Again, on p. 74, she argues that the king's rejection of Shakuntala does not become an issue, because of the ring. I have changed her spelling of Dusyanta and Sakuntala to agree with the conventions I am using throughout this book.

62. Thapar, *Sakuntala*, 59.

63. Thapar, *Sakuntala*, 256.

64. A. K. Ramanujan, "No Amnesiac King."

65. *Kathasaritsagara* 30–34.

66. Wendy Doniger, "Magic Rings and the Return of the Repressed."

67. He returned to it briefly in *Jokes and Their Relation to the Unconscious* (1903), before spelling it out in some detail in *Moses and Monotheism* (1937).

68. Sigmund Freud, *The Interpretation of Dreams*, 297.

69. Freud, *Moses and Monotheism*, 162.

70. In *The Future of an Illusion* (1927) and in *Civilization and Its Discontents* (1929).

71. A. K. Ramanujan, "Telling Tales," 250.

72. What Ovid actually said was *nihil interit, omnia mutantur,* in *Metamorphoses* 15.165.

73. Sigmund Freud, *Three Essays on the Theory of Sexuality,* III.V [88].

74. Doniger, *Splitting the Difference,* 140–146.

75. Gail Hinich Sutherland, unpublished essay, "Manu and the Fish: Three Versions of the Flood Legend in Indian Mythology," May 1982; cited in Doniger O'Flaherty, *Dreams,* 223.

76. James Fenton, introduction to Diana Scarisbrick, *Rings: Jewelry of Power, Love and Loyalty,* 7.

CHAPTER 4

1. Tom Peete Cross, "The Celtic Origin of the Lay of Yonec," 415.

2. Marie de France, *The Lais of Marie de France,* "Yonec," 137–152; here, 148, lines 414 ff.

3. George Frederick Kunz, *Rings for the Finger,* 306–307, citing the *Gesta Romanorum* (*Die Gesta Romanorum,* ed. Wilhelm Dick, Erlangen, 1890), 10–11.

4. Béroul, *Le Roman de Tristran,* lines 3483 ff.

5. Béroul, *Le Roman de Tristran,* lines 4140 ff.

6. Bédier, *Tristan,* 135.

7. Joseph J. Duggan, "Afterword," to Burton Raffel's translation of *Yvain, The Knight of the Lion,* 212.

8. *The Red Book of Hergest,* a fourteenth-century Welsh text, translated by Lady Charlotte Guest and published in Jeffrey Gantz, *The Mabinogion,* where it appears as "The Lady of the Fountain."

9. Chrétien de Troyes, *Yvain, Le Chevalier au Lion,* verses 4566–4640, 6510–6818; translated by D. D. R. Owen, *Chrétien de Troyes: Arthurian Romances,* 342–343, 369–373; and by W. Wistar Comfort, *Arthurian Romances by Chrétien de Troyes,* verses 4533–6813.

10. Alexander Penrose Forbes, *The Lives of S. Ninian and S. Kentigern,* 123–132, 243–252.

11. *Yvain, The Knight of the Lion,* trans. Burton Raffel.

12. This Welsh version, which calls the hero Owein and the maid Luned, does not come next after the Scottish text chronologically, however; the version by Chrétien de Troyes is older. Duggan, 216, writes, "It was once thought that *Yvain* and 'The Lady of the Fountain' derived from a common source. It is much more likely, however, that a reading of Chrétien's romance was heard by some Welsh storyteller who retold the tale using elements familiar to his audience."

13. Duggan, "Afterword," 217.

14. Wendy Doniger, *Splitting the Difference*, 192–196; Wendy Doniger, *The Bedtrick*, 107–118. In "Beauty and the Beast," it is the woman who marries the man from the other world and insists on returning to visit her sisters, or her father, and breaks her promise to her husband.

15. Duggan, "Afterword," 211.

16. Ogier is best known from the *Geste de Doon de Mayence*; his story is retold in Thomas Bulfinch's *Legends of Charlemagne, or Romance of the Middle Ages* (chapter 26, "Ogier the Dane, continued").

17. William Jones, *Finger-ring Lore*, 121–122.

18. The *Vita Merlini* composed between 1148 and 1151 by Geoffrey of Monmouth (who calls her Guanhamara); the English prose *Merlin* composed between 1215 and 1235 by Robert de Boron (who calls her Gonnore); *Lancelot* (also known as the *Lancelot* proper), a French romance composed during the same period (Guenièvre); and *Lancelot of the Lake*, the so-called non-cyclic French prose version of the story from roughly the same period (Guinevere). All of these names probably stem from the Welsh *Gwenhwyfar*, which seems to be cognate with the Irish name Findabair (see chapter 2, p. 26). "Jennifer" and "Gwen" are the modern English variants.

19. *Lancelot of the Lake*, 584–613; summarized in Corin Corley translation, 413–418.

20. *Lancelot: roman en prose du 13e siècle*, part 4, 53–6, #119, "Bors spurns King Brandegoore's daughter."

21. Sir Thomas Malory, *Morte d'Arthur*, Book 11, chapters 2, 3, and 6.

22. Malory, Book 11, chapter 1.

23. Gottfried von Strassburg called the lovers Tristan and Isolde; the German text (c. 1180) of Eilhart von Oberg called them Tristrant and Isalde; the French text (c. 1160) by Thomas of Britanny called them Tristran and Ysolt; the incomplete French text (c. 1190) of Béroul called them Tristran and Iseut; French fragments translated by Joseph Bédier called them Tristan and Iseult; and a Norwegian prose adaption (*Tristans saga ok Isondar, The Saga of Tristram and Isond*, in 1226) calls them Tristan and Isond. There are many more, including Richard Wagner's (German) opera, *Tristan und Isolde* (which does not include either of the episodes that concern us here).

24. Like Yvain (in a passage we have not considered), Tristan wins the love of a woman who has reason to hate him for killing a man she loves and (in a passage we did consider) tricks a woman into accepting him and making a promise to him when she does not know who he is.

25. There are several Tristans in some versions, Isolde's Tristan plus a dwarf named Tristan and a man named Tantris who turns out to be Isolde's Tristan. But let's not go there.

26. There is actually a third Isolde, Queen Isolde, the mother of Isolde the Fair, but I will try to leave her out of this discussion. Enough is enough.

27. Gottfried, *Tristan*, 297.

28. The *Tristan* of Thomas, in Gottfried, 301.

29. Bédier, *Tristan*, 114–116, citing Eilhart von Oberg.

30. Béroul, *Le Roman de Tristran*, 2708–2792.

31. Gottfried, *Tristan*, 281–282.

32. *The Saga of Tristram and Isond*, 121; *The Romance of Tristan & Ysolt*, 196.

33. The *Tristan* of Thomas, in Gottfried, *Tristan*, 306–307

34. *The Romance of Tristan & Ysolt*, 196, 154.

35. *The Saga of Tristan and Isond*, 108.

36. Bédier, *Tristan*, 114–116, citing Eilhart von Oberg.

37. This, in fact, has been true of him for most of his adult life: the poisoned wound in his thigh that he got at the start of the tale is reactivated in the poisoned wound in his loins that will be his death. His wound also opens and bleeds when he is in bed with Isolde, leaving proof—the male counterpart of the blood of defloration—that he was, in fact, in bed with her and forcing Mark to prosecute them.

38. The *Tristan* of Thomas, in Gottfried, *Tristan*, 310–311.

39. Bédier, *Tristan*, 114–116, citing Eilhart von Oberg.

40. The *Tristan* of Thomas, in Gottfried, *Tristan*, 317.

41. The *Tristan* of Thomas, in Gottfried, 310–311

42. Béroul, *Le Roman de Tristran*, 1804–2024.

43. The *Tristan* of Thomas, in Gottfried, *Tristan*, 323

44. Bédier, *Tristan*, 139, citing a French poem.

45. This episode may be modeled on the recognition scene between Odysseus and Penelope (*Odyssey* 19 and 23), in which the dog recognizes Odysseus before Penelope submits him to her test.

46. The *Tristan* of Thomas, in Gottfried, *Tristan*, 343–347.

47. The *Tristan* of Thomas, in Gottfried, *Tristan*, 347.

48. Béroul, *Le Roman de Tristran*, 2136–2196.

49. The *Tristan* of Thomas, in Gottfried, *Tristan*, 321.

50. It is related by Fordun in his "Scotichronicon," by Matthew of Westminster, and by Roger of Wendover; see William Jones, *Finger-ring Lore*, 128. Maurizio Bettini, *Portrait of the Lover*, 131, gives a number of other citations.

51. P. F. Baum, "The Young Man Betrothed to a Statue" (1919), 523ff; David Freedberg, *The Power of Images*, 333 ff; Theodore Ziolkowski, *Disenchanted Images: A Literary Iconology*. There is also a parody by F. Anstey (in *The Tinted Venus: A Farcical Romance* [1885]), which inspired the Broadway musical *One Touch of Venus* (1944, with a book, based on Anstey, by Ogden Nash and S. J. Perelman, lyrics by Nash, and music by Kurt Weill).

52. William of Malmsbury, *De gestis regum Anglorum* 2.205; cited by Bettini, *Portrait of the Lover*, 131.

53. Robert Burton, *Anatomy of Melancholy*, 649.

54. Thomas Moore, *The Poetical Works of Thomas Moore*, 61–64.

55. Prosper Mérimée, "La Vénus d'Ille," 18.

56. Vincent of Beauvais, *Speculum historiale* 8.87, and others, cited by Bettini, *Portrait of the Lover*, 276. See also Jones, *Finger-ring Lore*, 130. In a Norse telling, a statue of the goddess Freyja at first resists and then allows Earl Hakon (the son of Sigurd) to take a gold ring from her own arm and give it to his friend Sigmund; Sigmund is later murdered in his sleep for the ring (as is his kinsman, Sigurd, in the *Völsunga Saga*).

57. Bettini, *Portrait of the Lover*, 133.

58. In the film *Never On Sunday* (Jules Dassin, 1960), she plays a Piraeus whore who retells the Greek tragedies and gives them upbeat endings.

CHAPTER 5

1. An Old Norse text written in Norway c. 1250, the *Thidreks Saga af Bern*, or *Saga of Thidrek of Berne*, was composed sometime during the reign of King Hákon Hákonarson (1217–63), but scholars hesitate to be much more precise than that.

2. An Icelandic text, c. 1270. For the dates of the texts I am indebted to an essay by Kevin Wanner, "The Virgin and the Valkyrie: A Comparison of Three Medieval Germanic Texts," 1999.

3. A text written in German, in Austria, c. 1200, but drawing on Christian and European courtly sources. Byock, "Introduction," *Völsunga Saga*, 4. The relative dates are misleading, since the three texts draw on many of the same older sources, including the Eddas, which I will cite only in passing.

4. In 1848 Wagner published "The Nibelungenmyth: A Scheme for a Drama." By 1853 he had completed the poetic scenario for the cycle of operas, though the full libretto was first published in 1863 and the full cycle first performed in 1876.

5. He is called Sigurd in the *Thidreks Saga*, *Völsunga Saga*, and Ibsen, Siegfried in the *Nibelungenlied*.

6. She is called Brynhild in the *Thidreks Saga* and *Völsunga Saga*, Brünhild in the *Nibelungenlied*, Hjördis in Ibsen—strangely, since Hjordis is the name of Sigurd's *mother* in the *Völsunga Saga*.

7. He is called Gunnar in the *Thidreks Saga*, *Völsunga Saga*, and Ibsen, Gunther in the *Nibelungenlied*.

8. She is called Grimhild in the *Thidreks Saga* (strangely, since Grimhild is the name of Gudrun's *mother* in the *Völsunga Saga*), Gudrun in the *Völsunga Saga*, Kriemhild in the *Nibelungenlied*, and Dagny in Ibsen.

9. I discussed these texts at length in *The Woman Who Pretended to Be Who She Was*, but there I concentrated on the elements of sexual deception and self-imitation. Here I will trace a different theme, the ring.

10. Siegfried is then killed, usually by Hagen. What part Brünnhilde plays in his death, and what happens to Brünnhilde after that, varies, as do the motives for the murder of Siegfried.

11. Tom Shippey, "Tolkien Out-Wagners Wagner," 4.
12. Tom Shippey, "Tolkien Out-Wagners Wagner," 5.
13. Tom Shippey, "Tolkien Out-Wagners Wagner," 5.
14. Claude Lévi-Strauss, "The Story of Asdiwal," 29–30; *Structural Anthropology*, 229; *The Savage Mind*, 22.
15. This detail of this episode is very old indeed, for it is shared by Siegfried's Irish counterpart, Cuchlulain, who learned the language of the birds when he inadvertently tasted the flesh of a magic salmon (licking his burned fingers as he roasted it on a spit for someone else); Siegfried, too, tastes the dragon blood at first only by licking his burned fingers. Yvain and the protagonists of "The Two Brothers" (a story told by the Grimm brothers) have this gift of understanding animal language; King Solomon's ring, too, gave him the ability to understand animal speech (see chapter 2, pp. 27–28).
16. He chooses the horse with the help of Odin (Wotan), who knows that Grani is a descendant of Odin's own eight-legged horse Sleipnir. For Sleipnir's own bedtrick, see *The Prose Edda of Snorri Sturluson*, 36 (Gylfaginning 42–43).
17. Queen Isolde, the mother of Isolde the Fair, was also the mistress of magic love potions, a role played by the nurse in many of the other medieval romances.
18. For an argument that certain Norse and German texts suppressed the rape of Brünnhilde by Siegfried, see Theodore M. Andersson, *The Legend of Brünnhilde*, 222–224. For the symbolic equation of taking a ring and taking a maidenhead, see A. T. Hatto, *The Nibelungenlied*, 298–299.
19. William Archer's translation.
20. No production of the opera that I have ever seen has devised a way to keep the audience from laughing at this point.
21. Or, perhaps, Béroul's story of Tristan, who, at her request, gives Isolde his dog in exchange for her ring; Béroul, *Le Roman de Tristran*, 2696.
22. In the *Völsunga Saga*, too, there is an earlier encounter of actual seduction between Siegfried and Brünnhilde and a later one of chastity, though they are never conflated in any actual argument. This same talking-past-one-another occurs when they argue about where he got the ring: he goes for the original acquisition, from Fafner, while she focuses on the proximate acquisition, on the rock.
23. Jesse Byock, "Introduction," 28.
24. Wagner may also have had in mind the "helmet of dread" that Fafner wears when he takes the form of a dragon, in the Norse *Poetic Edda* and in the *Lay of Fafnir*. Sigurd takes the helmet along with the sword and a gold mailshirt (the equivalent of the protective skin that he gets from bathing in the dragon's blood, in other texts). See *The Poetic Edda*, trans. Larrington, 150 and 156.
25. I am indebted to Philip Kitcher for this insight; personal communication, December 8, 2015.

26. Wagner objects to Sieglinde's unwilling marriage to Hunding, from which Wotan's son Siegmund rescues her at the cost of his life.

27. Byock, "Introduction," 28.

28. *Mahabharata* 13.56.4–6; 1.169.16–26; 1.170.1–21; 1.171.1–23.

29. *Matsya Purana* 175.23–63; *Harivamsha* 1.45.20–64; Doniger O'Flaherty, *Women, Androgynes*, 226–227.

30. *Skanda Purana* 7.1.32.1–128, 33.1–103. Doniger O'Flaherty, *Women*, 228–233; *Siva*, 289–292.

31. He drew particularly on the *Voluspa*, "a powerful Eddic poem that presents all of cosmic history as inevitably leading to the cataclysmic doom of Ragnarok," and from Snorri Sturluson's *Prose Edda*. Byock, "Introduction," 27–28.

32. The oldest English source is "Deor's Lament" (date and author unknown); the story is also told in the *Thidreks Saga* and *Volundarkvida*.

33. Jean-Jacques Nattiez, *Wagner Androgyne*, 49.

34. Ursula Dronke, *The Poetic Edda*, II, 246–251.

35. *Thidreks Saga*, 57–79. Volundr's older brother Egil, whom we have encountered as the son of Hjördis and Gunnar in Ibsen's play, also marries a Valkyrie, and together they help Volundr to escape.

36. Wendy Doniger, *Splitting the Difference*, chapter 1.

37. Wagner published this draft in *The Art Work of the Future*, in 1849.

38. Richard Wagner, *The Art Work of the Future*, 210–213.

39. This is the version that Oskar Schlemm used to compose a libretto for the composer Jan Levoslav Bella's opera between 1880 and 1890. Summarized in Nattiez, 46–48.

40. *Swan Lake*, composed by Pyotr Ilyich Tchaikovsky in 1875–76, may have been inspired by *Wieland the Smith*, though stories of swan maidens are much older, one (the story of Urvashi) even narrated in the ancient Indian *Rig Veda*, c. 1500 BCE. See Barbara Fass Leavy, *In Search of the Swan Maiden*.

41. But, unlike Gunther, Gram too is affected by the power of the ring. Nattiez, *Wagner Androgyne*, 49.

42. Nattiez, *Wagner Androgyne*, 51.

43. Lorraine Daston, personal communication, February 27, 2016.

44. Hugo von Hofmannsthal, "Die ägyptische Helena"; Doniger, *Splitting the Difference*, 34–36.

45. "Social Amnesia in Mice Lacking the Oxytocin Gene," *Nature Genetics* (August 2000), 284–288.

46. *Nature Genetics* and the *New Yorker* called them mice, but the animals in the Yerkes experiment were, in fact, monogamous voles.

47. Helen Fisher, *Why We Love*, 89.

48. James Collins, "Dept. of Mating," 30.

49. See Doniger, *Splitting the Difference* and *The Bedtrick*, for the asymmetry of these gendered stories.

50. Doniger, *The Bedtrick*, 137–139.
51. Ralph Harper, *On Presence*, 65.
52. Harper, *On Presence*, 96.

CHAPTER 6

1. Wendy Doniger, *The Bedtrick*.
2. Carol Thomas Neely, *Broken Nuptials in Shakespeare's Plays*, 78
3. Artin Pacha, *Contes populaires*, 239, 324, "Le Fille du Menusier," tale 20.
4. Kamil Zvelibil, *Two Tamil Folktales*, 153–64, "The Story of King Matanakama."
5. James C. Scott, *Weapons of the Weak*.
6. *Kathasaritsagara* 124 (18.5) 131–237. The story is translated on pp. 77 ff. of vol. 9 of the Tawney Penzer edition (chapter 124, or 171g).
7. The riddles in the Sanskrit text are religious, dealing with the mythology of the god Vishnu's incarnations as a boar and as a dwarf.
8. *Kathasaritsagara* 98.31 (12.24.31).
9. Muladeva may be one of the semi-mythical authors of a lost antecedent of the *Kamasutra*. Maurice Bloomfield ("The Character and Adventures of Muladeva," 621) suggests that Muladeva may be the Gonikaputra ("Son of a Courtesan") whom Vatsyayana, the author the *Kamasutra*, cites frequently as an earlier authority. Yashodhara, commenting on *Kamasutra* 6.1.17, gives as a notorious example of rivalry the fact that "Devadatta and Anangasena fought over Muladeva."
10. *Kathasaritsagara* 139 (163.15).
11. Kamil Zvelebil, *Two Tamil Folktales*, 153–164.
12. H. Parker, *Village Folk-tales of Ceylon*, 75–79.
13. James Hinton Knowles, "Shabrang, Prince and Thief," in *Folk-Tales of Kashmir*, 104–23; here, 110–121.
14. Hesiod, *Works and Days*, 235.
15. Zvelebil, *Two Tamil Folktales*, 153–164.
16. Parker, *Village Folk-tales of Ceylon*, 75–79.
17. Zvelebil, *Two Tamil Folktales*, 153–164.
18. So, too, in Richard Brome's *The Novella* (1632), the heroine comes to Venice "disguised as a new courtesan in order to find the man she loves. She entices men to visit her house, in the hope that her beloved will be drawn there, but she sets a high price on her maidenhead to discourage these other suitors, even as she readily accepts costly gifts from them." To avoid one particular man, she substitutes her Moorish servant, who is actually a disguised eunuch, though the customer discovers the trick before proceeding. Marliss C. Desens, *The Bed-Trick*, 100.
19. This happens in Li Yu's seventeenth-century Chinese novel, *The Carnal Prayer Mat*, 140, 147, 292–294, and in a contemporary novel by Javier Marias, *Tomorrow in the Battle Think on Me*.

20. Zvelebil, *Two Tamil Folktales,* 153–164.

21. Parker, *Village Folk-tales of Ceylon,* 75–79.

22. A. K. Ramanujan, *A Flowering Tree,* 198–206, #72: "A Wager."

23. Natesa Sastri, *Dravidian Nights,* 246.

24. Marina Warner, *Stranger Magic.*

25. Knowles, *Folk-Tales of Kashmir,* "The Young Gambling Merchant," 287.

26. Zvelebil, *Two Tamil Folktales,* 153–164.

27. Galit Hasan-Rokem, *Proverbs in Israeli Folk Narrative,* 78–79.

28. The ring that reveals the name of the dud dad was folded into a modern Hindi variant of the *Mahabharata,* which was narrated in the Himalayas by Bacan Singh in 1986. In this text, the other children tease Arjuna's abandoned child by calling him "cor-jar-putra," the equivalent of "bastard" but more literally "son of a thief-lover" (which is precisely what the boy is in the Muladeva story). Then his mother shows him the ring that has Arjuna's ten names written on it. Translated by William Sax, *Dancing the Self,* 69–70.

29. Natesa Sastri, *Dravidian Nights,* 246.

30. Zvelebil, *Two Tamil Folktales,* 153–164.

31. Knowles, *Folk-Tales of Kashmir,* 104.

32. Hasan-Rokem, *Proverbs in Israeli Folk Narrative,* 78–79.

33. Pacha, *Contes populaires,* 247. In the *Arabian Nights,* too, Scheherezade at the end presents Shahriyar with the three children to whom, unnoticed by her groom, she has given birth during her three or so years under sentence of death. Warner, *Stranger Magic,* 5.

34. Ramanujan, *A Flowering Tree,* 199–206.

35. Blackburn, *Moral Fictions,* 218–220, Tale 81: "A Clever Woman's Riddle."

36. Knowles, *Folk-Tales of Kashmir,* 292–293, "The Young Gambling Merchant."

37. Zvelebil, *Two Tamil Folktales,* 153–164, "The Story of King Matanakama,"

38. Parker, *Village Folk-tales of Ceylon,* vol. 2, #92, "The King Who Became a Thief," 75–79.

39. Natesa Sastri, 246, "The Story of Madana Kama Raja."

40. Pacha, *Contes populaires,* 245.

41. Maive Stokes, *Indian Fairy Tales,* 216, "The Clever Wife," Tale 28.

42. Hasan-Rokem, *Proverbs in Israeli Folk Narratives,* 78–79.

43. Knowles, *Folk-Tales of Kashmir,* 105–106, "Shabrang, Prince and Thief."

44. *Manasabijay* of Bipradas, 1–235; cited by Pradyot Kujmar Maity, *Historical Studies in the Cult of the Goddess Manasa,* 79. Parvati also becomes a ferrywoman in the *Manasa-mangal* of Ketaka Das.

45. "Siva and Parvati," from Karnataka, #48, *Folktales of India,* ed. Brenda E. F. Beck et al., 171–174. I have changed the spelling of the god's name from Siva to Shiva to conform with my usage elsewhere in this book. Cf. also Peter Claus, "Playing *Cenne,*" 290–293; David Shulman, *God Inside Out,* 108; Doniger, *The Bedtrick,* 17–20.

46. Translated by William Sax, *Dancing the Self*, 69–70.
47. Genesis 38:12–26. My summary of a translation by Robert Alter, *The Art of Biblical Narrative*, 5–10. See also Doniger, *The Bedtrick*, for a longer analysis of this text.
48. It is one of the apocryphal and apocalyptic books of the Bible.
49. *Testament of Judah* 12.3–10. See Esther Marie Menn, *Judah & Tamar*, 150.
50. Thomas Mann, *Joseph and His Brothers*, 1039.
51. The sources of Boccaccio, including the *All's Well* theme, are discussed by M. Landau, *Die Quellen des Dekameron*, and A. C. Lee, *The Decameron; Its Sources and Analogues*.
52. Thus N. M. Penzer, the editor of the translation of the story of Muladeva in the *Ocean of the Rivers of Story*, remarks in the footnote: "This story is known in Europe and may perhaps be the original source of Shakespeare's *All's Well That Ends Well*. At any rate there is a slight resemblance in the leading idea of the two stories. It bears a close resemblance to the story of Sorfarina, No. 36 in Gonzenbach's *Sicilianische Märchen*, and to that of Sapia in the *Pentamerone* of Basile."
53. Gary Tubb (in an unpublished essay) has established striking correspondences between Book 2, chapter 12, of the *Kathasaritsagara*, in which a Brahmin seduces a woman by impersonating the god Vishnu, and Day 4, Story 2, of Boccaccio, in which a friar seduces a woman by impersonating the archangel Gabriel; and between Book 2, chapter 13, of the *Kathasaritsagara*, in which a chaste wife dresses like a man, and Day 2, Story 9 of Boccaccio, ditto. (Personal communication from Gary Tubb, Chicago, November 21, 2015.)
54. Cited by Sir Arthur Quiller-Couch on p. xiii of his introduction to *All's Well that Ends Well*.
55. Giovanni Boccaccio, *Decameron*, the Ninth Story of the Third Day; John Payne translation, 267–276, my condensation of Payne's phrasing.
56. Neely remarks that the twin sons who look exactly like their father are "the fulfillment of a male fantasy prominent elsewhere in Shakespeare." Neely, *Broken Nuptials*, 88.
57. Isabella is the heroine not in *All's Well* but in the other Shakespeare play with a bed-trick, *Measure for Measure*.
58. Quiller-Couch, Introduction, xiii.
59. W. W. Lawrence, *Shakespeare's Problem Comedies*, 51.
60. Howard C. Cole, *The All's Well Story from Boccaccio to Shakespeare*, 5.
61. In the National Theatre's production of *All's Well* in 2009, directed by Marianne Elliot and designed by Rae Smith, the two rings were illuminated: Helena's ring was blue and Bertrand's ring was white, to help the audience trace the rather complex progress of the two rings through the play.
62. Barbara Hodgdon, "The Making of Virgins," 67.

63. The insistence that the ring was given by a parent is also a crucial part of the argument for the most famous piece of sexual evidence in all of Shakespeare, the handkerchief in *Othello*, which Othello describes in terms that apply equally well to the importance of Bertram's ring and indeed to many of the rings in these stories. The woman that gave it to his mother "told her, while she kept it / 'Twould make her amiable and subdue my father / Entirely to her love; but if she lost it / Or made a gift of it, my father's eye / Should hold her loathed and his spirits should hunt / After new fancies." 3.4.60–65.

64. John F. Adams, "*All's Well That Ends Well*: The Paradox of Procreation," 268.

65. From the standpoint of the audience, Helena's ring travels in a direction opposite to Bertram's: where we see Bertram's ring first on Bertram, then on Diana, we later notice Helena's ring, too, first on Bertram, but learn to trace it backward in time, to Helena-as-Diana, and then to Helena, and then backward farther to the king, who recognizes it in the final Act.

66. Neely, *Broken Nuptials*, 82.

67. In a Norwegian ballad, a woman whose royal husband goes off to war and tells her to have a child by him follows him to Scotland in disguise and gets him to impregnate her; "the king gives her a ring with his name on it, which serves as a proof of the paternity of the child when he returns home." M. B. Landstad, *Norske Folkeviser*, Christiania, 1853, "Kong Kristian og hans dronning," no. 73, 585 ff.; cited by W. W. Lawrence, *Shakespeare's Problem Comedies*, 44.

68. Janet Adelman, "Bed Tricks: On Marriage as the End of Comedy," 157.

69. Adams, "*All's Well That Ends Well*: The Paradox of Procreation," 268.

70. Adams, "*All's Well That Ends Well*," 268.

71. Adams, "*All's Well That Ends Well*," 263.

72. Adams, "*All's Well That Ends Well*," 262.

73. Manu 3.45.

74. From Lorraine Daston's remarks, Einstein forum, December 9, 1997. See Wendy Doniger, *Der Mann, der mit seiner eigenen Frau Ehebruch beging. Mit einem Kommentar von Lorraine Daston*.

75. Knowles, *Folk-Tales of Kashmir*, "Shabrang, Prince and Thief," 108.

76. Knowles, *Folk-Tales of Kashmir*, "The Young Gambling Merchant," 296.

77. Notes by A. Norman Jeffers on Yeats's poem, "He mourns for the change that has come upon him and his beloved, and longs for the end of the world," in Yeats, *Collected Poems*, 211.

78. Zwi Jagendorf, "In the morning," 56.

79. Adelman, "Bed Tricks," 152.

80. This psychological truth inspired Mark Twain's take on Genesis 3: "Adam was but human—this explains it all. He did not want the apple for the apple's sake; he only wanted it because it was forbidden. The mistake was in not forbidding the serpent; then he would have eaten the serpent." Mark Twain, *Pudd'nhead Wilson and Other Tales*, epigram for chapter 2.

81. Thomas Hardy, *Far from the Madding Crowd*, chapter VIII ("The Malthouse; the Chat; News"), 47.
82. Stanley Cavell, *Pursuits of Happiness*, 31.

CHAPTER 7

1. The trick of a woman having a baby when she is *always* asexual was accomplished only in Christian mythology, where Mary's perpetual virginity satisfies the desire to know that the son of God was in fact actually God's, and no one else's.
2. Artin Pacha, *Contes populaires*, 249.
3. Stanley Insler, "The Shattered Head," 120 and 125.
4. Wendy Doniger, *The Bedtrick*.
5. This paragraph is a modified quotation from Wendy Doniger, *The Woman Who Pretended*, 62–63.
6. Stephen Marcus, *The Other Victorians*.
7. Though Aelius Donatus (in his commentary on the *Mother-in-Law*) says the Terence play comes from Apollodorus of Carystus.
8. There is a subplot here, in which Habrotonon might win her freedom, according to Greek law, were she to prove that she bore her master's child. In fact, Charisios gives her freedom in the end anyway. A similar law was in effect in ancient India, and a similar subplot is found in the ancient Indian play, *The Little Clay Cart*, that we considered in chapter 3, p. 63, when a maid buys her freedom, not from a man but from a courtesan.
9. I have relied primarily on the Loeb edition, with the translation by W. G. Arnott; but I have also used fragments in the editions by Edward Capps and Maurice Balme.
10. The term is related to the word for recognition, which appears at the end of the play in Onesimos's statement that Pamphile and Charisios recognized one another (*anagnorismos*), 1123.
11. Terence, *The Mother-in-Law*, S. Ireland edition, p. 25. Radice translation. All of the quoted excerpts are from the Radice translation.
12. Terence, ll, 120–135 and 170–175.
13. nam vitium est oblatum virgini olim a nescioquo inprobo.
14. The play was inspired by *Controversia* 1.5 of the elder Seneca.
15. Fletcher et al., *The Queen of Corinth*, 74, 4.3.
16. I am indebted to Nicholas Rudall for this background information, and indeed for his general insights into the two plays.
17. He used it in his first play, *The Girl from Andros* (even using the same name for the main character, Pamphilus) and in his last play, *The Brothers*.
18. Henry Thomas Riley, *The Comedies of Terence*, note 42, *Committed upon her*)—Ver. 401.

19. Terence, *The Mother-in-Law*, Radice, 850 ff.
20. Ovid, *Metamorphoses* 6.440 ff.
21. A woman named Philumena is mentioned in the other Terence play in which someone named Pamphilus is the protagonist, *The Girl from Andros*, and there, too, she never appears.
22. Wendy Doniger O'Flaherty, *Dreams, Illusion*, 61–64.
23. Manjhan's *Madhumalati*, 70 to 72. In *Madhumalati*, trans. Aditya Behl and Simon Weightman.
24. *Kathasaritsagara* 12.6.[73]325–397; Tawney Penzer vol. VI, pp. 124–126.
25. Within "The Story of the Three Apples," *Arabian Nights*, Haddawy, vol. 2, 157–206.
26. Robert Irwin, *The Arabian Nights: A Companion*, 97. It is one episode within "The Story of Qamar al-Zaman and his Two Sons."
27. Marina Warner, *Stranger Magic*.
28. "They so thoroughly accepted Deronda as an ideal, that when he was gone the youngest set to work, under the criticism of the two elder girls, to paint him as Prince Camaralzaman." George Eliot, *Daniel Deronda*, 111; "'I declare she is like the Queen Budoor,'"124; "[Mab] now spoke bashfully, as was her wont in the presence of Prince Camaralzama," 221; "Prince Camaralzaman, who had heard the finest things, preferred Mirah's singing to any other," 288.
29. "The Two Viziers" may well have contributed to the story of Budur and Qamar, as it is probably the older of the two stories. Scholars generally locate the tale of Qamar and Budur on the fringes of the oldest core of the *Arabian Nights*, and "The Story of the Two Viziers" as a part of that core. We might therefore speculate that the author of the story of Budur knew the story of the two viziers. Robert Irwin, *The Arabian Nights: A Companion*, 97.
30. *The Arabian Nights*, trans. Haddaway, vol. 2, 165–268. In the Burton translation it is the 216th Night, vol. 3, second half.
31. The *Arabian Nights' Entertainment* omits the entire episode in which Budur-as-Qamar takes Qamar to bed in drag, and therefore also omits all the obscene poetry; in this text, she brings him to her bedroom but then changes into women's clothing. Burton, of course, delights in the scene of cross-dressing, and invents a number of stunningly obscene verses.
32. He also grows up to become one of the two protagonists of the second half of the story of what Haddawy calls "The Story of Qamar al-Zaman and his Two Sons, Amjad and A'sad."
33. *The Arabian Nights' Entertainment*; but it is not in the Mahdi/Haddawy edition.
34. *Arabian Nights' Entertainment*, 369–370.
35. *Arabian Nights' Entertainment*, 388.
36. *Arabian Nights' Entertainment*, 377.
37. Andras Hamori, "The Magian and the Whore," 26.
38. *Arabian Nights' Entertainment*, 391.

39. Hamori, "The Magian and the Whore," 34.
40. It is a ring with a blood-red stone in Robert Laffont's translation of the Mardrus version, cited by Jamal Eddine Bencheikh, "Le Conte de Qamar Az-Zaman," 98.
41. In a story in the *Kathasaritsagara*, a queen bathes in a tank filled with red dye and a bird mistakes her for raw flesh and carries her off. *Kathsaritsagara* 2.9; Tawney Penzer, I, 97–99.
42. Howard Schwartz, *Gabriel's Palace: Jewish Mystical Tales*, #78, 158–160, "The Miracle of the Ring," from the "Persian oral tradition."
43. One Jewish clever wife disguises herself as a man. Galit Hasan-Rokem, *Proverbs in Israeli Folk Narratives*, 90, citing IFA 3566.
44. Maive Stokes, *Indian Fairy Tales*, 42.
45. Knowles, *Folk-Tales of Kashmir*, "The Young Gambling Merchant," 292–293.
46. Jamal Eddine Bencheikh, "Le Conte de Qamar Az-Zaman," 106.
47. In the *Arabian Nights' Entertainment* (406) the excuse is merely that "she put a constraint on herself, believing that it was for both their interests that she should act the part of a king a little longer before she made herself known."
48. Galit Hasan-Rokem, *Proverbs in Israeli Folk Narratives*.
49. This verse appears only in Richard Burton's translation (3, 303), and it is very loose; indeed, he may have invented it himself.
50. The word in the text, Diwä, designating a kind of powerful djinnic giant, is related to the Persian "diva/div" and to our own "devil," and seems to designate a person of giant size and unusual physical power, something like a "djinn" in Arabic. The Iranians called the early Arab invaders "divan," and the medieval Indian chroniclers in Persian characterized the opposing army of the Hindu princes as "lashkar-i divan." To the impotent king in this story, the queen's lover is like a "div." I am grateful to Muzaffar Alam for glossing the word for me; personal communication, February 10, 2003. As for the blackness of the lover, recall that the king to whom Scheherazade tells her stories was cuckolded by a black slave; it is a very old stereotype.
51. W. Radloff, "Der Kluge Wesirs-Tochter," 191–198.
52. The tale of Kisagotami, in the parables of Buddhaghosha in the fifth century CE, is retold by T. W. Rhys Davids, *Buddhism*, 133–134. It is the parable of the mustard seed: A young girl named Kisagotami had just one child, a son, who died "when he could run alone." The mother begged the Buddha for "medicine that will be good for my child." He said he could make such medicine out of mustard-seed which the woman must obtain "from some house where no son, or husband, or parent, or slave has died." She failed to find such a house, but people taught her that "the living are few, but the dead are many." And so she left the dead body of her child in a forest, returned to the Buddha and became his disciple.
53. Wendy Doniger, *The Implied Spider*, 122–125.

54. The tale of Rhiannon in the Welsh *Mabinogion*; see Patrick Ford, *The Mabinogi and Other Medieval Welsh Tales*, 37–56; Wendy Doniger O'Flaherty, *Women, Androgynes*, 185–190.

55. *Magussaga*, 874. See also H. Suchier, "Die Quellen der Magussaga," 273–291 and W. W. Lawrence, *Shakespeare's Problem Comedies*, 44.

56. See Wendy Doniger and Gregory Spinner, "Misconceptions"; Wendy Doniger, "The Symbolism of Black and White Babies in the Myth of Maternal Impression."

57. The story was told to her by a sixty-three-year-old housewife named Ghaya, a woman who knew classical Arabic but told the story in the urban Tunis dialect of Arabic.

58. Monia Hejaiej, *Behind Closed Doors*, 104–117.

59. A. K. Ramanujan, "Towards a Counter-System: Women's Tales."

60. Doniger, *The Implied Spider*, 33–34.

61. *Ramayana* 7.41.22, followed by 7.42.

62. *Aitareya Brahmana* 7.13.18. Translated in full in Wendy Doniger O'Flaherty, *Textual Sources for the Study of Hinduism*, 20–25. The text goes on to say, "All the beasts know this, and therefore a son mounts his mother or his sister. This is the broad path, easy to use, on which those who have sons travel without sorrow. The beasts and birds look at it, and therefore they have intercourse even with their mother."

63. Manu 9.8–9. Some commentaries interpret the verb "make love" (*bhaj*) simply as a reference to the physical act of sexual intercourse; some take it as an indication that the woman's heart must be given to that man at the moment of union, too, for the child to resemble him.

64. Aristotle, *Generation of Animals*, 1.21, 729b17–18; *The Complete Works of Aristotle*, vol.1, p. 1132.

65. Lorraine Daston, "Succession Sealed." Citing Aristotle, *On the Soul*, 3.12, 424a20; in *The Complete Works of Aristotle*, vol 1, 674.

66. Lorraine Daston, personal communication, May, 2013. See also Lorraine Daston, "Perfection and Perfect Passivity."

67. The phrase *paternitas incerta* also occurs.

68. Doniger, *The Bedtrick*, 220–224; this paragraph is largely taken from Doniger, *The Woman Who Pretended*, 72.

69. Maurizio Bettini, *The Portrait of the Lover*, 187–192, citing Augustine's *Soliloquia: mater est falsitatis*.

70. This belief goes all the way back to the story of Jacob and the striped rods held before the ewes, in Genesis, and to the *Ethiopika* that we encountered in chapter 2, pp. 40–41. But it was fully developed as a theory in early modern Europe.

71. Billy Wilder wrote a line into the radio-play version of his film, *A Foreign Affair*, drawing upon this belief; after John Lund kissed Marlene Dietrich he said, "Your mother must have been frightened by a blow torch."

72. Doniger, "The Symbolism of Black and White Babies in the Myth of Maternal Impression."

73. Personal communication from Lorraine Daston, September 16, 2015.

74. Doniger and Spinner, "Misconceptions"; Doniger, "The Symbolism of Black and White Babies." This paragraph is also from chapter 4 of Doniger, *The Woman Who Pretended to Be Who She Was.*

75. Manu 9.32–55.

76. Marliss C. Desens, *The Bed-Trick*, 107.

77. Poggio Bracciolini, facetiae, Number 225.

78. Benjamin Mueller, "Paternity Case for a New Jersey Mother of Twins Bears Unexpected Results: Two Fathers," *New York Times*, May 7, 2015.

79. That great source of contemporary mythology, the *Globe* (September 9, 2013, pp. 6–7), ran an article alleging that Camilla, Duchess of Cambridge, wished "to subject newborn Prince George to DNA testing to confirm William is his real father!" Camilla was allegedly not charging infidelity (on Kate's part, though she had publicly claimed that "William, 31, would cheat—like all royal men"), but merely contamination from fertility treatments from a "sperm donor."

80. Robert Pippin, personal communication, email, February 21, 2016.

CHAPTER 8

1. John Hinton Knowles, *Folk-tales of Kashmir*, 126–136.

2. Galit Hasan-Rokem, *Proverbs in Israeli Folk Narratives*, 92.

3. Thomas Carlyle, *The Diamond Necklace*, 1 and 29.

4. Jonathan Beckman, *How to Ruin a Queen*, 4.

5. Beckman, *How to Ruin a Queen*, 237. The exception was Jeanne's lawyer Doillot, who was in his late sixties at the time of the trial.

6. Beckman, *How to Ruin a Queen*, 101.

7. People differ about the price. It's usually said to have been valued at 1,600,000 or 1,800,000 livres (approximately, $10,000,000); Carlyle valued it, in 1833, at $450,000 dollars, or 90,000 pounds; Carlyle, *The Diamond Necklace*, 27, 51.

8. Simon Schama, *Citizens: A Chronicle of the French Revolution*, 205.

9. Carlyle, *The Diamond Necklace*, 50–51. Jean Plaidy (in *The Queen of Diamonds*, 168) said more: "It consisted of a string of diamonds, all specially selected for their size and lustre, from which hung pendants of pear-shaped stones surrounded by clusters; from this string hung another, looped and composed of equally fine stones, and from this looped string hung more pear-shaped clusters. Then there was the double string of diamonds with an enormous centre-piece from which hung tassels of dazzling gems."

10. Beckman, *How to Ruin a Queen*, 101.

11. Schama, *Citizens*, 204.

12. Marcia Pointon, *Brilliant Effects*, 159.

13. Beckman, *How to Ruin a Queen*, 101.
14. Carlyle, *The Diamond Necklace*, 28.
15. Pointon, *Brilliant Effects*, 150
16. Schama, *Citizens*, 205.
17. Joan Haslip, *Marie Antoinette*, 78.
18. In Henry Vizetelly, *The Story of the Diamond Necklace*, 125; also Sarah Maza, *Private Lives and Public Affairs*, 199.
19. Carlyle, *The Diamond Necklace*, 28.
20. Antal Szerb, *The Queen's Necklace*, 102. Carlyle, *The Diamond Necklace*, 28, calls it the Hornbeam Arbor.
21. Vizetelly, *The Story of the Diamond Necklace*, 255.
22. Plaidy, *The Queen of Diamonds*, 200–201.
23. The queen had, in the interval, on March 27, 1785, given birth to her second son, but this time there was apparently no talk of marking the event with a gift of jewelry.
24. Jeanne's lawyer, Maître Doillot, argued that Jeanne's real first name was Marie-Antoinette, and that since a Valois descended from royalty could claim to be "of France," Jeanne had signed her own name to the document (Maza, *Private Lives*, 197). In the novel by Dumas, when the jewelers confront the queen with that signature, she points out that it is not in her hand and that, moreover, she is Marie Antoinette of Austria (Alexandre Dumas, père, *The Queen's Necklace*, 365).
25. Beckman, *How to Ruin a Queen*, 309.
26. Beckman, *How to Ruin a Queen*, 217, 221.
27. Frantz Funck-Brentano, *The Diamond Necklace*, 262.
28. At other times she accused Cagliostro of taking it. Funck-Brentano, *The Diamond Necklace*, 265.
29. Funck-Brentano, *The Diamond Necklace*, 257.
30. Maza, *Private Lives*, 185.
31. Plaidy, *The Queen of Diamonds*, 232.
32. Maza, *Private Lives*, 185.
33. Pointon, *Brilliant Effects*, 152.
34. Plaidy, *The Queen of Diamonds*, 232.
35. Vizetelly, *The Story of the Diamond Necklace*, 136–138.
36. Szerb, *The Queen's Necklace*, 106. Vizetelly, *The Story of the Diamond Necklace*, 133
37. Maza, *Private Lives*, 201; Vizetelly, *The Story of the Diamond Necklace*, 133.
38. Szerb, *The Queen's Necklace*, 255.
39. Funck-Brentano, *The Diamond Necklace*, 264.
40. Beckman, *How to Ruin a Queen*, 270.
41. Szerb, *The Queen's Necklace*, 270.
42. Beckman, *How to Ruin a Queen*, 287.
43. Isaac and Janet Asimov, *Norby and the Queen's Necklace*, 41.
44. Beckman, *How to Ruin a Queen*, 309

45. In Jean Plaidy's novel, *The Queen of Diamonds* (69 ff.), the Cardinal lusts after Jeanne the moment he meets her and makes her his mistress right then and there. He also has a terrible crush on the queen, but she continues to loathe him.

46. Beckman, *How to Ruin a Queen*, 236.

47. Schama, *Citizens*, 205.

48. Schama, *Citizens*, 205.

49. Szerb, *The Queen's Necklace*, 256.

50. Funck-Brentano, *The Diamond Necklace*, 284, citing Bachaumont, December 16, 1785.

51. Schama, *Citizens*, 225.

52. Maza, *Private Lives*, 206.

53. Maza, *Private Lives*, 207.

54. Pointon, *Brilliant Effects*, 162.

55. Beckman, *How to Ruin a Queen*, 290.

56. Szerb, *The Queen's Necklace*, 256.

57. Funck-Brentano, *The Diamond Necklace*, 284, citing Journal de Hardy, March 26, 1786.

58. Robert Darnton, "The Grub Street Style of Revolution," 316.

59. Maza, *Private Lives*, 196.

60. Beckman, *How to Ruin a Queen*, 276–277.

61. Isaac and Janet Asimov, *Norby and the Queen's Necklace*, 41.

62. Dumas, *The Queen's Necklace*, 322.

63. Dumas, *The Queen's Necklace*, 357.

64. Dumas, *The Queen's Necklace*, 421.

65. Dumas, *The Queen's Necklace*, 358.

66. Dumas, *The Queen's Necklace*, 353–354.

67. Dumas, *The Queen's Necklace*, 342.

68. Dumas, *The Queen's Necklace*, 374.

69. This leads into several other Dumas novels.

70. Dumas, *The Queen's Necklace*, 412.

71. Dumas, *The Queen's Necklace*, 418.

72. Dumas, *The Queen's Necklace*, 419.

73. Dumas, *The Queen's Necklace*, 422.

74. Max Ophüls, speaking to introduce the Screen Directors' Guild Presentation of his play about Charles II, *The Exile*, January 23, 1949.

75. *The Queen's Necklace*, by Maurice Leblanc (1905) (An Arsène Lupin Story); *The Rose of Versailles*, by Riyoko Ikeda; and *The Queen of Diamonds*, by Jean Plaidy (1958) are the best of a large crop.

76. *Le Collier de la reine*, a short, silent film, directed by Etienne Arnaud and Louis Feuillade, 1909; *Le Collier de la reine*, directed by Tony Lekain and Gaston Ravel, 1929; *Marie Antoinette*, directed by W. S. Van Dyke, starring Norma Shearer, 1938; *L'Affaire du collier de la reine*, directed by Marcel L'Herbier, 1946,

based on Stefan Zweig's *Marie Antoinette: The Portrait of an Average Woman* (*Bildnis eines mittleren Charakters*, 1932); *The Affair of the Necklace*, directed by Charles Shyer, with elements drawn from the novel by Alexandre Dumas, starring Hilary Swank, 2001.

77. Or, as Jonathan Beckman puts it, "It does not take much force to make a choker choke." Beckman, *How to Ruin a Queen*, 309.

78. Schama, *Citizens*, 203.

79. Schama, *Citizens*, 203, citing the *Moving Tableau of Paris*, 1787.

80. Maza, *Private Lives*, 203.

81. Beckman, *How to Ruin a Queen*, 91.

82. Maza, *Private Lives*, 204.

83. Imbert de Saint-Amand, *Marie Antoinette and the End of the Old Regime*, 60.

84. Szerb, *The Queen's Necklace*, 235. "[Marie Antoinette's] phobia about Ronan was such that it even made her fear that he and his co-conspirators might have hidden the necklace in her bedroom with the intention of 'finding' it at a suitable moment and laying a false charge, the way people did in medieval legends."

85. Szerb, *The Queen's Necklace*, 255.

86. Beckman, *How to Ruin a Queen*, 5.

87. Beckman, *How to Ruin a Queen*, 5.

88. Carlyle, *The Diamond Necklace*, 45.

89. Carlyle, *The Diamond Necklace*, 81.

90. Carlyle, *The Diamond Necklace*, 95.

91. Carlyle, *The Diamond Necklace*, 117–118.

92. Carlyle, *The Diamond Necklace*, 99.

93. Maza, *Private Lives*, 189.

94. Karl Marx, *The Eighteenth Brumaire*.

95. Beckman, *How to Ruin a Queen*, 91.

96. Maza, *Private Lives*, 204.

97. Beckman, *How to Ruin a Queen*, 306.

98. Carlyle, too, notes the significance of the timing.

99. Saint-Amand, *Marie Antoinette*, 86.

100. Saint-Amand, *Marie Antoinette*, 60.

101. Maza, *Private Lives*, 204.

102. Saint-Amand, *Marie Antoinette*, 56.

103. Figaro complicates the plot with several triangles of his own that need not concern us here (Figaro-Almaviva-Susanna and Figaro-Marcellina-Bartolo), and Rosina's intimacy with the young page, Cherubino, makes Almaviva suspect yet another triangle (Almaviva-Rosina-Cherubino).

104. Beaumarchais, *The Marriage of Figaro*, Act V, p. 136.

105. Isaac and Janet Asimov, *Norby and the Queen's Necklace*.

106. Isaac and Janet Asimov, *Norby and the Queen's Necklace*, 64–65.

107. Isaac and Janet Asimov, *Norby and the Queen's Necklace*, 112.

CHAPTER 9

1. See Lise Sanders, *Consuming Fantasies: Labor, Leisure, and the London Shopgirl.*

2. Elizabeth Taylor, quoted in "Crown Jewels," *People Magazine*, April 11, 2011, p. 72.

3. Larry McMurtry, "A Life for the Star."

4. Katherine Dunagan Osborne, "Inherited Emotions: George Eliot and the Politics of Heirlooms," 466–467.

5. Henry James, "Paste." In *The Novels and Tales of Henry James*, vol. 16, 315–337.

6. W. Somerset Maugham, "Mr Know-All."

7. It was one of three segments in *Trio*, also known as *W. Somerset Maugham's Trio*. Ken Annakin directed the "Mr. Know-All" segment. The narrator is played by Wilfred Hyde-White, Max Kelada by Nigel Patrick, Mrs. Ramsay by Anne Crawford, and Mr. Ramsay by Naunton Wayne.

8. Though the plot was spotted by one IMDB blogger—"lucy-19 from London, 23 January 2007," who wrote this comment on *China Seas*: "And the 'fake' pearls are definitely Somerset Maugham—they turn up again in a film that's a compendium of his short stories" (apparently a reference to *Trio*).

9. In this production, Mr. Timmons is played by Edward Brophy, Mrs. Timmons by Lillian Bond.

10. W. Somerset Maugham, "A String of Beads."

11. See the hilarious lyrics of "I Love a Film Cliché," by Dick Vosburgh, from *A Day in Hollywood, a Night in the Ukraine* (1979).

12. The film was based on James Hilton's *Random Harvest* (1941). See Wendy Doniger, *The Woman Who Pretended to Be Who She Was*, 97–106, for an analysis of other aspects of this film.

13. Thorold Dickinson's 1940 version of the film just has a locket with rubies, which she thinks are fake, though they are real; Cukor added the touches of the costume and the painting.

14. The verb, from the title of the film, even got into the *OED* in 1969.

15. The film was based on *D'entre les morts* (*The Living and the Dead*, 1954) by Pierre Boileau and Thomas Narcejac and further draws upon another novel, *Bruges-la-Morte* (*The Dead City of Bruges*, Paris, 1892), by Georges Todenbach. In *Bruges-la-Morte*, a man in deep mourning for his beloved wife sees a prostitute who resembles her. He dresses her more and more to look like his wife, but when he sees that she does not really resemble his wife, and that she hates him, he strangles her.

16. The clue of the necklace in the painting in *Vertigo* may have been "borrowed" from the painting-with-telltale-jewelry in *Gaslight*.

17. Pierre Boileau, *The Living and the Dead*, 11.

18. Boileau, *The Living and the Dead*, 127.

19. Boileau, *The Living and the Dead*, 131.

20. Also called *Diamond Earrings* and, in the French original, *Madame de . . .*, based on Louise Leveque de Vilmorin's 1951 novel, *Madame de.*

21. In Louise Leveque de Vilmorin's novel, *Madame de*, the general persuades her to put an end to the rumors that the earrings were stolen by making a public statement that she had found them again. She does so, and tells people that she is so frightened of losing them again that she is never going to wear them in public any more. Thus his is the second lie, which returns, twisted, when she pretends to find the earrings again in order to be able to wear them in public.

22. In de Vilmorin's novel, the general assumes that Donati is just her friend, not her lover, and that she had told Donati the truth she could not tell her husband: that she had sold the jewels and lied about it. And he assumes that by coincidence— and coincidences do happen (he muses)—Donati happened to have the jewels, and gave them to her so that she could repair the lie she had told. And so, in male comradeship, the general tells Donati that of course he knew she had not found among her gloves the earrings he had given her as a wedding present, as she had doubtless told Donati. And if she wore them now, he alone would know that they were a gift from Donati. But since he couldn't allow that, would Donati please deposit them with the jeweler and tell him to let the general know what he owed him for them.

23. In the book, the niece comes to Louise and tries to sell the earrings directly to her, but since Louise has no money, she tells the niece to sell them to the jeweler.

24. As a woman remarks of another woman in Peter de Vries, *The Tunnel of Love*, 35, "Deep down she's shallow."

25. This film technique was copied to express sexual vertigo in *Vertigo* (Alfred Hitchcock, 1968) and in *The Thomas Crown Affair* (Norman Jewison, 1968), to the tune of "The Windmills of Your Mind," all about circles.

26. Kelly also gave himself the two best partners, two great ballerinas: Diana Adams and Tamara Toumanova.

27. *The New Yorker*, March 14, 2011, 20–21, Lizzie Widdicombe, "Girls' Best Friend."

28. Perhaps it was Elizabeth Taylor. There was a joke going around in the 1950s that Ms. Taylor, landing at Orly airport in Paris, was asked what she intended to do in Paris, and replied, "Visit relatives," to which someone commented, "Yeah, Uncle Van Cleef and Aunt Arpels."

29. Anita Loos, *Gentlemen Prefer Blondes*, 72.

30. Elizabeth Taylor, *My Love Affair with Jewelry*, 43.

31. Marcia Pointon, *Brilliant Effects*, 35–36.

32. Loos, *Gentlemen Prefer Blondes*, 72–73.

33. Personal communication from Felix Salmon, at Tree Tops, Lalibela, South Africa, October 24, 2010.

34. Personal communication from Cynthia Read, May 9, 2016.
35. Julie Creswell, "Real Fur, Masquerading as Faux," *New York Times*, May 19, 2013.

CHAPTER 10

1. Tom Zoellner, *The Heartless Stone*, 285.
2. Zoellner, *The Heartless Stone*, 32.
3. Zoellner, *The Heartless Stone*, 41.
4. J. Courtney Sullivan, *Engagements*, 337.
5. Mircea Eliade, *Cosmos and History: The Myth of the Eternal Return*.
6. Zoellner, *The Heartless Stone*, 28.
7. *Economist*, "The Diamond Business: Glass with Attitude," 2. No author cited.
8. *Economist*, "The Diamond Business," 8.
9. Philip Roth, *Everyman*, 57. Roth sets this speech in 1933, a bit too early.
10. Lilliana Leopardi, "Ludovico Dolce's Treatise on Precious Gems."
11. Janine Roberts, *Glitter and Greed*, preface.
12. Robert J. Proctor, "Anti-agate," 395.
13. Sullivan, *Engagements*, 5.
14. Tara Siegel Bernard, "With Engagement Rings, Love Meets Budget."
15. Zoellner, *The Heartless Stone*, 42–43.
16. Ann Rower (Leo Robin's niece), "Gentlemen: A Musical Is Made," 27.
17. George Frederick Kunz, *Rings for the Finger*, 305, citing Mauricii Pinder, "De adamante," Berolini, 1829, 68.
18. Proctor, "Anti-agate," 398.
19. Proctor, "Anti-agate," 383 fn.
20. James Remington McCarthy, *Rings through the Ages*, 88; Kunz, *Rings for the Finger*, 184. The Latin of Buchanan's poem reads:
    Quod te jampriden fruitur, videt, ac amat absens,
    Haec pignus cordis gemma, et imago mei est.
    Non est candidior, non est haec purior illo,
    Quamvis dura magis, non magis firma.
    It has also been rendered:
    The gem which saw thee near and loves thee still,
    Is pledge and image of my heart and will.
    My heart is not less white or pure than this,
    And though less hard, 'tis quite as firm I wis.
21. Zoellner, *The Heartless Stone*, 28.
22. Zoellner, *The Heartless Stone*, 186.
23. Proctor, "Anti-agate," 387.
24. Proctor, "Anti-agate," 388.
25. Kohinoordiamond.org and other websites.

26. Richard Kurin, *Hope Diamond*, 19.

27. Anita Loos, *Gentlemen Prefer Blondes*, 158.

28. Kurin, *Hope Diamond*, 185.

29. Diana Scarisbrick, *Rings: Jewelry of Power, Love and Loyalty*, 82.

30. Kurin, *Hope Diamond*, 185.

31. Proctor, "Anti-agate," 394.

32. *Economist*, "The Diamond Business," 5.

33. Kurin, *Hope Diamond*, 186.

34. Rebecca Tushnet, "Rules of Engagement," 2591; see also Margaret F. Brinig, *Rings and Promises*.

35. *Economist*, "The Diamond Business," 5.

36. Proctor, "Anti-agate," 391.

37. *Economist*, "The Diamond Business," 5.

38. Proctor, "Anti-agate," 396.

39. Proctor, "Anti-agate," 382 fn.; he also cites Gary S. Becker and George J. Stigler, "De Gustibus Non Est Disputandum," 76–90.

40. Proctor, "Anti-agate," 381.

41. *Economist*, "The Diamond Business," 5.

42. Proctor, "Anti-agate," 392.

43. Loos, *Gentlemen Prefer Blondes*, 75.

44. Zoellner, *The Heartless Stone*, 49–50.

45. Rower, "Gentlemen," 67, cites Alex Gottlieb, in a conversation with Leo Robin in the early 1990s at the Motion Picture Home and Hospital in Calabassas. "I said, 'Where'd you get the idea for "Diamonds Are a Girl's Best Friend"?' He said, 'I stole it from Anita Loos.'"

46. Rower, "Gentlemen," 27ff; the verses were found jotted on some of Joe Field's stationery. Another was: "Get that rock rock rock on your finger. / A kiss on the hand may be grand but it doesn't linger."

47. Rower, "Gentlemen," 90.

48. Rower, "Gentlemen," 91.

49. *Economist*, "The Diamond Business," 7.

50. *Economist*, "The Diamond Business," 2.

51. Proctor, "Anti-agate," 395.

52. Perhaps infected by the James Bond film title, Proctor uses the plural where De Beers was so careful never to use it.

53. Proctor, "Anti-agate," 384.

54. Kurin, *Hope Diamond*, 311.

55. "Hope springs eternal in the human breast; / Man never is, but always to be blessed." Alexander Pope, "An Essay on Man."

56. Rower, "Gentlemen," 95.

57. The producers had had great difficulty in raising the $200,000 they needed, scrounging it together with assorted $5,000 commitments from a motley group—Anita Loos's brother Clifford, most of the writers involved in the show, a group of gamblers in Cleveland, Alfred Lunt and Lynn Fontanne, Marie and Antoinette Arnstein, Lucia Chase, and, finally, Rodgers and Hammerstein, Joshua Logan and Leland Hayward. An item, placed strategically in the *New York Times*, noting that the latter four show-biz greats had put their money in the show, inspired more than enough angels to give them the money they needed (Rower, "Gentlemen," 67). But nothing from De Beers.

58. Sullivan, *Engagements*, 85.

59. Zoellner, *The Heartless Stone*, 49.

60. Rower, "Gentlemen," 10.

61. Though Ettinger later claimed that she knew nothing about De Beers. Zoellner, *The Heartless Stone*, 50.

62. Ian Fleming, *James Bond: Diamonds Are Forever*, 184, 192.

63. Zoellner, *The Heartless Stone*, 53.

64. John Beckman, *How to Ruin a Queen*, 309.

65. Zoellner, *The Heartless Stone*, 51.

66. Wendy Doniger, *The Implied Spider*.

67. Proctor, "Anti-agate," 17.

68. *Economist*, "The Diamond Business," 6.

69. Kunz, *Rings for the Finger*, 235.

70. Chiara Atik, "Will 'Divorce Rings' Catch On?" Today.com, September 2, 2011.

71. Atik, "Will 'Divorce Rings' Catch On?"

72. Sullivan, *Engagements*, 165.

73. Style News, Style Watch, "A look back at Vanessa Bryant's 'Apology' Ring," December 17, 2011.

74. Adam Mars-Jones, in a review of *Roth Unbound* by Claudia Roth Pierpont, in the *London Review of Books*, January 23, 2014. Citing Claire Bloom's 1996 memoir, *Leaving a Doll's House*.

75. Tim Clayton and Phil Craig, *Diana: Story of a Princess*, 75.

76. Tracy Moore, "Eight Reasons Why the Mangagement Ring Should Totally Be a Thing," filed on "I Thee Dread," February 2, 2014, http://jezebel.com/eight-reasons-why-the-mangagement-ring-should-totally-1524567911.

77. Kunz, *Rings for the Finger*, 231.

78. Mary Schwager, "Mangagement Rings," Huff Post Weddings, November 30, 2011.

79. Doniger, *Implied Spider*, 87–113.

80. Scarisbrick, *Rings*, 82.

81. Michael Carré and Jules Barbier, Libretto for *Tales of Hoffmann*, Act III.

> Scintille, diamant, fascine, attire-la
>
> L'alouette ou la femme a cet appât vainqueur
>
> Vont de l'aile ou du coeur
>
> L'une y laisse la vie
>
> Et l'autre y perd son âme.

82. I am certain that I copied these lines years ago from a version of the libretto, but I cannot now find the source, or the French version of the text, and would welcome hearing from any reader who can place the passage.

83. Kunz, *Rings for the Finger*, 227, citing Thomas Fuller, "Holy State," chap. xxii, "Of Marriage."

84. Edwards, *The History and Poetry of Finger-Rings*, 232.

85. Annette S. Beveridge, trans., *Baburnama*, p. 477, Folio 268b. Wheeler Thackston, in *The Baburnama*, p. 328, Folio 268b, translates it as "half a day's food." See also Henry Beveridge, "Babur's Diamond; Was It the Koh-i-nur?"

86. Sullivan, *Engagements*, 149. Another woman, hearing about the brutality in the diamond mines, is so ashamed that she turns her diamond engagement ring around to hide the diamond. (Sullivan, *Engagements*, 152). She is trying to make the diamond invisible, or even to become invisible herself, just as Yvain (see p. 90) turned the diamond in his ring around to make himself invisible.

87. Sullivan, *Engagements*, 151–152. In the De Beers mines, the black workers but not the white were locked up at night, stripped naked and made to submit to a search of every inch of their bodies after work, because it was assumed they would steal.

88. *Economist*, "The Diamond Business," 2.

89. Elizabeth Taylor, *My Love Affair with Jewelry*, 49. Taylor had converted to Judaism in 1959.

90. Sullivan, *Engagements*, 196.

91. *Economist*, "The Diamond Business," 5.

92. Proctor, "Anti-agate," 391.

93. Proctor, "Anti-agate," 391. Citing Stefan Kanfer, *The Last Empire: De Beers, Diamonds, and the World*, 272. See also Margaret F. Brinig, *Rings and Promises*: "The [diamond] industry enjoyed a phenomenal success during the period following 1935, and by 1965, 80 percent of all brides chose diamond engagement rings."

94. Rebecca Tushnet, "Rules of Engagement," 2604, fn. 107. Citing Lois Smith Brady, "Christian Engagement Rings," *Commonweal*, October 21, 1949, 38; "Rock Me: A Girl and Her Ring," *Mademoiselle*, March 1990, 177.

95. Rebecca Okrent, "Ring Cycle." I've rearranged the order of two of the sentences, to keep the chronology.

96. Edwards, *The History and Poetry of Finger-Rings*, 207.

97. Diana Scarisbrick, cited by Kurin, *Hope Diamond*, 184.

98. McCarthy, *Rings through the Ages*, 166.

99. Marcia Pointon, *Brilliant Effects*, 25. Citing Horace Walpole to Horace Mann, February 25, 1742, *Walpole's Correspondence*, vol. xvii (1954), p. 343; and to Conway, August 5, 1761, vol. xxxviii (1974), 35.

100. Shivani Vora, "Brides: Steal His Heart, but Borrow the Jewelry," *New York Times*, July 31, 2013.

101. Loos, *Gentlemen Prefer Blondes*, 130.

102. Loos, *Gentlemen Prefer Blondes*, 85–95.

103. Lorraine Daston, personal communication, May 2013.

104. Linda K. Kerber, "Why Diamonds Really Are a Girl's Best Friend," 92.

105. Peter Evans and Ava Gardner, *Ava Gardner: The Secret Conversations*, 20.

106. According to Wikipedia, the original rough diamond was found in 1966 and weighed 241 carats (48.2 g), later cut by Harry Winston to 69.42 carats (13.884 g) in the shape of a pear, and recut to 68.0 carats (13.60 g) in 1980.

107. Alex Kuczynski, "Good Times and Bum Times, but She's Here," *New York Times*, Sunday, September 29, 2002, section 9, pp. 1 and 15, here 15.

108. Tushnet, "Rules of Engagement," 2585, 2584.

109. Tushnet, "Rules of Engagement," 2585, 2584.

110. Proctor, "Anti-agate," 396.

111. Pointon, *Brilliant Effects*, 44.

112. *Oxford English Dictionary*, s. v. "fortune-hunter."

113. Tushnet, "Rules of Engagement," 2594, 2595.

114. Tushnet, "Rules of Engagement," 2591, 2601.

115. Proctor, "Anti-agate," 384.

116. Tushnet, "Rules of Engagement," 2601, fn. 91.

117. Kerber, "Why Diamonds Really Are a Girl's Best Friend," 92.

118. Tushnet, "Rules of Engagement," 2591. See also Margaret F. Brinig, *Rings and Promises*.

119. Elizabeth Taylor, *My Love Affair with Jewelry*, 117.

120. Judith Martin, "Finding a Way to Stop Passengers from Taking Control," *Chicago Tribune*, January 25, 1996.

121. Tushnet, "Rules of Engagement," 2602.

122. Tushnet, "Rules of Engagement," 2606, 2591, 2604, fn. 108.

123. Tushnet, "Rules of Engagement," 2606.

124. Tushnet, "Rules of Engagement," 2602, citing Gigi Barnes, "Diamonds Aren't Forever," *Mademoiselle*, September 1995, 30.

125. Tushnet, "Rules of Engagement," 2606.

126. Two of the rings she sold could have been engagement gifts, since they married twice, divorcing in between.

127. An online ad for Joint Venture Jewelry, Celebrities and Famous Jewels, October 18, 2012: "When Celebs Split, What Happens to the Jewelry?"

128. Liz Taylor's affection for diamonds was so compelling that when she marketed her line in perfumes, she named the scents White Diamonds, Black Pearls, White Diamonds Brilliant, White Diamonds Sparkling, Diamonds and Rubies, Diamonds and Sapphires, and Diamonds and Emeralds.

129. Online advertisement for Joint Venture Jewelry, on October 18, 2012, in "Celebrities and Famous Jewels."

130. I am indebted to Kathleen Geier for telling me about this website.

131. Nora Ephron, *Heartburn*, 166–168.

132. Kunz, *Rings for the Finger*, 231.

133. I am indebted to my niece, Emma Doniger, for telling me about *Sex and the City*.

134. Ruth La Ferla, "Ellen Unloads," *New York Times*, September 21, 2006.

135. Zoellner, *The Heartless Stone*, 285.

136. Zoellner, *The Heartless Stone*, 199.

137. Zoellner, *The Heartless Stone*, 285.

138. Sullivan, *Engagements*, 273.

139. Zoellner, *The Heartless Stone*, 285.

140. "4 Timeless Lessons from Single and Happy Sushmita Sen," *Yahoo News*, South Africa, May 15, 2013.

141. Sampada Sharma, "Sushmita Sen Just Gave Us Another Reason To Love Her With This Instagram Post." *Scoop Whoop*, May 10, 2016.

142. Thanks to Laurie Patton for telling me about this website.

143. Proctor, "Anti-agate," 408.

144. Zoellner, *The Heartless Stone*, 37, 59–63.

145. Sarah Maza, *Private Lives and Public Affairs*, 43.

146. *Economist*, "The Diamond Business," 2.

147. David Bario, "Power to the Pure: Rutland Herald Online," Rutlandherald.com. March 29, 2005.

148. Bario, "Power to the Pure."

149. Their interpretation of "chastity" is a rough Christian equivalent of the Jewish Sabbath elevators, which run constantly, automatically, with open doors, to get around the law against operating a machine on the Sabbath. See Alan Dundes, *The Shabbat Elevator*.

150. Ceci Connolly, "Teen Pledges Barely Cut STD Rates, Study Says," washington-post.com, March 19, 2005.

151. Montana Miller, "Vernacular Abstinence," *Practical Matters Journal*, November 9, 2001.

CHAPTER 11

1. Simon Schama, *Citizens: A Chronicle of the French Revolution*, 205.

2. Claude Lévi-Strauss, *The Elementary Structures of Kinship*, 48. See also Gayle Rubin, "The Traffic in Women: Notes on the 'Political Economy' of Sex."

3. Manu 3.51, 54. Manu rails against the bride-price again at 9.98–99, but he cheerfully discusses the legal ways to do it at 9.97 and at 8.204, .366, and .369.
4. From the website of the Paris restaurant Lapérouse. I am indebted to Daryl Otte for this information.
5. Charles Edwards, *The History and Poetry of Finger-rings*, 203. Also George Frederick Kunz, *Rings for the Finger*, 133.
6. Kunz, *Rings for the Finger*, 193.
7. Ann Rower, "Gentlemen: A Musical Is Made," 18. Whiting was Leo Robin's adopted niece and the daughter of his first Hollywood partner (Rower, "Gentlemen," 47); she may have had Leo in mind when she said this, as he was a little man married to a very tall gorgeous blonde showgirl.
8. James C. Scott, *Weapons of the Weak*.
9. Linda K. Kerber, "Why Diamonds Really Are a Girl's Best Friend," 92.
10. Manu 9.78–79.
11. Nandini Bhattacharyya Panda, "Women in the Sastric Traditions." Also Henry Thomas Colebrooke, in *Essays in the Religion and Philosophy of the Hindus*.
12. Carla Higgins, "Jewelry."
13. Higgins, "Jewelry."
14. From a BBC World Radio Service story on alternatives to banks, Sunday, October 10, 2010, on the show "Business Weekly," the episode titled "Islamic Pawn Shops," http://www.bbc.co.uk/programmes/p00b3lhf.
15. For a similar source of funds for jewelry in Florida, see http://www.cappelloloans.com/not-bank-pawn-broker.html.
16. Thanks to Sarah Jacoby for this information. Personal communication, May 2015.
17. This remark was made by Marilyn Waldmann and told to me, on May 24, 2016, by Bruce Lincoln.
18. I blame this pun on Judith Martin ("Miss Manners"), who used it in the title of an article she published in the *Washington Post*, March 15, 1998 ("Engagement Rings: Carat and Stick").
19. Claude Lévi-Strauss, "Split Representation in the Art of Asia and America."
20. Robert Pippin, personal communication, February 21, 2016.
21. Wendy Doniger, *The Implied Spider*, xi, 2–5.
22. Doniger, *The Implied Spider*, 6–8.
23. *Die Fledermaus*, act three, scene 12. Falke: "Ah, wie ich sehe, hat's hier schon eine Erkennungsszene gegeben!"
24. Terence Cave, *Recognitions*, 489.
25. Alexander Goldenweiser, "The Principle of Limited Possibilities," 45; Doniger, *The Implied Spider*, 139–145.
26. Goldenweiser, "The Principle of Limited Possibilities," 35–58; Doniger, *The Implied Spider*, 139–145.
27. Cave, *Recognitions*, 489.
28. Cave, *Recognitions*, 495, 489.

29. Marina Warner, *Stranger Magic*, 5.

30. Thanks to Simi Chavel for this idea, in Chicago, 2011.

31. George Orwell, "Rudyard Kipling."

32. Max Horkheimer and Theodor W. Adorno, *Dialectic of Enlightenment*.

33. The film's director, Nicholas Hytner, as well as its star, Nigel Hawthorne, have denied this, but Bennett himself said it in "Madness: The Movie," *London Review of Books*, February 9, 1995.

34. Warner, *Stranger Magic*, 80.

35. W. R. Shedden Ralston, "Cinderella," 41–42.

36. A. S. Byatt, *The Children's Book*, 15.

37. Doniger, *The Implied Spider*, 122–153.

38. From Lorraine Daston, conversation, June 5, 2015.

39. Lorraine J. Daston and Peter Galison, *Objectivity*; Lorraine J. Daston, Peter Erickson, et al., *How Reason Almost Lost Its Mind*.

40. Lévi-Strauss, "The Structural Study of Myth."

41. *Economist*, "The Diamond Business," 8.

42. Herodotus, *History*, 1.8. When the queen learned that Gyges had looked upon her naked, she insisted that he sleep with her and kill her husband.

43. Plato, *Republic* 2, 359D–360D.

44. Adam Gopnik, "What Did Jesus Do?," 75.

45. Joseph Bédier, *The Romance of Tristan and Iseult*, 140.

46. Marina Warner, *Once upon a Time*, 2.

47. William Butler Yeats, *Fairy and Folk Tales of the Irish Peasantry*, 52–59, "Jamie Freel and the Young Lady." A Donegal tale, from Miss Letitia Maclintock.

48. *Mahabharata* 3.298.

49. The commentary on the very first verse of the *Kamasutra* says, "You can, of course, learn about pleasure from other teachings, just as you can read meaning into a hole shaped like a letter of the alphabet that a bookworm has eaten out of a page, but you do not understand what you should do and what you should not do. And so people say:

    A man should not be congratulated
    if he happens to succeed at something without knowing its science,
    for it is pure chance, like a bookworm eating a hole
    in the shape of a letter of the alphabet."

50. Wendy Doniger, *The Woman Who Pretended*, 229–232.

51. Thomas Kuhn's concept of the paradigm shift and Leon Festinger's syndrome of cognitive dissonance help us to understand the power that traditional rationality has over individual reason. Thomas Kuhn, *The Nature of Scientific Revolutions*; Leon Festinger, *A Theory of Cognitive Dissonance*.

52. For this important function of myth, which is beyond the range of this present inquiry, see Bruce Lincoln's work, particularly *Discourse and the Construction of Society*.

53. Heliodorus, *Ethiopika* 9.24.7.
54. Thanks to Paul Harrison for this idea, at Stanford, in 2010.
55. Thanks to Lanier Anderson for this formulation, at Stanford, in 2010.
56. Thanks to Stuart Blackburn for this formulation and for several of the ideas in this paragraph. Reader's Report, March 21, 2014.
57. Marina Warner said this of fairy tales, on p. xxiii of *Once upon a Time*, but it is equally true of myths.
58. Cited by Warner, *Once upon a Time*, xxiv.
59. Zoellner, *The Heartless Stone*, 292.

Bibliography

ANCIENT, MEDIEVAL, AND PRE-MODERN SOURCES (BY TITLE)

Abhijnanashakuntalam of Kalidasa, with the commentary of Raghava. Bombay: Nirnaya Sagara Press, 1958.

Aitareya Brahmana, with the commentary of Sayana. Anandashrama Sanskrit Series 32. Poona, 1896.

Aithiopika [Ethiopika] of Heliodorus. In *Collected Ancient Greek Novels,* ed. B. P. Reardon. Berkeley: University of California Press, 1989.

Amores of Ovid. *Heroides, Amores.* Latin text and English translation. Loeb Classical Library. Cambridge, MA: Harvard University Press, 1914.

Amores of Ovid, trans. Anthony S. Kline. *The Love Poems (Translated, Illustrated): The Amores, Ars Amatoria and Remedia Amoris.* CreateSpace Independent Publishing Platform, 2015.

The Arabian Nights, trans. Husain Haddawy, based on the text edited by Muhsin Mahdi. New York: W. W. Norton, 1990.

The Arabian Nights, trans. Richard Burton. *The Arabian Nights* and *The Supplementary Nights.* 16 vols. Benares: Printed by the Kamashastra Society for Private Subscribers Only, 1885.

The Arabian Nights' Entertainment, trans. Robert L. Mack. Oxford: Oxford World Classics, Oxford University Press, 1995, based on Antoine Galland's twelve volume *Mille et une Nuit* (1704–17, translated anonymously into English between 1706 and 1721).

The Arabian Nights II: Sindbad and Other Popular Stories, trans. Husain Haddaway. New York: W. W. Norton, 1995.

The *Arbitrators* of Menander. In *Four Plays of Menander: The Hero, Epitrepontes, Periceiromene and Samia,* ed. Edward Capps. Boston: Ginn, 1910.

The *Arbitrators* of Menander. In *Menander,* Vol. 1., ed. and trans. W. G. Arnott. Cambridge, MA: Harvard University Press, Loeb series, 1979.

The *Arbitrators* of Menander. In *Menander: The Plays and Fragments,* trans. Maurice Balme. Oxford: Oxford World Classics, 2001.

Arthashastra of Kautilya. Critical edition, ed. R. P. Kangle. 3 vols. Bombay: University of Bombay, 1960.

Brahmavaivarta Purana. Poona: Anandasrama Sanskrit Series #102, 1935.

Bhagavata Purana, with the commentary of Shridhara. Benares: Pandita Pustakalaya, 1972.

Brihadaranyaka Upanishad. In *The Early Upanisads,* ed. and trans. Patrick Olivelle. New York: Oxford University Press, 1998.

(*Cilappatikaram*) *The Tale of an Anklet: An Epic of South India* (*The Cilappatikaram of Ilanko Atikal*), trans. R. Parthasarathy. New York: Columbia University Press, 1993.

Decameron of Giovanni Boccaccio, trans. John Payne; revised and annotated by Charles S. Singleton. Berkeley: University of California Press, 1982.

Edda. The Poetic Edda. Vol. 1: *Mythological Poems,* edited with translation, introduction, and commentary by Ursula Dronke. Oxford: Clarendon Press, 1997.

Edda. The Prose Edda of Snorri Sturluson: Tales from Norse Mythology, trans. Jean I. Young. Berkeley: University of California Press, 1954.

Epitrepontes. See *The Arbitrators.*

Generation of Animals, of Aristotle. In *The Complete Works of Aristotle,* ed. Jonathan Barnes. 2 vols. Princeton, NJ: Princeton University Press, 1984.

Gregorius vom Stein (*Gregory of the Rock*), by Hartmann von Aue. In *Arthurian Romances, Tales, and Lyric Poetry: The Complete Works of Hartmann von Aue,* trans. with commentary by Frank J. Tobin, Kim Vivian, and Richard H. Lawson. University Park: Pennsylvania State University Press, 2001.

Harivamsha. Poona: Bhandarkar Oriental Research Institute, 1969.

Hecyra. See *The Mother-in-Law.*

History of Herodotus, trans. David Grene. Chicago: University of Chicago Press, 1987.

Jataka Stories, ed. E. B. Cowell. London: Pali Text Society, 1973.

Kamasutra of Vatsyayana, trans. Wendy Doniger and Sudhir Kakar. London: Oxford World Classics, 2002.

Kamasutra of Vatsyayana, with the commentary of Sri Yasodhara. Bombay: Laksmivenkatesvara Steam Press, 1856.

Kathasaritsagara (*The Ocean of the Rivers of Story*) of Somadeva. Bombay: Nirnara Sagara Press, 1930.

Kathasaritsagara. The Ocean of Story, ed. N. M. Penzer, trans. C. W. Tawney. 10 vols. London: Chas. J. Sawyer, 1924.

Lancelot of the Lake, trans. Corin Corley. Oxford: Oxford World Classics, 2008.

Lancelot: roman en prose du 13e siècle. 9 vols, éd. critique avec introd. et notes par Alexandre Micha. Genève: Droz, 1978–1983.

The Lives of S. Ninian and S. Kentigern, Compiled in the Twelfth Century, ed. Aexander Penrose Forbes. The Historians of Scotland Series, 5; Edinburgh: Edmonston and Douglas, 1874.

The Mabinogion, trans. Gwyn Jones and Thomas Jones. Everyman. London: J. M. Dent, 1949; revised, 1993.

The Mabinogion, trans. Jeffrey Gantz. Harmondsworth: Penguin Books, 1976.

The Mabinogion and Other Medieval Welsh Tales, trans. Patrick K. Ford. Berkeley: University of California Press, 1977.

Madhumalati: An Indian Sufi Romance, trans. Aditya Behl and Simon Weightman, Oxford: Oxford University Press, 2000.

The *Magussaga* or the *Bragoa-Magus saga*, from Pauli's *Grundriss*, Vol. 2. Strassburg, 1901–1909.

Mahabharata of Vyasa. Poona: Bhandarkar Oriental Research Institute, 1933–69.

Manu. [*Manusmrti*], *The Laws of Manu*, ed. Harikrishna Jayantakrishna Dave. Bombay: Bharatiya Vidya Bhavan, 1972–85.

Manu, The Laws of Manu, trans. Wendy Doniger, with Brian K. Smith. Harmondsworth: Penguin Books, 1991.

Matsya Purana. Poona: Anandashrama Sanskrit Series 54, 1907.

Metamorphoses of Ovid, trans. Frank Justus Miller. Cambridge, MA: Loeb Library, 1977.

Le Morte d'Arthur of Sir Thomas Malory. New Hyde Park, NY: University Books, 1961.

The Mother in Law [*Hecyra*] of Terence, ed. with translation, introduction, and commentary by S. Ireland. Warminster, Wiltshire: Aris and Philips, 1990.

The Mother in Law [*Hecyra*] of Terence, trans. Betty Radice. In *Terence: The Comedies*. Harmondsworth: Penguin Classics, 1965.

The Mother in Law [*Hecyra*] of Terence, trans. Henry Thomas Riley. *The Comedies of Terence*. New York: Harper, 1853 [1986].

The Mother in Law [*Hecyra*] of Terence. Commentary by Aelius Donatus. *Commentum in Terentii Comoedias.* Online from the Library of Congress.

Mudrarakshasa of Vishakhadatta. Sanskrit text with translation by M. R. Kale. Delhi: Motilal Banarsidass, 2011.

The Nibelungenlied [*Das Ring des Nibelungen*], trans. A. T. Hatto. Harmondsworth: Penguin Books, 1965.

Oedipus Tyrannus [*Oedipus the King*] of Sophocles. Text, with trans. by F. Storr. Cambridge, MA: Loeb Classical Library, 1913.

The One Hundred New Tales (*Les Cent nouvelles nouvelles*), trans. Judith Bruskin Diner. Garland Library of Medieval Literature, Vol. 30, series B. New York: Garland, 1990.

Il Pentamerone: or The Tale of Tales of Giovanni Batiste Basile, trans. Sir Richard Burton. New York: Horace Liveright, 1927.

The Poetic Edda, trans. Carolyne Larrington. Oxford: Oxford University Press, 2014.

Priyadarshika and *Ratnavali* of Harsha, trans. Wendy Doniger. *The Lady of the Jewel Necklace and the Lady Who Shows Her Love.* Clay Sanskrit Series. New York: New York University Press, J J C Foundation, 2006.

Ramayana of Valmiki, trans. Robert P. Goldman et al. 6 vols. Princeton, NJ: Princeton University Press, 1984–2009.

Ramayana of Valmiki. Baroda: Oriental Institute, 1960–75.

Ratnavali of Harsha, ed. Ashokanath Bhattacharya and Maheshwar Das. Calcutta: Modern Book Agency, 1967.

Shatapatha Brahmana. Benares: Chowkhamba Sanskrit Series, 1964.

Skanda Purana. Bombay: Shree Venkateshvara [Venkatesvara] Steam Press, 1867.

Testament of Judah. In *The Testaments of the Twelve Patriarchs: A Critical Edition of the Greek Text*. Pseudepigrapha Veteris Testamenti Graecae. 2 vols. Leiden: E. J. Brill, 1978.

Die Thidrekssaga, oder Dietrich von Bern und die Niflungen. Übersetzt durch Friedrich Heinrich von der Hagen. Mit neuen geographischen Anmerkungen versehen von Heinz Ritter-Schaumburg. St.-Goar: Otto Reichl Verlag, 1989.

Die Geschichte Thidreks von Bern. Sammlung Thule XXII, uebertragen von Fine Erichsen. Duesseldorf: Eugen Diederichs Verlag, 1967.

(Although *Tristan* is a character rather than a title, the following seven works are known as the "Tristan"s of various authors and should be considered together.)

Tristan. Bédier, Joseph. *The Romance of Tristan and Iseult*, trans. Hilaire Belloc and Paul Rosenfeld. New York: Pantheon, 1945; Vintage, 1965.

Tristan. Béroul, *Le Roman de Tristran*. The Romance of Tristran, ed. and trans. Norris J. Lacy. Vol. 36. Series A, Garland Library of Medieval Literary. New York: Garland, 1989.

Tristan of Eilhart von Oberg. *Tristrant [und Isalde]*, trans. J. W. Thomas. Lincoln: University of Nebraska Press, 1978.

Tristan. *La Folie Tristan d'Oxford*, ed. Ernest Hoepffner. Publications de la faculté de l'université de Strasbourg, 8. Paris: Les Belles Lettres, 1963.

Tristan of Gottfried von Strassburg. *Tristan*, trans. A. T. Hatto and supplemented with the surviving fragments of the *Tristan* of Thomas. Harmondsworth: Penguin Books, 1960.

Tristan. *The Romance of Tristan & Ysolt* of Thomas of Britain, trans. from the Old French and Old Norse by Roger Sherman Loomis. New York: E. P. Dutton, 1923.

Tristan. *The Saga of Tristram and Isond*, trans. Paul Schach. Lincoln: University of Nebraska Press, 1973.

Vishnu Purana, with the commentary of Shridhara. Calcutta: Sanatana Shastra, 1972.

Völsunga Saga (The Saga of the Volsungs), trans. Jesse L. Byock. *The Saga of the Volsungs: The Norse Epic of Sigurd the Dragon Slayer*. Berkeley: University of California Press, 1990; Penguin, 1999.

Works and Days of Hesiod. Text with trans. Hugh G. Evelyn-White. Cambridge, MA: Loeb Classical Library, 1914.

Yogavasishtha [*Yogavasishtha-Maha-Ramayana* of Valmiki], ed. W. L. S. Pansikar. 2 vols. Bombay: Nirnaya Sagara Press, 1918.

Yvain, The Knight of the Lion. Chrétien de Troyes: Arthurian Romances, trans. D. D. R. Owen. London: Everyman's Library [No. 698], 1987.

Yvain, Le Chevalier au Lion of Chrétien de Troyes. Manchester, UK: Manchester University Press, 1967.

Yvain, The Knight of the Lion. Arthurian Romances by Chrétien de Troyes, trans. W. Wistar Comfort. Halle: Max Niemeyer Verlag, 1887.

Yvain, The Knight of the Lion. Arthurian Romances by Chrétien de Troyes, trans. William W. Kibler. Harmondsworth: Penguin, 1991. Yvain, pp. 295–517.

Yvain, The Knight of the Lion. Trans. Burton Raffel. Afterword by Joseph Duggan. New Haven, CT: Yale University Press, 1987.

MODERN SOURCES (BY AUTHOR)

Adams, John F. "*All's Well That Ends Well*: The Paradox of Procreation." *Shakespeare Quarterly* 12 (1961), 261–270.

Adelman, Janet. "Bed Tricks: On Marriage as the End of Comedy in *All's Well That Ends Well* and *Measure for Measure*." In *Shakespeare's Personality*, ed. Norman Holland, Sidney Homan, and Bernard J. Paris. Berkeley: University of California Press, 1989, 151–174.

Afanasiev, A. N. *Russian Fairy Tales*, collected by Aleksandr Afanas'ev, trans. Norbert Guterman. New York: Pantheon Books, 1945.

Alter, Robert. *The Art of Biblical Narrative*. New York: Basic Books, 1981.

Andersson, Theodore M. *The Legend of Brynhild*. Ithaca, NY: Cornell University Press, 1980.

Arnim, Achim von, and Clemens Brentano. *Des Knaben Wunderhorn*. Berlin: Insel Verlag Anton Kippenberg, 2000.

Asimov, Isaac, and Janet Asimov. *Norby and the Queen's*. New York: Walker, 1986.

d'Aulnoy, Marie-Catherine Le Jumel de Barneville, Baroness. *The Fairy Tales of Madame d'Aulnoy*. Newly Done into English with an introduction by Anne Thackeray Ritchie. Translated by "Miss Lee." Honolulu: University Press of the Pacific, 2003.

Babb, Lawrence. A. *Alchemies of Violence*. New York: Sage, 2004.

Badalanova, Florentina. *Folkoren Erotikon*, Vol. 1. Sofia: Rod Publishing House, 1993.

Basile. See *Pentamerone*.

Battke, Heinz. *Geschichte des Rings in Beschreibung und Bildern*. Baden-Baden: Woldemar Klein, 1953.

Baum, P. F. "The Young Man Betrothed to a Statue." *Publications of the Modern Language Association* 34 (1919), 523 ff.

Beaumarchais, Pierre-Auguste Caron de. *The Barber of Seville/The Marriage of Figaro*, trans. John Wood. Harmondsworth: Penguin Books, 1964.

Beaumarchais, Pierre-Auguste Caron de. *Théatre de Beaumarchais: Le Barbier de Séville, Le Mariage de Figaro, La Mère coupalbe*, ed. Maurice Rat. Paris: Éditions Garnier Frères, 1956.

Beck, Brenda E. F. et al., eds. *Folktales of India*. Chicago: University of Chicago Press, 1987.

Becker, Gary S., and George J. Stigler. "De Gustibus Non Est Disputandum." *American Economic Review* 67 (1977), 76–90.

Beckman, Jonathan. *How to Ruin a Queen: Marie Antoinette and the Diamond Necklace Affair*. Boston: Da Capo Press, 2014.

Bédier, Joseph. See *Tristan*.

Béroul. See *Tristan*.

Bettini, Maurizio. *The Portrait of the Lover*, trans. from the Italian by Laura Gibbs. Berkeley: University of California Press, 1999.

Bencheikh, Jamal Eddine. "Le Conte de Qamar Az-Zaman." In *Les mille et une nuits or la parole prisonniere*. Paris: Gallimard, 1988, chapter 3 (97–135).

Benchley, Robert. "Opera Synopses." In *The Benchley Round-up*. New York: Delta Books, 1962, 65–72.

Bernard, Tara Siegel. "With Engagement Rings, Love Meets Budget." In the "Your Money" section of the *New York Times*, January 31, 2014.

Beveridge, Annette S., trans. *Baburnama*. Lahore: Sang-E-Meel, 2002.

Beveridge, Henry. "Babur's Diamond; Was It the Koh-i-nur?" *Asiatic Quarterly Review*, April 1899.

Bevington, David, ed. *The Complete Works of Shakespeare*. 4th ed. New York: Harper Collins, 1992.

Bhattacharyya-Panda, Nandini. "Women in the Sastric Tradition: Colonialism, Law, and Violence." In *Blackwell Companion to Religion and Violence*. Oxford: Wiley Blackwell, 2011, 389–405.

Blackburn, Stuart. *Moral Fictions: Tamil Folktales in Oral Tradition*. Helsinki: Suomalainen Tiedeakatemia, Academia Scientiarum Fennica, FF Communications No. 287. Vammala: Vammalan Kirjapaino Oy, 2001.

Bloomfield, Maurice. "The Character and Adventures of Muladeva." *Proceedings of the American Philosophical Society* 52 (1913), 618–649.

Boccaccio. See *Decameron*.

Boileau, Pierre, and Thomas Narcejac. *D'entre les morts*. Paris: Editions Denoel, 1954. Trans. Geoffrey Sainsbury as *The Living and the Dead*. London: Hutchinson, 1956.

Boswell, John. *Same-Sex Unions in Premodern Europe*. New York: Villard Books, 1994.

Bright, Janette, and Gillian Clark. *An Introduction to the Tokens at the Foundling Museum*. London: Foundling Museum, 2011.

Brinig, Margaret F. "Rings and Promises." *Journal of Law, Economics, and Organization* 203, 206 (1990).

Brown, Judith C. *Immodest Acts: The Life of a Lesbian Nun in Renaissance Italy*. New York: Oxford University Press, 1986.

Bulfinch, Thomas. *Legends of Charlemagne, or Romance of the Middle Ages*. Boston: J. E. Tilton, 1867.

Burton, Richard. See *Arabian Nights*.

Burton, Robert. *Anatomy of Melancholy*. New York: Tudor, 1927.

Byatt, A. S. *The Children's Book*. New York: Vintage, 2010.

Bynum, Carolyn Walker. *Holy Feast and Holy Fast: The Religious Significance of Food to Medieval Women*. Berkeley: University of California Press, 1987.

Byock, Jesse L. See *Völsunga Saga.*

Campbell, Joseph. *The Hero with a Thousand Faces.* New York: Pantheon, 1949.

Carré, Michael, and Jules Barbier. *Les Contes d'Hoffmann.* Libretto. New York: G. Schirmer, 1986.

Carlyle, Thomas. *The Diamond Necklace*, cd. W. F. Mozier. Boston: Leach, Shewell & Sanborn, 1892. First published in *Fraser's Magazine*, Nos. 85 and 86.

Carré, Michael, and Jules Barbier. *Tales of Hoffmann.* Libretto dialogue version French/English, *Les Contes d'Hoffmann.* G. Schirmer's Collection of Opera Librettos. New York: Schirmer, 1986.

Carter, Isabel G. "Mountain White Folklore: Tales from the Southern Blue Ridge." *Journal of American Folklore* 6 (1925), 356–363.

Cave, Terence. *Recognitions: A Study in Poetics.* Oxford: Clarendon Press, 1990.

Cavell, Stanley. *Pursuits of Happiness: The Hollywood Comedy of Remarriage.* Cambridge, MA: Harvard University Press, 1981.

Chavannes, Édouard. *Cinq cents contes et apologues extraits du Tripitaka Chinois.* 4. vols. Paris: E. Leroux, 1910.

Chrétien de Troyes. See *Yvain, Le Chevalier au Lion.*

Claus, Peter. "Playing *Cenne*: The Meanings of a Folk Game." In *Another Harmony: New Essays on the Folklore of India*, ed. Stuart Blackburn and A. K. Ramanujan. Berkeley: University of California Press, 1986, 265–293.

Clayton, Tim, and Phil Craig. *Diana: Story of a Princess.* London: Atria Books, 2003.

Cole, Howard C. *The All's Well Story from Boccaccio to Shakespeare.* Urbana: University of Illinois, 1981.

Colebrooke, Henry Thomas. *Essays on the Religion and Philosophy of the Hindus.* London: Williams and Norgate, 1858.

Collins, James. "Dept. of Mating. Science Explains Why Men Are Like That." *New Yorker*, August 7, 2000, 30.

Crooke, William, ed. *North Indian Notes and Queries*, vol. 3 (April 1893).

Cross, Tom Peete. "The Celtic Origin of the Lay of Yonec." *Revue Celtique* 31 (1918), 413–437.

cummings, e. e. *The Complete Poems: 1904–1962*, ed. George J. Firmage. London: Liveright, 1994.

Darnton, Robert. *The Great Cat Massacre and Other Episodes in French Cultural History.* New York: Basic Books, 1984.

Darnton, Robert. "The Grub Street Style of Revolution: J.-P. Brissot, Police Spy." *Journal of Modern History* 40.3 (1968), 301–327.

Daston, Lorraine J. "Projection and Perfect Passivity." In *Affektive Dinge: Objektberührungen in Wissenschaft und Kunst*, ed. Natascha Adamowsky et al. Göttingen:Wallstein, 2011, 24–50.

Daston, Lorraine J. "Succession Sealed." Max Planck Institute for the History of Science, *Wissenschaftskolleg Seminar on Hamlet*, May 24–25, 2013.

Daston, Lorraine J., and Peter Galison. *Objectivity.* New York: Zone Books, 2010.

Daston, Lorraine J., with Peter Erickson et al. *How Reason Almost Lost Its Mind: The Strange Career of Cold War Rationality.* Chicago: University of Chicago Press, 2013.

Davids, T. W. Rhys. *Buddhism: A Sketch of the Life and Teachings of Gautama the Buddha.* London: C and J B Young, 1894.

de France, Marie. *The Lais of Marie de France*, trans., with an introduction and notes, by Robert Hanning and Joan Ferrante. Durham, NC: Labyrinth Press, 1978.

De La Sale [Salle], Antoine. *Les cent nouvelles nouvelles, dites les Cent Nouvelles du Roi Louis XI* (Par Antoine de La Salle): Nouvelle édition revue sur l'édition originale, avec des notes et une introduction par P. L. Jacob. Paris: Adolphe Delahays, 1858. Translated into English as *One Hundred Merrie and Delightsome Stories* by Robert B. Douglas, 1899; Project Gutenberg.

De Morgan, Mary. *The Necklace of Princess Fiorimonde and Other Stories.* London: Macmillan, 1880.

Desens, Marliss C. *The Bed-Trick in English Renaissance Drama: Explorations in Gender, Sexuality, and Power.* Newark, NJ: University of Delaware Press, 1994.

de Vries, Peter. *The Tunnel of Love.* Boston: Little, Brown, 1949.

Dickens, Charles. *Oliver Twist.* Harmondsworth: Penguin Classics, 2003.

Diderot, Denis. "Les bijoux indiscrets." In *Oeuvres Complètes de Diderot, Philosophie IV, Belles-Lettres I* [Romans, contes, critique littéraire]. Paris: Garnier Frères, 1875, 130–378.

Diderot, Denis. "The Indiscreet Jewels," trans. Sophie Hawkes. In *The Libertine Reader: Eroticism and Enlightenment in Eighteenth-Century France*, ed. Michel Feher. New York: Zone Books, 1997, 342–531.

Diner, Judith Bruskin. See *The One Hundred New Tales* (*Les Cent nouvelles nouvelles*).

Dinesen, Isak. "The Roads Round Pisa." In *Seven Gothic Tales.* New York: Vintage Books, 1934, 165–216.

Doniger, Wendy. *The Bedtrick: Tales of Sex and Masquerade.* Chicago: University of Chicago Press, 2000.

Doniger, Wendy. "Gli Anelli Magici della Memoria." Traduzione di Vincenzo Vergiani, in *Adelphiana.* Milan, May 30, 2001, 1–36.

Doniger, Wendy. *The Hindus: An Alternative History.* New York: Penguin Books, 2009.

Doniger, Wendy. *The Implied Spider: Politics and Theology in Myth.* New York: Columbia University Press, 1998.

Doniger, Wendy. "Jewels of Rejection and Recognition in Ancient India." *Journal of Indian Philosophy* 26 (1998), 435–453.

Doniger, Wendy. "Magic Rings and the Return of the Repressed." In *Spirituality and Religion: Psychoanalytic Perspectives.* Vols. 34–35 (2006–7) of *The Annual of Psychoanalysis*, ed. Jerome A. Winer and James William Anderson. Catskill, NY: Mental Health Resources, 243–256.

Doniger, Wendy. *Der Mann, der mit seiner eigenen Frau Ehebruch beging. Mit einem Kommentar von Lorraine Daston.* Berlin: Suhrkamp, 1999.

Doniger, Wendy. "Menander, Terence, and the Rape of the Clever Wife." In the Festschrift for James Redfield, ed. Lillian E. Doherty and Bruce King. New York: Routledge, forthcoming.

Doniger, Wendy. "Myth, Reason, and Rationality." In *What Reason Promises: Essays on Reason, Nature, and History*, ed. Wendy Doniger, Peter Galison, and Susan Neiman. Berlin: De Gruyter, 2016, 63–70.

Doniger, Wendy. "Narrative Conventions and Rings of Recognition." In *Recognition: The Poetics of Narrative. Interdisciplinary Studies on Anagnorisis*, ed. Philip R. Kennedy and Marilyn Lawrence. New York: Peter Lang, 2009, 13–25.

Doniger, Wendy. "The Ring of the Forgetful Husband in World Mythology." The 1999 Adams Lecture at San Diego State University.

Doniger, Wendy. "The Rings of Budur and Qamar." In *Scheherazade's Children: Global Encounters with the Arabian Nights*, ed. Marina Warner and Philip Kennedy. New York: New York University Press, 2013, 108–126.

Doniger, Wendy. *Splitting the Difference: Gender and Myth in Ancient Greece and India*. Chicago: University of Chicago Press, 1999.

Doniger, Wendy. "The Symbolism of Black and White Babies in the Myth of Maternal Impression." *Social Research* 70.1 (Spring 2003), 1–44.

Doniger, Wendy. *The Woman Who Pretended to Be Who She Was*. New York: Oxford University Press, 2005.

Doniger, Wendy, with Gregory Spinner. "Misconceptions: Male Fantasies and Female Imaginations in Parental Imprinting." *Daedalus* 127.1 (Winter 1998), 97–130.

Doniger O'Flaherty, Wendy. *Asceticism and Eroticism in the Mythology of Siva*. New York: Oxford University Press, 1973. Paperback, retitled *Siva: The Erotic Ascetic*. New York: Galaxy, 1981.

Doniger O'Flaherty, Wendy. *Dreams, Illusion, and Other Realities*. Chicago: University of Chicago Press, 1984.

Doniger O'Flaherty, Wendy. *Karma and Rebirth in Classical Indian Traditions*. Berkeley: University of California Press; Delhi: Motilal Banarsidass, 1980.

Doniger O'Flaherty, Wendy. *Textual Sources for the Study of Hinduism*. Chicago: University of Chicago Press, 1990.

Doniger O'Flaherty, Wendy. *Women, Androgynes, and Other Mythical Beasts*. Chicago: University of Chicago Press, 1980.

See also *Kamasutra, Manu, Ratnavali*.

Doyle, Sir Arthur Conan. "The Case of Lady Sannox." In *The Conan Doyle Stories*. London: John Murray, 1929, 495–506.

Dronke, Ursula. See *Edda*.

Duggan, Joseph J. "Afterword" to Burton Raffel's translation of *Yvain, The Knight of the Lion*. See *Yvain, The Knight of the Lion*.

Dumas, Alexandre, père. *The Queen's Necklace*. In *The Complete Works*. New York: P. F. Collier and Son, 1904.

Dundes, Alan. *Cinderella: A Casebook*. New York: Wildman Press, 1983.

Dundes, Alan. "The Psychoanalytic Study of the Grimms' Tales with Special Reference to 'The Maiden Without Hands' (AT 706)." *Germanic Review* 62.2 (Spring 1987), 50–65.

Dundes, Alan. *The Shabbat Elevator and Other Subterfuges: An Unorthodox Essay on Circumventing Custom and Jewish Character*. Lanham, MD: Rowman & Littlefield, 2002.

Dundes, Alan. "'To Love My Father All': A Psychoanalytic Study of the Folktale Source of *King Lear*." In Dundes, *Cinderella*, 229–244.

Economist (no author listed), "The Diamond Business: Glass with Attitude." December 18, 1997, 113–115.

Edwards, Charles. *The History and Poetry of Finger-Rings*. New York: John W. Lovell, 1855.

Eilhart von Oberg. See *Tristan*.

Eliade, Mircea. *Cosmos and History: The Myth of the Eternal Return*. New York: Pantheon, 1954.

Eliot, George. *Daniel Deronda*. Harmondsworth: Penguin Classics, 1996.

Ephron, Nora. *Heartburn*. New York: Vintage Books, 1996.

Euripides. See *Medea*.

Evans, Peter, and Ava Gardner. *Ava Gardner: The Secret Conversations*. New York: Simon & Schuster, 2013.

Fauset, Arthur Huff. "Negro Folk Tales from the South." *Journal of American Folklore*, Vol. 40. New York: American Folk-lore Society, 1927, 243–245.

Festinger, Leon. *A Theory of Cognitive Dissonance*. Stanford, CA: Stanford University Press, 1957.

Fisher, Helen. *Why We Love: The Nature and Chemistry of Romantic Love*. New York: Holt, 2004.

Fiske, John. *Myths and Mythmakers: Old Tales and Superstitions Interpreted by Comparative Mythology*. Boston: Houghton, Mifflin, 1988.

Fleming, Ian. *James Bond: Diamonds Are Forever*. London: Coronet, 1988 [1956].

Fletcher, John, Nathaniel Field, and John Massinger. *The Queen of Corinth*. In *The Dramatic Works in the Beaumont and Fletcher Canon*, ed. Robert Kean Turner. Vol. 8, ed. Fredson Bowers. Cambridge: Cambridge University Press, 1992, 1–112.

Forbes, Aexander Penrose. See *The Lives of S. Ninian and S. Kentigern*.

Ford, Patrick K., trans. *The Mabinogi and Other Medieval Welsh Tales*. Berkeley: University of California Press, 1977.

Foucault, Michel. *History of Sexuality*, trans. Robert Hurley. 3 vols. New York: Vintage, 1990.

Freedberg, David. *The Power of Images: Studies in the History and Theory of Response*. Chicago: University of Chicago Press, 1989.

Freud, Sigmund. *Collected Papers*, ed. James Strachey. 5 vols. London: Hogarth Press, 1950.

Freud, Sigmund. "Family Romances." In *Collected Papers* 5, 74–78.

Freud, Sigmund. *The Future of an Illusion*, trans. James Strachey. New York: W. W. Norton, 1989.

Freud, Sigmund. *The Interpretation of Dreams*, trans. James Strachey. New York: Basic Books, 1965.

Freud, Sigmund. "Medusa's Head." In *Collected Papers* 5, 105–106.

Freud, Sigmund. *Moses and Monotheism*, trans. Katherine Jones. New York: Vintage Books, 1939.

Freud, Sigmund. *Three Essays on the Theory of Sexuality*, trans. James Strachey. New York: Basic Books, 1962.

Freud, Sigmund, and D. E. Oppenheim. *Dreams in Folklore*, trans. A. M. O. Richards. New York: International Universities Press, 1958.

Funck-Brentano, Frantz, trans. H. Sutherland Edwards. *The Diamond Necklace*. London: Greening, 1911.

Gantz, Jeffrey. *Early Irish Myths and Sagas*. Harmondsworth: Penguin Classics, 1982. See also *The Mabinogion*.

Geertz, Clifford. *After the Fact: Two Countries, Four Decades, One Anthropologist. The Jerusalem-Harvard Lectures*. Cambridge, MA: Harvard University Press, 1995.

Ginzburg, Carlo. "Morelli, Freud and Sherlock Holmes: Clues and Scientific Method." *History Workshop* 9 (1980), 5–36.

Ginzberg, Louis. *The Legends of the Jews*. Baltimore: Johns Hopkins University Press, 1998.

Goldenweiser, Alexander. "The Principle of Limited Possibilities in the Development of Culture." In *History, Psychology, and Culture*. London: Kegan Paul, Trench, Trubner, 1933, 35–58.

Goldman, Robert P. "Karma, Guilt, and Buried Memories: Public Fantasy and Private Reality in Traditional India." *Journal of the American Oriental Society* 105.3 (1985), 413–425.

Gopnik, Adam. "What Did Jesus Do? Reading and Unreading the Gospels." *New Yorker*, May 24, 2010, 72–77.

Gottfried von Strassburg. See *Tristan*.

Green, Cynthia Whidden. *Saint Kentigern, Apostle to Strathclyde: A Critical Analysis of a Northern Saint*, with a translation of Jocelyn, a monk of Furness: *The Life of Kentigern* (Mungo). Master's Thesis Presented to the Faculty of the Department of English, University of Houston, 1998. http://legacy.fordham.edu/halsall/basis/Jocelyn-LifeofKentigern.asp.

Gregor, Walter. *The Folklore of North East Scotland*. London: Folklore Society, 1881.

Gurdon, Eveline Camilla, Lady. "The Suffolk 'King Lear.' Cap o' Rushes." A. W. T., "Suffolk Notes and Queries." *Ipswich Journal*, 1877; *County Folk-Lore: Printed Extracts No. 2*, Suffolk, 40–43.

Hamori, Andras. "The Magian and the Whore: Readings of Qamar al-Zaman," pp. 25–40 of *Studia Islamica*, No. 43 (1976), *The 1001 Nights: Critical Essays and Annotated Bibliography*. Cambridge, MA: Dar Mahjar, 1985.

Hardy, Thomas. *Far from the Madding Crowd*. Tustin, CA: Xist Publishing, 2015.

Harper, Ralph. *On Presence: Variations and Reflections*. Baltimore: Johns Hopkins University Press, 2006.

Hasan-Rokem, Galit. *Proverbs in Israeli Folk Narratives: A Structural Semantic Analysis*. Folklore Fellows Communications No. 232. Helsinki: Academia Scientiarum Fennica, 1982.

Haslip, Joan. *Marie Antoinette*. New York: Grove Press, 1988.

Hatto, A. T. *The Nibelungenlied*. Harmondsworth: Penguin Books, 1965.

Hejaiej, Monia. *Behind Closed Doors: Women's Oral Narratives in Tunis*. New Brunswick, NJ: Rutgers University Press, 1996.

Higgins, Carla. "Jewelry." In *Saudi Arabia and the Gulf Arab States Today: An Encyclopedia*, Vol. 1, ed. Sebastan Maisel and John A. Shoup. New York: Greenwood, 2009, 240–241.

Hilton, James. *Random Harvest*. New York: Carroll and Graf, 1969 [1941].

Hodgdon, Barbara. "The Making of Virgins and Mothers: Sexual Signs, Substitute Scenes and Doubled Presences in *All's Well That Ends Well*." *Philological Quarterly* 66.1 (Winter 1987), 47–71.

Hofmannsthal, Hugo von. "Die ägyptische Helena" [1928]. In *Gesammelte Werke*. Vol. 4, *Dramen*, ed. H. Steiner. Frankfurt: S. Fischer, 1958, 473–476.

Horkheimer, Max, and Theodor W. Adorno. *Dialectic of Enlightenment* (*Cultural Memory in the Present*) (1947), trans. Edmund Jephcott. Stanford, CA: Stanford University Press, 2007.

Ibsen, Henrik. *The Vikings at Helgeland* (1858), trans. James Walter McFarlane. *The Oxford Ibsen*, Vol. 2. London: Oxford University Press, 1962, 27–94.

Ibsen, Henrik. *The Vikings of Helgeland*. In *The Prose Dramas of Henrik Ibsen*, Vol. 3, trans. William Archer. Project Gutenberg.

Idris, Yousef, trans. Catherine Cobham. "House of Flesh." In *Rings of Burnished Brass*. Cairo, Egypt: American University in Cairo Press, 1992.

Ingledew, J. C. Davison. *Ballads and Songs of Yorkshire*. London: Bell and Daldy, 186 Fleet Street, 1860.

Insler, Stanley. "The Shattered Head Split and the Epic Tale of Sakuntala." *Bulletin d'Etudes Indiennes* 7–8 (1989–90), 97–139.

Irwin, Robert. *The Arabian Nights: A Companion*. London: Allan Lane, 1994.

Jagendorf, Zvi. "'In the Morning, Behold It Was Leah': Genesis and the Reversal of Sexual Knowledge." In *Biblical Patterns in Modern Literature*, ed. David H. Hirsch et al. Brown Judaic Studies 77. Chico, CA: Scholars Press, 1984, 51–60.

James, Henry. *The Last of the Valerii* (1874). In *The Novels and Tales of Henry James*, Vol. 26. New York: Charles Scribner's Sons, 1909.

James, Henry. "Paste." In *The Novels and Tales of Henry James*, Vol. 16. New York: Charles Scribner's Sons, 1909, 315–337

James, Henry. "The Real Thing." In *The Real Thing and Other Tales*. New York: Macmillan, 1893, 1–44.

Jones, William. *Finger-ring Lore: Historical, Legendary, Anecdotal*. 2nd ed. London: Chatto and Windus, 1890.

Kanfer, Stefan. *The Last Empire: De Beers, Diamonds, and the* World. New York: Farrar, Straus and Giroux, 1993.

Kerber, Linda K. "Why Diamonds Really Are a Girl's Best Friend: Another American Narrative." *Daedalus: Journal of the American Academy of Arts and Sciences*, Winter 2012, 89–100.

Kipling, Rudyard. "The Butterfly That Stamped." In *Just So Stories*. New York: Doubleday, 1912.

Knowles, James Hinton. *Folk-Tales of Kashmir*. London: Kegan Paul, Trench, Trübner, 1892.

Kuhn, Thomas. *The Nature of Scientific Revolutions*. 2nd. ed. Chicago: University of Chicago Press, 1970.

Kunz, George Frederick. *Rings for the Finger*. New York: Dover, 1917.

Künzig, Johannes. "Der im Fischbauch Wiedergefundene Ring in Sage, Legende, Märchen und Lied." In *Volkskundliche Gaben*, for John Meier. Berlin: Walter de Gruyter, 1934, 85–103.

Kurin, Richard. *Hope Diamond: The Legendary History of a Cursed Gem*. New York: Harper Collins, 2006.

Landau, M. *Die Quellen des Dekameron*. Stuttgart: Scheible, 1884.

Landstad, M. B. "Kong Kristian og hans dronning," no. 73, 585 ff. In *Norske Folkeviser*. Christiania, Copenhagen, 1853.

Lawrence, W. W. *Shakespeare's Problem Comedies*. New York: Frederick Ungar, 1960.

Leavy, Barbara Fass. *In Search of the Swan Maiden: A Narrative on Folklore and Gender*. New York: New York University Press, 1994.

Lee, A. C. *The Decameron: Its Sources and Analogues*. London: Nutt, 1909.

Levertov, Denise. *Life in the Forest*. New York: New Directions, 1978.

Leopardi, Lilliana. *"Speculum Lapidum*: Some Reflections on Sixteenth-Century Intaglios and Astral Magic." *Abraxas, International Journal of Esoteric Studies*. Special Issue No. 1. Summer 2013, 53–64.

Leopardi, Lilliana. "Ludovico Dolce's Treatise on Precious Gems." Paper presented at Kalamazoo College in 2010.

Lévi-Strauss, Claude. *The Elementary Structures of Kinship*. Boston: Beacon Press, 1971.

Lévi-Strauss, Claude. *The Savage Mind*. Chicago: University of Chicago Press, 1966.

Lévi-Strauss, Claude. "Split Representation in the Art of Asia and America." In *Structural Anthropology*, trans. Claire Jacobson and Brooke Grundfest Schoepf. Harmondsworth, England: Penguin, 1963, 245–268.

Lévi-Strauss, Claude. "The Story of Asdiwal." In *The Structural Study of Myth and Totemism*, ed. Edmund Leach, trans. Nicolas Mann. London: Tavistock, 1967, 1–48.

Lévi-Strauss, Claude. *Structural Anthropology*, trans. Claire Jacobson and Brooke Grundfest Schoepf. Harmondsworth, England: Penguin, 1963.

Lévi-Strauss, Claude. "The Structural Study of Myth." In *Structural Anthropology*, 206–31.

Lincoln, Bruce. *Discourse and the Construction of Society*. Comparative Studies of Myth, Ritual, and Classification. New York: Oxford University Press, 1992.

Loomis, Roger Sherman. See *Tristan*.

Loos, Anita. *Gentlemen Prefer Blondes: The Illuminating Diary of a Professional Lady*. New York: W. W. Norton, 1998.

Lopez, Don S., ed. *Religions of India in Practice*. Princeton Readings in Religion. Princeton, NJ: Princeton University Press, 1995.

Lorenz, Konrad. *King Solomon's Ring*. New York: Crowell, 1952.

Maity, Pradyot Kujmar. *Historical Studies in the Cult of the Goddess Manasa*. Calcutta: 1966.

Mann, Thomas. *Joseph and His Brothers*, trans. H. T. Lowe-Porter. New York: Alfred Knopf, 1948.

Marcus, Stephen. *The Other Victorians: A Study of Sexuality and Pornography in Mid-Nineteenth-Century England*. New York: Basic Books, 1966.

Marias, Javier. *Tomorrow in the Battle Think on Me*, trans. Margaret Jull Costa. New York: Harcourt Brace, 1996.

Marx, Karl. *The Eighteenth Brumaire*. Peking: Foreign Language Press, 1978.

Maugham, W. Somerset. "Mr Know-All," 317–322, and "A String of Beads," 412–417 in *Collected Short Stories*, Vol. 1. New York: Penguin Books, 1977.

de Maupassant, Guy. *The Necklace and Other Short Stories*. New York: Dover, 1992.

Maury, L. F. Alfred. *Croyances et Légendes du Moyennes Ages*. Paris: H. Champion, 1896.

Maza, Sarah. *Private Lives and Public Affairs: The Causes Celebres of Prerevolutionary France*. Berkeley: University of California Press, 1993.

McCarthy, James Remington. *Rings through the Ages: An Informal History*. New York: Harper and Brothers, 1945.

McCarthy, Cathleen. "Sex and the City: The Jewelry." Thejewelryloup.com. May 13, 2010.

McMurtry, Larry. "A Life for the Star." Review of M. G. Lord, *The Accidental Feminist; How Elizabeth Taylor Raised Our Consciousness and We Were Too Distracted by Her Beauty to Notice*. *New York Review of Books*, April 26, 2012.

Menander. See *The Arbitrators*.

Menn, Esther Marie. *Judah & Tamar (Genesis 38) in Ancient Jewish Exegesis*. Leiden: Brill, 1997.

Mérimée, Prosper. "La Vénus d'Ille." In *The Venus of Ille and Other Stories*, trans. Jean Kimber. London: Oxford University Press, 1966, 1–18.

Middleton, Thomas. "The Changeling." In Thomas Middleton, *Five Plays*, ed. Bryan Loughrey and Neil Taylor. New York: Penguin Books, 1988, 345–421.

Moore, Thomas. *The Poetical Works of Thomas Moore*, ed. A. D. Godley. London: Oxford University Press, 1929.

Morris, William. See *Volsungasaga*.

Moule, Thomas. *The Heraldry of Fish, Notices of the Principal Families Bearing Fish in Their Arms.* London: Jones, 1842.

Natesa Sastri, S. M. *Dravidian Nights: Being a Translation of Madanakamarajankadai.* Madras: Excelsior Press, 1886.

Nattiez, Jean-Jacques. *Wagner Androgyne: A Study in Interpretation*, trans. Stewart Spencer. Princeton, NJ: Princeton University Press, 1993.

Neely, Carol Thomas. *Broken Nuptials in Shakespeare's Plays.* New Haven, CT: Yale University Press, 1985.

Okrent, Rebecca. "Ring Cycle." Sunday *New York Times*, September 23, 2007, back page of the magazine section.

Orwell, George. "Rudyard Kipling," a review of T. S. Eliot's *A Choice of Kipling's Verse*, in *A Collection of Essays*. Garden City, NY: Doubleday, 1954, 116–131.

Osborne, Katherine Dunagan. "Inherited Emotions: George Eliot and the Politics of Heirlooms." *Nineteenth-Century Literature* 64.4 (March 2010), 465–493.

Ovid. See *Amores, Metamorphoses.*

Pacha, S. E. Yacoub Artin. *Contes populaires inedits de la vallée du Nil.* Paris: Maisonneuve, 1893.

Parker, H. *Village Folk-tales of Ceylon.* 2 vols. Dehiwala, Ceylon: Tisara Prakasakayo, 1972 [1910]. Vol. 2, #92, "The King Who Became a Thief," 75–79.

Partridge, Eric. *Shakespeare's Bawdry.* Rev. ed. New York: E. P. Dutton, 1969.

Penzer and Tawney. See *Kathasaritsagara.*

Plaidy, Jean. *The Queen of Diamonds.* London: Harper Collins, 1998 [1958].

Pointon, Marcia. *Brilliant Effects: A Cultural History of Gemstones and Jewellery.* New Haven, CT: Yale University Press, 2009.

Poggio Fiorentino. *Poggii Facetiae: Latin Jokes.* CreateSpace Independent Publishing Platform, 2010.

Porter, Andrew. See Wagner.

Proctor, Robert N. "Anti-Agate: The Great Diamond Hoax and the Semiprecioius Stone Scam." *Configurations, a Journal of Literature, Science, and Technology* 9 (2001), 381–412.

Proust, Marcel. *À la recherche d'un temp perdu* (1871–1922). New York: Apple-Century-Crofts, 1952.

Quiller-Couch, Arthur. Introduction to the Cambridge University Press edition of *All's Well that Ends Well.* Cambridge: Cambridge University Press, 1968.

Rabelais, François. *Gargantua and Pantagruel*, trans. Jacques LeClercq. New York: Heritage Press, 1936.

Rabelais, François, trans. Sir Thomas Urquhart and Peter Motteux. In Robert Maynard Hutchins, ed., *Great Books of the Western World.* Vol. 24, *Rabelais*, 185. Chicago: Encyclopaedia Britannica, 1952.

Radloff, W. "Der Kluge Wesirs-Tochter." In *Proben der Volkslitteratur der nördlichen türkischen Stämme.* Vol. 6, *Dialect der Tarantschi.* St. Petersburg: Der Dialect der Tarantschi. St. Petersburg, 1886, 191–198.

Raffel, Burton. See *Yvain*.

Ralston, William Ralston Shedden. "Cinderella." In Dundes, *Cinderella*, 30–56.

Ralston, William Ralston Shedden. *Tibetan Tales, Derived from Indian Sources, Translated from the Tibetan of the Kah-gyur by F. Anton von Schiefner, done into English from the German, with an Introduction, by Shedden Ralston*. London: Trubner, 1882.

Ramanujan, A. K. *A Flowering Tree, and Other Oral Tales from India*. By A. K. Ramanujan, eds. Stuart Blackburn and Alan Dundes. Berkeley: University of California Press, 1997.

Ramanujan, A. K. *Folktales from India*. New York: Pantheon Books, 1992.

Ramanujan, A. K. "Hanchi: A Kannada Cinderella." In Dundes, *Cinderella*, 259–275.

Ramanujan, A. K. "No Amnesiac King." First published in *Second Sight*. Delhi: Oxford University Press, 1986, 16–17; reprinted in *The Collected Poems of A. K. Ramanujan*. Delhi: Oxford University Press, 1995, 126.

Ramanujan, A. K. "Telling Tales." *Daedalus* 118.4 (Autumn 1989), 239–261.

Ramanujan, A. K. "Towards a Counter-System: Women's Tales." In *Gender, Discourse, and Power in South Asia*, ed. Arjun Appadurai et al. Philadelphia: University of Pennsylvania Press, 1991, 33–55.

Rank, Otto. *The Myth of the Birth of the Hero*. 1914. Republished in *In Quest of the Hero*, by Otto Rank et al. Princeton, NJ: Princeton University Press, 1990.

Réage, Pauline. *Story of O*, translated from the French by Sabine d'Estrée. New York: Ballantine Books, 1973; Paris, 1954; Grove Press, 1965.

Roberts, Janine. *Glitter and Greed: The Secret World of the Diamond Cartel*. New York: Disinformation Company, 2003.

Roberts, Leonard W. *South from Hell-fer-Sartin: Kentucky Mountain Folk Tales*. Lexington: University of Kentucky Press, 1955; Boston: Houghton Mifflin, 2002.

Roth, Philip. *Everyman*. New York: Vintage Books, 2006.

Rower, Ann. "Gentlemen: A Musical Is Made." Unpublished ms., February 14, 1995, 102.

Rubin, Gayle. "The Traffic in Women: Notes on the 'Political Economy' of Sex." In *Toward an Anthropology of Women*, ed. Rayna Reiter. New York: Monthly Review Press, 1975, 157–210.

Saint-Amand, Imbert de. *Marie Antoinette and the End of the Old Regime*, trans. Thomas Sergeant Perry. New York: Charles Scribner's Sons, 1894.

Saintyves, Pierre. "L'anneau de Polycrate et le statère dans la bouche du poisson in des Verfs." In *Essais de folklore biblique: Magie, Mythes et Miracles dans l'ancient et le nouveau testament*. Paris: Emile Nourry, 1923, 366–404.

Sanders, Lise. *Consuming Fantasies: Labor, Leisure, and the London Shopgirl*. Columbus: Ohio State University Press, 2006.

Sax, William. *Dancing the Self: Personhood and Performance in the Pandav Lila of Garhwal*. New York: Oxford University Press, 2002.

Scarisbrick, Diana. *Rings: Jewelry of Power, Love and Loyalty*. London: Thames and Hudson, 2007.

Schach, Paul. See *Tristan*.

Schama, Simon. *Citizens: A Chronicle of the French Revolution*. New York: Vintage, 1990.

Schwartz, Howard. *Gabriel's Palace: Jewish Mystical Tales*. New York: Oxford University Press, 1993.

Scott, James C. *Weapons of the Weak: Everyday Forms of Peasant Resistance*. New Haven: Yale University Press, 1985.

Shakespeare. All citations, unless otherwise noted, are from *The Arden Shakespeare. Complete Works*, ed. Richard Proudfoot et al. London: Thomas Learning, 2001.

Shippey, Tom. "Tolkien Out-Wagners Wagner." A review of J. R. R. Tolkien's *The Legend of Sigurd and Gudrun. Times Literary Supplement*, May 6, 2009.

Shulman, David, with Don Handelman. *God Inside Out: Siva's Game of Dice*. New York: Oxford University Press, 1997.

Spencer, Sharon. "Beyond Therapy: The Enduring Love of Anais Nin for Otto Rank." In Suzanne Nalbantain, *Anais Nin: Literary Perspectives*. New York: St. Martin's Press, 1997, 97–111.

Stern, Alfred. "Der Ring im Märchen, in der Novelle, im Drama, im Recht." In *Hessische Blätter für Volkskunde* 30 (1931), 106–125.

Stokes, Maive S. H. *Indian Fairy Tales*. London: Jacobs, Joseph, 1880.

Suchier, H. "Die Quellen der Magussaga." *Germania* 20 (1875), 273–291.

Sullivan, J. Courtney. *Engagements*. New York: Alfred A. Knopf, 2013.

Szerb, Antal. *The Queen's Necklace*, trans. Leonard Rix. London: Pushkin Press, 2010.

Tagore, Rabindranath. "Sakuntala, Its Inner Meaning." In *Sakuntala, Its Inner Meaning*, ed. K. N. Das Gupta and Laurence Binyon. Calcutta: Macmillan, 1920, v–xiii.

Taylor, Elizabeth. *My Love Affair with Jewelry*. New York: Simon & Schuster, 2002.

Terence. See *Hecyra*.

Thackston, Wheeler. *The Baburnama; Memoirs of Babur, Prince and Emperor*. New York: Oxford University Press, 1996.

Thapar, Romila. *Sakuntala: Texts, Readings, Histories*. New Delhi: Kali for Women, 1999.

Thomas, Chantal. Introduction to Diderot, "Les bijoux indiscrets," 333–341.

Thompson, Stith. *Motif-Index of Folk Literature*. 6 vols. Bloomington: Indiana University Press, 1955–1958.

Todenbach, Georges. *Bruges-la Morte (The Dead City of Bruges*; Paris, 1892), trans. Philip Mosley. Scranton: University of Scranton Press, 2007.

Tolkien, J. R. R., and Christopher Tolkien. *The Legend of Sigurd and Gudrun*. New York: Houghton Mifflin Harcourt, 2009.

Tushnet, Rebecca. "Rules of Engagement." *Yale Law Review* 107.8 (1998), 2583–2618.

Twain, Mark. *Pudd'nhead Wilson and Other Tales*, ed. R. D. Gooder. London: Oxford University Press, 1992.

Vartanian, Aram. Preface to 1978 edition of Diderot, *Oeuvres Complètes de Diderot*. Paris: Hermann, 1978.

de Villiers, Pierre. See *The One Hundred New Tales.*

de Vilmorin, Louise Leveque. *Madame de,* translated by Duff Cooper. Canada: Helen Marx Books, 1968.

Vizetelly, Henry. *The Story of the Diamond Necklace, Told in Detail for the First Time, Chiefly by the Aid of Original Letters, Official and Other Documents, and Contemporary Memoirs Recently Made Public.* 2 vols. London: Tinsley Brothers, Catherine Street, Strand, 1867.

Vora, Shivani. "Brides: Steal His Heart, but Borrow the Jewelry." *New York Times,* July 31, 2013.

Wagner, Richard. *The Art-Work of the Future.* In *The Art-Work of the Future and Other Works.* Trans. William Ashton Ellis. Lincoln: University of Nebraska Press, 1993.

Wagner, Richard. *The Ring of the Niebelung,* trans. Andrew Porter. New York: W. W. Norton, 1976.

Wanner, Kevin. "The Virgin and the Valkyrie: A Comparison of Three Medieval German Texts." Ms., 2000.

Warner, Marina. *Once upon a Time: A Short History of Fairy Tale.* New York: Oxford University Press, 2014.

Warner, Marina. *Stranger Magic: Charmed States and the Arabian Nights.* New York: Belknap Press, 2012.

Wilbur, Richard. *Collected Poems: 1943–2004.* New York: Harcourt, 2006.

Wilde, Oscar. *The Picture of Dorian Gray,* ed. Donald L. Lawler. New York: W. W. Norton, 1988 [London, 1890; 1891].

Williams, Howard. *Superstitions of Witchcraft.* London: Longman, Green, 1865.

Williams, Tennessee. *Cat on a Hot Tin Roof.* In *Tennessee Williams, Plays 1937–1955.* New York: Library of America, 2000, 873–1009.

Yeats, William Butler. *Fairy and Folk Tales of the Irish Peasantry,* ed. William Butler Yeats. London: Walter Scott, 1888.

Yeats, William Butler. *W. B. Yeats: Selected Poetry,* ed. A. Norman Jeffers. London: Pan Books, 1974.

Yu, Anthony C. *The Journey to the West.* Rev. ed., 4 vols. Chicago: University of Chicago Press, 2012.

Yu, Li. *The Carnal Prayer Mat,* trans. Patrick Hanan. New York: Ballantine, 1990.

Zimmer, Heinrich. *The King and the Corpse: Tales of the Soul's Conquest of Evil,* ed. Joseph Campbell. Princeton, NJ: Bollingen, 1948. ("Die Geschichte vom indischen König mit dem Leichnam," 1935).

Ziolkowski, Theodore. *Disenchanted Images: A Literary Iconology.* Princeton, NJ: Princeton University Press, 1977.

Zoellner, Tom. *The Heartless Stone: A Journey through the World of Diamonds, Deceit, and Desire.* New York: Picador, 2007.

Zvelebil, Kamil. *Two Tamil Folktales: The Story of King Matanakama; the Story of Peacock Ravana.* Delhi: Motilal Banarsidass, 1987.

Index